Crash Course in Artificial Intelligence and Expert Systems

Louis E. Frenzel, Jr.

Howard W. Sams & Co.
A Division of Macmillan, Inc.
4300 West 62nd Street, Indianapolis, IN 46268 USA

FIRST EDITION
SECOND PRINTING — 1987

International Standard Book Number: 0-672-22443-7
Library of Congress Catalog Card Number: 86-62223

Acquisitions Editor: *Greg Michael*
Manuscript Editor: *Betty White*
Production Editor: *Albright Communications, Inc.*
Designer: *T.R. Emrick*
Illustrator: *Wm. D. Basham*
Cover Artist: *Joe LaMantia*
Technical Reviewer: *Leed Associates Computer Publications*
Indexer: *New England Editorial Services*
Compositor: *Impressions, Inc.*

Printed in the United States of America

Contents

Trademark Acknowledgments

All terms mentioned in this book that are known to be trademarks or service marks are listed below. In addition, terms suspected of being trademarks or service marks have been appropriately capitalized. Howard W. Sams & Co. cannot attest to the accuracy of this information. Use of a term in this book should not be regarded as affecting the validity of any trademark or service mark.

Apple is a registered trademark of Apple Computer Inc.

Macintosh is a trademark licensed to Apple Computer Inc.

dBASE II and dBASE III are registered trademarks of Ashton-Tate

GCLISP is a registered trademark of Gold Hill Computers Inc.

IBM is a registered trademark of International Business Machines Corp.

INTELLECT is a trademark of Artificial Intelligence Corporation

ZETALISP is a registered trademark of Symbolics Inc.

Lotus is a registered trademark of Lotus Development Corporation

1-2-3 is a registered trademark of Lotus Development Corporation

Personal Consultant is a trademark of Texas Instruments

Explorer is a trademark of Texas Instruments

Q&A is a trademark of Symantec Corporation

Rulemaster is a registered trademark of Radian Corporation

Symbolics is a registered trademark of Symbolics Inc.

Teknowledge is a registered trademark of Teknowledge, Inc.

Turbo Prolog is a registered trademark of Borland International

UNIX is a registered trademark of AT&T

VAX is a registered trademark of Digital Equipment Corporation

WordStar is a registered trademark of MicroPro International Corporation

Xerox is a registered trademark of Xerox Corporation

R:BASE is a trademark of Microrim, Inc.

NaturalLink is a trademark of Texas Instruments

XENIX is a registered trademark of Microsoft Corporation

Insight is a service mark of Whitney Educational Services

Preface

Everybody is talking about artificial intelligence (AI). Two years ago you could hardly find anyone who had heard of AI, much less knew what it was. Today there's not only a lot of talk about it, but also a lot of action. All kinds of AI hardware and software products are now on the market, and many more are expected this year and next. The whole field is booming. What was only a tiny research-oriented community a few years ago is now one of the fastest growing segments of the computer business.

So what's in it for you? Well, for starters it's still a very young and underdeveloped discipline. There's a tremendous amount of opportunity to develop and also to use AI products. AI has been around about thirty years, but now all the work of three decades has reached critical mass, and it is resulting in many practical new products and fresh solutions to old problems.

Take expert systems, for example. These advice-giving consultation programs contain the knowledge of one or more experts in a given field. They make it easy for non-experts to get the information they need to solve problems or make decisions on the job.

Natural language processing software is making computers easier to use by allowing users to communicate with the computer via English rather than some artificial intermediate language. AI is giving the computer a new lease on life. This means that there may be a good chance for you to create an expert system or adopt AI techniques to solve some nagging problem.

In any case, AI will be impacting you in some way. It'll make your computer easier to use and far more powerful. On top of that, you'll be able to solve a wider range of problems. But to take advantage of these benefits, you'll need to know something about AI and expert systems. Thus this book.

There are a number of good AI books around, but the bulk of them were written as college texts for computer science graduate students or as advanced references for experienced practitioners. Most are designed to supplement a lecture and are extremely difficult to use for personal learning; some are too simple. I've tried to hit a happy medium somewhere between these two extremes.

This book was written for engineers, programmers, and technical managers who want to learn something about AI quickly and easily by self study. I've taken all the gory details and boiled them down into a concise text that will bring you up to speed fast. This book is a cheap seminar substitute.

The purpose of this book is to take the rather broad and complex subject of AI, with all its many arcane, complex, and diverse AI concepts and techniques, and explain them so that anyone can understand and use them. It is NOT the purpose of this book to exhaustively catalog and explain all AI methods and applications. Instead, the book covers only the most important and useful concepts and techniques. The emphasis is on the practical rather than the theoretical. Topics are not selected for their historical significance or their intellectual curiosity. Instead, the book focuses on those subjects that are the most relevant and useful in the real world.

Overall, this book is a general introduction to the whole field of AI, but with special emphasis on expert systems. Chapter 1 introduces AI and gives you the big picture. In Chapters 2 and 3, I get into the computer techniques unique to AI, such as search methods and knowledge representation schemes. With these three chapters under your belt, you will be ready to tackle any of the other chapters that interest you.

In Chapters 4 and 5, I cover expert systems, the largest and most active subfield of AI. You'll learn the basic concepts in Chapter 4. In Chapter 5, I show you how to build a simple expert system of your own using available software development tools on a personal computer.

Natural language processing concepts are covered in Chapter 6. You will probably never have to create a natural language program, but you will most surely encounter one as an interface or front-end to another type of software package such as a DBMS.

In Chapter 7, I cover computer vision. Using AI techniques, a computer can look at visual information, analyze it, and extract useful information from it. That has all kinds of applications, one of them being robotics, covered in Chapter 8. After a quickie overview of robotics, I show how AI makes robots more useful by making them "smarter."

In Chapters 9 and 10, I get into programming, specifically covering the two main languages of AI, LISP and Prolog. These chapters certainly won't make you an AI programmer by any means, but you will at least learn how these languages look, how they work, and what common functions they perform.

I wrap things up in Chapter 11 by discussing some of the special AI hardware available. Topics include LISP machines, supercomputers, parallel processing, and the new RISC architectures.

At the end of each chapter is a summary called Key Points. It highlights the major facts and concepts. It is a good way to review the chapter or to get a "quickie" introduction before reading it.

Oh yes, don't overlook the Glossary at the end of the book. It is the largest and most complete collection of AI terms available. Learning AI is largely a matter of understanding a lot of new terminology. Use the Glossary liberally as you read this book and related articles and books.

Welcome to the exciting world of AI and expert systems.

Lou Frenzel
Oakton, Virginia

1

Making Computers More Useful by Making Them Smarter

Intelligence . . . is the faculty of making artificial objects, especially tools to make tools.

HENRI BERGSON

Artificial intelligence (AI) is a subdivision of computer science devoted to creating computer software and hardware that imitates the human mind. The main goal of AI is to make computers smarter by creating software that will allow a computer to mimic some of the functions of the human brain in selected applications. The idea is not to replace human beings, but to provide us a more powerful tool to assist us in our work.

Computers already emulate some of the simpler activities of the human mind. They can perform mathematical calculations, manipulate numbers and letters, make simple decisions, and perform various storage and retrieval functions. In these applications, the computer is exceptional and usually exceeds the human mind in performance. Computers can calculate larger, more complex problems faster than the human mind, and they can store huge quantities of data that can be accessed easily. Extremely useful tools, computers greatly speed up and simplify some aspects of the human thought process. As a result, they greatly improve our ability to accomplish work.

Intelligence: Acquiring Knowledge and Applying It

Artificial intelligence gives computers added computing capability, allowing them to exhibit more intelligent behavior. Intelligence, the ability of a human being to acquire knowledge and apply it, means the capability of thinking and reasoning. To a limited degree, artificial intelligence permits computers to accept knowledge from human input, then use that knowledge through simulated thought and reasoning processes to solve problems.

A key part of any artificial intelligence application is knowledge, an understanding of some subject area obtained through education or experience. Although a computer cannot have experiences or study and learn as the human mind can, it can acquire knowledge given to it by human experts. The knowledge consists of facts, concepts, theories, procedures, and relationships. Knowledge is also information that has been

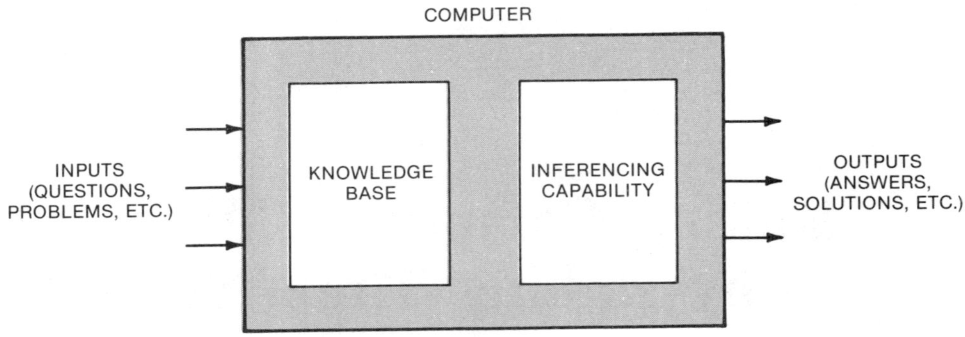

Figure 1–1. ***Applying AI concepts with a computer.***

organized and analyzed to make it understandable and applicable to problem solving or decision making. Most knowledge bases are limited in that they typically focus on some specific subject area or domain.

Once a knowledge base is built, artificial intelligence techniques are used to give the computer thought and reasoning capability. The computer will be able to think, reason, and make inferences and judgments based on the facts and relationships contained in the knowledge base. It will be able to look through the knowledge base and reach conclusions based on the content.

With a knowledge base and the ability to draw inferences from it, the computer can now be put to some practical use as a problem solver and decision maker. Figure 1–1 illustrates the concept of a computer using AI in an application. By searching the knowledge base for relevant facts and relationships, the computer can reach one or more alternative solutions to the given problem. The computer's knowledge base and inferencing capability augment those of the user.

Artificial intelligence gives a computer the ability to solve a wider range of problems than calculation, data storage and retrieval, or simple control. Table 1–1 summarizes some of the ways traditional computers process data. Whenever we give the computer a knowledge base and inferencing capability, the computer can be applied to applications that heretofore were restricted to human solutions only. As a result, the computer becomes a far more useful tool, supplementing and enhancing our own capabilities for increased performance.

Discovering How Our Brains Work

A secondary goal of AI is understanding human intelligence. By attempting to model human intelligence on the computer, we are forced to learn how we store knowledge and use it. We begin to understand our own thought patterns, reasoning techniques, and problem-solving approaches. We learn how we learn, and our strengths and weaknesses are revealed. The result is a better understanding of our minds which can lead to improved ways of learning and applying our intelligence to real world problems. The field of AI devoted to such studies is called *cognitive science.*

Table 1–1. ***How Computers Process Data***

THE PROCESS	THE MANIPULATION
1. Calculate	Perform mathematical operations such as add, subtract, multiply, divide, square root, etc. Solve formulas.
2. Logic	Perform logical operations such as AND, OR, invert, etc.
3. Store	Remember facts and figures in files.
4. Retrieve	Access data stored in files as required.
5. Translate	Convert data from one form to another.
6. Sort	Examine data and put it into some desired order or format.
7. Edit	Make changes, additions, and deletions to data and change its sequence.
8. Make Decisions	Reach simple conclusions based on internal or external conditions.
9. Monitor	Observe external or internal events and take action if certain conditions are met.
10. Control	Take charge of or operate external devices.

How AI Differs from Conventional Computing

Artificial intelligence is software that permits virtually any digital computer to duplicate some functions of the human brain in a limited way. Although special artificial intelligence hardware can be built, most AI is software that will run on mainframes, minicomputers, and even personal computers.

AI programs can be written in virtually any computer language and have been written in assembly language, BASIC, Fortran, Pascal, C, and Forth. However, AI programming languages have been developed especially for AI applications. The two most popular AI programming languages are LISP and Prolog, both of which will be covered later in the book.

Conventional Computing

The techniques for creating AI programs vary considerably from the software we associate with digital computers. In conventional software, we tell the computer how to solve the problem, whereas in AI we tell the computer what the problem is but not how to solve it. Ordinarily, the computer is given data and a step-by-step program that specifies how the data is to be used to reach an answer. In artificial intelligence computing, the computer is given knowledge about the problem subject area plus some inferencing capability. We do not tell the computer specifically how to solve the problem. Instead, the computer and software determine the method of arriving at a solution.

Conventional computer programs are based on an *algorithm,* a clearly defined, step-by-step procedure for solving a problem. It may be a mathematical formula or a clearly defined sequential procedure that will lead to a solution. The algorithm is converted into a computer program, a sequential list of instructions or commands that tell the computer exactly what operations to carry out. The algorithm then uses data such as numbers, letters, or words to solve the problem. New data can be used to solve the same problem.

AI Computing

AI software is not based on an algorithmic process. Instead, it is based on symbolic representation and manipulation. In AI a symbol is a letter, word, or number that is used to represent objects, processes, and their relationships. It can be in printed or electronic form. Objects can be people, things, ideas, concepts, events, or statements of fact. By using symbols, it is possible to create a knowledge base that states facts, concepts, and the relationships between them. Then various processes are used to manipulate the symbols to solve a problem. The process is qualitative rather than quantitative as it is in algorithmic computing.

Virtually all digital computers are algorithmic in their operation, based on the Von Neumann concept: instructions stored in memory are executed sequentially to perform some desired operation. The question is, how is symbolic processing implemented on an algorithmic machine? Algorithm software is written in such a way as to permit symbolic representation and manipulation.

Once a knowledge base of facts and their logical associations is built, some means of using it to solve problems must be developed. How does the AI software reason or infer with this knowledge base? The basic techniques are *search* and *pattern matching.* Given some initial start-up information, the AI software searches the knowledge base looking for specific conditions or patterns. It looks for match ups that satisfy the criteria set up to solve the problem. The computer literally hunts around until it finds the best answer it can give based on the knowledge it has.

While AI problem solving does not take place directly by algorithmic processes, algorithms, of course, are used to implement the search process. Algorithmic programs perform symbolic manipulations that cause problems to be solved in a way that more closely approximates the way a human mind works.

Figure 1–2 shows block diagram representations of a digital computer implementing both conventional and AI operations.

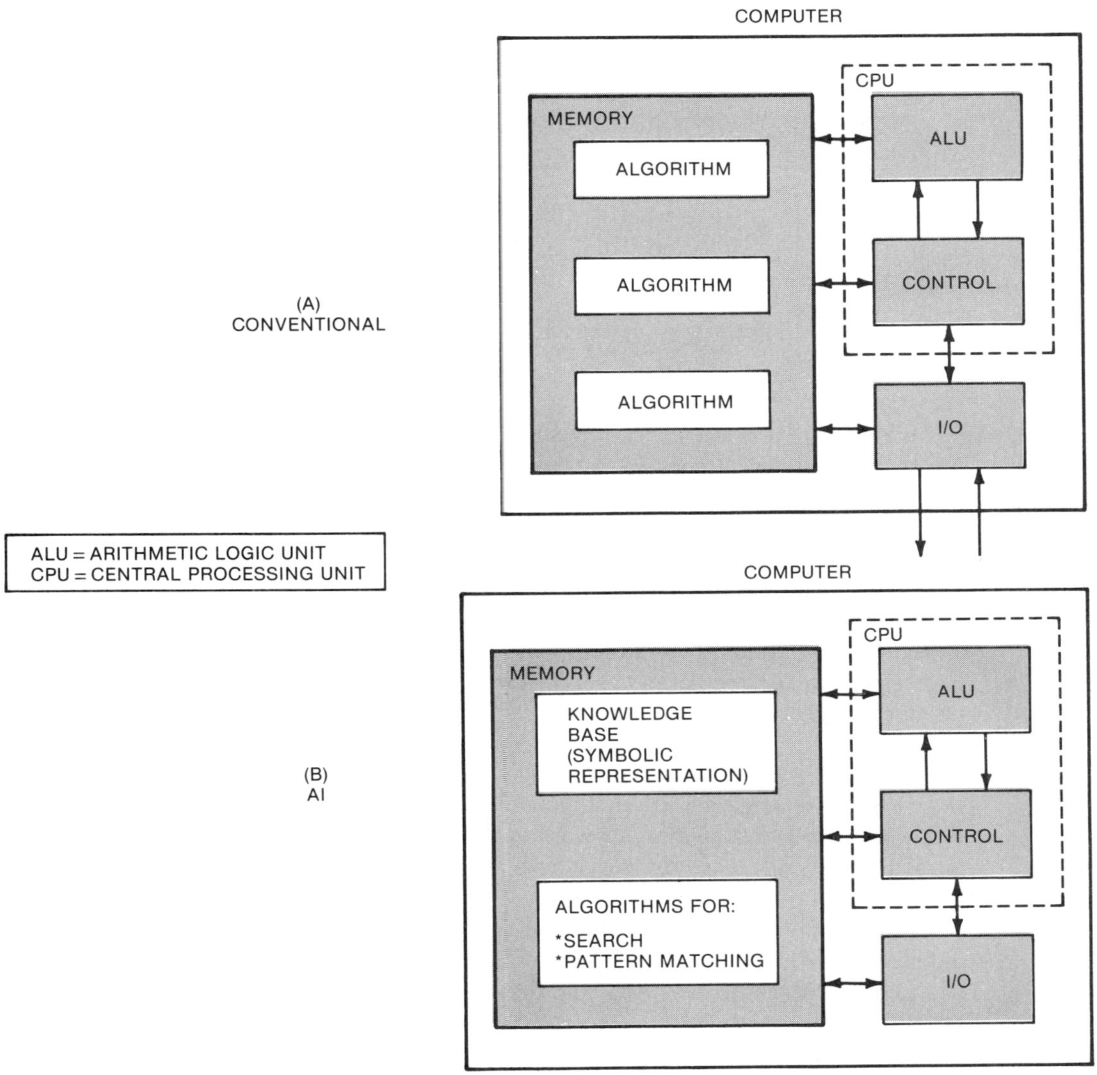

Figure 1–2. ***How digital computers work with conventional (A) and AI (B) methods.***

> *I think, therefore I am.*
>
> DESCARTES

Does a Computer Really Think?

Knowledge bases and search techniques certainly make computers more useful, but can they really make computers more intelligent? AI specialists, computer scientists,

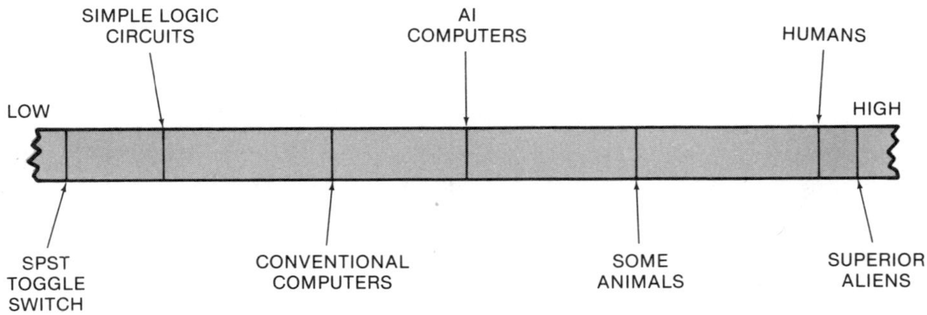

Figure 1–3. ***Spectrum of intelligence or "brain power."***

and others regularly debate that question. The fact that most AI programs are implemented by search and pattern matching techniques leads to the conclusion that computers aren't really intelligent. You can give the computer a lot of information and some guidelines for using it. Using that information and those criteria, the computer can come up with a solution. All it does is test the various alternatives and attempt to find some combination that meets the designated criteria. When that's done, typically a solution is achieved. So although the computer isn't really intelligent, it certainly appears to be "thinking" and often gives a satisfactory solution. Obviously, there are degrees of intelligence as Figure 1–3 shows. The human mind occupies the high end on an intelligence spectrum and simple logic circuits the low end. AI lies somewhere between.

Actually, the whole thing may be a moot point. Does it really matter whether the computer is as intelligent as a human as long as it performs some useful function? If it speeds up and simplifies our work and increases our productivity and ability to do a good job, then who cares how it was accomplished or what degree of intelligence was exhibited?

This brings up another question. Just how do you tell if a computer exhibits intelligence? What are the criteria for making such a judgment? AI researchers have had to deal with those questions, and they have developed some tests that can be used to tell if a system has intelligence.

The most widely known is the Turing test devised by AI pioneer and British mathematician Alan Turing. Basically, the test has a human query a computer via a remotely located computer terminal. At the end of the terminal is either a computer with AI software or another terminal and human operator. The human making the query doesn't know which. Assume it is the computer. If during the exchange the operator believes he is talking to another human, then the computer is said to be intelligent.

Then there is the Chinese room analogy. Assume that you speak only English, and you are isolated in a room with a set of rules and procedures for translating Chinese characters into other Chinese characters. You are then fed Chinese characters to translate. Using your rule book, you create other characters which you send out. The inputs may be questions, the outputs, answers. Does this successful translation process mean you are intelligent? Or does rote following of the rules and procedures presuppose the lack of intelligence?

Even though you got the right answers, can you really say that you know and understand Chinese? No, yet you achieved useful work. All a computer does in AI applications is translate input symbols to appropriate output symbols according to a set of rules in a program.

It is tough to identify intelligence. Any test for intelligence has only limited value and effectiveness. It may work for some cases and not others. The big problem is that intelligence is difficult to define and visualize, because it means so many things.

Let's face it. Although AI is making computers smarter and more powerful, the dream of building a machine that can fully duplicate the human brain will probably not be realized in our lifetime. Despite major advances in all areas of computer science, many question whether we will ever be able to create a computer that will accurately emulate the function of a human mind. Hubert Dreyfus[1], a philosopher at the University of California at Berkeley, feels that the public is being misled about AI, that its usefulness is overblown and its goals impossible. Dreyfus says we will never be able to establish rules for all of the ways we think. It is just too complex.

Of course, researchers are getting closer to a smart machine each year, but there are still too many unanswered questions. For example, how do you represent skills, manual dexterity, learning ability, moods, imagination, emotions, creativity, and "gut feel"? To answer such questions, researchers are turning to related fields such as philosophy, psychology, linguistics, and neuroscience as well as computer science. Thus, the interdisciplinary field of cognitive science was born. Research in microbiology suggests that future computers will use molecular logic circuits rather than silicon electronic circuits, thereby greatly increasing circuit density and reducing size. Still, practical machines based on such techniques are many years away, if ever.

Nevertheless, despite the criticism, AI methods are valuable. They are showing us how we think and how to better apply our intelligence. AI techniques will make computers easier to use and make greater knowledge available to the masses. Perhaps it doesn't matter if we don't fully duplicate the human brain. Even if we can simulate parts of it, the resulting software or hardware will be useful. Besides, computers were created as a tool to assist us, not replace us.

> *The test of a first rate intelligence is the ability to hold two opposed ideas in the mind at the same time, and still retain the ability to function.*
>
> FRANCIS SCOTT FITZGERALD

Applications of Artificial Intelligence

Because of the incredible flexibility of the artificial intelligence process, AI software can be tailored to any problem requiring its special qualities. For example, there are all kinds of problems with no algorithmic solution. Non-numerical problems often don't yield to the algorithmic process. Neither do problems with uncertainty and ambiguity,

[1]Dreyfus, Hubert. 1979. *What Computers Can't Do: The Limits of Artificial Intelligence,* Rev. Ed. New York: Harper & Row.

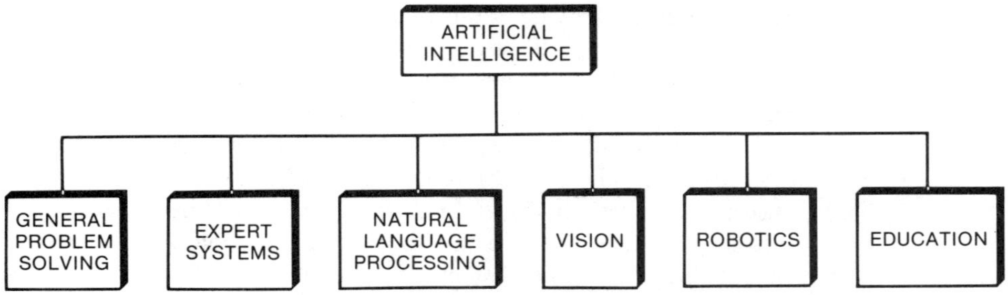

Figure 1–4. ***The major application areas of AI.***

but both are readily solved with AI techniques. With algorithmic software, the problem is guaranteed to be solved; with AI, there can be partial solutions or even no solution. As a result, AI often fits the disorganized, imperfect real world better than conventional software because it can deal with shades of gray.

Games

The first applications of AI were game playing and puzzle solving. Researchers felt that the ability of a computer to play a game was an excellent demonstration of human intelligence, and it is, in a controlled and limited way. AI programs to play chess, checkers, backgammon, tic-tac-toe, and others were written, tested, and improved. AI programs were also written to solve puzzles and riddles. For example, AI programs have been written to solve the Rubik's cube puzzle. These first applications proved the symbolic processing concepts of AI, and games and puzzles are still used as examples in teaching AI.

But AI researchers also discovered the limitations of computers in these initial applications. Huge memories were needed to store the knowledge base (game rules, how pieces move, opening strategies, etc.), and the search process usually required a long time. Even if a computer had enough memory, its speed limited the performance so that the response was often maddenly slow. As a result, only the largest and fastest mainframes could be used on AI problems.

Fortunately, technological developments have virtually eliminated speed and memory size limitations for all but the largest AI programs. Today, minicomputers routinely run AI software, and most of the newer personal computers are capable of dealing with AI software.

Although games are interesting, they are not particularly useful. Computer users are looking for programs that will help their performance and productivity, and artificial intelligence has found some specific niches in which it excels. These applications areas include general problem solving, expert systems, natural language processing, computer vision, robotics, and education. These are illustrated in Figure 1–4. All of these applications employ a knowledge base and inferencing techniques to solve problems or help make decisions in specific domains.

General Problem Solving

General problem solving is something AI does well, and that ability can be applied to a very wide range of subjects. For people with tough problems to solve or problems that don't fit algorithmic computer processes, AI offers a fresh alternative.

Some early attempts were made to create a general purpose AI problem-solving program. Although limited success was achieved, the approach was just not suitable for all types and sizes of problems. As a result, virtually all AI software is custom designed for the application. The best AI software is designed and optimized for the specific job.

Some of the toughest jobs that a mathematician, scientist, or engineer does are theorem proving or formula reduction. Their work frequently leads to the expression of some concept or physical system in mathematical form. In analyzing or designing a system, for example, the mathematical formulas representing that system must be solved. This involves reducing the formulas to their simplest form, then plugging in real world values to get the final result. Some formulas are so large and complex that they take an enormous amount of time, thought, and trial-and-error. Some even defy human solution.

Occasionally, a theorem describing how a system works must be proved. Hours, even weeks or months, of difficult mathematical work are required to prove the theorem. Computers can help, of course. Special theorem proving AI programs have been developed to help solve these large complex problems. A good example is MACSYMA. Its basic skill is algebraic manipulation, but it can also perform over 500 different math operations, including calculus, trigonometry, and series. It does all of its processing symbolically, manipulating the input expressed in symbols into a simplified formula for proving or disproving a theorem.

Another problem-solving application is planning, the process of setting up a step-by-step sequence of actions to achieve some goal. Coming up with a good plan, that takes the least time and effort and has the lowest cost and fewest steps, is the key to running a business or a manufacturing operation. When many complex steps are involved, generating the plan is difficult because there are so many possible combinations. By giving these steps to an AI program along with some criteria to judge the output, an optimized plan can be generated. The program searches through the steps combining them in various ways until a solution is reached. Similar programs are also excellent for complex scheduling problems where many events must be properly timed and sequenced.

Expert Systems

The major use of artificial intelligence today is in *expert systems,* AI programs that act as intelligent advisors or consultants. Drawing on stored knowledge in a specific domain, an inexperienced user applies inferencing capability to tap the knowledge base. As a result, almost anyone can solve problems and make decisions in a subject area nearly as well as an expert.

An expert system permits the knowledge and experience of one or more experts to be captured and stored in a computer. This knowledge can then be used by anyone

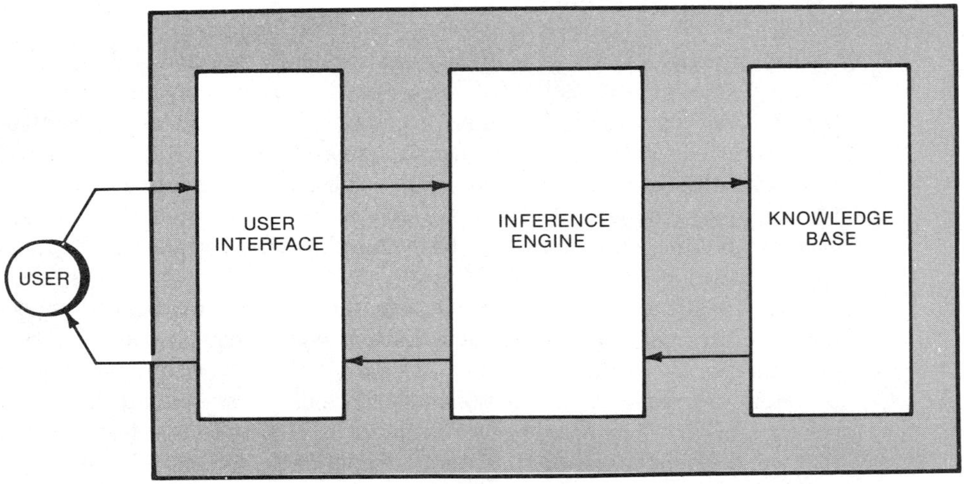

Figure 1–5. ***General block diagram of an expert system.***

requiring it. The purpose of an expert system is not to replace the experts, but simply to make their knowledge and experience more widely available. Typically there are more problems to solve than there are experts available to handle them. The expert system permits others to increase their productivity, improve the quality of their decisions, or simply to solve problems when an expert is not available.

Valuable knowledge is a major resource and it often lies with only a few experts. It is important to capture that knowledge so others can use it. Experts die, retire, get sick, move on to other fields, and otherwise become unavailable. Thus the knowledge is lost. Books can capture some knowledge, but they leave the problem of application up to the reader. Expert systems provide a direct means of applying expertise.

> *Knowledge is the only instrument of production that is not subject to diminishing returns.*
>
> J. M. Clark

An expert system consists of three major components: a knowledge base, an inference engine, and a user interface. These are illustrated in Figure 1–5. The knowledge base contains all the facts, ideas, relationships, and interactions of a narrow domain. The inference engine analyzes the knowledge and draws conclusions from it. The user interface software permits new knowledge to be entered into the knowledge base and implements communication with the user.

To use an expert system, the user boots up the expert system software. The expert system then asks the user various questions to gather some initial information about the problem to be solved. The user can key in the information requested or select it from alternatives presented in menu form. Once the expert system has the input it needs, it proceeds to search for a solution and reach a conclusion. The output may be a recommended course of action or the selection of the best alternative from a number of choices.

The user may also direct the expert system to explain the process by which the conclusion was reached. Often users do not trust expert systems and are unwilling to apply the results to critical decision making unless they understand the reasoning process. Some expert systems have the ability to present the steps used in arriving at the answer, thus allowing the user to follow the logic involved and to become more comfortable with the outcome.

Expert systems are ideal when it is necessary for an individual to select the best alternative from a long list of choices. Based on the criteria supplied to it, the expert system can choose the best option. For example, there are expert systems that will help you select one of the many places to invest your money based on your own financial condition, goals, and personality traits.

An expert system can be created to help an individual troubleshoot and repair a complex piece of equipment. The various troubles and symptoms can be given to an expert system which then identifies the problem and suggests courses of action for repair.

Expert systems also can be used to aid in diagnosing medical cases. Symptoms and test results can be given to the expert system which then searches its knowledge base in an attempt to match these input conditions with a particular malady or disease. This results in a conclusion about the illness and some possible suggestions on how to treat it. Such an expert system can greatly aid a doctor in diagnosing an illness and prescribing treatment. It does not replace doctors, but helps them confirm their own decisions and may provide alternative conclusions.

Expert systems perform financial analysis. Some expert systems can evaluate stocks and recommend buy, sell, or hold positions. Other expert systems can be used in tax planning and budgeting.

Expert systems have been used to help locate oil and mineral deposits or to configure complex computer systems and recommend a specific policy in a variety of insurance applications. Expert systems also have been used to locate oil spills and provide speedy critical advice to commanders in battlefield situations. The variety of potential applications is enormous. If one or more experts exist in the domain of interest, and the knowledge can be codified and represented in symbolic form, then an expert system can be created.

Natural Language Processing

A second widely used AI application is natural language processing (NLP). Natural language refers to our native tongue, whether it be English or any other language. Natural language processing programs use artificial intelligence techniques to permit a computer to understand and generate natural language. It has been said that the key to intelligence is the understanding of language.

Computers are controlled and programmed by using complex languages, a cross or compromise between the machine language of the computer and our natural language. Other forms of computer software use a wide variety of special languages, commands and syntax. To use a computer, you must adjust to these special languages and procedures. Just think how much simpler it would be if we could apply our own natural language instead. Computers would be far easier to use, and more people could take advantage of their power.

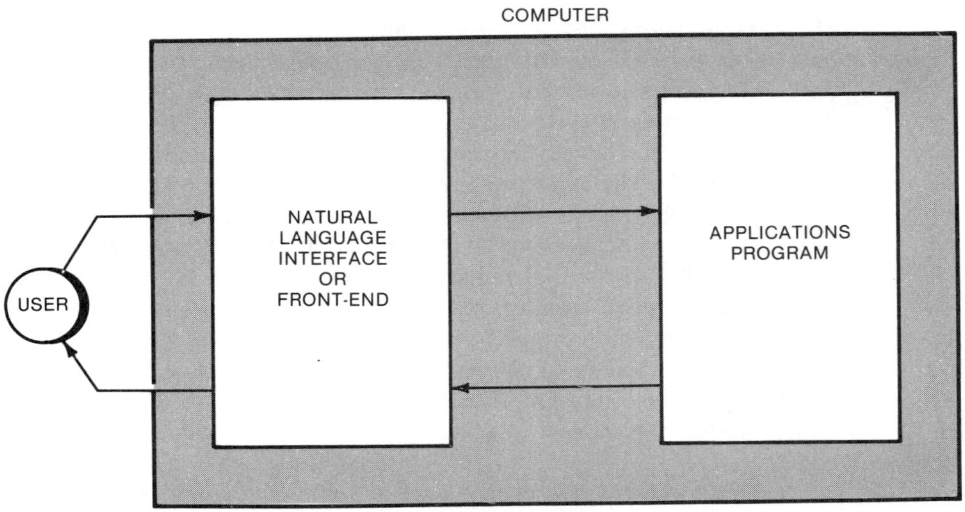

Figure 1–6. ***A natural language interface.***

Natural language processing programs use AI techniques to analyze natural language inputs typed in on the computer keyboard. These programs attempt to identify the syntax, semantics, and context contained within a sentence to extract meaning from the natural language input. If such a program can understand what is said, it can then respond. For example, the computer could initiate the commands specified by the user. Usually, such an action would have to be programmed in a special language or implemented by a unique sequence of commands, but with an NLP program, a simple English statement could cause it to happen.

A typical application for an NLP program is as a "go-between" to other forms of computer software as shown in Figure 1–6. Such programs are called natural language interfaces or natural language front-ends. They permit the user to interact with other software using natural language rather than the usual complex systems and procedures. A natural language front-end might be used on an operating system, a data base management system, a spreadsheet, or in a variety of other ways.

Natural language understanding programs can also be used for language translation. Such a program might read the Spanish language, understand it, and produce an accurate English translation. Another natural language program may read existing sources of information and abstract them. Such a program would search the masses of data available and provide a summary of the key facts, thus saving time and effort.

So how does a natural language processing system work? The whole idea behind a natural language processor is to understand the words and sentences entered. That is, the natural language processing software has to extract meaning from the input. For this purpose, most natural language processors have three basic parts: a parser, a knowledge representation system, and an output translator, as shown in Figure 1–7. The parser takes the natural language input sentence and breaks it down into the various parts of grammar (nouns, verbs, adjectives, prepositions, etc.). This is the first step in determining the function of each word in the sentence and the way the words relate to one another. This analysis usually results in the construction of a tree-like

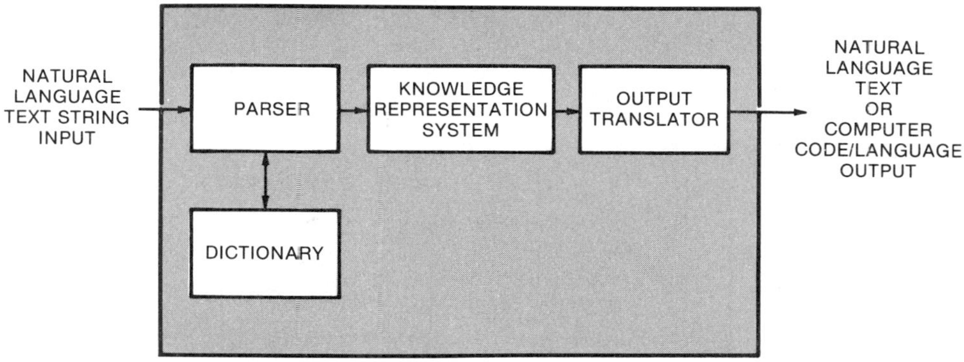

Figure 1–7. ***The major components of an NLP system.***

graph that organizes the words according to their meaning and purpose. This tree is a variation of the old sentence diagramming process that many of us used in learning English grammar.

A dictionary associated with the parser helps determine word meaning, but it often has a limited vocabulary. It can't know everything. So, like expert systems and other AI programs, NLP systems are usually limited or dedicated to a specific subject area or application.

The knowledge system then analyzes the parsed output to determine meaning. Based on its knowledge, the NLP system tries to understand the input so it can take some appropriate action.

Finally, the output translator takes the interpretation of the knowledge system and initiates some action. It may respond with a natural language reply or create special outputs that match other computer programs. For example, a natural language input may elicit a response that is nothing more than a "canned" natural language phrase set up especially for that purpose. Or it may generate a special code or command that the computer operating system or an applications program can use to trigger further action.

A special AI field related to NLP is *speech recognition.* AI software also can be created to allow a computer to respond to voice input. Voice or speech recognition uses an electronic process of converting voice input to a microphone into electronic signals that can be understood and used by the NLP system. Typically, voice recognition is typically a hardware process, but some advanced systems use AI software techniques. Thus natural language processing and voice recognition can be combined.

The output of the voice recognizer can be used to drive a natural language processing system so that a computer can be operated by voice. Instead of typing in natural language inquiries, all you do is speak into a microphone. The voice recognition equipment converts the sound waves into electronic signals that a natural language interface can understand. Then NLP takes over and interprets what is said and causes other actions to take place. There are several commercial voice recognition systems available, but like natural language processors, their vocabulary is limited and they cannot deal with foreign languages. Nevertheless, they make it possible to operate a computer in an entirely new and easier way.

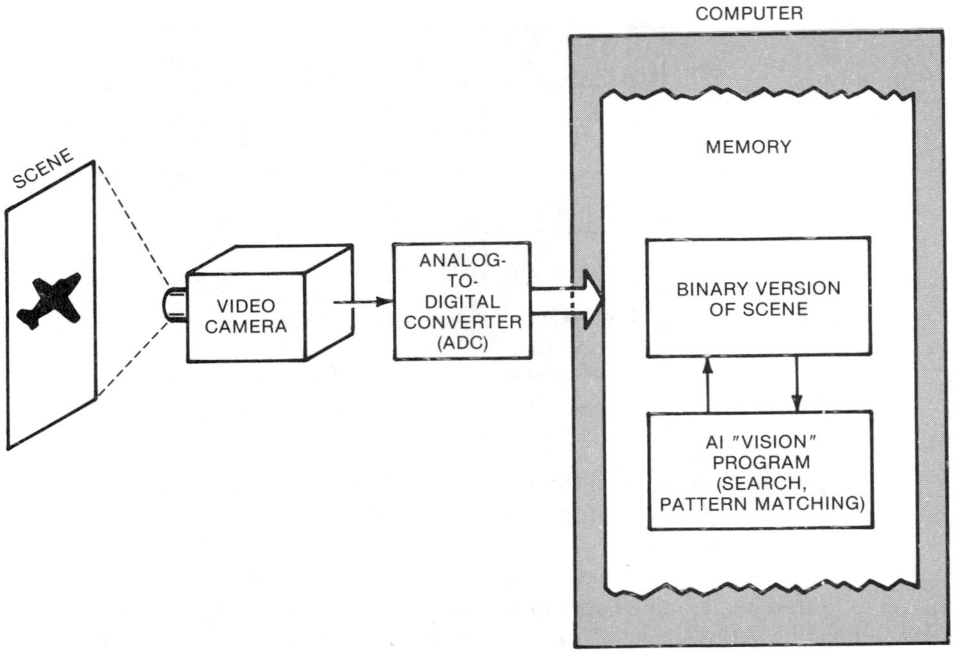

Figure 1–8. ***A computer vision system.***

Computer Vision

Computer vision is another application for artificial intelligence. Computer vision is the use of a computer to analyze and evaluate visual information. Artificial intelligence techniques allow the computer to examine a picture or real life scene to identify particular objects, features, or patterns.

By using search and pattern-matching techniques, a computer can pick out key features and search and identify information that a human eye may miss. Computer vision AI software attempts to extract knowledge from visual information to help a user solve a problem or make a decision. The examination of aerial photographs for intelligence information is an example application.

For a computer to perform artificial intelligence operations on visual inputs, the picture or real life scene must first be converted into digital signals compatible with the computer. A typical system for doing this is shown in Figure 1–8. A video camera is pointed at the picture or scene and a video signal generated. A high speed analog-to-digital converter (ADC) changes the analog video signal into binary numbers that are stored in the computer memory. The AI software then uses this input data for its content analysis.

Robotics

Artificial intelligence is also used in the field of *robotics.* Robotics is that field of engineering devoted to duplicating the physical capabilities of human beings, a natural

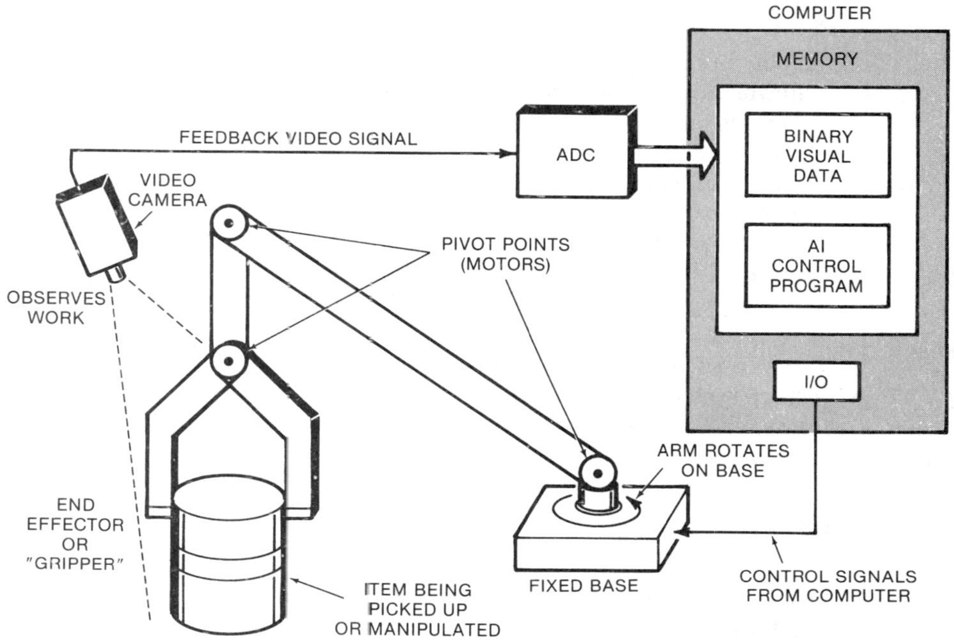

Figure 1–9. ***An "intelligent" robot.***

complement to the field of AI which attempts to mimic human mental abilities. Robots are machines or manipulators capable of carrying out limited physical functions. The typical robot is a manipulator arm that can be used to pick up and place parts in a manufacturing operation, weld, paint, attach bolts and screws, and perform other intricate mechanical manipulations.

Robotic manipulator arms are operated by special electronic controllers or in some cases a computer. The controller or computer supplies commands to the robot and causes it to move the way it has been programmed to move. The program algorithm determines what the robot does.

Robots cannot respond to unusual or changing conditions. They cannot make their own decisions. However, if a robot is controlled by a computer, then it can be given artificial intelligence software which can make it more powerful and flexible. The robot with intelligence can then respond to changing conditions. Instead of blindly carrying out a preprogrammed sequence of operations, the robot may decide to change the order of its process, eliminate some steps, or otherwise modify its operation to fit the situation.

To use artificial intelligence software, however, a robot must receive inputs about its environment. This means it must use sensors to detect the position of its arm and other conditions in its surroundings. Typical robotics arms can be outfitted with pressure sensors, temperature sensors, light sensors, and a variety of other kinds of transducers that provide environmental information. The most useful sensor is visual input from a video camera. With information about its own conditions and environment, the robot can use artificial intelligence software to adapt to its surroundings. This makes the robot far more flexible and useful as it can more closely duplicate the work of human beings. Figure 1–9 shows an example of an "intelligent" robot.

Education

AI can also be used in education and training. Using AI methods, new forms of computer-based training (CBT) software can be created that allow the computer to act as an intelligent tutor. In conventional computer-based training applications, "canned" sequences of instructional material are presented. Interaction with the program helps the student learn, but the main disadvantage of such CBT is that it presents a fixed content and sequence to all students regardless of their background or capability.

Unlike traditional CBT, AI-based CBT can adjust its tutorial to the student's knowledge, experience, strengths, and weaknesses. It may even be able to carry on a natural language dialogue. Intelligent CBT is far more effective than conventional CBT as a result.

In addition, students can also learn from expert systems. The knowledge in an expert system can be tapped by assuming problems and finding solutions. In some cases, education or training may not even be necessary if the knowledge in an expert system is available.

Other Applications

There are literally hundreds of other ways AI can be applied. Automatic programming is an example. Here AI techniques are used to help a programmer develop and code an algorithmic program for a special problem. Ideally, the desired program may be stated in natural language while the output is machine code that solves the problem. As computers and the problems they solve get more complex, they become more difficult to program. It is a time consuming and costly process. Further, there is a continuing shortage of good programmers. An AI-based automatic programming system can greatly improve programmer productivity by simplifying, shortening, and lessening the expense of programming.

Another important application is computer-aided design (CAD). General purpose computers and special engineering workstations are now routinely used for CAD in electronic, mechanical, and architectural fields. AI techniques give them design knowledge and problem-solving capability that help an engineer design useable products and systems in record time with minimum effort. The future will bring many other similar applications.

Advantages and Disadvantages of AI

AI is sure to be a big hit with computer users once it becomes more widely known and firmly established. But there is also a down side. Let's examine some of the pros and cons of AI software.

The Good News

For openers, AI software can make any computer, be it a $500 home computer, a powerful mini, or a multi-million dollar supercomputer, more user friendly than any of these machines are now. Users will be able to communicate with the computer in their own natural language—English or any other language—rather than having to use the cryptic commands and syntax of operating systems, languages, and applications programs. With AI, an untrained user can approach the machine and achieve useful work. Computers will be no more difficult to use than the telephone.

Special natural language interfaces will have to be written to achieve this ambitious result, and already many commercial natural language interfaces are available for popular computers and software packages. Data base management systems (DBMS) are one of the first types of conventional software to take advantage of natural language front-ends. They permit fast, easy access to data stored in the DBMS without tricky programming. Spreadsheets, word processing packages, operating systems, and other applications programs are expected to eventually incorporate AI methods to improve user friendliness and thus increase productivity.

Another major benefit is that computers will be far more useful. It has been said that computers are a solution looking for a problem. There's a lot of truth in that statement (you can say the same thing about AI), but computers have found problems to solve. They are excellent data processors and they find a wide range of uses in business, industry, government, military, schools, and even the home. However, not all problems yield to an algorithmic or data processing solution. Not all problems require calculation or data storage and retrieval. There are many problems to be solved that do not fit the capabilities usually associated with a computer.

Then along comes AI to change all of that. With AI techniques, a whole new realm of opportunities open up. New kinds of problems can be solved. The same computers that do your data processing can now address problems associated with acquiring and accessing knowledge, making decisions, and otherwise performing some functions heretofore reserved only for humans. AI is great for "messy" problems where the data is unknown or incomplete or where there are no known algorithms. Such capabilities, combined with your own expertise, can lead to improved performance and productivity. AI techniques as used in expert systems have the potential to make problem solving and decision making in specific domains faster and easier.

The Bad News

But surely, as with everything, there must be a down side to AI. As far as applications go, AI offers only advantages or benefits, but not without a price. Overall, computers will become a more powerful and useful tool, but the increased cost might represent a disadvantage to some. AI applications usually require very powerful computers with fast CPUs and lots of memory. AI is currently not practical on the smaller home or personal computers, for example. Most AI research and many AI applications are implemented on mainframes and big minicomputers such as Digital Equipment Corporation's (DEC) VAX series. Typical systems sell from $150,000 to nearly a half million dollars.

However, microcomputers are getting faster and more powerful. Sixteen-bit machines are commonplace, and 32-bit micros are just coming on the market. Memory chips are getting denser and cheaper. The 256K chips are common and inexpensive. One and four megabit chips are on their way. As a result, many AI applications can be readily implemented on the larger PCs, such as the IBM PC/XT and AT models and their compatibles. The Apple Macintosh is another PC capable of small scale AI. The cost disadvantage is slowly going away, but for now, it is a problem to deal with.

Another disadvantage is the difficulty of AI software development. AI programs are incredibly complex. As a result, they take more time to develop and they are far more expensive. Software development tools such as improved AI programming languages and expert system generators help speed up and simplify AI software development, but they, too, are expensive and require some talent to use.

On top of this, there are few programmers around who are capable of dealing with AI. As the colleges graduate more AI computer scientists and as the field grows, there will be more programmers to write the software, but now there is a severe shortage. AI programmers can literally name their price and position.

Finally, there are few practical commercial AI products on the market. There are several natural language interfaces, a few expert systems, and lots of languages and software development tools, but that's about it. Of course, many future products are expected.

The Early Days

As a specialized field of computer science, artificial intelligence is said to have begun in the summer of 1956 when a group of computer scientists met at Dartmouth College to discuss the potential of computers for simulating human intelligence. Researchers from academia, industry, and various "think tanks" got together to discuss their work and exchange ideas. From that point on, AI has grown, changed, and developed into a full fledged field of inquiry. It is finally emerging from the labs to perform useful work.

Table 1–2 shows a time line of AI history, indicating some of the most notable events. AI has existed primarily in universities and research labs, and few, if any, practical products were developed. By the late 1970s and in the 1980s, many AI techniques had been developed, and practical commercial products were possible. Much of the research during the past several decades is now being converted into real products that bring the benefits of AI to the computer user.

Influencing Factors

Although AI has been painfully slow in reaching a commercially viable state, during the past several years it has become more visible and practical for several important reasons.

First, developments in computer technology have made AI applications more practical. Most AI applications require exceptional computer performance. Very high speed operation and mass storage capability are required for even the simplest AI functions. Faster computing circuits and cheap semiconductor mass storage have made computers more powerful but at the same time smaller and more affordable. Practical hardware is now available for AI applications at reasonable cost.

The same is true of software development. Over the years, considerable AI software has been created. New languages and programming tools are now commercially available and have made AI software faster and easier to develop.

Table 1–2. ***Time Line of AI History***

Event	Year
•Alan Turing conceives the "Turing Machine"	1937
•John von Neumann states the "stored program" computer concept	1945
•Eckert & Mauchly dedicate the first general purpose electronic calculator ENIAC at the University of Pennsylvania	1946
•Turing proposes his "Turing Test" for intelligence	1950
•Early chess-playing programs demonstrated	1955
•Dartmouth AI conference	1956
•LISP language created by John McCarthy at MIT	1957
•First major expert system, DENDRAL, started at Stanford	1965
•Second major expert system, MACSYMA, started at MIT	1966
•First implementation of the Prolog language	1970
•First microprocessor by Intel	1971
•Milestone expert system MYCIN developed at Stanford	1972
•SHRDLU natural language robot demonstrated at MIT	1972
•First commercial natural language processing system, "Intellect," available from Artificial Intelligence Corp.	1981
•Japanese begin their 5th generation computer development program	1982
•First practical AI programs available for personal computers	1984

The personal computer is another factor that has influenced the emergence of AI techniques. Today millions of people know how to use a computer and seek the advantages and benefits they bring. Users are demanding more and better software for their machines, and AI promises to deliver. Personal computer software companies trying to stay competitive and give customers what they want are rapidly incorporating AI techniques.

Further, the potential of AI has attracted venture capitalists, who provide money to finance new companies and to help existing companies expand and grow. Many new companies are now forming to take advantage of AI opportunities and the available funding. Many existing software companies are planning to incorporate AI as soon as it makes sense. Most major computer and electronic companies have AI programs. These include IBM, Sperry, DEC, General Motors (Hughes and Teknowledge) and others.

Finally, there is a kind of self-imposed pressure on the AI community to step up research efforts and create more practical AI products sooner. This pressure comes partially from wanting to take advantage of the incredible opportunities to serve the growing needs of those who use computers and make money doing it. But the pressure also comes from a desire to respond to Japan's announced quest for world computer leadership.

Japan and the Fifth Generation

In 1982, the Japanese told the world of their plans to create the new fifth generation of computers based on AI techniques. The U.S. computer community moved quickly to assess its own position. Should the Japanese succeed in their effort, they could become the dominant world computer power, a position the U.S. now holds and jealously guards. The Japanese AI effort is supported by Japanese industry which funds and staffs the Institute for New Generation Computer Technology (ICOT) where most of the research and development on the 5th generation machines takes place. ICOT is also funded by the Japanese government to the tune of $450 million over the next ten years. The Japanese claim they will have commercially viable machines by the early 1990s.

In the U.S., twenty-one computer and electronic companies have formed a consortium called Microelectronics and Computer Technology Corporation (MCC) in Austin, Texas, to do AI and other related research in advanced computer and electronic technologies. These companies fund the research and hope to cash in on the results by incorporating it in future products.

The U.S. government does not fund such commercial efforts. However, it does indirectly fund R&D in AI. For example, the Defense Department's Defense Advanced Research Projects Agency (DARPA) has been a major contributor to AI projects in universities and research companies over the years. AI has many positive implications for military applications, but the research is applicable to many other commercial applications.

Despite the major Japanese effort, most assessments say that the U.S. is already far ahead of Japan as well as Britain, France, Germany, and other countries with major AI programs. U.S. computer leadership does not appear to be in jeopardy, because the healthy competition not only among countries but also among corporations will help keep the U.S. ahead. It is expected that U.S. companies will also be offering the first 5th generation computers in the early 1990s.

As the field of computer science has evolved, technological developments have caused computers to change from one stage to the next. Each stage is referred to as a generation. Table 1–3 indicates the various generations of computer hardware and software and the characteristics of each. We are now assumed to be in the fourth generation with the fifth generation under development. The fifth generation typically means computers based on parallel processing and artificial intelligence concepts. These knowledge-based machines will also have conventional computing capability and even greater power and ease of use.

Great Expectations

So what does the future hold? Plenty. First, AI R&D will continue and all of the various subfields will evolve and improve. New software techniques will be discovered. Improved software development tools will be created making it easier to develop new expert systems and other AI programs.

Advances will also occur in hardware. In addition to the usual on-going developments in semiconductor technology that will bring us larger and faster microprocessors and RAM chips, entirely new devices will be created. Special search, pattern matching, and symbolic computing chips will be developed. The new parallel computer architectures with multiple CPUs operating simultaneously will bring a whole new dimension to AI, offering the opportunity of different and far more powerful AI software. The fifth generation machines will make it a whole new ball game.

Table 1–3. ***The Computer Generations***

GENERATION	HARDWARE	SOFTWARE
1st 1945-1957	*Vacuum tubes *Delay line, CRT and drum memories	*Machine code *Plug boards
2nd 1957-1963	*Transistors *Magnetic core memories	*Higher level languages (COBOL, FORTRAN)
3rd 1963-1971	*Integrated circuits *Semiconductor memory *Minicomputers *Magnetic disk storage	*Operating systems *Virtual memory *Timesharing
4th 1971-1989	*Microprocessors & personal computers *VLSI *Faster denser RAM *Networking	*DBMS *4th Generation languages
5th 1989-2000	*VHSIC *Parallel processing architectures *RISC architectures	*Knowledge-based software *Expert systems *Natural language processing
6th 2000-?	*Optical processors and storage	*Automated programming

For the immediate future, you can expect to see AI added to existing software. Natural language front-ends will become a common feature on many applications programs. Internally, programs will use segments of AI to make some performance improvement. Expert systems on important topics will become more widely available.

Generally speaking, however, there will be few stand-alone AI software products. Expert systems are the exception. The predictions are that AI software will in most applications be combined with conventional algorithmic software. That is, AI subroutines, including expert systems, will be embedded in traditional software or vice versa. The AI will be virtually transparent to the user.

There is great concern within the AI and software communities that too much will be expected of AI. AI researchers are particularly upset over the excessive amount of PR and hype that AI has been receiving during the past few years. They fear that the public's expectations will be far beyond what AI can really deliver. That is certainly a legitimate concern, but such build-ups occur on most new high tech methods and products. The press and others often exaggerate the potential of new "whiz-bang" technology just to get attention, creating false hope and enormous expectations.

For years home computers were hyped beyond belief. Everyone expected them to be the end-all/do-everything electronic appliance of the 20th century. People were actually afraid of not having a home computer for themselves and their kids, so millions were purchased. Then the public quickly discovered that there were very few good applications for a home computer. As a result, many of these machines are now in closets, basements, attics, and garage sales. Despite the disappointment, the public survived and so did the industry.

Even with all the hype, AI will survive and prosper. It is too complex a subject for the average person, so most people will not really be affected. It will be the knowledgeable end users that may get burned by unrealistic expectations. That could waste time and money, not to mention ruin careers and give AI a bad name.

So, while AI is an excellent technology, it is not the panacea we might like it to be. Look at it for what it really is: some special software techniques now developed to the point that they can be practical and useful. Where possible, consider AI as an alternative, a possible factor in your application. Look for ways to use it, just don't expect miracles. On rare occasions, AI may give a miracle-like solution, but more likely it will not. It will deliver evolutionary rather than revolutionary improvements.

> *We are drowning in information but starved for knowledge.*
>
> JOHN NAISBITT IN MEGATRENDS

Dealing with Info Glut

One place we are likely to see major improvements is in the general handling of information. Most of us are voracious users, generators, and dispensers of information of all kinds. There is so much information that there is simply no way to track, catalog, or access all of it. Industries have grown up in an attempt to tackle various aspects of information handling. Libraries have been established to help collect and dispense information.

But despite all these efforts, most of us are still in information overload. There is simply too much information to deal with. Further, we don't always know that it exists or how to obtain it once we know that we need it. And while the information glut is real, we need that information desperately. We need it to do our jobs competently, and we want it so that we can live an informed, intelligent life.

Computers can help immensely to conquer the information problem even though most of us would agree that they are just as much a part of the problem as they are the solution. There is no way to stop or even slow down the generation of new information, and we probably wouldn't want to even if we could. The secret is to find a way to use the computer to collect, catalog and dispense the information in an organized way. Huge computer data bases are being built which permit the convenient storage and retrieval of information. Information utilities are being formed to catalog and store information of all varieties that may be accessed by anyone via a computer terminal over the telephone lines.

Artificial intelligence will help relieve our information overload. It will provide new means of finding and accessing the information you need. Natural language interfaces will make computer data bases easier to tap.

But perhaps the most important aspect of AI is that it will force or encourage the conversion of information into knowledge. Typically you have to analyze the information, organize it, sift through it, and extract from it what's important to you. It is at that point that information becomes knowledge that can be applied to the solving of a problem or the making of a decision.

Since AI programs like expert systems are knowledge-based, then some means must be used to convert the information into knowledge. While this is a difficult, time

Book Mark

HOWARD W. SAMS & COMPANY
Excellence In Publishing

DEAR VALUED CUSTOMER:

Howard W. Sams & Company is dedicated to bringing you timely and authoritative books for your personal and professional library. Our goal is to provide you with excellent technical books written by the most qualified authors. You can assist us in this endeavor by checking the box next to your particular areas of interest.

We appreciate your comments and will use the information to provide you with a more comprehensive selection of titles.

Thank you,

Vice President, Book Publishing
Howard W. Sams & Company

SUBJECT AREAS:

Computer Titles:
- ☐ Apple/Macintosh
- ☐ Commodore
- ☐ IBM & Compatibles
- ☐ Business Applications
- ☐ Communications
- ☐ Operating Systems
- ☐ Programming Languages

Electronics Titles:
- ☐ Amateur Radio
- ☐ Audio
- ☐ Basic Electronics
- ☐ Electronic Design
- ☐ Electronic Projects
- ☐ Satellites
- ☐ Troubleshooting & Repair

Other interests or comments:
____
____

Name ____________________
Title ____________________
Company ____________________
Address ____________________
City ____________________
State/Zip ____________________
Daytime Telephone No. ____________________

HOWARD W. SAMS & COMPANY

A Division of Macmillan, Inc.
4300 West 62nd Street
Indianapolis, Indiana 46268 USA

22443

consuming, expensive process, it is one that will get a handle on the information explosion. It will help us get the knowledge we need, not just the raw data.

By now you should have AI in the proper perspective. It is indeed an exciting and unusual technology. In the remaining chapters, you will be exposed to a wide range of applications and techniques. You are certain to find something of interest.

Key Points

- AI is a subfield of computer science devoted to making computers and software that mimic the human brain.
- The main purpose of AI is to make computers smarter, more powerful and thus more useful.
- Intelligence is the ability to acquire knowledge and apply it. Knowledge comes from education and experience.
- Conventional computing uses algorithms for data storage and retrieval, calculation, control and other processing functions.
- AI computers process symbols which represent objects, concepts, and relationships.
- AI is software that consists of a knowledge base and a mechanism that solves problems and makes decisions by search and pattern matching techniques.
- The main applications areas for AI are general problem-solving, expert systems, natural language, vision, robotics, and education.
- An expert system is an advice-giving or consultation program containing the knowledge and experience of one or more experts in a specific domain that anyone can tap as an aid in solving problems.
- An expert system consists of a knowledge base that stores the expertise, an inference engine that thinks and reasons, and an interface that communicates with the user.
- Natural language processing (NLP) refers to the understanding and generation of a natural language such as English, using AI methods.
- Typical uses of NLP include front-ends or interfaces to make software easier to use and language translation.
- Computer vision refers to the use of AI methods in analyzing and understanding visual information.
- AI can make robots smarter and more useful.
- The two main benefits of AI are (1) it can make computers easier to use and (2) more useful by solving a wider range of problems.
- The disadvantages of AI are (1) complexity and (2) high cost.
- AI is approximately 30 years old, but the first successful commercial AI products didn't appear until the 1980s.

- AI has been made practical by faster CPUs, cheap mass memory, and software development tools.
- The fifth generation refers to (1) an effort by the Japanese to achieve dominance in the computer market and (2) the forth-coming new generation of computers based on AI techniques and parallel processing.
- Despite its age, AI is still an infant technology with much work to be done and much progress yet to be made.
- There will be few stand-alone AI programs, instead AI will simply be a part of conventional software and essentially transparent to the user. An exception is expert systems.
- AI is not a panacea. While it will improve conventional software and permit new uses for computers, it will not produce miracles. As a result, hopes and expectations for AI should not be blown out of proportion.

2

Knowledge Representation

The whole machinery of our intelligence, our general ideas and laws, fixed and external objects, principles, persons and gods, are so many symbolic, algebraic expressions. They stand for experience; experience which we are incapable of retaining and surveying in its multitudinous immediacy. We should flounder hopelessly, like the animals, did we not keep ourselves afloat and direct our course by these intellectual devices. Theory helps us to bear our ignorance of fact.

GEORGE SANTAYANA

Most artificial intelligence systems are made up of two basic parts: a knowledge base and an inference mechanism. The knowledge base contains facts about objects in the chosen domain and their relationships. Most AI programs focus on a specific domain or sphere of interest. The knowledge base can also contain concepts, theories, practical procedures, and their associations. The knowledge base forms the system's source of intelligence and will be used by the inference mechanism to reason and draw conclusions.

The inference mechanism is a set of procedures that are used to examine the knowledge base in an orderly manner to answer questions, solve problems, or make decisions within the domain. A way for the computer to "think" about the subject area, the inference mechanism searches through the knowledge base looking for answers and solutions.

In this chapter we discuss just how knowledge is represented to form a knowledge base, and examine various techniques for creating an inference mechanism. As you will discover, there are many different ways of representing knowledge and applying it. A variety of schemes have been devised to put almost any kind of knowledge into symbolic form suitable for storage in and manipulation by computer.

Because there are so many different knowledge representation schemes, this chapter can be only an introduction, a survey of the most popular methods used throughout the AI field. You are introduced to the whole scope of techniques as a sound base for more detailed study if that is desirable or necessary.

In later chapters on AI programming languages and in the programming experiments, you will see how some of these knowledge representation and search schemes are implemented in real programs. In practice, you will probably never have to develop such schemes yourself because there are so many useful development software tools that will do this for you. The knowledge in this chapter will simply allow you to better understand the processes used in those programs.

Knowledge Representation Schemes

The first step in constructing an artificial intelligence program is to build a knowledge base. In order to act intelligently, a computer must have knowledge about the domain of interest. In most cases, the knowledge already exists. It may be carried around in the heads of one or more human experts, or it may exist in printed form in books, articles, memos, procedures, or whatever. Regardless of its form, the knowledge of the domain must be collected and codified. It must be organized, outlined, or otherwise arranged in a systematic order.

This process of collecting and organizing the knowledge is called *knowledge engineering.* It is perhaps the most difficult and time-consuming part of any AI software development process. We will discuss knowledge engineering in greater depth in the next two chapters on expert systems. For now, we will concentrate on what to do with the knowledge once we have acquired it. Just how do we format this knowledge and convert it into a form suitable for storage and use in a computer? We will attempt to answer this question.

Although a variety of knowledge representation schemes have been developed over the years, these representation schemes share two common characteristics. First, they can be programmed with existing computer languages and stored in memory. Second, they are designed so that the facts and other knowledge contained within them can be used in reasoning. That is, the knowledge base contains a data structure that can be manipulated by an inference system, the other major part of an AI program. The inference system uses search and pattern matching techniques on the knowledge base to answer questions, draw conclusions, or otherwise perform an intelligent function.

Knowledge representation schemes have generally been categorized as either *declarative* or *procedural.* A declarative scheme is one used to represent facts and assertions. A procedure representation scheme deals with actions or procedures.

Declarative knowledge representation methods include logic, semantic networks, frames, and scripts. Procedural knowledge representation schemes include procedures or subroutines and production rules. A brief overview of each of these schemes is presented in this section. The key to the success of any AI program is the selection of a knowledge representation scheme that best fits the domain knowledge and the problem to be solved. That choice is best left to the knowledge engineer with considerable AI software design experience.

Logic is the anatomy of thought.

JOHN LOCKE

Logic

Perhaps the oldest form of knowledge representation is logic, the scientific study of the process of reasoning and system of rules and procedures that aid in the reasoning

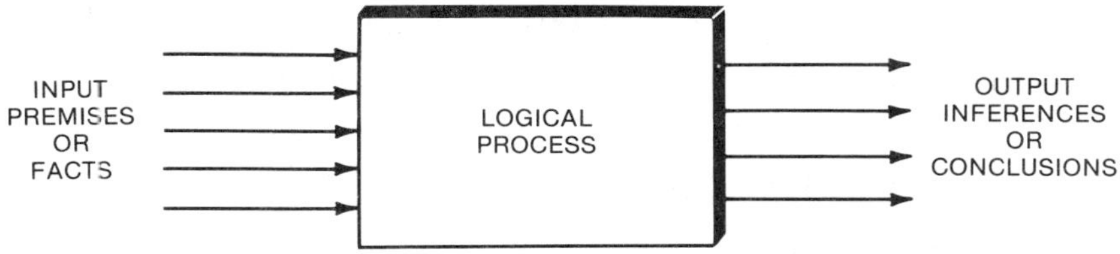

Figure 2–1. ***Using logic to reason.***

process. Logic is considered to be a subdivision of philosophy. The development and refinement of its processes are generally credited to the ancient Greeks.

The general form of any logical process is illustrated in Figure 2–1. First, information is given, statements are made, or observations are noted. These form the inputs to the logical process and are called *premises*. The premises are used by the logical process to create the output which consists of conclusions called *inferences*. With this process, facts that are known to be true can be used to derive new facts that also must be true.

There are two basic types of reasoning: *deductive* and *inductive*. Both types are used in logic to make inferences from premises.

Deductive Reasoning

When general premises are used to obtain a specific inference, the process is called deductive reasoning or deduction. Reasoning moves from a general principle to a specific conclusion. To illustrate this process, let's take a look at an example.

The deductive process generally begins with a syllogism or statement of the premises and inferences. It generally consists of three parts: a major premise, a minor premise, and a conclusion. Almost any problem or argument can be put into this form for deductive reasoning purposes. For example:

Major premise: I do not run when the temperature exceeds 90 degrees.

Minor premise: Today the temperature is 93 degrees.

Conclusion: Therefore, I will not run today.

To use deductive reasoning, the problem must generally be formatted in this way. Once this format has been achieved, the conclusion must be valid if the premises are true. Again, the whole idea is to develop new knowledge from previously given knowledge.

Inductive Reasoning

Inductive reasoning uses a number of established facts or premises in order to draw some general conclusion. An example will illustrate this process. Again, a syllogism is used to express the problem.

Premise: Faulty diodes cause electronic equipment failure.

Premise: Defective transistors cause electronic equipment failures.

Premise: Defective integrated circuits cause electronic equipment malfunction.

Conclusion: Therefore, defective semiconductor devices are a major cause of electronic equipment failure.

The interesting thing about inductive reasoning is that the conclusion is never final or absolute. Conclusions can change if new facts are discovered. There will always be some uncertainty in the conclusion unless all possible facts are included in the premises, and this is usually impossible. As a result, the outcome of the inductive reasoning process will always contain some measure of uncertainty. However, that uncertainty will be reduced as more facts or premises are used in the reasoning process. The more knowledge you have, the more conclusive your inferences can be.

Propositional Logic

For a computer to perform reasoning using logic, some method must be used to convert syllogisms and the deductive or inductive reasoning process into a form suitable for manipulation by a computer. The result is what is known as symbolic logic or mathematical logic. It is a system of rules and procedures that permit the drawing of inferences from various premises using a variety of logical techniques. These methods are generally known as *computational logic.*

There are two basic forms of computational logic, *propositional logic* or calculus and *predicate logic* or calculus. The term calculus here does not refer to differential and integral calculus which we ordinarily associate with the term. Instead, calculus simply refers to a system for computing. In this section we will take a look at propositional logic while predicate logic will be covered separately.

A proposition is nothing more than a statement that is either true or false. It is a premise which can be used to derive new propositions or inferences. Rules are used to determine the truth (T) or falsity (F) of the new proposition.

In propositional logic we use symbols such as letters of the alphabet to represent various propositions, premises, or conclusions. For example, consider the propositions used below in this simple deductive process:

A = The mailman comes Monday through Saturday.

B = Today is Sunday.

C = The postman will not come today.

Single simple propositions like these are not very interesting or useful. Real world problems involve many interrelated propositions. To form more complex premises, two or more propositions can be combined using logical connectives. These connectives or operators are designated as AND, OR, NOT, IMPLIES, and equivalent. The meanings of each of these connectives and the symbols used to represent them are given in Figure 2-2.

Those of you familiar with digital logic will recognize these connectives. They are the same as those used in Boolean algebra. In fact, because propositional logic involves only the truth or falsity of propositions, Boolean algebra and all of the related techniques

CONNECTIVE	SYMBOL
AND	∧, &, ∩
OR	V, U, +
NOT	¬, ∼
IMPLIES	⊃, →
EQUIVALENT	≡

Figure 2–2. ***Logical connectives or operators and their symbols.***

used in analyzing, designing, or simplifying binary logic circuits can be used in propositional logic.

Connectives are used to join or modify propositions to make new propositions. Some examples will show what we mean.

1. NOT

A = It is raining today.

NOT A = It is not raining today.

A truth table can be used to show all possible combinations of this connective.

A	NOT A
T	F
F	T

This truth table shows that if proposition A is true, then NOT A is false. If proposition A is false, then NOT A is true.

2. AND

When the AND connective is used to combine two propositions, the resulting new proposition is true only if both of the original propositions are true.

D = The car is black.

E = The car has a six cylinder engine.

F = The car is black AND has a six cylinder engine.

F = D AND E

In this case above, F is true only if D AND E are true.

Although the connective AND or any of the symbols shown in Figure 2–2 can be used in the symbolic representation of propositions, sometimes they are omitted and the two letters representing the propositions are simply written next to one another (D AND E = DE). In the case above, F is true only if D AND E are true.

Again, a truth table can be used to illustrate all possible combinations of the two propositions. This is illustrated below.

D	E	F
F	F	F
F	T	F
T	F	F
T	T	T

As you can see, the new proposition F is true only if propositions D and E are both true.

3. OR

When the OR connective is used to combine propositions, the new proposition is true if either one or both of the original propositions are true.

P = The moon is a satellite.

Q = The earth is a satellite.

R = P OR Q - The moon OR the earth is a satellite.

A truth table can be used to illustrate all possible combinations of the OR connective.

P	Q	R
F	F	F
F	T	T
T	F	T
T	T	T

You can see that the new proposition R is true if P is true, Q is true, or both P and Q are true.

This form of OR is known as the inclusive OR. Another form of OR connective is the exclusive OR which means that either one proposition (P OR Q) or the other is true, but not both. Expressed logically, the exclusive OR is P AND NOT Q OR NOT P AND Q. When converting problems into logical representations, care should be taken so that the correct representation, inclusive or exclusive OR, is used.

In the AND and OR examples above, we have used only two premises for simplicity. But keep in mind that more may be used as required to express the problem.

4. IMPLIES

The IMPLIES connective means that if proposition A is true, then proposition B is also true. The truth of A implies the truth of B or:

$$A \rightarrow B$$

Example: A = The car's engine is defective.

B = I cannot drive today.

C = A IMPLIES B

Another way to explain IMPLIES is to use an IF-THEN arrangement. In the above example, we can say that IF the car's engine is defective, THEN I will not drive today.

The truth table below illustrates the *IMPLIES function.*

A	B	C
F	F	T
F	T	T
T	F	F
T	T	T

The IMPLIES function is somewhat difficult to understand. The way to look at this is that the new proposition C is true if A is false OR B is true. Written logically, this is NOT A OR B. You can see that B is true in the second and fourth entries in the truth table. A is false in the first and second entries. As a result, the first, second, and fourth entries are true. The only time C is false is when A is true and B is false or A AND NOT B.

Let's analyze this example a bit closer. The first condition in the truth table states if A is false and B is false, C will be true. This can be stated as: "If the car's engine is not defective, then I can drive today." A IMPLIES B is true.

The second condition in the truth table says that if A is false and B is true, C is true. This is stated as "If the car's engine is not defective, then I cannot drive today." While this does not make much sense, it is allowed according to the definition of IMPLIES. The possibility exists that even if the engine is not defective that you cannot drive today for some other reason.

In the third case, if A is true and C is false, then A IMPLIES B is false. This is the only combination that gives a false result. It is stated as "If the car's engine is defective, then I can drive today." That is false.

Finally, if both A and B are true, then A IMPLIES B is true.

By using symbols for the various propositions and relating them with connectives, a complete set of premises with resulting conclusions can be expressed. The resulting symbolic expression looks very much like a math formula. It can then be manipulated using the rules of propositional logic or Boolean algebra to infer new conclusions. The truth or falsity of a conclusion can be determined from a wide variety of premises.

Predicate Calculus

Although propositional logic is a knowledge representation alternative, it is not very useful in artificial intelligence. Since propositional logic deals primarily with complete statements and whether they are true or false, its ability to represent real world knowledge is limited. Consequently, AI uses *predicate logic* instead.

Predicate logic is a more sophisticated form of logic that uses all the same concepts and rules of propositional logic. Also known as predicate calculus, it gives added ability to represent knowledge in finer detail. Predicate calculus permits you to break a statement down into component parts, namely an object, a characteristic of the object, or some assertion about the object. As you will see, predicate calculus allows you to separate a statement or proposition into the objects something is being asserted about and the assertion itself. In addition, predicate calculus also lets you use variables and functions of variables in a symbolic logic statement. The result is a more powerful knowledge representation scheme that is far more applicable to practical problem solving on a computer.

Predicates and Arguments

In predicate calculus, a proposition or premise is divided into two parts, the arguments (or objects) and the predicate (or assertion). The arguments are the individuals or objects an assertion is made about. The predicate is the assertion made about them. In a common English language sentence, objects and individuals are nouns that serve as subject and object of the sentence. In a sentence the predicate would be the verb or part of a verb. The two are combined to create a proposition:

PREDICATE (Individual [object] 1, Individual [object] 2)

For example, the proposition:

The car is in the garage

would be stated as follows:

IN (car, garage)

In = Products (assertion)
Car = Argument (object)
Garage = Argument (object)

Another example:

Proposition: John likes Mary.
Predicate Calculus Expression: LIKES (John, Mary)

Other formats are also used such as:

(in car garage) or
(likes John Mary)

Here the knowledge is contained not only in the words but also in their sequence (i.e., predicate, individual 1, individual 2). You will see this form when a programming language such as LISP is used to implement logic.

In some cases, the proposition may have only one argument. Some examples are:

The door is open.
OPEN(door)

The tire is flat.

FLAT(tire)

Chris is a man.

man(Chris)

In this last case, the predicate man is called a function and is written in lower case. Functions are different from predicates in that functions simply show a relationship while predicates express conditions about the arguments.

Variables

In predicate calculus, letters may be substituted for the arguments. The symbols x or y could be used to designate some object or individual. The previous example "John likes Mary" could be expressed in variable form if x = John and y = Mary. Then the proposition becomes:

LIKES(x,y)

If variables are used, then the stated proposition must be true for any names substituted for the variables.

Using this system, a knowledge base can be formed. The knowledge, expressed in predicate calculus, can be manipulated to generate inferences. Here's a simple example.

John likes Mary.

Ramon likes Mary.

John = x, Mary = y, Ramon = z

LIKES(x,y) AND NOT LIKES (z,y) IMPLIES

NOT LIKES(x,z)

This expression says that if John likes Mary and Ramon likes Mary, then John does not like Ramon.

Instantiation

Instantiation is the fancy term given to the process of assigning the name of a specific individual or object to a variable. That object or individual becomes an "instance" of that variable. In the previous example, plugging in John, Mary, and Ramon for x, y, and z respectively in the logic expression is a case if instantiation.

Quantifiers

A quantifier is a symbol that permits you to state the range or scope of the variables in a logical expression. Two basic quantifiers are used in logic: ∀, the universal quantifier, which means "for all," and ∃, the existential quantifier, which means "there exists." Some examples will make this clear.

All Texans are U. S. citizens.

Using the quantifier, this would be expressed as:

$(\forall x)[\text{Texan}(x) \rightarrow \text{U.S. Citizen}(x)]$

The ∀ symbol states that the expression is universally true. That is "for all" values of x, if x is a Texan, then it is true that x is also a U.S. citizen.

Consider the proposition:

Some cars are red.

This could be stated as:

$(\exists x)[\text{car}(x) \text{ AND IS RED}(x)]$

This means that there is a particular car x that satisfies the expression. There exists an object x that is a car AND that object is red.

Quantifiers are just a way to determine when things are true and under what conditions, all of the time or just some of the time. The cryptic notation makes them a bit harder to understand than just a simple verbal statement of the proposition. Incidentally, these logical expressions made up of variables, predicates, quantifiers, and connectives like the ones above are referred to as well formed formulas (wff or WFFs).

Reasoning with Logic

So far, all we have shown here is a system for expressing facts and knowledge in a symbolic form. What we really want is to use that knowledge to make inferences. How do we use this knowledge to answer questions, reason, or draw conclusions? We use various rules of inference to manipulate the logic expressions to create new expressions. If the original propositions are true, then the conclusions will be true.

The simplest rule of inference is *modus ponens.* Modus ponens says that if propositions A and A IMPLIES B are true, then proposition B is true. Expressed logically, this is:

$[A \text{ AND } A \rightarrow B)] \rightarrow B$

A and (A → B) are propositions in a knowledge base. Given the above expression, we can replace them both with the proposition B. In other words, we can use modus ponens to draw the conclusion that B is true if the first two expressions are true. Here's an example:

A —It is sunny.

B —We will go to the beach.

A → B—If it is sunny, then we will go to the beach.

The first premise simply states that it is a sunny day. The second says we will go to the beach. Further, A IMPLIES B. So if both A AND A IMPLIES B are true, B is true. Using modus ponens you can then deduce that we will go to the beach.

Actually, all of this seems to be just common sense. Anyone can figure it out. Except for a computer. Simple deduction like this comes naturally to our brains, but a computer must be told how to make simple inferences like modus ponens.

Numerous other techniques are used to make deductions from given premises or to prove the truth or falsity of a proposition. All of them require an extensive knowledge of logic and are complex in their implementation. They are beyond the scope of this course. Furthermore, they are already programmed into some AI languages and development tools. For example, one of the main reasoning methods in logic called resolution is built into the Prolog programming language. Prolog (meaning programming in logic) permits you to solve problems by putting them in predicate calculus form. Inferences are drawn automatically by the resolution algorithm that is part of Prolog.

> *Men are apt to mistake the strength of their feeling for the strength of their argument. The heated mind resents the chill touch and relentless scrutiny of logic.*
>
> GLADSTONE

Lists and Trees

Lists and trees are simple structures used for representing *hierarchical knowledge.* So much knowledge is of this type that you will make wide use of these structures in building knowledge bases.

Lists

A list is a written series of related items. It can be a list of names of people you know, things to buy at the grocery store, things to do this week, or products in a catalog. There are just about a jillion ways to list various items.

Lists are normally used to represent hierarchical knowledge where objects are grouped, categorized, or graded according to rank or relationship. Objects are divided into groups or classes of similar items. Then, their relationships are shown by linking them together. The simplest form is one list, but a hierarchy is created when two or more related lists are combined.

Figure 2–3 shows a generalized format for a list. The list has a name to identify it (LIST A) and two or more elements. You can see that an element in one list can be the name of another list containing sub-elements. One or more of the sub-elements can, in turn, be the name of another list and so on.

Another way to look at related lists is as an outline. An outline is nothing more than a hierarchical summary of some subject. The various segments of the outline are lists.

Trees

A tree is a graphical structure of a hierarchy. It is simply a way of illustrating lists and other hierarchical knowledge.

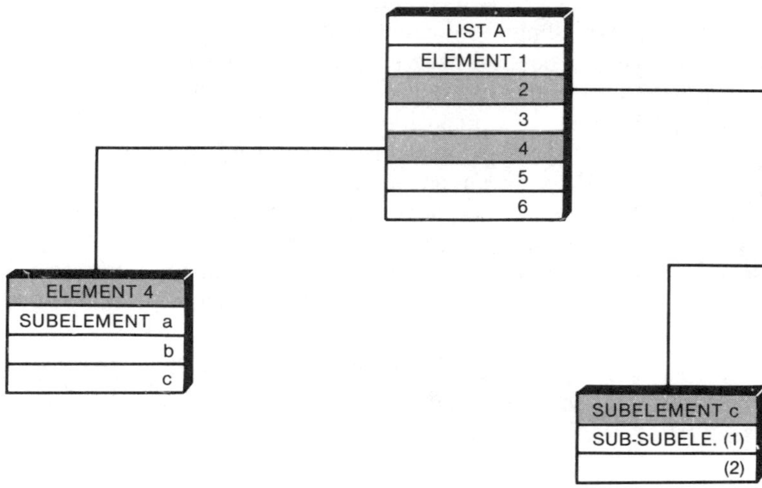

Figure 2–3. ***Using lists to represent hierarchical knowledge.***

A tree is shown in Figure 2–4. It consists of nodes that correspond to list names and elements. The nodes are connected by lines called arcs that show the relationships between the nodes. This structure or graph is called a tree because it has multiple branches, but the tree graph is inverted from a normal tree. Incidentally, the tree in this figure represents the same knowledge as the lists in Figure 2–3.

Lists, and trees, are so commonly used to represent knowledge that you will deal with them regularly in virtually every area of AI. In fact, lists are so widely used that a special programming language has been created to deal with them. It is called LISP, short for LISt Processing. LISP is the main programming language for AI work. We'll talk more about lists, trees, and LISP later.

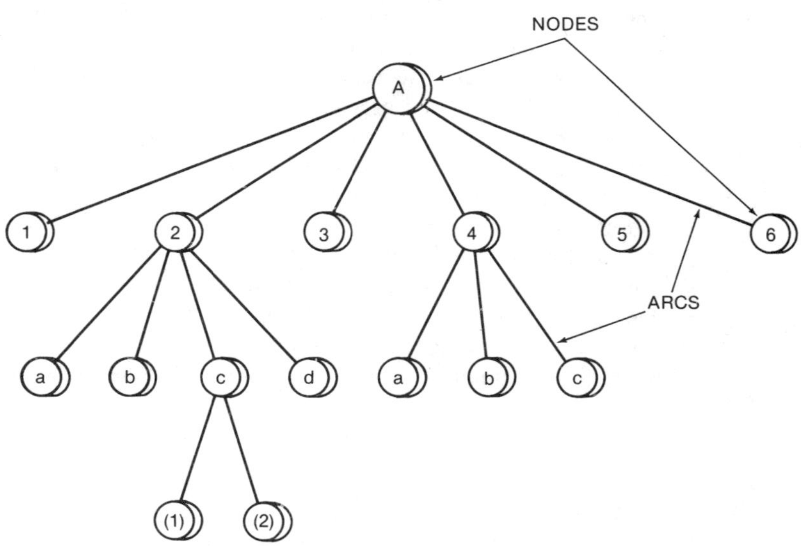

Figure 2–4. ***Tree graphs for illustrating hierarchical knowledge.***

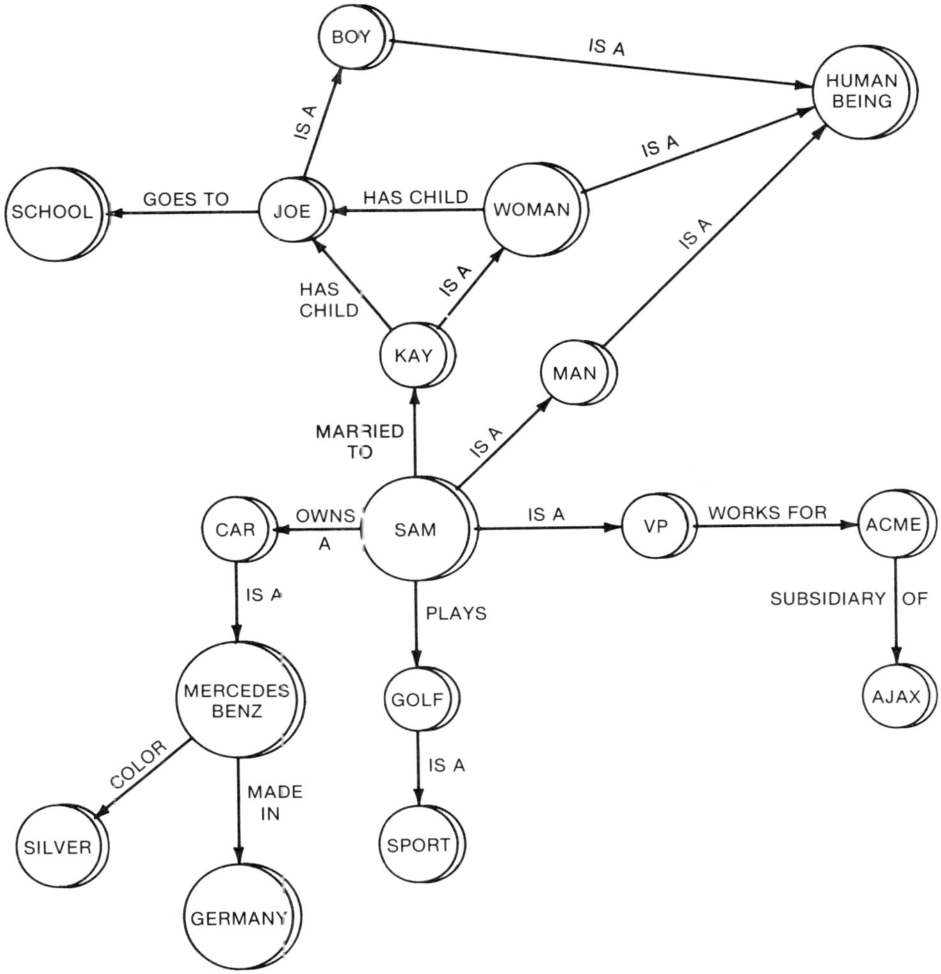

Figure 2–5. ***Example of representing knowledge in a semantic net.***

Semantic Networks

One of the oldest and easiest to understand knowledge representation schemes is the *semantic network* or semantic net. Semantic networks are basically graphical depictions of knowledge that show hierarchal relationships between objects.

A simple semantic network is shown in Figure 2–5. It is made up of a number of circles or nodes which represent objects and descriptive information about those objects. Objects can be any physical item such as a book, car, desk, or even a person. Nodes can also be concepts, events, or actions. A concept might be Ohm's Law; an event, a picnic or an election; an action, building a house or writing a book. Attributes of an object can also be used as a node. These might represent size, color, class, age, origin, or other characteristics. In this way, detailed information about objects can be presented.

The nodes in a semantic network are also interconnected by links or arcs. These arcs show the relationships between the various objects and descriptive factors. Some of the most common arcs are of the is-a or has-a type. Is-a, usually just designated as isa, is used to show class relationship; that is, that an object belongs to a larger class or category of objects. Has-a links are used to identify characteristics or attributes of the object nodes. Other arcs are used for definitional purposes. In general, a link designating almost any relationship can be used to interconnect objects.

Now refer to the example in Figure 2–5. As you can see, the central figure in this domain of knowledge is a person called Sam. One link shows that Sam is a man and that man is a human being or is part of a class called humans. Another arc from Sam shows that he is married to Kay. Additional arcs show that Kay is a woman and that a woman is, in turn, a human being. Other links show that they have a child, Joe, who is a boy and goes to school.

Some nodes and arcs show other characteristics about Sam. For example, he is a vice president for Acme, a company which in turn is a subsidiary of Ajax, a large corporation. We also see that Sam plays golf which is a sport. Further, Sam owns a Mercedes Benz whose color is silver. We also see that Mercedes Benz is a type of car which is made in Germany.

The semantic network is a very flexible method of representing knowledge. Almost any kind of object, attribute, concept, or whatever can be defined and relationships created with links. There are no hard rules about putting knowledge in this form. You can do almost anything.

Once the semantic network has been constructed, it can be used for problem solving. For example, you can ask questions about the domain represented by the network. Usually the network will provide the answers. We can ask the question, "Who is Sam married to?" Of course, the "married to" link shows that he is married to Kay. Or you might ask, "Does Sam have any children?" Of course, the link "has child" to son Joe shows that he does. We could also ask, "What sport does Sam play?" The "plays" link to golf provides the answer. The computer simply searches forward or backward through the arcs from a starting node to seek the answers.

One of the most interesting and useful facts about a semantic network is that it can show inheritance. Since the semantic network is basically a hierarchy, the various characteristics of some nodes actually inherit the characteristics of others. As an example, consider the links showing that Sam is a man and a man is, in turn, a human being. Here, Sam inherits the property of human being. We can ask the question is Sam a human being and because of the inheritance links, we can say that he is.

Another example of inheritance is the relationship between the Acme Company for whom Sam works and its parent corporation, Ajax. Again we can ask the question, "Does Sam work for the Ajax Corporation?" The answer is yes, because it owns Acme. This inheritance characteristic of semantic networks makes it possible to make a variety of deductions from the information provided.

The amount of detail that you include in a semantic network is dependent upon the kinds of problems that must be solved. If the problems are general, less detail is required. If the problems involve a lot of nitty-gritty, more explanation must be given

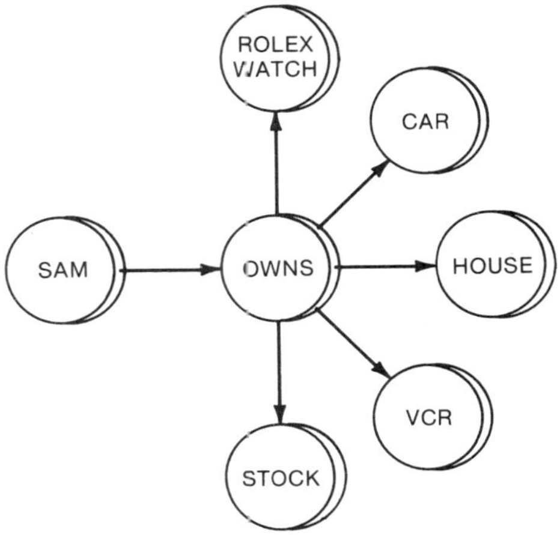

Figure 2–6. ***Example of adding detail to a semantic net.***

in the original network. For example, the link showing that Sam owns a car might be expanded to show that he owns many other things. Figure 2–6 illustrates the idea. Here Sam is linked to a new node called owns. Keep in mind that nodes may also represent conditions, situations, and actions as well as specific objects and their attributes. Here the situation is that he owns a car. Further, we also see that he owns a house, a VCR, a Rolex watch, and some stock. Additional links could be created defining everything that Sam owns, although the problem itself may not require it.

Another example involves the attributes of various objects in the net. For example, suppose that we want to show the ages of Sam and Kay. This could be done by the network shown in Figure 2–7A. Here the ages are given as numerical values in the related nodes. A more flexible way of representing this information is given in Figure 2–7B. Here we assign both Sam and Kay an age node. The age node, in turn, is given the actual value. This representation is much better because a factor such as age will change. Further, we can show the relationship between the ages better in this format. The "greater than" link accomplishes that.

Although the semantic network is graphic in nature, it does not appear this way in a computer. Instead, the various objects and their relationships are stated in verbal terms, and these are programmed into the computer using one of several different kinds of languages. To use the resulting program, a starting point is given at some particular node. This starting point is usually determined by a question. The computer then uses various search and pattern-matching techniques to look through the network structure to identify the desired objects and determine their relationship as posed by the question.

Schemas

Much knowledge used in our everyday reasoning process is fixed and well-known. It is based on previous exposure to typical objects and situations as well as experience

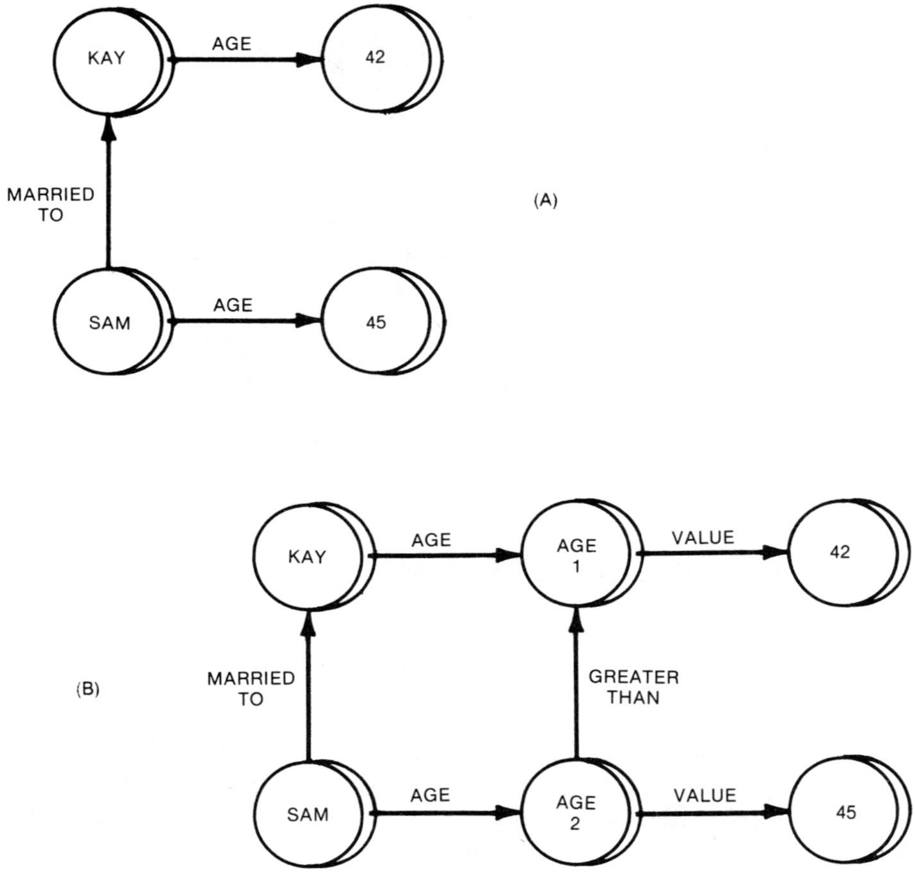

Figure 2–7. ***Other methods of expanding the knowledge in a semantic net.***

with conventional, unvarying processes. We call it stereotyped knowledge. We represent such knowledge with *schemas.* A schema is a method of organizing, presenting, and using stereotyped knowledge for computer reasoning. There are two basic types of schemas: frames and scripts.

Frames

A *frame* is a relatively large block or chunk of knowledge about a particular object, event, location, situation, or other element. The frame describes that object in great detail. The detail is given in the form of slots which describe the various attributes and characteristics of the object or situation.

Frames are normally used to represent stereotyped knowledge or knowledge based on well-known characteristics and experiences. We all have a great deal of common sense knowledge and experiences stored away in our brains that we call upon to analyze a new object or experience to solve a problem. Frames can be used to represent that kind of knowledge. The reasoning process that takes place with frames is essentially

AUTOMOBILE FRAME

Class of: Transportation
Name of Manufacturer: Audi
Origin of Manufacturer: Germany
Model: 5000 Turbo
Type of Car: Sedan
Weight: 3300 lb.
Wheelbase: 105.3 inches
Number of Doors: 4 (default)
Transmission: 3-speed automatic
Number of Wheels: 4 (default)
Engine: (Reference Engine Frame)
- Type: In-line, overhead cam
- Number of cylinders: 5
Acceleration (procedural attachment)
0 - 60 10.4 seconds
Quarter Mile 17.1 seconds, 85 mph
Gas Mileage: 22 mpg average (procedural attachment)

ENGINE FRAME

Cylinder bore: 3.19 inches
Cylinder stroke: 3.4 inches
Compression ratio: 7.8 to 1
Fuel system: Injection with turbocharger
Horsepower: 140 hp
Torque: 160 ft/LB

Figure 2–8. ***Example of a frame.***

the seeking of confirmation of various expectations. This amounts to filling in the slots and verifying that they match the current situation. With frames, it is easy to make inferences about new objects, events, or situations because they provide a base of knowledge drawn from previous experience.

A frame provides a means of organizing knowledge in slots that contain characteristics and attributes. In physical form, a frame is somewhat like an outline with categories and subcategories. A typical frame describing an automobile is shown in Figure 2–8. Note the slots describing attributes such as name of manufacturer, model, origin of manufacturer, type of car, number of doors, engine, and other characteristics.

Note that some slots contain default values. For example, one default value is that the number of wheels on the car is four. Default value simply means that we can assume the car has four wheels unless contradictory information to the contrary indicates otherwise. Another default value is the number of doors, in this case four. Because the type of car is a sedan, four doors are assumed because most sedans have four doors.

Another type of slot is the procedural attachment. This is a slot that permits new information to be added on an if-needed basis. In Figure 2–8, both acceleration and gas mileage are procedural attachments. These refer to a step-by-step procedure that would define how to acquire this information. For example, to determine acceleration, timing runs for both zero to 60 mph and quarter mile elapsed time and speed would be described. A procedural attachment to determine gas mileage would state a procedure for filling the gas tank, driving a certain number of miles, determining the amount of gasoline used, and then computing the gas mileage in terms of miles per gallon.

Another type of slot is one that references another frame. Such a frame may provide greater detail on the particular attribute of the given slot. For example, the

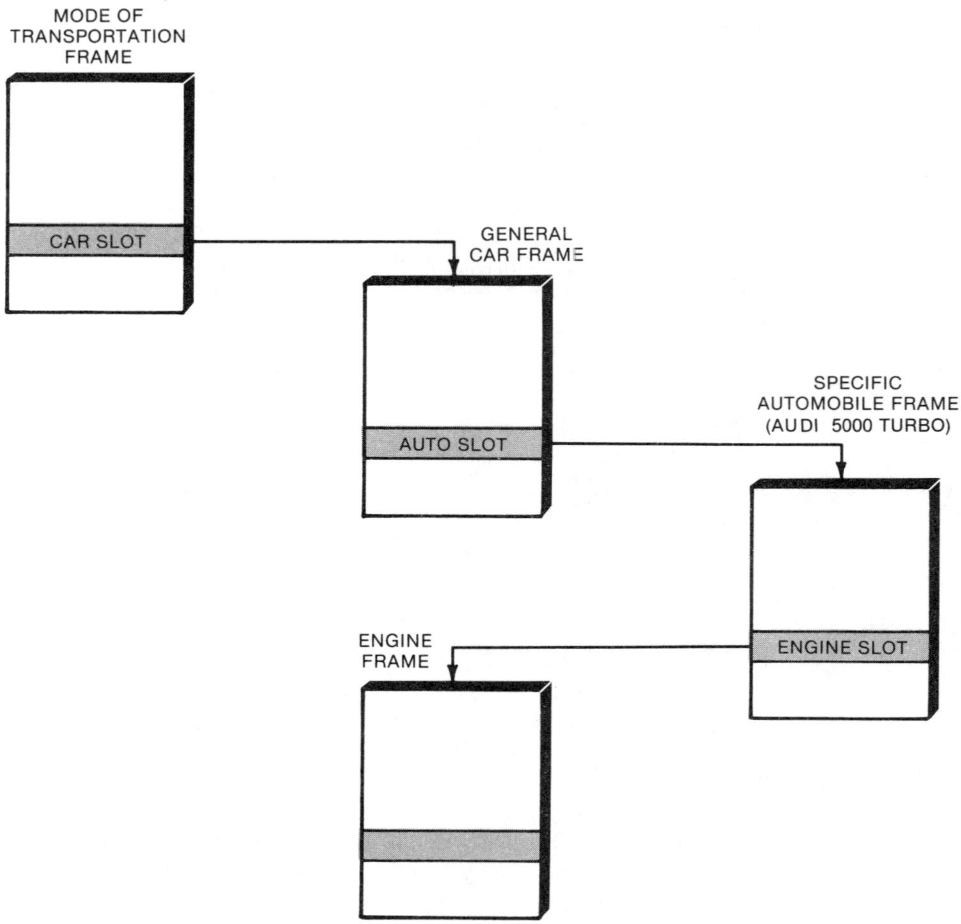

Figure 2–9. ***Knowledge represented in a hierarchy of frames that inherit properties from higher level frames.***

engine slot in Figure 2–8 simply states that an in-line 5 cylinder OHC engine is used. This slot references an engine frame in Figure 2–8 that gives the specific details about the engine, such as cylinder bore and stroke, horsepower, torque, compression ratio, type of fuel induction system, etc.

Most artificial intelligence systems using frames are made up of a collection of frames that are linked together in this way. Together they form a hierarchy that may be used for reasoning purposes. When hierarchies of frames are used, then one frame may also inherit the properties of another frame. For example, the automobile frame in Figure 2–8 would inherit all the properties of a general car frame or a more general frame describing modes of transportation. See Figure 2–9.

To use the frame system, the frame itself is programmed using an AI programming language. A slot hierarchy is set up, say, using the LISP language, then addressed to derive the answer to a question. Special frame-based software development tools are also available. A tool is a program that helps a user create another program. Tools require no programming skill as they provide a pre-established format of slots that simply permit you to enter the various characteristics. Once the frames are stored in memory, various search and pattern matching techniques are invoked to answer questions or otherwise make deductions from the knowledge available.

Scripts

A *script* is a knowledge representation scheme similar to a frame, but instead of describing an object, the script describes a sequence of events. Like the frame, the script portrays a stereotyped situation. Unlike the frame, it is usually presented in a particular context. To describe a sequence of events, the script uses a series of slots containing information about the people, objects, and actions that are involved in the events.

Some of the elements of a typical script include entry conditions, props, roles, and scenes. The entry conditions describe situations that must be satisfied before events in this script can occur or be valid. *Props* refer to objects that are used in the sequence of events that occur. Roles refer to the people involved in the script. The result is conditions that exist after the events in the script have occurred. *Track* refers to variations that might occur in a particular script. And finally, *scenes* describe the actual sequence of events that occur. Track refers to variations that might occur in a particular script.

A typical script is shown in Figure 2–10. It is a variation of the classical restaurant that has been used in AI as an example of representing knowledge in script format. Going to a restaurant is a stereotyped situation with predictable entry conditions, results, props, roles, and scenes. As you can see, such a script accurately describes what occurs in almost every fast food restaurant situation. The scenes are mini-scripts within the main script that describes the various subdivisions of the entire process. Note the optional scene that describes a take-out rather than an eat-in situation. Another option may be a drive-thru scene. Finally, note the results.

A script is useful in predicting what will happen in a certain situation. Even though certain events have not been observed, the script permits the computer to predict what happens to whom and when. If the computer triggers a script, questions can be asked and accurate answers derived with little or no original input knowledge. Like frames, scripts are a particularly useful form of knowledge representation because there are so many stereotype situations and events which humans use everyday. Knowledge like this is generally taken for granted, but in computer problem-solving situations, such intelligence must often be simulated to solve a particular problem using artificial intelligence.

To use the script, you store knowledge in the computer in symbolic form. This is done using LISP or another language. You can then ask questions about various persons and conditions. A search and pattern matching process examines the script for the answers. For example, what does the customer do first? Well, he parks the car, then goes into the restaurant. Whom does he pay? The server, of course. The whole thing is totally predictable.

> *What is all knowledge too but recorded experience, and a product of history, of which, therefore, reasoning and belief, no less than action and passion, are essential materials?*
>
> THOMAS CARLYLE

```
RESTAURANT SCRIPT

Track: Fast food restaurant
Roles: Customer (C)
       Server (S)
Props: Counter
       Tray
       Food
       Money
       Napkins
       Salt/Pepper/Catsup/Straws
Entry Conditions: Customer is hungry.
                  Customer has money.

Scene 1: Entry
 - Customer parks car.
 - Customer enters restaurant.
 - Customer waits in line at the counter.
 - Customer reads the menu on the wall and makes a decision
   about what to order.

Scene 2: Order
 - Customer gives order to server.
 - Server fills order by putting food on tray.
 - Customer pays server.

Scene 3: Eating
 - Customer gets napkins, straws, salt, etc.
 - Customer takes tray to an unoccupied table.
 - Customer eats food quickly.

Scene 3A (option): Take-out
 - Customer takes food and exits.

Scene 4: Exit
 - Customer cleans up table.
 - Customer discards trash.
 - Customer leaves restaurant.
 - Customer drives away.

Results:
 - Customer no longer hungry.
 - Customer has less money.
 - Customer is happy. *
 - Customer is unhappy. *
 - Customer is too full. *
 - Customer has upset stomach. *

* Options
```

Figure 2–10. ***Example of a script.***

Production Rules

One of the most popular knowledge representation schemes is *production rules.* Production rules, sometimes just referred to as rules or productions, are two-part statements that embody small pieces of knowledge. The first part of the rule, called the *antecedent,* expresses a situation or premise while the second part, called the *consequent,* states a particular action or conclusion that applies if the situation or premise is true. The most common forms of production rule are of these formats:

ANTECEDENT	—	CONSEQUENT
SITUATION	—	ACTION
PREMISE	—	CONCLUSION

The first or left-hand part of the rule is a statement with the prefix IF. The second or right-hand part of the rule is a statement with the prefix THEN.

A typical rule is illustrated below:

IF the price of the stock drops below $250

THEN buy 100 shares

The action, consequence, or conclusion stated in the THEN part is valid if the IF part of the rule is true or meets certain conditions.

Production rules are one of the most flexible forms of knowledge representation. They are easy to create and understand. And their format is compatible with the way that our own minds store and apply knowledge. A wide range of knowledge types can be represented in production rule format. Production rules have become by far the most popular and widespread means of converting human knowledge into a format suitable for symbolic representation in a computer. Some additional examples of rules illustrate their flexibility in representing different kinds of knowledge.

1. IF the temperature exceeds 90 degrees
THEN turn on the cooling fan.

All this rule says is that if the temperature is less than 90 degrees, then the cooling fan will not be turned on. However, if the temperature is above 90 degrees, then the fan will be actuated.

2. IF it is a fourth down
AND the ball is inside the opponent's 30 yard line
THEN make a field goal attempt.

Again the rule is easy to understand. The key point here is the use of the conjunction AND. Here two conditions must exist prior to taking the action specified. It must be the fourth down AND the ball must be inside the opponent's 30 yard line. Both conditions must be true. If either one of these conditions does not exist, then the specified action will not take place. This is the logical AND function, and all of the conditions connected with it must be satisfied. Any number of conditions may be linked with ANDs in the IF part of the rule as required to represent the desired knowledge.

3. IF you need a tax deduction
OR you need a retirement plan
THEN purchase an IRA (individual retirement account)

Note here the use of the logical OR function between conditions in the IF part of the rule. In this case, the rule advises to purchase an IRA IF you need a tax deduction OR you need a retirement plan. The purchase is suggested for either one or both conditions. Again, you may link as many conditions as required with logical OR operators to encode the knowledge. In fact, both AND and OR logical functions may be combined in an IF statement if the knowledge representation requires it.

To define some domain of knowledge accurately, many production rules are usually necessary. The rules provide details about objects, their characteristics, and actions to take. It takes a lot of details to accurately cover a subject. The rules are usually interrelated and reference or point to one another. These rules form a knowledge base which then becomes part of a production system. A *production system* consists of a knowledge base plus some working memory and a control or inference mechanism. The working memory is given some initial conditions or goals to be achieved. The inference and control mechanism then searches through the knowledge base looking for rules that match the initial conditions or goals stored in the working memory. Those rules matching the desired goals or conditions then provide the basic knowledge to solve the problem.

The most common example of a production system is the expert system. In fact, an expert system is a production system and the terms can be used interchangeably. An expert system uses rules to encode the knowledge of an expert in a particular domain. This knowledge is then converted into a computer program. The resulting expert system software allows anyone with access to the computer to solve problems and make decisions comparable to those achievable by an expert.

Expert systems are the most widely used form of artificial intelligence software. Additional coverage of rules and expert systems is given in Chapters 3 and 4.

Representing Uncertainty

So far all of the knowledge representation schemes we have discussed assume the various statements of facts or premises are either true or false. There are many knowledge representation instances where such black and white procedures are applicable. However, in the real world there is a lot of uncertainty. There are many times when we cannot state with absolute certainty that a particular fact, premise, or conclusion is 100% true or false. Fortunately, there are techniques that can be used to deal with these ambiguities or uncertainties.

Probability and Statistics

One method of dealing with uncertainty is to use conventional statistics and probability. For example, with the use of statistics, sufficient data may be available to compute the mean (average), median, and standard deviation. These new figures derived from the original data provide additional knowledge which will help in making a decision.

Standard probability can also be used. Recall that probability is simply a ratio of the number of times that a particular action will occur for a given number of attempts. For example, in rolling a standard die, the probability is one-sixth that any one of the numbers 1 through 6 will come up. This may also be expressed as a fraction, .16667, or as a percentage, 16.67%. In many knowledge representation cases, the probability

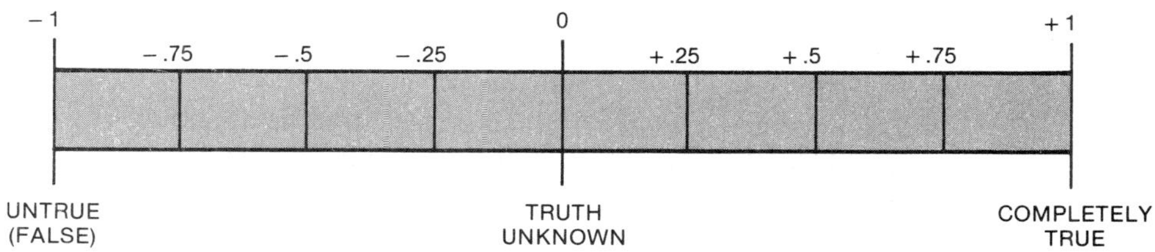

Figure 2–11. ***Certainty or confidence factors are used to deal with ambiguity and uncertainty.***

for a certain condition or action may be known or can be estimated. For example, if the probability of a certain event taking place is 70%, then it may be necessary to initiate some action if the probability is equal to or greater than 70%. If the likelihood is less than 70%, then perhaps an action may not be taken. For example, the production rule below uses probability:

IF the stone is clear, without color
THEN it is a diamond (probability 60%)

Certainty Factors

In expert systems, *certainty factors* (CF) are used to help deal with uncertain situations. A certainty factor is simply a number that indicates how confident we are that a particular fact is true. Based on our experience or available evidence, we are able to choose a certainty factor that indicates what we believe to be the level of truth. A typical range of certainty factors might be −1 to +1 where −1 indicates certainty that the information is false and +1 indicates complete certainty that the information is true. Zero indicates that the certainty is unknown. This is illustrated in Figure 2–11. A production rule using a certainty factor might look like this:

IF the patient has a runny nose, watery eyes and is sneezing,
THEN s/he has hay fever (certainly .3)

The certainty, or confidence, is only .3 because other conditions may cause those symptoms, such as a cold or an alergic reaction.

The important point to note is that a certainty factor is not the same as probability. Both are defined, computed, and used in different ways even though they represent methods of dealing with ambiguity and uncertainty in knowledge representation. More will be said about probability and certainty factors in the chapters on expert systems.

Logic is the art of going wrong with confidence.
JOSEPH WOOD KRUTCH

Key Points

- The two main parts of any AI software are (1) a knowledge base and (2) an inferencing system.

- The knowledge base is made up of facts, concepts, theories, procedures and relationships representing real world knowledge about objects, places, events, people, etc.
- The inference system or thinking mechanism is a method of using the knowledge base, that is, reasoning with it to solve problems.
- To build the knowledge base, a variety of knowledge representation schemes are used including logic, lists, semantic networks, frames, scripts and production rules.
- Logic is a set of rules and procedures used in reasoning.
- There are two basic types of reasoning (1) deductive and (2) inductive.
- In deductive reasoning, general premises are used to reach specific inferences.
- In inductive reasoning, specific premises are used to infer general inferences.
- Propositional logic is a system of using symbols to represent and manipulate premises, prove or disprove propositions, and draw conclusions.
- Predicate calculus is a form of propositional logic that is used to represent knowledge in the form of statements that assert information about objects or events and apply them in reasoning.
- A common way to represent hierarchical knowledge is to use lists.
- Hierarchical knowledge can also be represented visually with graphs called trees.
- Another knowledge representation scheme is semantic networks that uses circles called nodes that represent objects or events. The nodes are interconnected with lines called arcs that show relationships.
- Schemas are knowledge representation methods that can deal with stereotyped knowledge. Frames and scripts are the two types of schemas.
- Frames are used to represent facts about objects and events. Details are given in sub-elements called slots.
- Scripts describe knowledge that is a sequence of events or procedures.
- Frames and scripts permit a system to infer details of specific common objects and events.
- One of the most commonly used knowledge representation methods is production rules.
- Production rules are two part statements with a premise and a conclusion. They also may state a situation and a corresponding action.
- Rules take the form of an IF-THEN statement such as: IF you drank too much, THEN you should not drive.
- Probability, statistics, and certainty factors are numerical methods that help to reason with ambiguous and uncertain knowledge.

3

An Approach to Problem Solving

Seek and ye shall find; knock and it shall be opened unto you.

MATTHEW VII, 7

A knowledge base is nothing more than a collection of related facts about a certain subject. It is a highly organized assembly of information that has been uniquely formatted into what can be called a data structure. The knowledge base is not a program. But it is put into a form that can be stored in a computer memory. Once it's there, we can begin to use it.

To do that, we need some kind of inferencing mechanism that references the knowledge base to reason and draw conclusions. This is done by a program that employs search and pattern matching techniques. The inference mechanism searches the knowledge base for a solution, or it looks for patterns that match a desired goal or that satisfy the criteria set up for a particular hypothesis.

The search program uses one or more algorithms, but those algorithms do not solve the problem directly as a formula would. The algorithms only provide a means to examine the knowledge base in some orderly way in hopes of solving the problem. In this chapter, we will look at the various techniques used in AI search routines.

Once a knowledge base has been established, you can answer important questions, solve problems, tap expertise, and make important decisions.

The primary method of using the knowledge base is search, a trial and error technique of seeking the answer to a question by examining the alternatives in the knowledge base. Known facts are matched to the contents of the knowledge base. This leads to new facts and ultimately an answer or solution.

Search, unlike an algorithm which solves problems directly, is a more random and less organized approach to problem solving. Yet it is the technique widely used by humans in arriving at answers to questions or solutions to problems. We apply what we know to a given problem and search our memory for related facts, knowledge, relationships, and memories. The result may be an ideal solution to the problem. It may be only a partial or incompletely developed solution. In the real world, perfect solutions and complete problem solving are not always possible and, in fact, are not always necessary. In some applications any solution is better than no solution at all, and in many cases a good solution is just as acceptable as the best solution. It can be even more desirable if the time and cost involved are less.

Like knowledge representation schemes, search has been a major area of study in the field of artificial intelligence. Many techniques have been developed to search a knowledge base. This section will attempt to familiarize you with the most fundamental and widely used techniques.

Problem Solving Elements

The general process of solving any problem involves three major elements: problem states, a goal, and operators. Problem states define the problem situation and existing conditions. In starting to solve a problem, the initial state or states are given. These are known facts and conditions that provide a place to begin in searching for a solution. For example, assume the problem is to win a game of tic-tac-toe against an opponent which could be the computer. The initial state is an empty 3 × 3 grid of squares. As you and the opponent add X's and 0's, the problem state changes. If you are playing against the computer, it will record your move and search for the best location for its next move.

The goal, of course, is the objective to be achieved, a final answer, or solution. There may be more than one goal. In the tic-tac-toe game, the goal is to win the game, and there are several possible ways this can be achieved.

Operators are procedures used for changing from one state to another. An operator describes a process whereby some action is taken to change the initial state into another state that more closely approaches the goal. Operators move the problem from one state to the next following the guidance of a master control strategy until a goal is reached. An operator could be an algorithmic subroutine.

For example, in tic-tac-toe, the operator might assess the board state by counting the number of rows, columns, or diagonals still available to the computer and to you. The player with the greatest number of options has the best chance of winning. The computer then places its X where it will maximize its options and minimize yours. Your move will create a new state to be evaluated and responded to.

Figure 3–1 shows the relationship between the initial states, procedures, and goals. The initial conditions provide the states that are manipulated by procedures to achieve the goal. A control strategy selects or guides the procedures.

Figure 3–2 shows another method of viewing the relationship between these elements of a problem. The data base is a place to store the initial state, goal, current state or status, and any previous steps or transactions that took place. The data base is updated as the control strategy applies the operator to the current state. The control strategy is a basic technique chosen by the programmer to solve the problem, a subroutine that tells the program what to do next. More specifically, it designates how the operators or procedures will be applied to the problem states to achieve the goal. The control strategy selects the operator that manipulates the current state in the data base. Feedback from the data base guides the control strategy. If the goal is not achieved, the operator is applied again and again until the goal is reached.

It is important to point out that even though we may treat search as separate from the knowledge representation scheme, the two are very much interrelated. The selection of a particular knowledge representation method will greatly affect the type of search control strategy used. Not all operators are flexible enough to address different knowledge representation schemes.

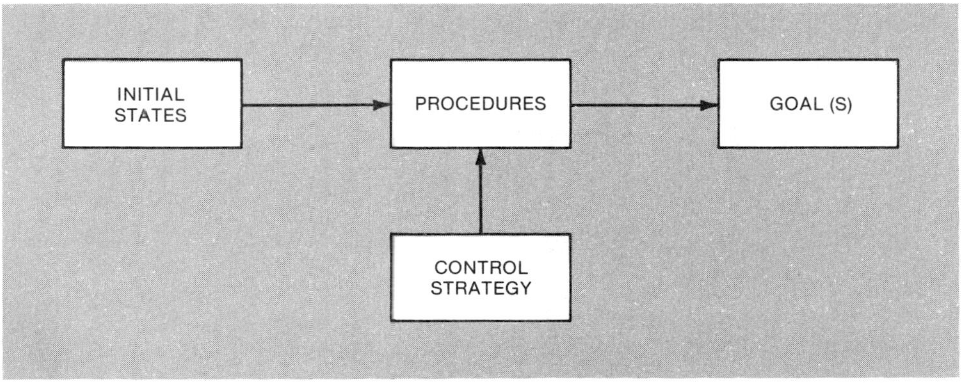

Figure 3–1. ***The relationship between the initial states, procedures, and goal(s) in the search process.***

State and Search Space

To define a problem, visualize a solution, or select a search method, it is often useful to express the problem in graphical terms. This can be done by drawing a graph of the problem showing the various problem states and how they are interconnected. The resulting graph is usually referred to as a *state graph* or the *state space.*

State Graph

Figure 3–3 shows a state graph for a simple problem, attempting to find the best path from one city, the source (S), to another city, the destination or goal (G). The state

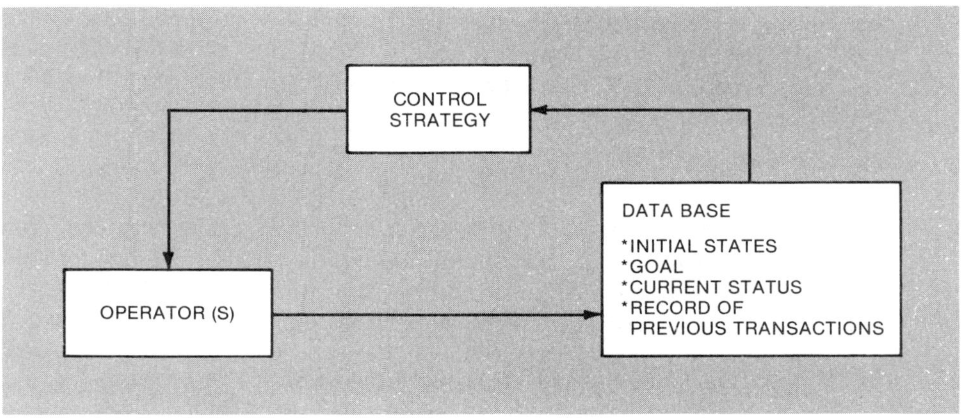

Figure 3–2. ***The basic search process.***

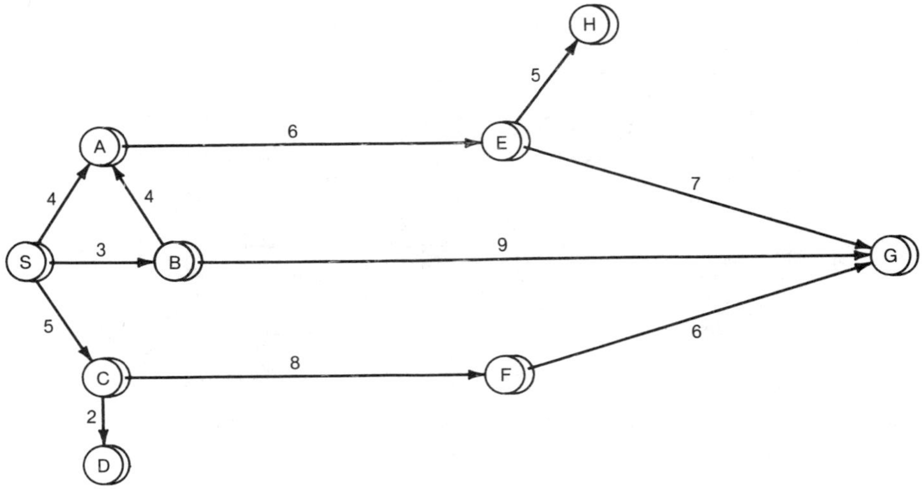

Figure 3–3. ***A state graph showing alternate routes from the start (S) to the goal (G).***

graph is a map showing the various possible intermediate towns and cities which would be passed through in reaching the desired destination. In such a problem, there often will be several alternative routes. The problem is to reach the destination in the least amount of time covering the shortest distance.

The state graph in Figure 3–3 uses nodes to define each of the various problem states or cities. Nodes correspond to the various systems states that can be achieved in applying the operators to the initial state to achieve new states in route to the goal. These intermediate states or nodes are often called subgoals.

The nodes in a state graph are interconnected by arcs or links. The arcs usually have arrows showing the direction from one state to the next. The arcs represent the application of an operator to a node. The numbers on the arcs represent the distance between nodes.

In practice, it is difficult to represent a state graph such as that in Figure 3–3 in software form. For example, some of the paths through the state graph can be retraced repeatedly. The path S to node B to node A back to node S could be repeated over and over again. Such endless loops cannot be tolerated in a computer program and, therefore, some procedure must be followed to eliminate undesired cyclical conditions such as this. This is done by converting the state graph into a search tree.

Search Trees

A *search tree* based on the state graph in Figure 3–3 is illustrated in Figure 3–4. The new tree diagram states the same problem but in a slightly different format. The network thus formed is more like a hierarchy. Note that some of the nodes are repeated to eliminate the cyclical loop problem described earlier. The resulting diagram is called a tree because it vaguely represents an upside down tree with its roots and trunk at the top and branches and leaves at the bottom.

A whole verbal language, using tree and genealogical terminology, has been developed to describe a search tree. For example, the initial state node is called the

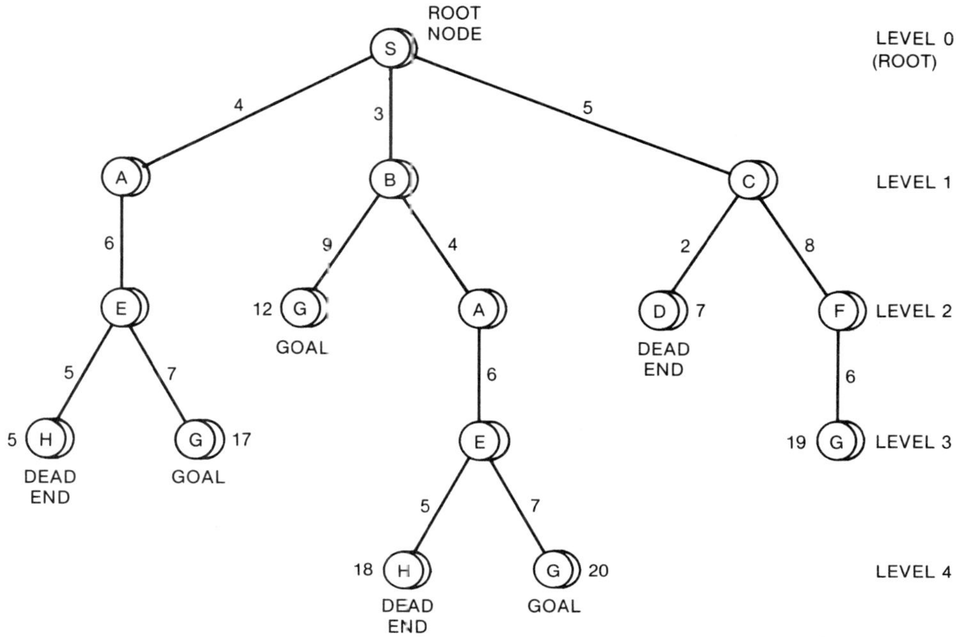

Figure 3–4. ***A search tree.***

root node. Other nodes branch out from the root. These successor or descendant nodes are also sometimes referred to as children. These nodes in turn have successors or children. Working backwards through the tree, nodes are also said to have predecessors, ancestors, or parents. Nodes with no children or successors are called leaves. The interconnecting arcs are referred to as branches.

Finally, note in Figure 3–4 that a search tree is divided into various levels that are a function of the hierarchy. These levels describe the depth of the tree. The root node is usually designated Level 0, and successive deeper levels are designated sequentially from numbers 1 through the highest level required to represent the state space.

It is not always possible to draw the state graph or search tree for a given problem. Most problems are simply too large and complex to draw. For that reason, most state graphs and search trees are implicit. This is not an unsatisfactory situation since most problems will be stated in terms of a program language anyway, and it is not usually necessary to actually draw the search tree.

There are two ways of looking at a search tree. The first is to assume that the entire hierarchy or network exists. All possible nodes and their arcs are illustrated. Another approach is to build or "grow" the tree a node at a time. The nodes are the various states in the search space. The arcs are operators used to move from one state to another. Beginning with the root node, operators are applied to achieve new states. As the operators are applied, the node is said to be expanded. Expanding a node generates children or successors. A node is said to be open until it is expanded. Once the node is expanded, it is said to be closed. Operators are applied and nodes are generated until the desired goal is achieved. Whether you look at the search tree as a

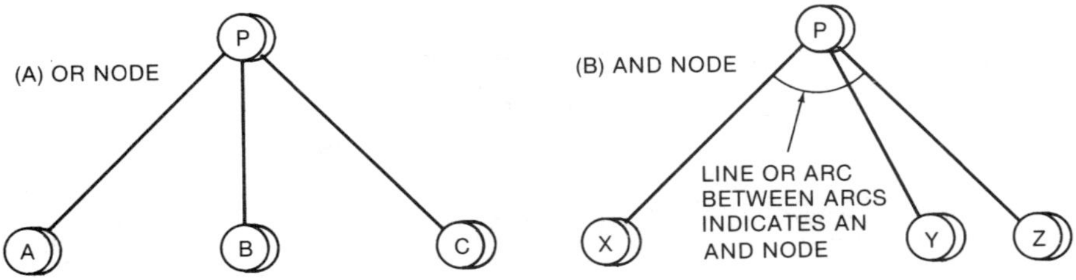

Figure 3–5. ***AND/OR nodes.***

final completed network or as a hierarchy that expands and grows as the search continues, the result is the same. A goal or solution to the problem is found.

One final thing about the search graph and tree. Note in Figures 3–3 and 3–4 that there are numbers on each arc. As we indicated earlier, these numbers represent the mileage between cities (nodes). Using these figures, you can add up the distance of each path from source to goal so you can see the shortest path. In Figure 3–4, the total distance of each path is given in miles at each goal or dead end node.

The mileage between cities is generally referred to as the "cost" of going from one node to the next. Cost could also be measured in time. The route (path) selected will have traffic conditions that will impact the speed you can travel, and, therefore, the time it will take you. In looking for the best path through a search tree, you always must state whether you prefer minimum time or minimum miles. One path may have the least miles, but because of traffic conditions your speed may be impeded, and it could take the most time. The longest route according to mileage may be on an interstate highway, and thereby take the least time.

AND/OR Trees

In the previous discussion of search trees, the branches from a node to its successors represented two or more alternative paths to subgoals. One path or another could lead to the goal. We can call these OR nodes because one branch, OR another, OR another could be the path to the goal.

In some problems, however, the successor nodes might represent problem states which must all be achieved or traversed before the goal is reached. These are referred to as AND nodes. One subgoal AND another subgoal (AND possibly others) must be achieved to solve the problem.

Figure 3–5A shows a simple OR node with problem P and three possible solution nodes A, B, or C. The problem is solved if A OR B OR C is chosen or achieved.

Figure 3–5B shows a simple AND node. Here problem P has the successor nodes X, Y, and Z. To solve the problem, subproblem nodes X AND Y AND Z must all be solved before P is solved. Note that to distinguish an OR node from an AND node, it is accepted practice to draw horizontal lines or arcs connecting the links between the parent and successor nodes of an AND tree as shown.

To define some problems, AND and OR nodes must be combined. These problems can be represented with an AND/OR tree. Such a problem is shown in Figure 3–6. In this AND/OR tree, there are three possible solutions. These are paths ABDEIJ, ACFGHK, and ACFGHL. In the first, I and J must both be solved to solve D. D and E must be

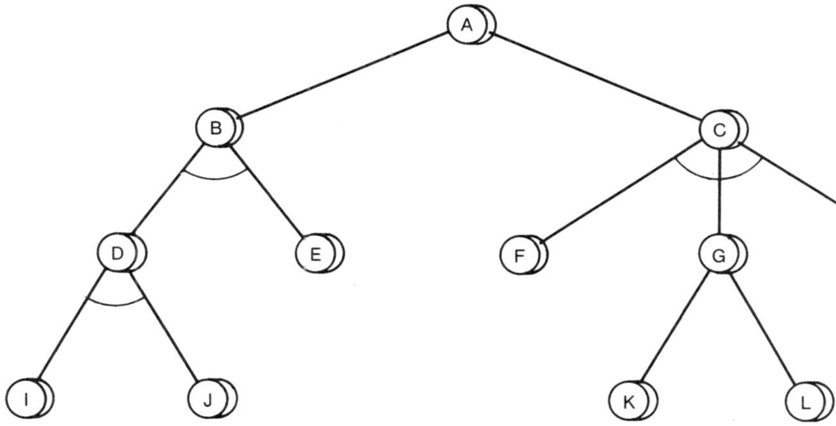

Figure 3–6. ***AND/OR tree.***

solved to solve B. And either B or C must be solved to solve the main problem, A. In the second and third cases, either K or L will solve G, but F, G, and H must be solved to satisfy C. C, of course, satisfies A.

Game Trees

A game tree is a graph showing all possible states or plays in a game between two players. As in other kinds of AI problems, the tree illustrates the nodes and paths that lead from the initial state to a goal or win state. Most game trees illustrate the play between two opponents, as in chess or checkers. The concept, however, is best illustrated with a simpler game with fewer possible moves. Tic-tac-toe is a good example.

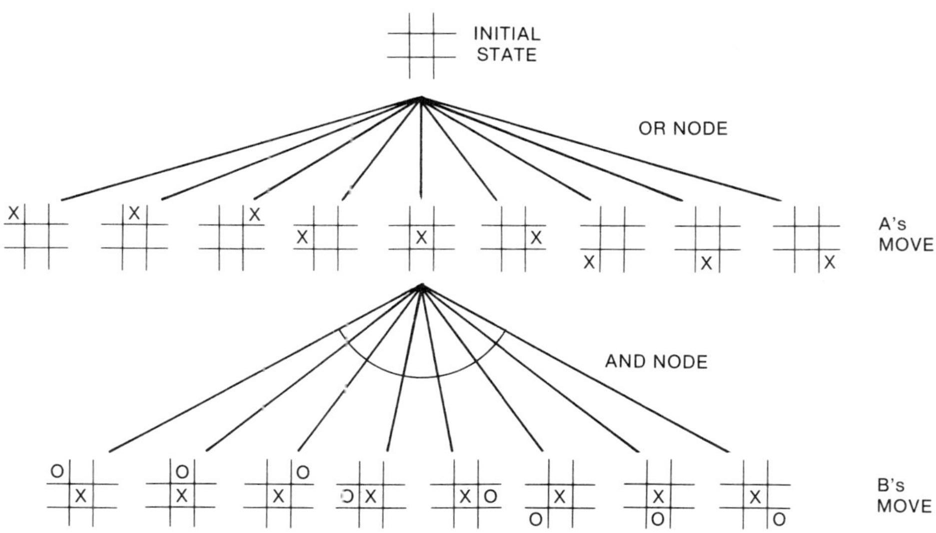

Figure 3–7. ***A game tree has alternate AND and OR nodes.***

Figure 3–7 shows the tree for a tic-tac-toe game between players A and B. The tree is shown from the viewpoint of A. From the initial state, player A begins and makes a move by entering an X somewhere in the 3 x 3 grid. Of course, there are nine possible choices as illustrated. This is a nine option OR node.

It is then player B's turn to enter a 0. There are eight possible choices. Notice that these options are interconnected by lines or arcs indicating that this is an AND node. The node at B's move is an AND node because A must be able to respond to all of B's moves as he has no control over the matter. At least one of these choices must lead to a win. So you can see that game trees are a special kind of AND/OR tree. The tree expands with alternative AND and OR nodes as the play continues and a win, lose, or draw goal is achieved.

Attempt the end, and never stand to doubt; Nothing's so hard but search will find it out.

ROBERT HERRICK

Search Methods

There are two basic approaches to searching a state space. The first is *blind search* and the second is *heuristic search.* Both are used in AI applications, but heuristic search is the primary method of problem solving in AI. Actually heuristic search is blind search that has been given some guidance or direction. Therefore, we will discuss blind search first.

Blind Search

Blind search is a collection of procedures used to search a state space. Beginning at the root node, operators are used to generate successor states. The search continues until a solution is found. The operators and the order in which they are tried have no meaning. The idea behind blind search is to examine the entire tree in an orderly manner, using all the operators and generating as many successor nodes as possible to find the desired solution.

Starting with the root node, there are several procedures for proceeding through the tree, but these approaches are inefficient, brute force techniques. In very large problems, a huge number of new states are generated and many alternatives are considered. As a result, it takes a considerable amount of time and effort to find the solution. For large problems, the practicality of blind search lies in the time it takes a computer to search the tree or generate all the alternatives. Often this translates into an unacceptably long computing time. Further, the volume of intermediate states may be so enormous that you simply run out of memory. However, for some smaller problems with fewer states, blind search may be perfectly acceptable. Very high speed computers also make blind search acceptable for some problems.

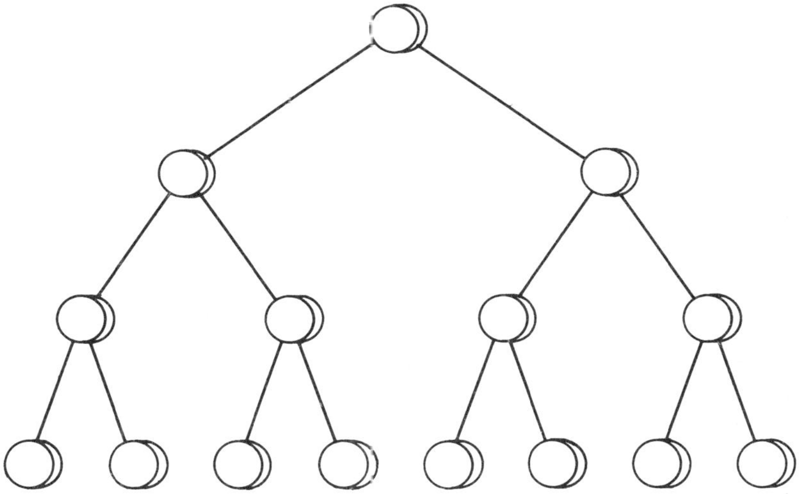

Figure 3–8. ***Combinational explosion in a search tree with two branches per node (N) to a depth of three levels (D) producing $N^D = 2^3 = 8$ possible outcomes.***

Combinatorial Explosion

Blind search takes so much time with large problems it suffers from something called *combinatorial explosion.* When many alternatives must be considered, the number of nodes to search expands exponentially. For example, consider one branch of a search tree. If each node can have an average number of N branches to other nodes, and you wish to expand that portion of the tree to a depth of D levels, the total number of nodes in the search space expands to N raised to the D power. In the simple tree of Figure 3–8, we are assuming an average of two branches per node to a depth of three levels. As you can see, this produces eight possible outcomes. If you wanted to expand a search tree with an average number of five branches per node to a depth of six levels, the total number of outcomes would be 15,625. It is easy to see that for large problems, the number of possibilities becomes enormous. The process of searching or generating each node usually becomes an impractical task.

For example, in a tree showing all possible states in a tic-tac-toe game, there are 362,880 nodes. That's what combinatorial explosion does to a problem like this. Just think of the number of possible moves in a chess or checker game. It has been estimated that there are 10 to the 120th power possible chess moves and 10 to the 40th power possible checker moves. Even if a computer could process each move in a microsecond, it would still take centuries to arrive at a solution.

A computer simply cannot be expected to handle such problems by blind search. Of course, it could easily deal with tic-tac-toe because the total number of moves is small enough. But in more complex games, some means of limiting and thus speeding up the search must be used. As you will see, that is the purpose of heuristic search.

In the sections that follow, we will examine a number of basic blind search techniques. Most of these techniques are widely used. However, the process is usually modified by heuristics to improve the efficiency of the search and reduce the number of alternatives that must be considered before a goal is found.

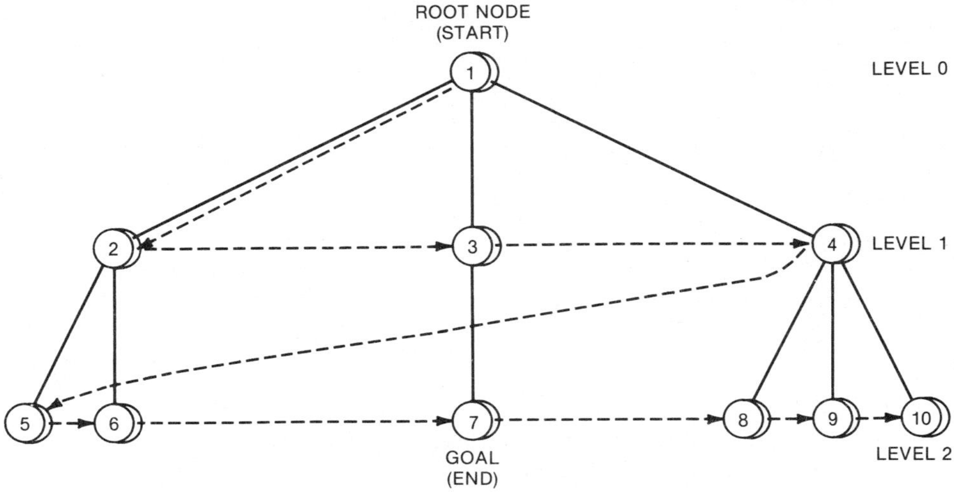

Figure 3–9. ***A breadth first search.***

Breadth First Search

Blind search methods differ primarily in the order in which the various nodes in the tree are examined. The two main search techniques are *breadth first* and *depth first* search.

A breadth first search examines all of the nodes in a search tree, beginning with the root node. The nodes in each level are completely examined before moving on to the next level. A simple breadth first search is illustrated in Figure 3–9. The numbers inside the node circles designate the sequence in which the nodes are examined. In this instance, the search would end at node 7 as that is the goal.

A breadth first search of the state space will always find the shortest path between the initial state and the goal state, with the least number of steps.

In a blind search procedure, we assume that any one path is as good as another. For that reason, there is no particular reason to choose one path over another in beginning a search. The process usually starts at the initial state node and works downward in the tree from left to right. This downward/left-to-right procedure is, of course, used in the breadth first search. A variation of this technique is used in a depth first search as well.

Depth First Search

A depth first search begins at the root node and works downward to successively deeper levels. An operator is applied to the node to generate the next deeper node in sequence. In other words, a child or successor node is generated by a parent node. This process continues until a solution is found or backtracking is forced by reaching a dead end.

A simple depth first search is illustrated in Figure 3–10. Again the numbers inside the nodes designate the sequence of nodes generated or searched. This process seeks

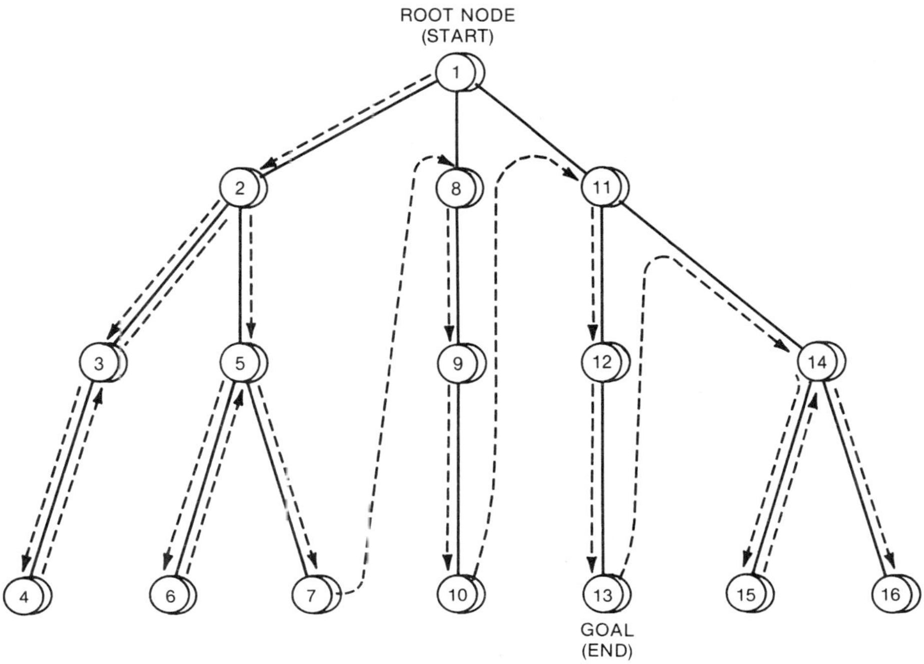

Figure 3–10. ***A depth first search.***

the deepest possible node. If a goal state is not reached in this way, the search process backtracks to the next highest level node where additional paths are available to follow. Again this process continues downward and in a left-to-right direction until a goal is discovered. Here the search ends at node 13.

When a dead end node is discovered, such as node 4 in Figure 3–10, the search process backtracks so that any additional branching alternative at the next higher node level is attempted. The search backs up to node 3. It has no alternate paths, so the search backtracks to node 2. Here, another path through node 5 is available. The path through node 6 is explored until its depth is exhausted. The backtracking continues until the goal is reached.

The depth first search guarantees a solution, but the search may be a long one. Many different branches will have to be considered to maximum depth before a solution is reached.

One of the main problems with depth first search is that it can often lead into deeper and deeper subnetworks that are far from the goal node which may exist at a much higher level. A considerable amount of time and effort is wasted in searching all of these possibilities. To minimize this problem, most depth first searches are accompanied by a depth limit, the maximum depth that a search process will take before backtracking. Such a search is said to be depth bound. It allows the search to move downward to a specific level. A depth first search can be considerably shortened or speeded up by this process. The trick is in knowing where to set the cut-off level. It is usually an educated guess or determined experimentally.

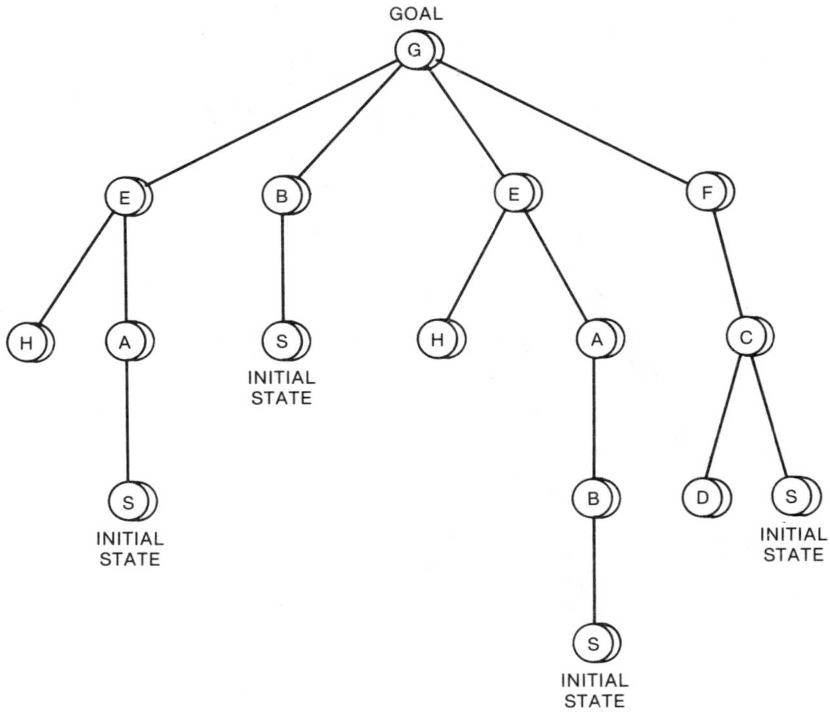

Figure 3–11. ***Backward chaining from goal to initial state.***

Forward and Backward Reasoning

In all of the search examples given so far, we have assumed there is a single starting point or initial state node. In practice, there may be two or more starting points. The problem may be defined in such a way that the search for a solution can begin at any one of several different entry points. We will continue to use a single initial state node for simplicity, but keep in mind that there may be more.

Further, in our examples we have started with the initial state node and used operators to generate successor nodes. This process of working from the initial state to the goal state is known as forward reasoning or forward chaining. A forward search process is said to be data driven. Forward chaining is a kind of deductive reasoning.

There is no reason why a backward reasoning approach cannot be taken. In this process you start with the goal node and work backward toward the initial state. In backward reasoning, the process is said to be goal directed. It is a kind of inductive reasoning. Starting at the goal node and using special inverse operators, it is possible to generate successor nodes to reach the initial state. Figure 3–11 is the search graph and search tree used in Figures 3–3 and 3–4, redrawn in a backward chaining manner.

You are probably wondering how you can identify the goal node as the starting point. If you know the goal, you wouldn't have to search for it. Actually, in backward chaining you simply pick one of several possible goal nodes and attempt to prove or justify it by searching backward.

In practice both forward and backward chaining are used. The choice of the direction, however, depends significantly on the shape of the search space. For instance, if there are more possible outcomes than there are initial states, a backward chaining process will produce the fastest search with the shortest path.

On the other hand, there are search trees in which there are many more initial start states than there are goal states. In these cases, forward reasoning is the better choice because having more starting points than goal states means that virtually any input starting point will lead very quickly to the goal.

In general it has been said that humans reason in a goal- directed manner. The human mind seems to prefer backward chaining. In AI practice, backward chaining techniques appear to be more widely used than forward chaining. However, keep in mind that the best approach really depends on the specific problem to be solved.

Finally, keep in mind that there is no reason why a control strategy adopting both forward and backward chaining cannot be used. The idea here is to start at an initial state as well as a possible goal state and work in both directions. In some problems, the search path and computing time can be shortened by taking a bidirectional approach. The search terminates when the forward and backward paths intersect at some node.

Blind Search Summary

The four basic blind search techniques used in almost any AI search process are depth first, breadth first, forward chaining, and backward chaining. Of course, these may be mixed in various ways. For example, a forward search can be depth first or breadth first. The same is true of a backward search which may be either breadth first or depth first. The best combination is chosen to optimize the search process for the given problem.

Heuristic Search

Heuristic is a term derived from a Greek word meaning to discover. A heuristic is something that helps us discover the path in a search tree leading to the solution of a problem. It is a rule of thumb, hint, trick, or other assistance that helps narrow or focus the search process. Heuristics help eliminate the search for or generation of nodes which clearly have no possibility of leading to the solution. The heuristics use experience and empirical knowledge to guide the search process, which may lead to a faster, more efficient solution. Heuristics can wipe out huge, unusable portions of the search tree leaving only those branches most likely to lead to a satisfactory goal. On the other hand, heuristics are not guaranteed to work. If properly chosen, they can be of major benefit, but in some problems, there is often no way of knowing their impact.

A variety of heuristic techniques have been devised to improve the efficiency of the search process. These fall into two categories: general purpose heuristics and domain specific heuristics. *General purpose heuristics* are flexible procedures that can be used on a wide variety of problems to prune the search space. The depth-bound technique mentioned earlier is an example.

Domain specific heuristics are special procedures that apply only to the given problem. One or both types of heuristics may be used depending upon the problem. In both cases, the goal of the heuristic is to provide knowledge that eliminates the problem of combinatorial explosion and shortens the search time.

A heuristic, in most cases, involves some mathematical evaluation. This is done by a so-called heuristic function which may be a formula to compute or a value to be determined. This computation evaluates a particular node and predicts the quality of successor nodes to determine their desirability as the next node in the path to the goal. Some examples of domain specific heuristic functions will illustrate this point.

An evaluation function in tic-tac-toe might be a count of the number of completely open rows, columns, and diagonals still available. The greater the number, the better the chance of winning. Another function might assign a value of one for each row, column, or diagonal in which a mark X or 0 already exists. It might assign a value of two for each two marks in a given row, column, or diagonal. Again, the higher the number, the better the chance of winning. In any case, the function gives the computer a numerical piece of data to work with in assessing the current status and in attempting to generate the next node.

In the traveling problem described earlier (Figures 3–3 and 3–4), the heuristic function may be the distance traveled so far. The function would add up the distance between the start node, and the nodes traversed to the present node. Another function may use the distances to all the successor nodes to decide which is shorter.

In moving from one node to the next in a search process, an operator must be applied. There is always a certain "cost" associated with the use of that operator. In the illustrated problem of finding the optimum path from one city to another, the cost was either time or miles. But cost can mean other things depending upon the problem. In a game, cost might represent the number of moves needed to achieve a win. The total cost of applying the operator to the various nodes between the initial state and the goal state will produce a total cost for the computation. The heuristic function attempts to determine the cost at each node.

The cost of a particular path through a search tree can be evaluated in terms of the number of arcs that must be traversed in going from the initial state to the goal state. This is illustrated in Figure 3–12. As you can see, there are several paths between the initial state and the goal state. Each arc has the same weight or value, in this case one. The cost of applying the operator is one each time it is used. The path with the least number of arcs, of course, has the least cost. The cost of each path is indicated at one each of the possible terminal nodes P,Q,F,L,R,N,I,S, and T. The goal nodes are Q and N. The preferred path of the search then is ACHN as it has the minimum cost.

One widely used general purpose heuristic function is called hill climbing. Hill climbing is a depth first search that employs a heuristic to estimate the remaining distance to the goal. The heuristic predicts the cost to the goal. The operators used on the initial state node generate successor nodes. These are then evaluated by the heuristic function and the one that appears to be the shortest distance from or lowest cost to the goal is selected. This process is repeated until the goal is reached.

In this technique, the goal is assumed to be at the top of a hill. The procedure it implements gradually moves the current node up the hill a step at a time until the goal is achieved. The problem with this method is that occasionally a node will be reached that is close to the goal, but where no further moves are possible. Successor nodes increase the cost or lengthen the distance to the goal instead of the opposite. Such false peaks are referred to as foothills, plateaus, or ridges. To get past such points,

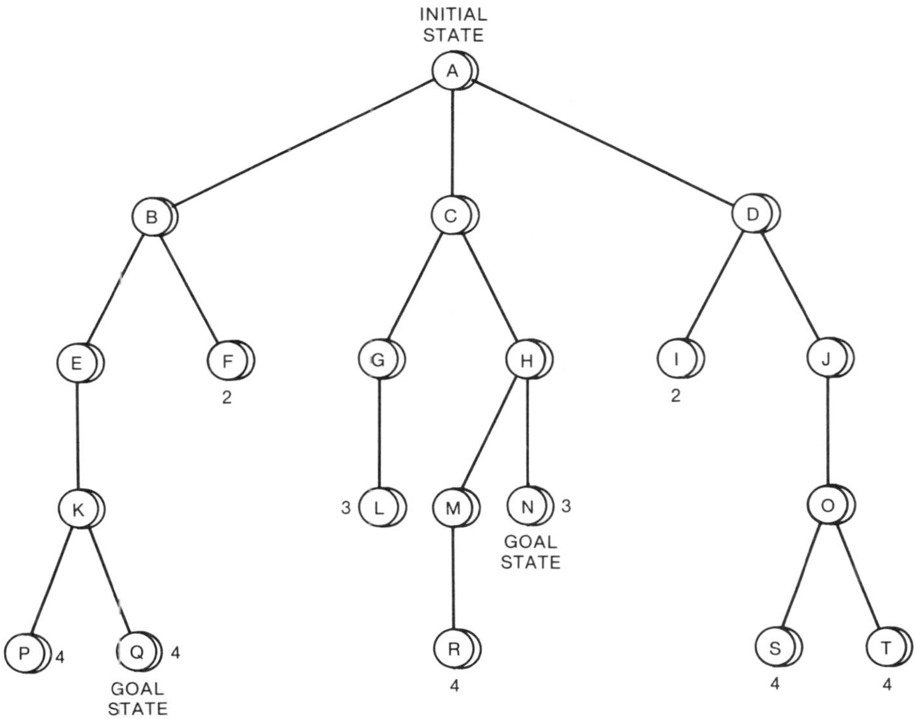

Figure 3–12. ***The "cost" of a search path.***

techniques for backtracking and jumping to a new point in the search space are used to get the system restarted in a better direction.

A Search Example

To help you understand the concepts of search trees and techniques, let's take an example. Refer to Figure 3–13. A computer-controlled robot arm is to be used to move the blocks on a table in a particular sequence from the initial state to the goal state. An AI search program will determine the sequence of movement of the arm.

The operator for this program is a command that says MOVE X to Y or rather to put block X on top of another block, Y, or the surface of the table. Here X and Y are general terms that refer to the individual blocks or the table surface. In Figure 3–13, X or Y may be A, B, C, or the table. A specific version of the operator might be to MOVE C to A. Here, X = C and Y = A. The operator says to put block C on top of block A. To use the operator, there must be nothing else on top of X, the block that is to be moved. If Y is a block and not the table surface, there should be nothing on top of Y.

Using the operator repeatedly, we can generate the complete search tree for this problem. That is, we can determine all possible moves beginning with the initial state.

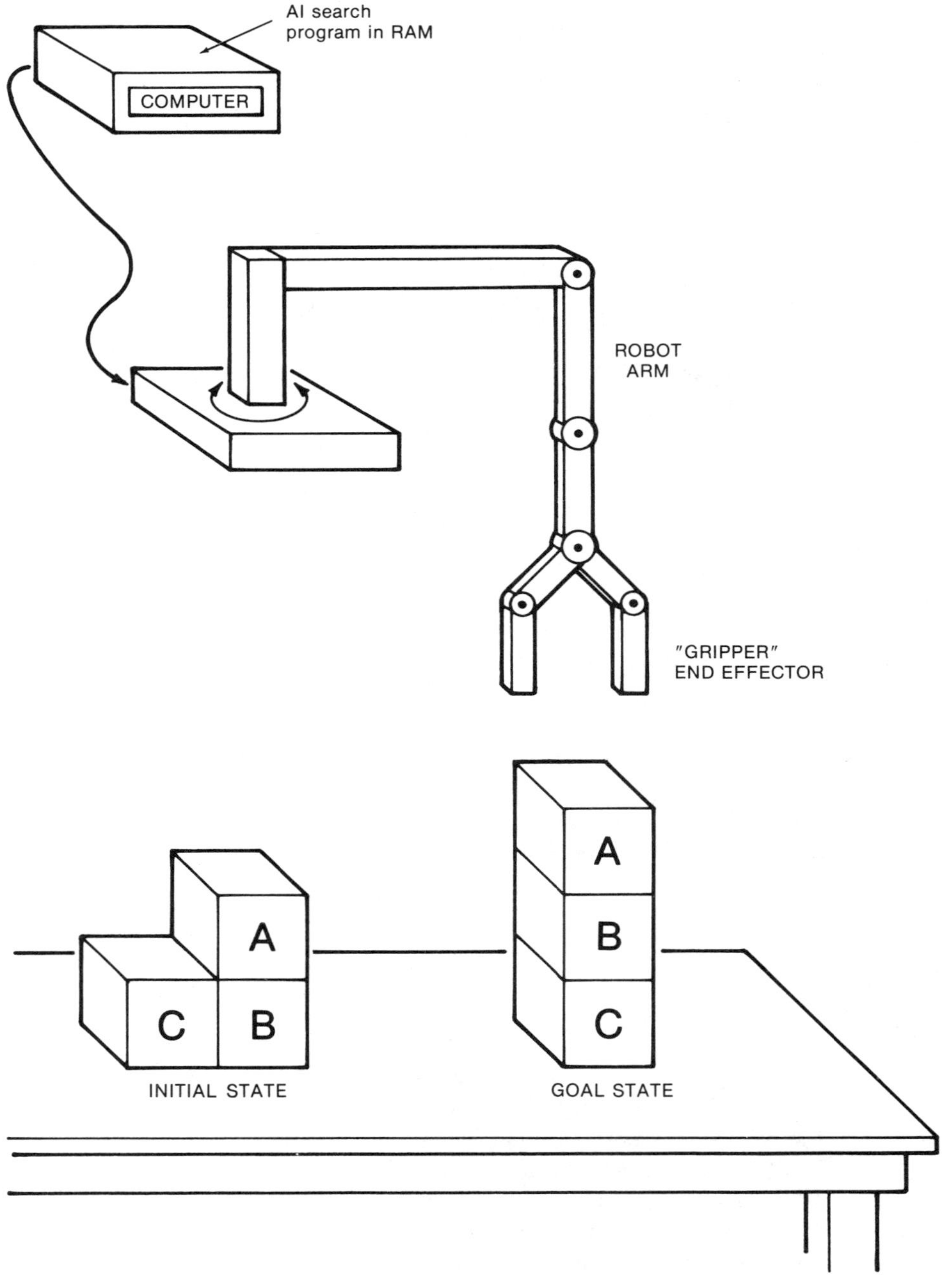

Figure 3–13. ***Example of a search.***

Each time you use the operator you will create a new mode. The initial and goal nodes are indicated in Figure 3–13.

Once the search tree is drawn, we can answer these questions:

a. Which produces the lowest "cost search from initial state to goal, a depth first or breadth first search?

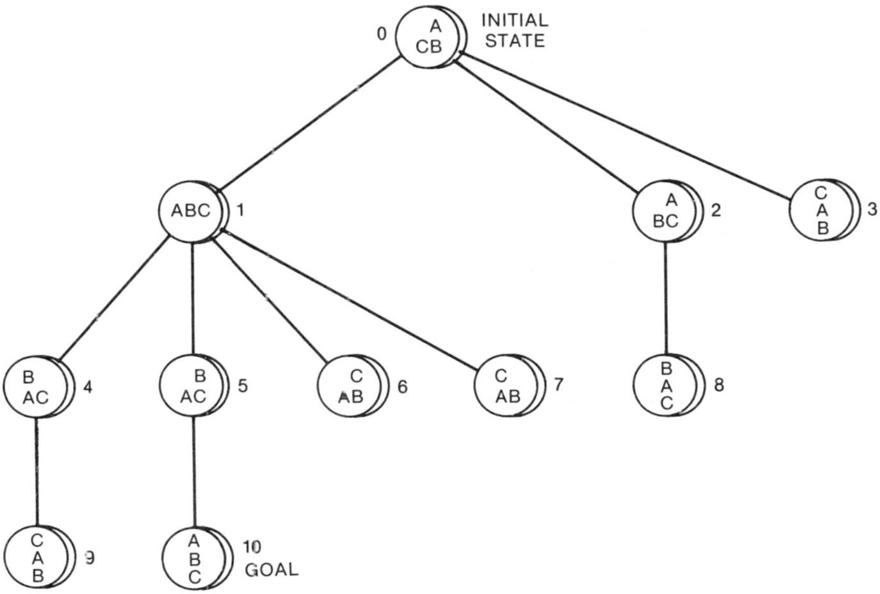

Figure 3–14. ***The search tree for the robot block mover problem.***

b. Is the search forward or backward?

The search tree for this problem is illustrated in Figure 3–14. All possible moves are illustrated. For example, node 1 is obtained by moving block A from block B to the surface of the table with the operator command MOVE A to table. Node 2 is obtained by moving A from B to C. Node 3 is obtained by moving C to A. The remaining nodes are generated in a similar manner.

The idea of the search is to get to the goal state as quickly as possible with the fewest moves. If we assume that the cost of any move from one node to another is one, then a depth first search produces the lowest "cost" solution. The cost is number of arcs traversed, including any in backtracking. The depth first search has the following node sequence: 0-1-4-9-4-1-5-10. That is seven node transitions. The breadth first search is 0-1-2-3-4-5-6-7-8-9-10, or ten node transitions. Thus the depth first search is faster and has the lowest cost. Work through this yourself to be sure you understand it. Forward reasoning is used in this example as we move from the initial state to the goal state.

Key Points

- The basic techniques used to reason with or draw inferences from the knowledge base are search and pattern matching.
- To solve a problem, answer a question or reach a conclusion, the knowledge base is methodically searched.

- The search process begins with an initial state or known fact. A control strategy uses procedures to manipulate the initial state to reach a goal or conclusion. This repetitive process is called search.
- Problems to be solved can be represented as a state space made up of nodes connected by arcs to show the various problem states and how they are interrelated.
- Most AI problems are represented in the form of a graph or network made up of nodes and arcs and called a search tree. The search tree has an initial or starting state, multiple intermediate problem states, and one or more goal states.
- The two primary methods of search are blind search and heuristic search.
- Blind search examines all possible states in the search tree looking for a solution. It is costly and time consuming but will always yield a conclusion.
- Combinatorial explosion is the geometric multiplication of search state possibilities that often makes blind search impractical for real world problems.
- The four methods of blind search are breadth first, depth first, forward chaining, and backward chaining.
- A breadth first search examines all states in a search tree one at a time from left to right and top to bottom one level at a time. Beginning with the initial state, a breadth first search looks at all the states on each level before proceeding to the next lower level.
- Depth first search examines all problem states seeking successively deeper problem states rather than those on the same level, and then backtracking, if required, until a goal state is found.
- A forward chaining search is one that begins at the initial state and continues to the goal state.
- A backward chaining search begins with a potential goal state and works backward through the search tree seeking proof, justification, or support.
- Heuristic search uses hints, tricks, rule of thumb, or knowledge about the state space to focus or limit the search process in an effort to zero in on a solution faster.

4

Introduction to Expert Systems

Knowledge is power.

HOBBES

Knowledge itself is power.

FRANCIS BACON

The biggest single use of artificial intelligence techniques today is in expert systems. More time and money is being invested in expert systems than in any other segment of the AI business. These new AI programs are becoming easier to develop and promise to make computers of all sizes more useful.

Because expert systems are so important, we will devote two complete chapters to expert system operation, application, and development. In this chapter, you will learn what expert systems are and how they work. Numerous famous commercial expert systems will be described. We will identify the major applications areas and walk you through the operation of a simple rule-based system.

Chapter 5 covers the development of expert systems. You will learn how to identify a potential expert system application. You will become familiar with the process of developing an expert system, including knowledge engineering and the use of some of the popular expert system development tools for personal computers. The procedures for converting knowledge into production rules will be outlined. With this knowledge, you will actually be able to develop a simple expert system of your own.

A Working Definition

An expert system is an artificial intelligence program incorporating a knowledge base and an inferencing system. It is a highly specialized piece of software that attempts to duplicate the function of an expert in some field of expertise. The program acts as an intelligent consultant or advisor in the domain of interest, capturing the knowledge of one or more experts. Non-experts can then tap the expert system to answer questions, solve problems, and make decisions in the domain.

The expert system is a fresh new, innovative way to capture and package knowledge. Its strength lies in its ability to be put to practical use when an expert is not available. Expert systems will make knowledge more widely available and will help overcome the age-old problem of translating knowledge into practical, useful results. And perhaps best of all, it is one more way that technology is helping us get a handle on the information glut. All AI software is knowledge-based as it contains useful facts, data, and relationships that are applied to a problem.

Expert systems, however, are a special type of knowledge-based system because they contain heuristic knowledge. As you learned in Chapter 3, heuristics are derived primarily from real world experience, not from textbooks. It is knowledge that comes directly from those people—the experts—who have worked for years within the domain. It is knowledge derived from learning by doing. It is perhaps the most useful kind of knowledge, specifically related to everyday problems, that works for us by producing solutions, decisions, and other positive outcomes.

It has been said that knowledge is power. Certainly there is truth in that statement, but in a more practical sense, knowledge becomes power only when it is applied. The bottom line in any field of endeavor is RESULTS, some positive benefit or outcome. Expert systems are one more way to achieve results faster and easier.

> *. . . building your power as an expert, that is, developing mastery of information that will satisfy individual and organizational needs, is a growing path to success.*
>
> THE PRYOR REPORT

Typical Expert Systems

One way to ensure that you understand what expert systems are and how they work is to give several examples of typical commercial systems. There are very few commercial expert systems now in operation, and they represent only a tiny percentage of all computer software in use. However, expert systems are growing in popularity as knowledge of their capability and ways to develop them become widespread. New software development tools make development faster and easier.

Although some commercial expert systems are now on the market, most operating expert systems are prototypes and laboratory experiments. Many organizations have been working with prototypes in an effort to learn how to develop commercial products, and graduate students are developing expert systems in universities. Now, low cost expert system development software is available for personal computers, giving anyone with a personal computer access to expert system technology. As knowledge of expert systems continues to grow, more commercial packages will become available.

Some software has unusually high visibility. This is particularly true of software packages for personal computers. Since there are many millions of personal computers in offices and homes, many people know and use them, and the software becomes well known. Typical famous personal computer software packages are Lotus' 1-2-3 spreadsheet, Ashton Tate's dBASE II/III DBMS, and MicroPro's WordStar word processing package. There is no well-known or widely used expert system.

The personal computer software packages mentioned here are generic programs that can be used to build special programs for many applications. An expert system, on the other hand, is a narrowly defined, highly dedicated piece of software. The expert system contains knowledge in a specific domain, and that field of expertise is extremely narrow. Because of the highly focused nature of an expert system, its market will naturally be more limited than the broad generic programs we hear so much about. It is not likely that you will hear about expert systems software in the same way, unless you happen to be working in the vertical field of interest and require knowledge in that domain.

Famous Expert Systems

If you do any additional reading or studying of artificial intelligence and expert systems, you will run across many of the systems we describe here. Several of these expert systems were milestones in AI development, representing real breakthroughs in artificial intelligence techniques. Many of the procedures used to develop the older systems are still widely used. As a result, they make good models for studying the structure of an expert system. Anyone working with artificial intelligence should be familiar with these particular systems.

MYCIN

MYCIN is probably the best known of all the expert systems. It was designed by Edward Shortliffe of Stanford University in the mid-1970s. It is a medical expert system that diagnoses bacterial infections and recommends antibiotic therapy. Here's how MYCIN helps a doctor identify patients with bacteremia, meningitis, and cystitis. The physician sits down at the computer and enters the patient's age and medical history, results of laboratory tests, and any additional relevant information. With this information plus its knowledge of the domain, MYCIN attempts to diagnose the cause of the infection. Then it recommends the type of drug and the dosage that might be used to cure the infection.

MYCIN has proved to be an extremely reliable medical advisor, but keep in mind that it was not intended to replace a physician. It can assist physicians who have little practical experience with the specific infections or diseases involved. It is also designed to help physicians check their diagnoses and therapy recommendations against those of a known expert or experts involved in creating the system. In any case, the use of such a program is optional, and the final decision on treatment is the responsibility of the physician. Nevertheless, expert systems have proven highly useful in medicine, and many more are being developed. Like other high tech developments in medicine, expert systems will increase the quality of medical care.

DENDRAL

Another early but well known expert system is DENDRAL. Like MYCIN, it is a product of researchers at Stanford University. Using its knowledge of molecular structures and chemistry, DENDRAL attempts to identify the molecular structure of unknown compounds. A sample of the unknown material is analyzed by a mass spectrometer and nuclear magnetic resonance equipment. When the data from the analyses is entered into DENDRAL, a special procedure goes about generating molecular structures that satisfy the constraints imposed by the data. The molecular structures thus generated are then checked against the chemical expertise stored in the knowledge base. This generating, testing, and sifting process eventually produces the inferred molecular structure.

The identification of unknown compounds is a long, difficult, tedious, and expensive process. Such a system can save scientists a considerable amount of time and effort.

XCON and XSEL

XCON, also known as R1 in its early prototype stages, is an expert system that helps configure large computer systems. Developed jointly by Digital Equipment Corporation (DEC) and researchers at Carnegie Mellon University (CMU), XCON helps translate a customer's order for a DEC VAX 11/780 series computer system into complete final system specifications. Large systems like the VAX are made up of hundreds of different components that can be mixed and matched to produce the exact configuration required by the customer. In addition, there are thousands of ways in which accessory PC boards, cables, disk drives, peripherals, software, and other items may be assembled into useful configurations. Days or weeks are spent in identifying all of the parts needed to assemble a system to meet the customer's specifications. XCON does it in minutes.

XSEL is another DEC-CMU expert system with knowledge of VAX 11/780 computer systems. XSEL was designed to help DEC sales persons select components for a VAX system. Because of the many options, the salesperson must often spend a considerable amount of time in putting together a suitable system for the customer. The knowledge in XSEL helps lead a prospective customer through the selection and configuration process. Given the desired specifications, XSEL selects a CPU, a memory configuration, peripheral devices, and recommendations for specific software packages. XSEL even assists in designing a floor layout for the specified system. Once the final configuration is available, it is passed along to XCON where it is further analyzed and the final configuration and components are decided upon.

XCON and XSEL are examples of practical, real world expert systems. They greatly increase the productivity of workers using them. The knowledge contained in such systems usually resides with only several experts within a company, but when their knowledge is put into the expert system, it can be tapped by anyone needing that information.

Prospector

Prospector is an expert system that helps geologists locate ore deposits. Its knowledge base contains rules and heuristic data derived from empirical data. It also contains a taxonomy of various kinds of minerals and rocks. Many geologists were interviewed and their expertise with particular types of ore deposits was captured.

The geologist searching for an ore deposit provides input information about a particular geological area, going into the field to observe the terrain and collect whatever evidence exists. Relevant geological features are noted and soil and rock samples are collected. Given this information, the expert system can evaluate the area in question and determine whether the potential exists for a particular kind of ore. Prospector gives a recommendation that indicates how favorable a particular site might be for further exploration or drilling.

Prospector can also look at data and suggest additional explorations, tests or data gathering. Once sufficient information is given, Prospector makes a final recommendation. The geologist can then pursue the recommended course based on his own judgment. Prospector has been credited with a $100 million molybdenum deposit find in Washington state.

Other Expert System Examples

Now let's take a look at several other expert systems to get a better feel for their scope, use, and value. While the expert systems described here are less well known, they are generally credited with advancing the art and science of expert system development. Some of the programs listed here are commercial systems while others are still research prototypes.

EL

This expert system analyzes electronic circuits made up of transistors, diodes, and resistors. A schematic diagram of the circuit is entered into the computer and EL performs a steady state analysis of it. The expert system works through the circuit and determines the characteristics of the circuit as well as the value of voltages and currents at all points in the circuit. Programmed into EL's knowledge base are many general principles of electronics, such as Ohm's Law, Kirchhoff's Law, component characteristics, and theory of transistor operation.

EL is an excellent tool for assisting the design engineer. A particular circuit can be described and analyzed quickly. A circuit operation and performance can be assessed without breadboarding a prototype. Problems can be spotted quickly and design changes can be made to achieve the desired circuit characteristics. EL can also be used as an aid in learning electronic circuit operation and design.

SOPHIE

SOPHIE was designed to help students learn to troubleshoot electronic circuits. The system presents a simulated electronic circuit and a problem, then permits the student to troubleshoot it. Test equipment is also simulated, allowing the student to make measurements in the circuit and thus help predict the fault. This program permits a step-by-step analysis of a problem while providing feedback. When a wrong move is made, the system detects the error and explains it. A considerable amount of troubleshooting experience can be obtained on a variety of circuits by using this program. It eliminates the need for designing and building special hardware for such training purposes.

DELTA

Developed by the General Electric Company, this program is used to assist maintenance personnel in locating problems in diesel electric locomotive engines. These systems are extremely large and complex and troubleshooting is difficult. Delta helps maintenance workers identify a malfunction and guides them through the entire diagnostic and repair procedure. An optional attached video disk system provides output in the form of schematic drawings, diagrams, and other repair information in video form. DELTA is just one of many expert systems designed for diagnostic and troubleshooting applications. For large complex systems of any kind, expert systems are ideal in helping maintenance personnel identify, locate, and service the system quickly.

FOLIO

This is an expert system that helps stock brokers and other portfolio managers in handling investments for their clients. The stock broker interviews clients to determine their resources and investment goals. With this information, FOLIO can select a portfolio that best meets their individual needs. FOLIO can provide recommendations for certain types of securities and has a knowledge base that permits it to evaluate high risk stocks, compute rates of return, and make decisions in the commodity markets.

FOLIO is one of a growing class of expert systems designed to assist financial planners. To minimize the loss of income to taxes, inflation, or other factors, many people are employing financial planners. Because the financial markets are so large and diverse, financial planners must be able to keep track of an enormous amount of information, including current events and the latest financial products. Expert systems that zero in on special areas can be invaluable tools for the financial planner attempting to structure a personal financial plan for a specific set of circumstances.

Miscellaneous Applications

There are so many uses for expert systems that it would be possible to fill an entire book with examples. Here are a few more to give you some additional ideas about the potential for this kind of software.

Weather Forecasting

Given inputs about the current weather situation, locally and in other parts of the country, an expert system can provide a relatively accurate prediction of the weather occurring over a period of several days.

Aircraft Identification

An observer who spots an airplane can record the various features and characteristics. These are entered into an expert system which will quickly provide an identification of the aircraft.

Battlefield Management

The Army, Navy, Air Force, and other services are rapidly developing expert systems that can be used to analyze battlefield situations. Both naval and military commanders can enter the current situation and the expert system will provide an analysis and recommendations for alternative courses of action.

Benefits of Expert Systems

These practical programs point out some of the major benefits of expert systems. First, like many other traditional forms of software, expert systems offer some of the following advantages:

1. Permit non-experts to do the work of experts
2. Improve productivity by increasing work output by improving efficiency
3. Save time in accomplishing a specific objective
4. Simplify some operations
5. Automate repetitive, tedious, or overly complex processes

Second, expert systems offer some additional benefits over conventional software, such as:

1. Permit new kinds of problems to be solved thereby making the computer more useful
2. Capture and store valuable knowledge that might be lost due to the resignation, retirement, or death of an expert.
3. Make expert knowledge available to a wider audience, thus increasing the problem solving ability of more people.

Note that cost savings is not listed. Expert systems, like most other software, rarely save money. They cost money to develop and use, but the benefits derived usually justify the cost.

The Down Side

Here are a few reasons why expert systems are not the panacea that the previously described benefits would have you believe.

1. Development of an expert system is extremely difficult, more difficult than creating more conventional software. Good experts are hard to find. Extracting their knowledge is a long, tedious job and coding that knowledge into software is a major chore.
2. Expert systems are expensive. It costs a lot to develop one, test it, and deliver it to the end-user.
3. Most expert systems still must be implemented and delivered on a big mainframe or minicomputer. Expert systems can be developed and used on personal computers, of course, but these are smaller, less sophisticated, and often less useful systems. The memory size and speed of a personal computer limits its usefulness.
4. Expert systems are not 100% reliable. Even with the best experts contributing to their design, expert systems aren't perfect or infallible. For that reason, their output recommendation must be weighed, tested, and otherwise scrutinized before it is used. A human being should always provide the final judgment.

These disadvantages are significant but certainly not impossible to overcome. They often can be surmounted or worked around, and despite their drawbacks, expert systems can be highly useful. Some of these disadvantages will gradually disappear or lessen as further technological improvements in hardware and software occur.

No man's knowledge here can go beyond his experience.

JOHN LOCKE

Stand-Alone vs. Embedded Systems

There are two basic types of expert systems: the stand-alone system and the embedded type. You will find real world examples of both types.

Stand-Alone

All of the expert systems we have talked about so far are of the stand-alone variety. This is a software package that runs on a personal computer, minicomputer, or mainframe. While the computer is running that program, it is totally dedicated to it. It stands alone in that application.

Embedded

Another type of expert system is the embedded type. See Figure 4–1. Here the expert system is just a portion of another larger program. The program may use conventional

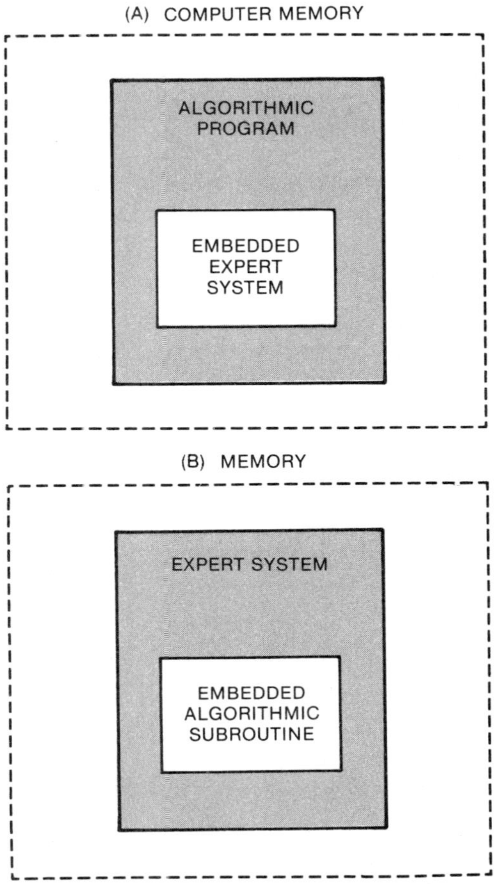

Figure 4–1. ***Types of embedded systems.***

algorithmic techniques but access the expert system as a subroutine when a particular type of information is required. This is illustrated in Figure 4–1A.

In another form of embedded system, an algorithmic program such as a mathematical subroutine is built into an expert system. See Figure 4–1B. During the reasoning or inferencing process, the expert system may have the subroutine perform a needed mathematical operation.

Links to Other Software

A variation of this arrangement is the expert system that links to an external software package such as a spreadsheet, data base management system (DBMS), or graphics program. During the inferencing process, the expert system may reach out and access data in the spreadsheet or DBMS to get enough knowledge to reach a solution. Or the graphics program may be called upon to display a visual output. While these programs are not really embedded, the effect is the same. They usually share memory with the expert system and have program links to it.

Dedicated Systems

Another kind of embedded system is the closed or dedicated system. Here the expert system is part of a special purpose computer dedicated to a single function. It may help analyze radar data in a fighter aircraft or make an intelligent decision about how to modify the process in a chemical plant. Regardless of the application, this kind of embedded system usually combines an expert system with conventional software to deal with a single or very narrow application. Today, millions of microprocessors are anonymously buried in electronic equipment and programmed to perform a specific dedicated function. In the future, many of those special purpose computers will contain expert systems.

The Trend

Presently, most expert systems are of the stand-alone variety. But as more progress is made in applying expert systems, there will be more and more unique designs. Embedded systems of all kinds are projected to grow considerably in popularity. In fact, some predict that the real future of the expert system lies more in embedded applications than stand-alone products.

Expert systems will most likely be one of the only stand-alone forms of AI software. Like expert systems, most other AI techniques will be employed as part of a larger, more conventional software. Natural language front-ends for DBMS and computer vision packages for robot systems are examples. The best way to look at AI is as a unique computer science process that complements and improves other software and hardware rather than as an entity unto itself.

> *That jewel knowledge is great riches, which is not plundered by kinsmen, nor carried by thieves, nor decreased by giving.*
>
> BHAVABHUTI

How Expert Systems Work

We are now ready to take an in-depth look at an expert system. We will identify its major components and show how they work together to produce an intelligent advisory program. As you can see, there is nothing complex, magical, or unusual about an expert system. It is simply a unique arrangement of software components that permits an expert's knowledge to be used by others for problem solving and decision making in a specific domain.

A general block diagram of an expert system is illustrated in Figure 4–2. The key components are the knowledge base, the inference system, the data base, and the user interface. In the following sections, each of these elements will be further explained.

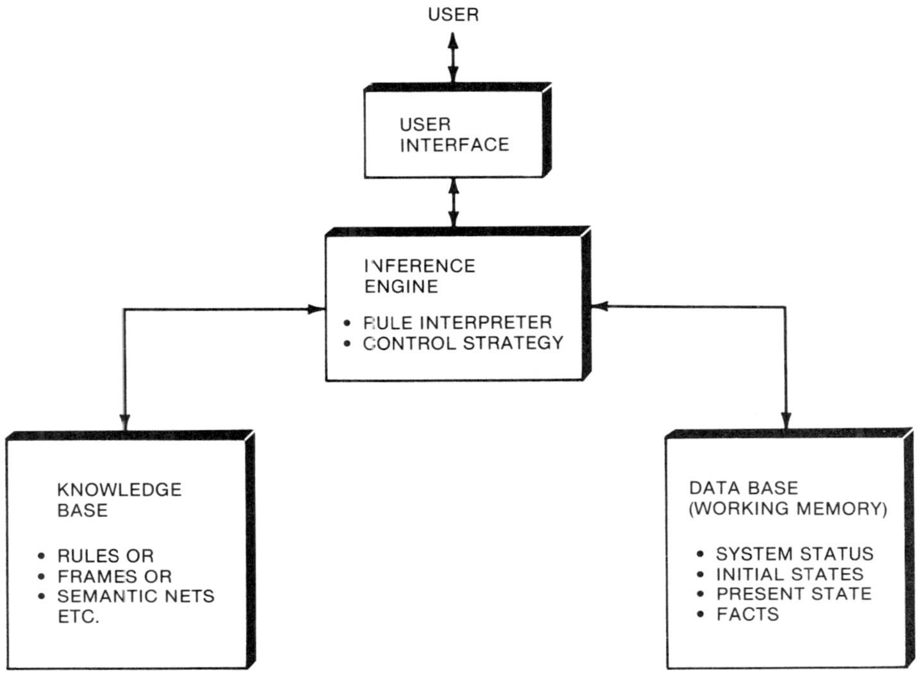

Figure 4–2. ***General block diagram of an expert system.***

The Knowledge Base

The heart of any expert system is its knowledge base, and there are many different methods for representing knowledge in AI software. The designer can choose among predicate calculus, lists, frames, semantic networks, scripts, and production rules. On the other hand, it has been determined through considerable experience that one of the best methods of knowledge representation for expert systems is production rules. Most commercial and experimental expert systems use the popular IF-THEN rule format described in Chapter 2.

Rules

Production rules are popular because their format is extremely flexible. Almost any kind of knowledge can be written to fit the IF-THEN rule format. Such rules are generally easy to write, and it is relatively easy to build an impressive knowledge base quickly. Production rules were covered previously, but let's take a minute to review this important topic.

First, keep in mind that the rule is formatted into two parts. The first (IF) part states some premise, condition, or antecedent. This is called the left-hand side of the rule. The second (THEN) part of A production rule states a conclusion, action, or consequence that will take place if the conditions on the left-hand side of the rule have been met. If the premises are true or the conditions met, the right-hand part is also true. The rule is said to be triggered. Then, when the right-hand side of the rule is implemented, the rule is said to have fired. Some rule examples given below show how certain types of knowledge are expressed in production rule format.

IF the animal lives in the water
AND the animal breathes water
THEN the animal is a fish, CF 1.0

IF the patient has frequent headaches
AND the patient has blurred distance vision
THEN the patient needs glasses, CF .8

IF the client is losing more than 20% of gross income to taxes
OR the client is looking for a tax free investment
THEN the client should have a tax shelter, CF .9

As you can see, each rule is made up of what we call clauses. A clause is like a sentence with a subject, a verb, and an object that states some fact. There is one IF clause and one THEN clause to every rule. The IF part of the rule may contain more than one premise, and will contain a clause for each. These are called compound clauses, and they are linked by the conjunctions AND or OR.

The CF means *certainty factor* and is a number between 0 and 1 that indicates the confidence we have in the truthfulness or validity of the conclusion. More on this later.

The kind of knowledge that can be represented with rules is extensive. Readily available theoretical knowledge from textbooks can usually be converted into rule format. But in most real world systems, we need knowledge that has been accumulated by an expert during years of solving problems in the area of specialization. This is usually empirical knowledge, the cut-and-try kind of experience that comes only from participation in practical problem solving. It is called heuristic knowledge.

Keep in mind too that while each production rule represents an individual chunk or piece of knowledge, it is usually associated with or related to many other rules. The rules link together to establish a line of reasoning. For example, the conclusion of one rule may become the premise of another. It is this collection or network of rules that forms the knowledge base. Since the basic element of most knowledge bases is production rules, you will often hear them referred to as the rule base.

Other Representations

Most expert systems use production rules, but other knowledge representation schemes have also been used. In some cases, depending on the subject matter, the extent of the knowledge, and the type of knowledge being represented, other representations may be more desirable. For example, frames, scripts, and semantic networks have all been used to produce expert systems. Further, two or more of these schemes have often been combined. Frames and rules or semantic networks and rules have been combined to form very large, complex expert systems.

A Key Benefit of Rules

In addition to the flexibility with which knowledge can be represented in rule format, rules offer another very important benefit to expert systems. With production rules, you can very easily modify or add to the knowledge base. The key to the success and value of an expert system is the integrity of its knowledge base. If the knowledge base is incorrect or incomplete, the system will be a poor problem solver and it may lead to wrong solutions. Therefore, it is extremely important that the knowledge base be kept up to date at all times. In some dynamic fields, new facts, figures, and knowledge are being added continually. Experts continue to gain new insights, different experiences, and improved problem-solving methods. All of this should be incorporated regularly into the expert system to keep it up to date. The rule format makes this easy because it breaks the knowledge down into small, manageable pieces. As a result, old rules can be rewritten to accommodate changes. Further, new knowledge is added by simply writing new rules and storing them in the knowledge base. Other knowledge representation schemes are less flexible in this regard.

Once all of the rules have been written, they are stored in the computer's memory. The knowledge base then becomes the search space in which the inference engine will work. Each rule becomes a node in a search tree that will develop as the inference system begins to tap the knowledge base.

The Data Base

Another important part of an expert system is the data base. It is sometimes called a global data base because it contains a broad range of information about the current status of the problem being solved. In practice, the data base is really a portion of working memory where the current status of the problem-solving process is stored.

The data base is also referred to as the fact base because it records facts about the problem. Known facts are stored there initially. Then new facts, as they are gleaned from the inference process, are added. The fact base keeps track of all that is known during the inferencing operations.

Among the important things stored in the data base are the initial conditions of the problem to be solved. Usually, the expert system asks the user for some beginning input. It may ask questions to which answers must be typed in, or it may present a menu of options from which the user must choose. This information gives the expert system a starting point to begin the search process.

The inference engine begins its search, matching the rules in the knowledge base against the information in the data base. As each rule is examined, actions caused when a rule fires may change the content of the data base, thereby updating the status of the problem. New facts become available to use in the decision-making process. In addition, special functions such as a request for additional information from the user, may be triggered.

The data base also stores a list of rules that have been examined, fired, and in what sequence. This helps to keep track of the process. The rule sequence can be given later if the user requires an explanation of the reasoning process.

The Inference Engine

The inference engine is software that implements a search and pattern-matching operation. It is sometimes called a rule interpreter because its operation is somewhat like a software interpreter for a computer language. Whereas a language interpreter looks at each line of code in a program and then implements the operations specified, the rule interpreter examines the rules in a particular sequence looking for matches to the initial and current conditions given in the data base. As rules matching these conditions are found, the rules are fired, thereby initiating the actions specified.

As the rules continue to fire, they will reference one another and form an inference chain. Each time a new rule is examined, it is checked against the current status of the problem solution stored in the data base. The firing of a particular rule may add new facts to the data base. This gives the rule interpreter additional information to go on, and it may modify the sequence in which the next rule is selected. This process continues until the solution is found.

In summary, we can say that the function of the inference engine is hypothesis proving. When the hypothesis is given to the expert system, the inference engine first checks to see if the hypothesis is stored in the data base. If it is, the hypothesis is considered to be a proven fact, and no further operation is necessary. Usually, however, the hypothesis is not there and must be proven by inferencing. As the various rules are fired, new facts are derived and ultimately the hypothesis is either proved or disproved.

Forward Chaining

The rule interpreter can take two basic approaches to search for an answer. These are forward and backward chaining. As you learned in Chapter 3, there are two approaches to implementing a search. The first is to begin with some initial information and work forward, attempting to match that information with a rule. This is called forward chaining. In forward chaining, the rule interpreter attempts to match a fact or statement in the data base to the situation stated in the left-hand or IF part of the rule.

Once a fact in the data base has been matched to the IF part of the rule, the rule is fired. The action or consequent stated could produce new knowledge or a new fact that is stored in the knowledge base. This new fact may then be used to search out the next appropriate rule. This searching and matching process continues until a final conclusion rule is fired.

To show how a forward chaining expert system works, let's consider a simple example. Figure 4–3 shows a rule base consisting of seven rules. The data base contains the initially known facts F and L. Letters F through N, of course, represent clauses.

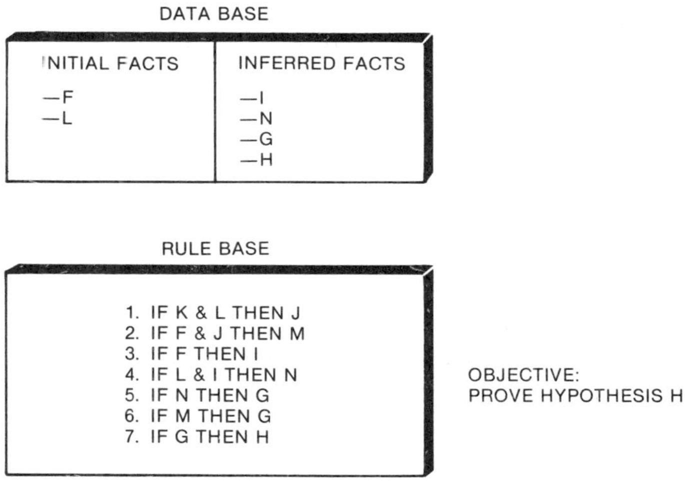

Figure 4–3. ***A simple hypothetical expert system example using forward chaining.***

The inference engine selects the first known fact F and begins searching the rule base looking for premises (the IF part of the rule) that matches it. It examines all of the rules sequentially. There is no match in rule 1, so it goes to rule 2. Here it finds F as a premise. But to fire the rule, J is also needed. The rule interpreter then looks back in the data base for J. It does not find it, so it abandons rule 2. In rule 3, F is again matched. Therefore, F infers I. The new fact I is added to the data base.

No additional rules contain F so the inference engine picks up L from the data base, then proceeds to look for matches. It discovers L in rule 4. I is also a condition for this rule, but the inference engine checks the data base and discovers I there. For that reason, rule 4 is fired and N is inferred. N is added to the data base.

The process continues as the rule interpreter uses the new facts in the data base, I and N, to match other premises. It finds none that matches I, but rule 5 fires when N is matched. G is, therefore, inferred. G is added to the data base. The inference engine then finds G in rule 7 inferring H. H, of course, is our hypothesis and, therefore, it is proved and the process concludes.

As you can see, the rules link together to form a chain or a line of reasoning to prove the hypothesis. This chain is better illustrated with a graph or network as shown in Figure 4–4.

Backward Chaining

Another approach is backward chaining. Here the rule interpreter starts with a fact in the data base, but this time it is the hypothesis. The rule interpreter then begins examining the right-hand or THEN parts of rules looking for a match. The inference engine searches for evidence to support the hypothesis originally stated. If a match is found, the data base is updated recording the conditions or premises that the rule stated as necessary for supporting the matched conclusion. The chaining process continues with the system repeatedly attempting to match the right side of the rule against the

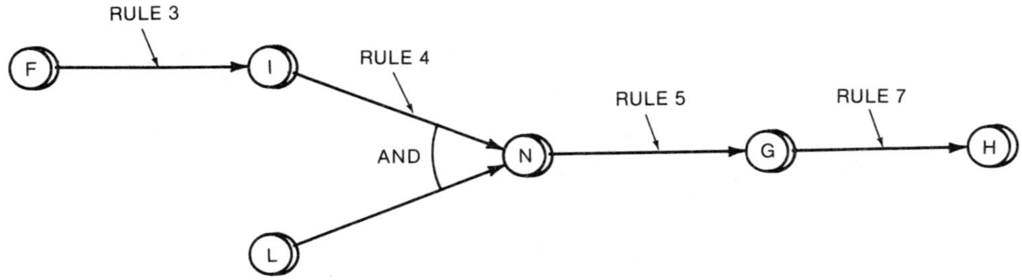

Figure 4–4. ***Forward chaining using the example in Figure 4–3.***

current system's status. The corresponding IF sides of the rules matched are used to generate new intermediate hypotheses or goal states which are recorded in the data base. Again, this backward chaining continues until the hypothesis is proved.

Now, using the same rule base and data base in Figure 4–3, we can illustrate backward chaining. We begin by telling the system we want to prove H. The inference engine first looks in the data base on the off chance H is there, and no further processing is necessary. Of course, it is not there, so the inference engine begins looking for conclusions of rules that infer H. It finds rule 7. It, therefore, looks for G in the data base. It is not there, so now the rule interpreter looks for rules with G on their right side. It finds rules 5 and 6. If it looks at rule 5 first, it will then look in the data base for N. N is not there so it searches for rules that conclude N. It now discovers rule 4 with premises L and I. The search continues for L and I. L is in the data base, so now I is looked for. I is found in rule 3. Therefore, the rule interpreter now looks for F and finds it in the data base.

At this point, F proves I, and L and I prove N. N, in turn, proves G. G then proves H, the original hypothesis.

You may have wondered what would happen if the rule interpreter looked at rule 6 first in trying to find G. It would, of course, have looked for M and would have found rule 2. Then it would have looked for F and J in the data base. Finding only F, it would proceed to search for J. J would be identified in rule 1, so the rule interpreter would look for K and L in the data base. L would be found, but not K. The system would now look for K. K is never located, so the system comes to a dead end. As a result, it would backtrack to the point where it found G in rule 6. It would look for G again. This time, it would find rule 5, then go on to prove H as we've already described.

In backward chaining expert systems, all of the hypotheses are known. In other words, all of the possible final outcomes, choices, or selections are identified in the beginning. That makes sense because the experts creating the system will know what all the answers are. The job of the expert system is to search through the hypotheses one at a time trying to prove one based on the data it is given.

During the backward chaining process, the rule interpreter will look for the various premises in the data base. If it does not find them, it goes on to what it can find. But backward chaining systems can be set up to ask the user questions. For example, if fact K is not found in the data base, as described previously, it will ask the user if he knows K. If he doesn't, he enters it. Then the system would go on to prove H using rules 1, 2, 6, and 7 instead of rules 3, 4, 5, and 7. Being able to ask when it does not know is a virtue of backward chaining systems.

Forward vs. Backward

The choice of a control strategy with either forward or backward chaining is determined by the design of the system. The choice is also dependent on the problem being solved. Often, however, it is not possible to determine which approach may be the best. In large systems with many rules, the forward chaining or data driven approach may be too slow as it will generate many sequences of rules. The search, as a result, can go off in undesired directions exploring alternatives that do not fit the problem. In such cases a backward chaining or goal driven approach may be more advantageous.

On the other hand, a backward chaining or goal directed approach has its problems also. Depending on the rules themselves, the backward chaining process could get a fixation on a particular hypothesis and continue to explore it although the data available to support it may not be there. The system doesn't know when to switch the emphasis or context to a more appropriate search sequence.

Some expert systems incorporate both forward and backward chaining. This usually speeds up the process and ensures a solution. The concurrent forward-backward search rapidly converges on an answer.

In practice, the user couldn't care less about the inference technique used. It doesn't matter whether it's forward or backward as long as a solution is supplied. On the other hand, the creator of the expert system must be concerned with such things. If the expert system is being programmed from scratch in a language such as LISP, a decision of forward versus backward chaining must be made. A language such as Prolog does not give much choice as its inference system is basically backward chaining. In addition, most expert system development tools have a fixed inference format, either forward or backward. In developing the system, you take what is supplied and do your best to make it work properly. Backward chaining is used in most expert system development tools.

Knowledge advances by steps, and not by leaps.

THOMAS B. MACAULAY

User Interface

The remaining element of the expert system shown in Figure 4–2 is the user interface. This is a piece of software that lets the user communicate with the system. The user interface asks questions or presents menu choices for entering initial information in the data base. It provides a means of communicating the answer or solution once it has been found. Any intermediate communications during the problem-solving process are taken care of by the user interface.

The user interface contains "canned" questions, statements, or menu sequences. It also has a means of selecting portions of the final rule to be displayed as the answer. Usually, in simple systems, the clauses used in the rules are used as outputs with appropriate prefaces. Some expert systems also can include blocks of text with each rule and at the beginning or the end of the expert system. These are built in by the designer and are used to provide supplementary information or explanations.

The user interface is like the user communications facilities in other types of software. It is not truly a natural language processing front-end where the user can simply type in questions or supply information in any form. Usually, information supplied by the user must be formatted in a special way or entered in a unique, restricted syntax.

As natural language processing programs become easier to develop, there is no doubt that they will be included in more expert systems. This will make the software far easier to use. Users will be able to use the system by simply asking questions in their own unique ways. The system will be able to tap the knowledge base, extract the desired answer, and supply it to the user in a carefully constructed natural language output. While natural language interfaces are now available for some data base management systems and other software, few have been incorporated in expert systems. However, look for this as one of the future advancements for larger and improved expert systems.

Desirable Expert System Features

Expert systems are far more useful if they have some additional features. These include an explanation facility, ease of modification, transportability, and adaptive learning ability. Let's take a look at each of these key features.

Explanation Facility

Expert systems are very impersonal and get right to the point. Many first time users are surprised at how quickly the expert system comes up with a recommendation, conclusion, or selection. The result is usually stated concisely and sometimes very curtly using rule clauses. A natural language interface will help improve this situation, but that's not the main problem. A more important issue is that often users have difficulty in "buying" the output decision. They question it or flat don't believe it. Users frequently want to know just how the expert system arrived at that answer. Most of the better expert systems have a means for explaining their conclusion. Typically, this takes the form of showing the rules involved in the decision and the sequence in which they were fired. All of the information is retained in the data base for that purpose. When users want to know the expert system's line of reasoning, they can read the rules and follow the logic themselves. Some rule formats permit the inclusion of an explanation statement that justifies or elaborates on the need for or importance of the rule.

The explanation facility is important because it helps the user feel more comfortable with the outcome. Sometimes the outcome is a surprise or somewhat different than expected. It is difficult for an individual to follow the advice of the expert system in these cases. However, once the expert system explains itself, the user better understands the decision and feels more at ease in making a decision based upon it.

Ease of Modification

As indicated earlier, the integrity of the knowledge base depends upon how accurate and up to date it is. In domains where rapid changes take place, it is important that some means be provided for quickly and easily incorporating this knowledge. If the expert system was developed using one of the newer development tools, it is usually a simple matter to modify the knowledge base by writing new rules, modifying existing rules, or removing rules. The better systems have special software subsystems that allow these changes to be made without difficulty. If the system has been programmed in LISP or Prolog, changes are much more difficult to make. In examining or evaluating an expert system, this feature should be considered seriously in context of the application.

Transportability

The wider the availability of an expert system the more useful it will be. An expert system is usually designed to operate on one particular type of computer, and this is usually dictated by the software development tools used to create the expert system. If the expert system will operate on only one type of computer, its exposure is limited. The more different types of computers for which the expert system is available, the more widely the expertise can be used. If possible, when the expert system is being developed, it should be done in such a way that it is readily transportable to several different types of machines. This may mean choosing a programming language or software development tool that is available on more than one target machine.

Adaptive Learning Ability

This is an advanced feature of some expert systems that allows them to learn from their own use or experience. As the expert system is being operated, the inference engine will draw conclusions that can, in fact, produce new knowledge. New facts are stored temporarily in the data base, but in some systems they can lead to the creation of a new rule which can be stored in the knowledge base and used again in a future problem. The more the system is used, the more it learns about the domain and the more valuable it becomes.

The term learning as applied to expert systems refers to the process of teaching the expert system new things by adding additional rules or modifying existing rules. On the other hand, if the system incorporates the ability to learn on its own, it will be a much more powerful and effective problem solver. Today few expert systems have this capability, but it is a feature that is sure to be further developed and incorporated into future systems.

Dealing with Uncertainty

One of the neat things about expert systems is their ability to deal with incomplete or uncertain information. There will be times when an expert system, in gathering its initial inputs, will ask a question for which you do not have the answer. In such cases, you simply say that you do not know. Expert systems are designed to deal with inputs such as this. Because you may not have a particular fact, the search process will undoubtedly take a different path. It may take longer to come up with an answer, but the expert system will give you an answer.

Traditional algorithmic software simply cannot deal with incomplete information. If you leave out a piece of data, you won't get an answer at all. If the data is incorrect, the answer will be incorrect. Garbage in-garbage out. This is where artificial intelligence programs, particularly expert systems, shine. When the inputs are ambiguous or completely missing, you can still get a solution to your problem. The system may qualify that solution, but at least it is an answer that can in most cases be put to practical use. And isn't this the way real life is? We rarely have all the facts before making a decision. Our common sense or knowledge of the problem tells us what is important to know and what is less important. Experts almost always work with incomplete or questionable information, but that doesn't stop them from solving the problem.

As you saw in Chapter 2, there are several methods of dealing with uncertain information. In rule based expert systems, numerical factors indicating the truth or probability of a premise or conclusion are used as a measure for uncertainty. These numerical factors are known as certainty factors (CF) and probability. In this section we want to take a look at these measures of uncertainty to be sure that you understand their use in rule based expert systems.

Certainty Factors

In a high percentage of expert system rules, there will be no ambiguity or uncertainty. We will know with confidence whether or not a particular premise or conclusion is true or false. If the information is not known at all, then the rule requesting it will not fire. In cases where there is the possibility that the information is not known, special rules can be created to deal with this problem. The rule might state that if a particular piece of information is not available, then a certain action will be initiated.

There are many cases where the information is known but we have less than 100% confidence in its truthfulness. Just as weather forecasters use a number to predict the likelihood of rain, so can a confidence number be used with production rules. Weather forecasters may say that there is a 70% probability of rain. What they're really saying is that they don't know for sure whether or not it is going to rain. On the other hand, they have enough information to be able to say that 70% of the time under similar circumstances it does rain. While a certainty or confidence factor is not really a probability, it is a number that helps you to represent the uncertainty. A certainty factor is simply a measure of the confidence you have that a particular fact or rule is true or not true. It is usually a number between 0 and 1 where zero indicates no confidence and 1 means full or complete confidence. You will also hear certainty factors called confidence factors or rule strength.

Certainty factors are used with both the premise (IF) and conclusion (THEN) portions of a rule. The two examples given below show how confidence factors are used.

IF the patient has hayfever, CF = .6
THEN prescribe an antihistamine

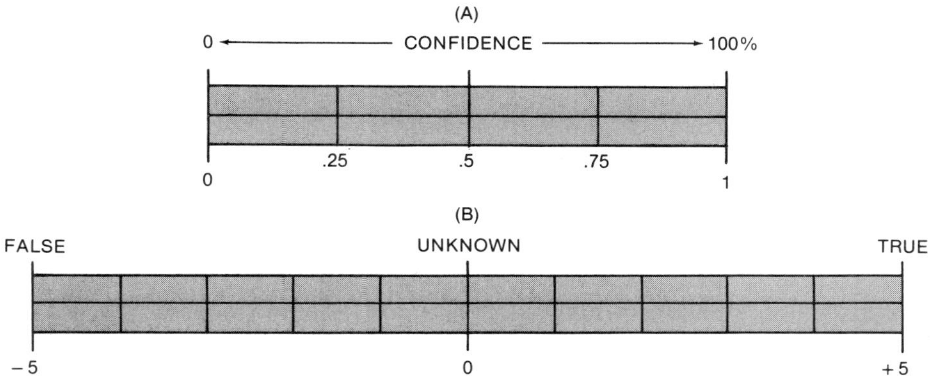

Figure 4–5. ***Confidence or certainty factor scales.***

IF the patient is sneezing
AND has a runny nose
AND has watery eyes
THEN the patient has a cold, CF = .5

Figure 4–5 shows several ways to use certainty factors. As you can see, the scale is pretty much up to the programmer. In example A, a scale of 0 to 1 is used where 1 = absolute certainty; that is, 100% truthfulness or validity of the premise or conclusion of a rule. The 0, of course, indicates absolute uncertainty or falsity. Intermediate values have varying degrees of truthfulness or uncertainty. You could also use a scale of 0 to 10 or 0 to 100 with the same result.

The + and − scale shown in example B in Figure 4–5 is another approach. A +5 indicates absolute certainty while a −5 indicates 100% falsity. The 0 in the center of the scale indicates unknown. You could also use a −1/0/+1 scale as well.

Determining whether a particular rule is to fire requires the inference engine to look at the confidence factor and evaluate it. For example, if you are using the 0 to 1 scale, you might want the rule to fire if the confidence factor is above a certain threshold level, say a .2. In Figure 4–5B, you may assign a threshold of +1 or −1 depending upon the circumstances as the minimum acceptable level for determining whether something is true or false. Other levels may be set depending upon the problem.

This brings up the point about who sets these levels. First, the confidence factors themselves are determined by the experts creating the knowledge base. Only the experts know how true or false something is or how confident they are of the various premises and conclusions in a rule. Most of the time these are simply intelligent estimates based upon experience, educated guesses. In some cases, reliable statistical data may be available which will help the expert put a more accurate figure on the truthfulness or confidence of the information.

Threshold level is assigned by the programmer. But the programmer listens to and uses the expert's advice as a guideline for the problem. In most expert systems development tools, the threshold may be set by the programmer by simply keying in a number. Various scales and systems are used. The validity of the threshold can be tested during actual usage.

In rules with compound premise clauses connected by AND or OR, each clause may have its own CF. For such situations, there must be a way to compute a composite CF for the rule. This is done by using the minimum CF of all clauses connected by AND or the maximum CF of all clauses connected by OR. Some examples will illustrate this.

Rule 1:

IF X (.4)
AND Y (.75)
THEN Z, Composite CF $= .4$

Rule 2:

IF D (.3)
AND E (.8)
THEN F, Composite CF $= .8$

If each rule in a reasoning chain has a CF, each will, of course, affect the other. The outcome has to be decided based upon some composite evaluation. One way this is done is with a special formula. Composite CF $= CF(X) + CF(Y) - CF(X)*CF(Y)$. This says that the CF for rule X is added to the CF for rule Y and from that is subtracted the product of the CFs for rules X and Y. Below are two rules to illustrate the point.

Rule 3:

IF P
AND Q
THEN R (.65)

Rule 4:

IF R
THEN S (.2)

The composite CF then is:

$$.65 + .2 - (.65)\,(.2) =$$

$$.85 - .13 = .72$$

Of course, there will usually be more than two rules in a chain. The formula above can be used by taking the composite CF of two rules and combining it with the CF of a third rule. That new composite CF is then combined with a fourth, and so on.

Probability

The strength of a rule, the belief or confidence in the premise or conclusion, can also be expressed as a pure probability. Probability is a number that expresses the chance of something occurring or not occurring. It is really a ratio as shown below:

$$P(X) = \frac{\text{Number of outcomes favoring the occurrence of}}{\text{Total number of events}}$$

The probability of X occurring, stated as P(X), is the ratio of the number of times X occurs to the total number of events that take place. An example will illustrate this. Suppose we ask ten engineers whether they can program in the BASIC language. Out of the ten, three say they can. We can use these figures to compute the probability:

$$P(\text{BASIC}) = \frac{3}{10} = .3$$

What this says is that the probability of an engineer being able to program in BASIC is .3. We can also express this as a percentage by simply multiplying the probability by 100. We say that the probability of engineers being able to program in BASIC is 30%. Probability figures like this can be used to determine rule strength if they fit the problem.

Multiple probability values will occur in many systems. For example, a rule may have three parts to its antecedent, each with a probability value. The overall probability of the rule then becomes the product of the individual probabilities, if the parts of the antecedent are independent of one another. In a three part antecedent, the probabilities may be .9, .7 and .65. The overall probability is:

$$P = (.9)(.7)(.65) = .4095$$

The combined probability is about 41%. But this is true only if the individual parts of the antecedent do not affect or interrelate to one another.

Sometimes one rule references another. Here the individual rule probabilities can propagate from one to another. There is a need to evaluate the total probability of a sequence of rules or a path through the search tree to determine if a specific rule fires. Or you may be able to use the combined probability to predict the best path through the search tree. In other words, the probabilities become the "costs" of the individual arcs in the tree.

There are numerous methods of computing combined probabilities. If the rules are independent, a simple product can be used as described before. However, most events and rules are dependent upon one another. In that case, a special procedure called Bayes' Rule or Theorem can compute the probability of event A occurring given that event B has already occurred. This is expressed as P(A:B). Bayes' Theorem is:

$$P(A{:}B) = \frac{P(B{:}A)P(A)}{P(B{:}A)P(a) + P(B{:}\text{not } A)P(\text{not } A)}$$

We won't attempt to explain this rule here as it is doubtful that you would ever need to program it. But you should know that many expert systems use Bayes' Theorem instead of certainty factors to deal with uncertainty. Several major expert system development tools use Bayesian probability.

Fuzzy Logic

Another method of dealing with imprecise or uncertain knowledge is to use *fuzzy logic.* Fuzzy logic is a system conceived by mathematician and computer scientist Lofti Zadeh for dealing in inexact or unreliable information. In this method, an attempt is made to assign numerical ranges with a possibility value between zero and one to concepts such as height, beauty, age, and other elements with values that are hard to pin down. It allows you to work with ambiguous or fuzzy quantities such as large or small, or data that is subject to interpretation.

For example, how tall is tall? Are you tall if you are 5 foot 7 inches? Is tall over 6 feet or over 6 feet 3 inches? Is short less than 5 foot 5 inches or what? Fuzzy logic gives you a way of expressing this kind of information. Tall might be expressed as some value of X where X is between 5′10″ and 6′2″ with a possibility of .8. A "0" possibility means that X is not in the range given while "1" means that X is between the values given. Values between 0 and 1 mean some degree of possibility that X is in the given range. Once you are able to express such imprecise knowledge, you can use it more reliably in the reasoning process. Fuzzy logic is not as widely used in AI as confidence factors and probability because it is more complex and difficult to implement. And often it does not offer any advantages over the simpler systems. But it is an alternative of growing importance as AI expands into new areas of application.

Expert System Applications

In an earlier section, we described numerous commercial and experimental expert systems to give you some idea about the kinds of applications being addressed with this type of software. Unquestionably, the applications are broad. But now let's take a closer look at expert system applications to come up with some generic guidelines for determining whether a particular application is suitable for an expert system. Expert systems are definitely not suitable for all situations. In this section we provide some specific details on the kinds of applications that best fit the way an expert system represents knowledge and draws inferences.

Generic Classification of Applications

Table 4–1 shows the main categories of applications suitable for expert systems. If the problem to be solved falls into one of these categories, it is a candidate for expert systems solution. This is not to imply that an expert system is the only answer. There may very well be a more conventional algorithmic program that will do the job. In any case, assuming the problem is one of these types, an expert system should most certainly be considered as an alternative. Now let's take a look at each category in more detail.

Control

Control is a very common computer application. In this application the computer is interfaced to some other component or system. For example, the computer may operate

Table 4–1. ***Generic Expert System Categories***

CONTROL — intelligent automation
DEBUGGING — recommends corrections to faults
DESIGN — developing products to specification
DIAGNOSIS — estimates defects
INSTRUCTION — optimized computer instruction
INTERPRETATION — clarification of situations
PLANNING — developing goal-oriented schemes
PREDICTION — intelligent guessing of outcomes
REPAIR — automatic diagnosis, debugging, planning and fixing.

a single component such as a motor or a complete system such as a factory. In any case, the computer governs the operation of the component or system.

There are two basic types of control, open loop and closed loop. In an open loop system, the computer follows some mathematical formula or step-by-step procedure to cause a particular type of behavior to occur in the system or component.

The other type of control is closed loop. Again an algorithm is used to cause certain events to take place in a particular sequence. However, a closed loop control uses feedback. Sensors provide signals from the component or process being controlled to tell the computer what is happening in the system. Feedback signals of all kinds can provide useful input information to the computer. These feedback signals may represent position, speed, temperature, pressure, light level, liquid level in a tank, flow rate in a pipe, or dozens of other characteristics. The computer program uses these to make adjustments in the control process.

While many applications are adequately dealt with by algorithmic control processes, an expert system can sometimes greatly improve the performance of the system. Sometimes an algorithm cannot be found to provide the kind of control desired.

The key to using an expert system in control applications is to have feedback that monitors the system or component status. This gives the expert system inputs to use in making decisions. With this kind of input information in addition to its own knowledge base, an expert system can adapt or adjust to changing conditions. It can also predict future performance, diagnose problems, and correct them by making adjustments in the control process. The system can anticipate problems and develop plans for overcoming them. Control by an expert system is far more intelligent, adaptable, and flexible than more conventional algorithmic control systems.

Debugging

Debugging is the process of troubleshooting, that finds problems or faults in a system and comes up with a corrective solution. Debugging is needed in those situations where the system is not operating to specifications.

Design

Design information for certain types of products and systems can be accumulated and stored in an expert system. A designer/user can then call upon the expert system to either design the product or assist in doing so. Given a set of product specifications that are in effect constraints, the expert system goes about developing or configuring the product to meet the specifications. Design expert systems are already widely used. Systems are available for designing printed circuit board layouts, electronic circuits, integrated circuit geometry, buildings and houses, and mechanical components of all kinds. Most automobile manufacturers use computer aided design techniques in producing new cars. Many incorporate expert systems.

Diagnosis

Expert systems can be used to diagnose a malfunction in a product or system. In this sense they are similar to debugging expert systems except that they do not prescribe a solution to the problem. A diagnosis system observes the behavior of the device or system and makes note of improper performance, irregularities, or unplanned actions. With this information, it can infer the possible cause of the problem. It does not suggest a correction for this malfunction, but leaves that up to the user.

Instruction

Expert systems also can be used for instructional purposes. An expert system domain can be used in teaching students how to solve problems in the field of expertise. The student can sit down with the computer and work through numerous problems with the expert system. By using the explanation subsystem, the student can note the sequence of rules being used to reach a conclusion. From this the student can get an idea as to what knowledge an expert needs and how it is used to solve problems of that type.

Special expert systems can be constructed to aid in the learning process. For example, an expert system can be part of a larger computer-aided instruction program. Computer-aided instruction (CAI) or computer-based training (CBT) are types of software implemented on a computer. The computer acts as a one-on-one tutor presenting information to the student. The student interacts with the computer through the keyboard by supplying answers to questions.

While such instructional software is effective, it is designed in a fixed manner to present a standard content and sequence to every student. However, not all students come to the program with the same knowledge, background, and skills. As a result, the program may not be suitable for all students. By building an expert system into the CAI, the program will be able to interpret the student's knowledge and behavior. It will be able to diagnose weaknesses and suggest corrective action. Instructional programs like this adjust the content and sequence of the material so that it is optimized for the student using it. In this way, smart, highly skilled students can get through the material quickly. Those who are slower and less knowledgeable can be provided with remedial material or extra instruction when understanding does not come quickly.

Interpretation

One of the best applications for an expert system is interpretation. Interpretation systems are given inputs that consist of observations and other data. Then, using its knowledge base and inferencing system, the interpretation program attempts to infer a particular situation from the input data. It attempts to clarify or explain the situation which it represents. Such systems help an individual to understand or put into perspective an event or situation. Examples of interpretation include intelligence analysis, surveillance, image and signal analysis.

Planning

A planner attempts to come up with a method, arrangement, or approach that will achieve a goal. Given the objective and starting point, as well as some possible intermediate steps, an expert system can work out an appropriate or optimum plan for achieving that goal with the given resources and limitations. For very complex projects or systems, planning is an incredibly difficult human task. But for an expert system with the appropriate knowledge and inputs, planning is a relatively easy task. Some planning applications are project management, military tactics and strategy, robot programming, and automatic software generation.

Prediction

Predicting means to foretell or prophesy the future. Like other expert systems, a prediction system receives input data about a given situation. Its job then is to infer the consequences or outcomes. The expert system will generate one or more scenarios which its best judgment creates based on the inputs and its knowledge base. Weather forecasting is a good example of an expert system of this type.

Prediction systems also do what is generally known as structured selection. Given the input conditions or facts, the system examines all of its possible output possibilities to see which one best fits the inputs. This is a good way to decide between various alternatives when there are many factors to consider.

Repair

Repair is the process of returning a broken, injured, or partially destroyed item to its original state. The output of a debugging type of expert system usually provides suggestions for remedies and clues to defective components. A repair expert system takes this one step farther and actually implements automatic repair of the system. To do this, a repair expert system must have built into it those capabilities normally associated with a diagnosis, debugging, and planning operating system. The system locates the trouble, suggests a course of action, works out a plan, and then implements it. An example of a repair system is a computer program that fixes or repairs another defective program.

Keep in mind that while many expert systems will fall into just one of the above categories, the application may require a mix of the various kinds. Two, three, or more of the various categories might have to be merged to carry out the objectives of the desired expert system.

Example Expert Systems

In this section, two small example expert systems are presented to further illustrate their operation and applications. Both are rule based. In addition, their small size and simplicity make them easy to understand although not very useful. These systems will provide a starting point and some guidelines in helping you develop your own expert system.

Restaurant Selection

This expert system helps you choose a restaurant. The questions are how much money do you wish to spend and what kind of food do you want? Given answers to those questions, the expert system will make a recommendation.

The rule base for this expert system is given below.

1. IF you want to pay less than $10 per person
   AND you have a taste for Mexican food
   THEN go to Montezuma's Revenge Restaurant
2. IF you want to pay less than $15 per person
   AND you want seafood
   THEN go to the Chesapeake Bay Fish House
3. IF you want to pay less than $20 per person
   AND you want some Italian food
   THEN go to Alfredo's
4. IF you want to pay less than $50 per person
   AND you want continental cuisine
   THEN go to Chez Francois
5. IF you want to pay less than $5 per person
   THEN stay home

The system would begin by asking you how much money you are willing to spend. It may ask you to type in an upper limit per person or it may give you a menu choice like this.

"What is the maximum you are willing to pay per person?"

1. $ 5
2. $10

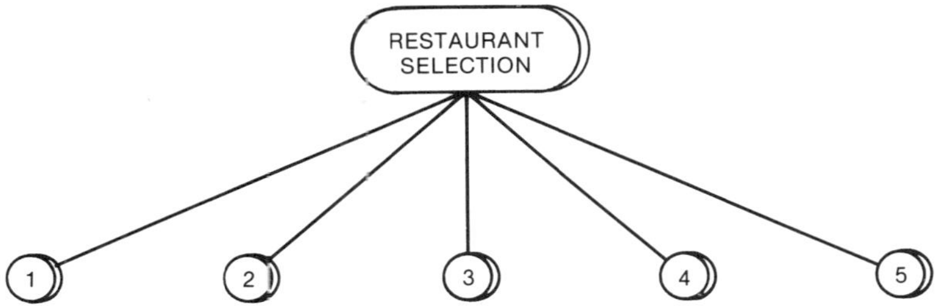

Figure 4–6. ***Search tree for restaurant selection expert system.***

3. $15
4. $20
5. $50

You would type in a number between 1 and 5.

Next, the system asks if you prefer a food type. Again you may just type in an answer or choose from a menu.

Desired food choice
1. Mexican
2. Italian
3. Seafood
4. Continental

You would enter the number corresponding to your choice.

This initial information is stored in the data base. Then the search begins. In this case, it is not very extensive because of the small rule base, but it should be obvious that you could easily expand this expert system to a very large size. You could add more qualifications such as location, distance, or occasion and increase the number of food types.

Figure 4–6 shows the search tree. It is unusual because it has only one level. The reason for this is that each rule corresponds to an output choice or answer. There is no categorization or hierarchy. There is no complex network with multiple choices to search. Answering the input questions satisfies only one rule. The numbers in the nodes designate the rules.

The inference engine looks at each rule attempting to match the initial inputs in the data base to the antecedents in the rule. Once a match is made, the rule fires, and the recommendation is made.

For example, if you chose a maximum of $20 per person and selected Italian, then you would get the recommendation Alfredo's. Incidentally, you would get the same recommendation if you selected $10 or $15 per person and Italian since both of these are less than $20.

This points up one important fact. Most expert systems can do simple math and make decisions based on numerical values. Here the system is looking for figures below a given threshold.

If you chose continental food and $15 per person, you would get no answer. These initial conditions don't match anything in the rule base. The expert system cannot deal with it. This points up the fact that to make the system practical, you will have to add one rule or more to take care of unexpected input choices like this. For example, such a rule might say:

IF you want to spend less than $15 per person
AND you want continental cuisine
THEN output the following statement:

"There are no continental restaurants in this price range. Try Mexican or seafood."

It is possible to create an expert system like this where all the conditions are contained within the left-hand (IF) side of the rule. But it is better to organize the knowledge into a hierarchy where chaining search procedures will be used.

Lamp Repair

The next example is an expert system that assists in diagnosing a fault in a lamp and suggests possible causes and remedies. Like the restaurant example, it is not very useful in the real world, but it will illustrate the concept of how larger diagnosis or debugging systems work.

The rules in the knowledge base are listed below.

1. IF the lamp does not work
   THEN check to see that power is on
2. IF the power is not on
   THEN check for blown fuse
3. IF the power is not on
   AND the fuse is good
   THEN check for a power failure
4. IF the power is not on
   AND there is no fuse
   THEN check for a tripped circuit breaker
5. IF the power is not on
   AND the circuit breaker is on
   THEN check for a power failure
6. IF there is a power failure
   THEN wait for power to come back on
7. IF the power is on
   THEN check the bulb
8. IF the bulb is bad
   THEN replace the bulb
9. IF the bulb is good
   THEN check the switch

10. IF the switch is bad
 THEN replace the switch
11. IF the bulb is good
 AND the switch is good
 THEN check the plug
12. IF the plug is bad
 THEN fix or replace the plug
13. IF the bulb is good
 AND the switch is good
 AND the plug is good
 THEN check the cord
14. IF the cord is bad
 THEN fix or replace the cord
15. IF the bulb is good
 AND the switch is good
 AND the plug is good
 AND the cord is good
 THEN check the wall outlet
16. IF the wall outlet is bad
 THEN fix or replace the outlet

The starting assumption is that the lamp does not work. The system attempts to discover the reason and suggest a course of action.

Figure 4–7 shows the search tree for this system. The numbers in the node circles are the rule numbers but could also represent the search sequence. Again, the numbers in the nodes designate the rules.

The system asks some questions as it goes. To begin with, it wants to ascertain that power is available. You must check for this, then answer. If the power is absent, the system has you check the fuses or circuit breakers or determine if there was a power failure. At each point, you have to answer before the system goes ahead.

If power is on, the system first has you check the bulb. Again you test and answer. This process continues as you check the switch, cord, plug and wall outlet until the problem is located.

Key Points

- An expert system is an AI program that clones or emulates a human expert within a specific domain.
- Users can tap the knowledge in an expert system to solve problems and make decisions without the need for the expert.
- Expert systems are a superior way to package and dispense knowledge as well as control information glut.

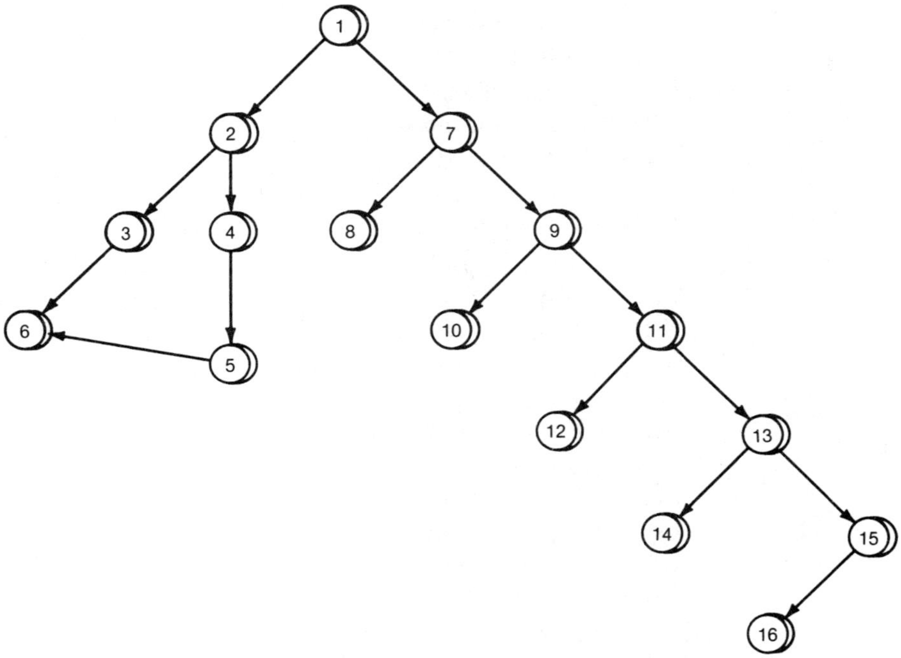

Figure 4–7. ***Search tree for the lamp repair expert system.***

- Expert systems are not generic problem solvers like spreadsheets and DBMS. They focus on only one subject.
- Commercial expert systems have been developed to perform medical diagnoses, identify unknown compounds, configure large computer systems, and locate ore and oil deposits.
- Other expert systems are used for computer-aided design, instruction, system troubleshooting, financial analysis and planning, tax decisions, weather forecasting, and battlefield management.
- The benefits of expert systems are productivity improvement by allowing inexperienced users to do the work of experts, saving time, simplifying work, and automating some tasks.
- Expert systems solve new kinds of problems not dealt with by traditional software. They allow valuable, irreplaceable knowledge to be captured and used.
- The main disadvantages of expert systems are difficulty of development, high cost, and less than 100% reliability.
- Expert systems can be a stand-alone piece of software or be part of an embedded system where the expert system is a part of a conventional program or vice versa.
- Most AI software will most likely be of the embedded rather than stand-alone variety.
- An expert system is made up of four major components: the knowledge base, the data base, the inference engine, and the user interface.

- The knowledge base contains the heuristic knowledge of one or more experts.
- Most knowledge bases are made up of production rules, although semantic nets, frames, scripts, and other knowledge representation methods are also used.
- A rule consists of two parts, the premise or condition and the conclusion or action. They are in the form of clauses that state facts or actions. These clauses appear in an IF-THEN format such as:

  IF noise appears on the power bus

  THEN there is insufficient decoupling

- Rules are preferred as they can represent a wide range of knowledge and the knowledge base can be easily updated.
- The data base holds facts about the status of the system. It contains initial conditions or facts and, later, inferred facts.
- The inference engine performs the reasoning function using the rules. It implements a search strategy and pattern-matching scheme to review rules and select those that apply.
- There are two basic types of inference methods, forward chaining and backward chaining.
- In forward chaining, the inference engine searches the knowledge base looking for the IF parts of rules that match initial and inferred facts.
- In backward chaining, the inference engine attempts to prove a hypothesis by matching facts in the data base to the THEN parts of rules.
- The user interface is that part of the expert system that communicates with the user.
- Four desirable expert system features are (1) explanation facility, (2) ease of modification, (3) transportability, and (4) adaptive learning capability.
- Expert systems can deal with ambiguous and uncertain knowledge by attaching certainty factors and probabilities to rules to specify their confidence or degree of truth.
- Expert systems have a wide range of applications. The major categories are control, debugging, design, diagnosis, instruction, interpretation, planning, prediction, and repair.

5

Developing an Expert System

Knowledge is of two kinds. We know a subject ourselves; or we know where we can find information upon it.

SAMUEL JOHNSON

It is one thing to know how an expert system works and how to use it, but another thing altogether to develop one. Most expert systems are relatively easy to use, and virtually anyone can learn the process of tapping the knowledge they contain. It is also relatively easy to understand the basic concepts of how an expert system works. However, designing and building expert systems is a major undertaking. It requires a lot of thought, design, programming, and debugging to create such a program from scratch. Expert systems are more complex than conventional software.

Despite the complexity of creating an original expert system, many attempt it and a large number of those attempts are successful. The purpose of this chapter is to describe in detail the process of creating an expert system. We will identify the key steps in the process and expand upon each of them so that you may attempt to develop an expert system of your own.

While there are clearly defined steps in the development of an expert system, keep in mind that size, scope, and subject matter will vary considerably. These steps can be only a general guideline. The only way to learn to develop an expert system is to actually create one. Following the basic guidelines here, choose a simple topic, then try it yourself. If you keep the problem small, you should be able to create a successful expert system. In the process, the experience you gain will enable you to tackle other more ambitious projects.

As you go through this chapter, keep two important things in mind. First, the development process we describe recommends that you use programming tools, software packages that help you to develop expert systems without having to program. Eliminating the need to program in an AI language such as LISP or Prolog or a conventional language such as Pascal or C will greatly speed up and simplify the process. We will describe briefly some of the types of expert system development tools available.

Second, we are emphasizing the development of expert systems on personal computers. The general development process is applicable to any size computer, but we are focusing on the personal computer because there are many development tools available for them. Further, there are many small-to-medium size problems that can be implemented quickly and easily on a personal computer. As you know, there are millions of personal computers in offices, factories, and homes everywhere. Expert systems that run on personal computers will have the greatest impact and widest commercial value. Finally, personal computers can be used as an initial development tool even for large systems. Often a prototype system is designed and implemented quickly on a personal computer to test the concept. If it works and the problem is beyond the capacity of a personal computer, the work can be transferred to a larger machine.

So let's begin by looking at the development process itself.

Creating an Expert System

There are ten basic steps in creating any expert system. Figure 5–1 shows the process. In this section we will amplify each of those steps. The remainder of the chapter will explain each step in detail.

To illustrate each step we will create a small, simple expert system as we go. This will show you how each step works as well as the procedures and techniques involved.

Identify the Problem and Need

Like many computer programs, expert systems are, in a sense, a solution looking for a problem. To justify the creation of an expert system, there must be a real problem to solve or need to meet. For that reason, your first step in developing an expert system should be to examine your situation and clearly decide what the problem is or why such a system may be helpful.

In attempting to achieve results, we often run into problems: time problems, productivity problems, or people problems. The problem you identify could be suitable for solution by an expert system.

Determine the Suitability of the Problem

Once the problem is clearly identified, you can then examine it in more detail to see if it is right for an expert system solution. Although you may be excited about the concept of expert systems and are looking for a way to apply them to your own work, keep in mind that only certain types of problems can be successfully solved with an expert system. Using the guidelines described in the previous chapter and the new ones we will present, you should have little difficulty in determining whether your problem is a suitable candidate. The key factor to look for is the application of expert knowledge to solve a problem.

To take advantage of an expert system, the user must have a computer or at least access to one. Today, many employees already use computers. That makes expert

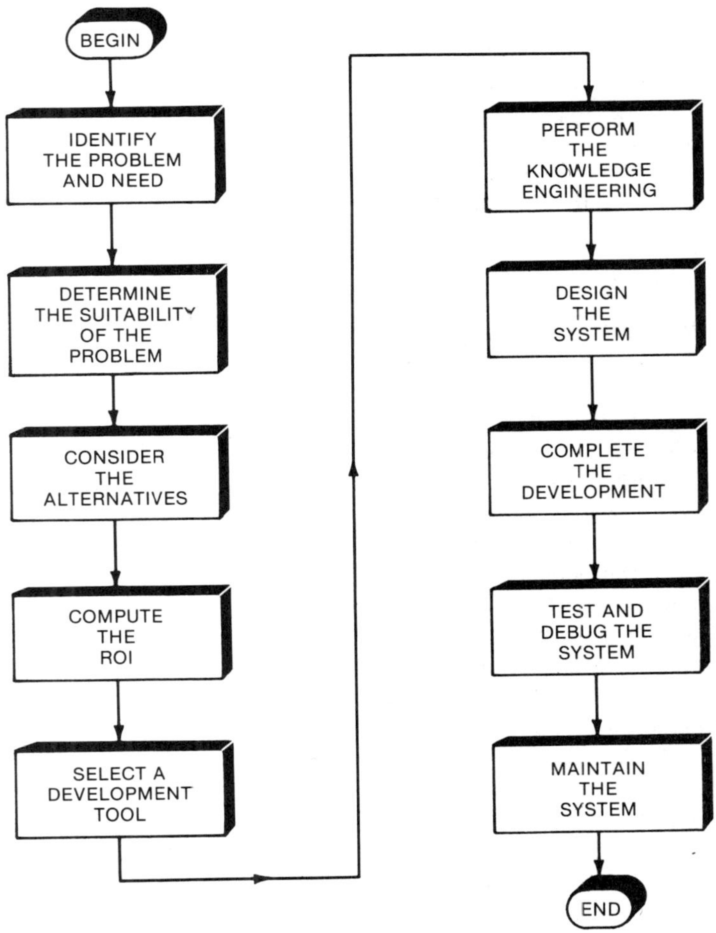

Figure 5–1. ***Ten steps in the process of developing an expert system.***

systems viable. This seems almost obvious, but many people overlook the fact that the knowledge in an expert system is worthless if an employee can't get to it quickly and easily.

Consider the Alternatives

Although your problem may fit the criterion for an expert system, don't overlook what might be simpler or equally as satisfactory alternative solutions. For example, certain kinds of employee performance problems might be corrected by training. Another solution is providing all employees with the information they need in a written manual or job aid. A non-computer solution may be not only the best solution, but also the simplest and least expensive.

Consider other software alternatives. A data base management system (DBMS) software package might better fit the problem than an expert system, by letting you store a significant amount of information and access it conveniently. The ability of the computer to reason may not be necessary.

Finally, don't overlook a conventional software solution. A straightforward algorithmic solution might be better than a symbolic or AI solution.

Having now looked at the alternatives, you can make your final decision. If an expert system is your choice, then you can begin the next steps.

Compute the ROI

If your choice is an expert system, your next step is to determine whether or not it is economically feasible. You must compute the return on your investment (ROI) by performing a cost/benefit analysis. This will help you estimate the cost of creating the expert system and determine whether its cost can be justified in terms of the savings or other benefits it produces.

Developing an expert system is not a simple job. It is going to cost a considerable amount not only in the purchase of software but in the hours it will take to create the system. Personnel must be available to do the work, and even the simplest of expert systems will take months to develop and cost thousands of dollars. Can the time and expense be justified? Is the problem to be solved bad enough or important enough to make the investment?

To compute the ROI, take a stab at estimating expert system development cost. At best this will be an educated guess as it is always difficult to size up a software development job and accurately determine its cost. We will give you guidelines later for coming up with a ball park figure for your project.

Next, you will need to determine, if possible, the savings that will result in using the expert system. The problem you are having may be costing you money, whether it is a direct expense or extra time used by employees. If the current loss is great enough, developing the expert system may offset this cost and produce a real savings over a period of time.

It may not be possible to compute any savings, yet there may still be justification for developing the expert system. You may derive benefits from using it that more than justify the cost of development.

Select a Development Tool

An expert system development tool is a software package that allows you to enter an expert's knowledge into the computer without having to program. Most expert system development tools are rule based. Some tools permit the implementation of frames and semantic networks, but they are usually more expensive and generally operate only on the larger computers. However, many tools are available to implement rule based systems. Your next job is to identify the available tools and choose one that fits your needs. Later in this chapter we will discuss some typical development tools, and the appendix contains a complete list of the various tools and their vendors.

Perform the Knowledge Engineering

At this point in the development process, you are finally ready to do some real creative work. Development of an expert system begins with knowledge engineering; that is, acquiring the knowledge. As you know, knowledge comes in many forms. It can be standard textbook knowledge that you can dig out of books, articles, and other references quickly and easily. This knowledge is important, but it is usually not the best kind of knowledge for an expert system. The real knowledge will come from individuals who are experts in the subject. In addition to acquiring textbook knowledge, you must locate one or more experts who are willing to spend some time on the project.

The format of the knowledge will guide you in selecting a particular knowledge representation scheme. However, unless the knowledge is very unusual, you will find that most knowledge can be represented in production rule form. For that reason, during the knowledge engineering phase, assume that the knowledge base will be made up of many rules. You will have a wide choice of software development tools if you use a rule-based knowledge format.

Design the System

Using the knowledge you have acquired and the tool you have selected, you can now begin the nitty-gritty design of the expert system. First, you will need to create an outline, a hierarchal flow chart, a matrix, decision table, or other format that will help you organize and understand the knowledge. Using these aids, you will convert the knowledge into IF-THEN rules. It is best to follow the specific procedures recommended by the software tool you are using. Once the basic design is complete, you can begin using the tool to create a prototype of one segment of the system. Translate a portion of the knowledge into rules and test the newly created segment. Your job here is to test the concept before going ahead with the entire program.

Complete the Development

Once you have satisfied yourself that the system is going to work satisfactorily, you can begin to expand the prototype into the final system.

The best way to go about this is to expand the prototype one segment at a time. Typically, the knowledge will divide itself conveniently into logical "chunks," each with a block of rules. Test each new segment as it is added to see that it works with the original prototype. You can do this a rule at a time if you like. In this way, you will make good progress, and end up with a final workable system without major bugs.

Test and Debug the System

After the expert system has been developed, you will need to spend some time testing and debugging it. No expert system will be perfect the first time, and a considerable amount of work will be required to validate it.

Take your expert system to the field and try it out on its intended users. User feedback will show you where to make final changes, corrections, and additions to achieve the desired performance.

Maintain the System

Few subjects or domains are static. Thus, an important part of expert system development is ongoing maintenance, updating the system with new knowledge, removing knowledge that is no longer applicable, and otherwise fine tuning the system to keep it fully current and applicable to the problem.

Don't overlook this vital step. If your system is not periodically updated, it will quickly become worthless and your investment in its development will be wasted. Be sure your ROI calculations take this into consideration.

In the remainder of this chapter, we will expand upon these ten steps.

Identifying the Problem

The first step toward the creation of an expert system is to identify the problem. Problems manifest themselves in several ways. They may show up as indicators of poor performance. The employee may not be able to get the job done fast enough or achieve the desired quality or quantity level. Key objectives are not being met. If the problem seems to have its roots in the need for more knowledge about the job, an expert system may be a potential candidate.

To get a feel for the wide range of problems suitable for an expert system, take a look at some of these examples:

- Computer store salespeople have difficulty matching hardware and software to specific applications and assembling complete systems because they do not have broad enough experience or sufficient knowledge of the products and inventory.

- The maintenance personnel of commercial airlines need constant help from the few specialists available. This slows up repairs and service operations.
- The operators of a nuclear power plant must watch dozens of indicators and recorders to monitor plant status, condition, and safety, and must determine the cause of a problem if a malfunction is noted. They must apply their knowledge quickly to prevent damage or correct the problem.

Two major conditions exist in these examples. First, the user does not know the information or does not have access to an expert who does. Second, the user needs the knowledge fast to do the job.

Problem Analysis

Begin the problem analysis by writing a statement of the perceived problem. The act of writing the problem down causes you to think through the situation.

Once you have written your statement, conduct follow-up analysis. Interview those individuals affected by the problem. During the interview, ask a variety of questions aimed at confirming your written statement. Get the real story from those involved.

If possible, plan to observe as well. Attempt to watch the employees performing their job and witness the problem firsthand. Have someone else join you in this effort to gain a different perspective.

When the interviewing and observation steps are complete, go back and refine your original statement. You may find that you were right on target. But chances are the problem analysis has revealed a somewhat different problem. You may have identified only the symptoms of the problem. Only when the cause is identified can you begin to formulate a practical solution.

This first step often is ignored or glossed over. Many people believe that the problem is obvious and requires no further analysis or definition. That may sometimes be the case, but the problem is often more complex and subtle than it appears. Only a formal analysis will reveal the real problem. Do not make the mistake of ignoring this initial problem identification stage.

Determining the Suitability of the Problem

If the problem is knowledge related, it is most likely suitable for an expert system solution. But let's be more specific. First, attempt to categorize the problem. In Table 5–1, we outline ten categories of expert systems and the kind of problems they address: control, debugging, design, diagnosis, instruction, interpretation, planning, prediction, and repair.

Using your problem definition statement, attempt to match the need to one of these ten categories. If your problem fits one or more of them, you are one step closer to an expert system solution.

Table 5–1. ***Problem Categories Suitable for Expert Systems***

CONTROL — intelligent automation
DEBUGGING — recommends corrections to faults
DESIGN — developing products to specifications
DIAGNOSIS — estimates defects
INSTRUCTIONS — optimized computer instruction
INTERPRETATION — clarification of situations
PLANNING — developing goal-oriented schemes
PREDICTION — intelligent guessing of outcomes
REPAIR — automatic diagnosis, debugging, planning and fixing

Even though you have decided the problem is knowledge related and does fit one of the ten categories generally associated with expert systems, there are still some important decisions to make before proceeding. Table 5–2 lists several additional factors to consider. Let's take a look at each of these in more detail.

Human Expertise

An expert system simulates a human expert, consultant, or advisor. Such a person has extraordinary knowledge, education, and experience in a particular domain. If having such an expert would solve your problem, chances are an expert system would also solve the problem.

The need for human expertise varies considerably with the type of problem. For example, the loss of a key person in your organization can bring about performance problems. Your expert may be retiring, resigning, or transferring. In any case, the loss of expertise can create severe problems.

The human expertise you need may be scarce, and even when experts exist, there may be more problems than the experts can solve in a given period of time. If you need more experts, an expert system will certainly multiply those you do have. Employees can then use the expert system to solve the problem almost as adequately as the expert can.

Expert systems also can provide expertise needed in a hostile environment, such as outer space, on the battlefield, or in unusually severe conditions in a manufacturing

Table 5–2. ***Additional Factors in Determining the Suitability of a Problem to an Expert System***

1. Relies on human expertise
2. Has a high payoff
3. No common sense required
4. Focuses on a specific area
5. A mental, not physical solution is required
6. Has a moderate level of difficulty
7. Can be solved with appropriate knowledge
8. Has a minimum number of solutions
9. Experts are available

plant. In such cases, the problem may be solved by a computer, controller, or other automatic or remote control device. A robot is a good example. Such machines can be designed to survive severe environments better than humans, and should the danger cause a loss, the loss is only a machine rather than a human life. The machine is not intelligent, but if the mission is narrowly focused, an expert system linked to the machine can solve the problem without the help of a human being.

High Payoff

The suitability of an expert system for problem solution must be justified. Keep in mind that there is a major cost involved in creating such a system, and the investment of time and money must produce a major return.

If the expert system can help diagnose illnesses and cure more people, the payoff is high. If the expert system helps in locating new deposits of oil worth billions, then obviously the payoff is high. If many individuals are experiencing the problem and an expert system will solve it, then the development can be justified.

Later in the expert system development process, you are going to have to compute the return on your investment. But now, you should determine in a broader, more general sense if that development will produce a payoff worth the effort.

No Common Sense Required

An expert system is useful if no common sense is required to solve the problem. Common sense, that great general storehouse of knowledge you have about the world, is based on an enormous amount of knowledge acquired through education and experience. An expert system simply cannot be expected to know what is right and what is wrong, or what is good and what is bad. It has not learned that a red light means stop or that gravity will cause objects to fall. It cannot know how people react in certain situations. If common sense is an important requirement in solving the kind of problem you have identified, you should immediately rule out an expert system solution.

Focus on a Specific Area

The problem you have discovered should be specific and limited to a particular field. In other words, the domain of knowledge must be clear, finite, and relatively narrow. If your problem requires drawing on more than one subject domain, it is going to be difficult if not impossible to develop an expert system. Perhaps in the future, larger, more complex expert systems capable of solving multiple problems will become available. But for now, your expert system has to be a specialist in only one limited area.

Mental Not Physical Solution

If the problem can be solved by mental processes rather than physical action, an expert system is a possibility. Expert systems cannot solve physical problems. An expert system cannot examine diagrams, listen to phone calls, detect odors, or perform manual manipulations. Expert systems, on the other hand, are superior in solving problems where the user can provide some initial facts and figures. The expert system can weigh that information, reason with it, and make a decision which leads to a satisfactory solution.

Moderate Level of Difficulty

If the problem is too simple, then it probably doesn't make sense to create an expert system to solve it. If the problem is vastly complex and difficult, it may not be possible or practical to develop an expert system. Expert systems seem to do best when the problem they solve is of moderate difficulty.

The level of difficulty is usually determined by the time it takes an expert system to solve the problem. If the problem can be solved in less than several minutes, it is probably too simple. If the problem takes more than several hours to solve, it is probably too difficult. Anything in between these two extremes fits best with an expert system solution.

Appropriateness of the Knowledge

Knowledge for an expert system must be represented in symbolic form and then manipulated by a computer. Appropriate knowledge can be expressed in IF-THEN rules. You should be able to analyze a small segment of the required knowledge and determine whether it can be put into the form of rules. Heuristic knowledge is particularly suitable for expression as rules. Verify that this is the type of knowledge you have before going on.

Minimum Number of Solutions

The output of your expert system is going to be a recommended outcome or solution. Based on the input information you give it, the system will search its knowledge base and reach a conclusion. In most successful expert systems, the number of possible output solutions or recommendations is limited.

There usually are only a few practical solutions for most problems. If there are only one or two solutions, an expert system may not be necessary. If, on the other hand, there are hundreds of possible outcomes, an expert system will not be practical. Expert systems typically have fewer than one hundred different outcomes but more than a half dozen.

Experts Are Available

One of the most critical requirements for judging whether your problem is suitable for expert system solution is the availability of experts. The knowledge must exist in one or more individuals, and those individuals are going to have to be involved in the development of the system. These experts should be able not only to solve the problem but also to express in simple terms the knowledge and procedures they use to solve it. They also should be willing to participate in the development process.

> *An expert is one who knows more and more about less and less.*
>
> NICHOLAS MURRAY BUTLER

Consider the Alternatives

If you completed an analysis of the suitability of your problem to an expert system solution, you probably have made your final decision either to go ahead or to seek another approach. If you have discovered your problem is not suitable for an expert system, you will want to take a look at the alternatives available to you. Even if your problem may be suitable for an expert system, you may want to examine some of the other options available to you. The alternative solutions generally fall into two categories, training and non-expert system computer solutions.

Training

Training and/or education are frequently good choices for solving performance problems. The solution may be as simple as sending an employee to an appropriate course, seminar, or workshop. You may have the employee work with an expert to gain the knowledge and experience required to do the job. On-the-job training is very common and particularly effective. In other words, you begin to create new experts.

If a source of training does not exist, consider developing it. This is certainly a viable alternative to developing an expert system. Often the expert gets involved in creating the training. Development of training courses or materials is usually far less expensive than creating a complex piece of computer software like an expert system.

Keep in mind that knowledge acquired through training stays with the individual. It may solve the problem, but if the individual leaves, the knowledge is lost. For this reason, investing in an expert system may be the best long term permanent solution. An employee may leave, but an expert system stays and another employee can use it.

Documentation

Formal training is not always necessary. If the knowledge can be packaged, it may not be necessary to conduct a formal course. The problem might be solved with pure information, facts and figures that can be accessed readily when they are needed. For that reason, an alternative solution can be a manual or job aid that the employee refers to when doing the job.

A manual, of course, is a printed book which contains information to use as reference. A job aid can be a collection of tables, charts, graphs, summaries, checklists, step-by-step procedures, and other aids and is usually presented in printed form. When a task must be done, the job aid is referred to and the problem is solved. Documentation is particularly useful when in-depth knowledge is not really required. Often the employee can execute a particular procedure without understanding how or why it may work.

Be sure to consider documentation as an alternative in solving the problem. It is far less expensive and easier and faster to develop than an expert system.

Traditional Software

You may be able to use readily available computer programs or to create a special new program particularly for the problem.

Consider the use of a standard algorithmic program. During your analysis, you will get a feel for whether the problem is algorithmic or symbolic. For example, if the problem involves a lot of math and computation, an algorithmic solution is probably best. Although written for a specific application, its development may not be as complex or expensive as creating an expert system.

You also may be able to use existing software packages. Some particularly useful packages are the so-called productivity tools, such as spreadsheets and data base management systems (DBMS). Recall that a spreadsheet is simply an electronic matrix of figures that can be manipulated in a variety of ways. It may be possible to create a spreadsheet that adequately solves your problem. A DBMS is a special case that bears further consideration.

Data Base Management Systems

One of the questions that always comes up when expert systems are first discovered is: What is the difference between a DBMS and an expert system? They both are used to store, retrieve, and manipulate information. Both use search techniques. The answer lies in the difference between data and knowledge. Data is simply facts, numbers, names, or other designators. Knowledge is information that embodies relationships of facts to other facts. Knowledge is understanding.

Consider the basic elements of a DBMS and an expert system. In the DBMS, the basic element is a record made up of fields of data. A typical record from a customer file might contain facts such as name, address, telephone number, last date of purchase, amount of purchase, and amount still owed. That's good, valuable information, but it is not knowledge.

In an expert system, the basic element is usually a rule. The rule might say: IF the car will not start, AND the ignition system is good, THEN the problem is in the fuel system. That is knowledge.

Rules also link to one another as a line of reasoning develops. Records in a file, on the other hand, stand alone and usually do not interrelate.

The expert system is capable of reasoning, making decisions, and giving an opinion or solution. The DBMS cannot reason, but it will manipulate and present information in ways that are easy for an individual to consume and understand. It is up to the individual to think, reason, and make a decision to solve the problem.

Data Base Primer

One of the most useful types of software packages is the DBMS or file manager. This software allows a user to create and manage large files of data that are stored (usually on a disk) and conveniently retrieved when needed. The data can also be sorted, searched, and edited to provide desired outputs.

The basic data storage unit, the record, is composed of specific data elements called fields. A record might be a name and address. Typical fields would include name, street address, city, state, zip code, and telephone number. Another type of record might be an inventory item consisting of fields such as item name, part number, and quantity on hand.

Similar records are grouped together into files, and related files can be grouped together into larger files. Several levels of files may be grouped together to form a data base. Figure 5–2 shows how all of the elements are related.

An often used analogy is that a piece of paper is a record on which are printed the various fields. Similar records are put into a manila folder to form a file. These file folders are, in turn, put into a file drawer in a file cabinet. Several file cabinets may make up the complete data base.

An important term you will hear when data bases are discussed is "key." The key designates one of the fields in the records as a reference in sorting or searching. For example, to sort a file by zip code, the search key would be a specific zip code. All zip codes would be compared to the key, and identical zip codes would be sorted into a new output file.

There are two major types of data base systems: file managers and data base management systems (DBMS). A file manager is the simplest type, and it will

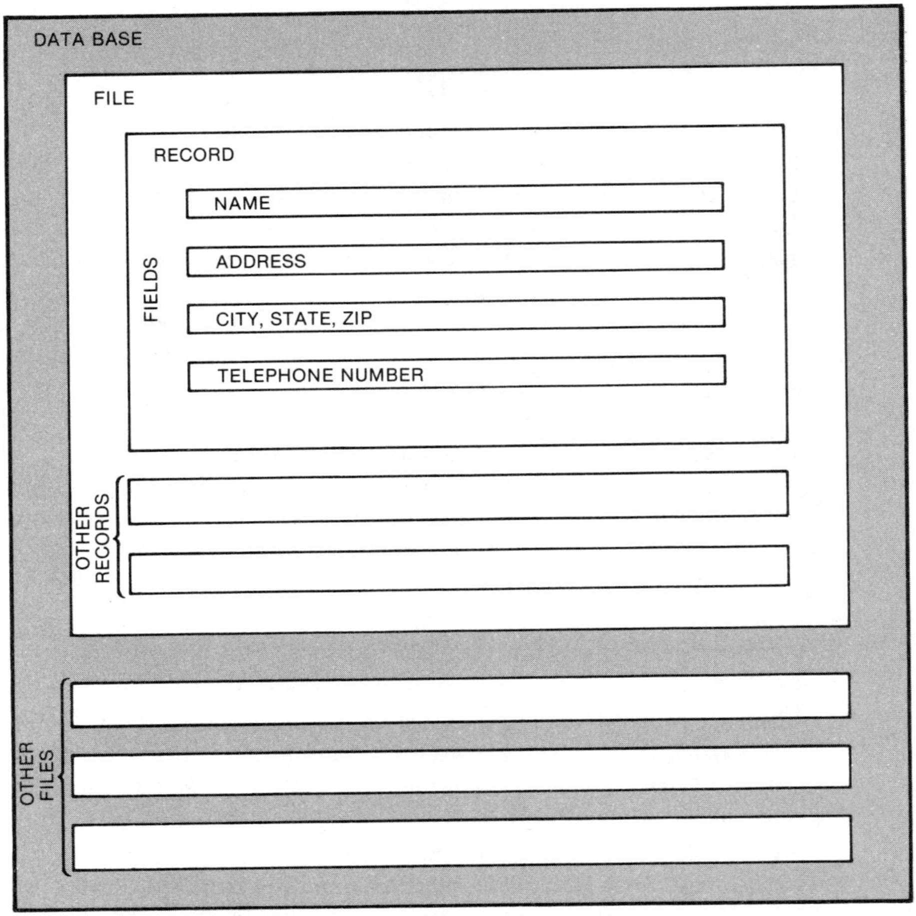

Figure 5–2. ***Elements of a data base.***

let you perform all of the functions described so far. A DBMS is a more sophisticated, and more capable file manager.

There are three types of DBMS: hierarchical, network, and relational. The first two are not widely used. The relational is the most powerful and most flexible, and therefore, the most popular. Figure 5–3 shows a typical relational DBMS.

A relational DBMS lets you "relate" records in two or more different files. You can match up similar fields in records, tying one record to another to give you an additional connection or link between pieces of information.

The standard format of a relational data base is a two dimensional table with rows and columns. The rows represent records, and the columns, the different fields. Figure 5–3A shows a simple relational file of customer names, products purchased, and date of purchase.

An inventory file of the products is shown in Figure 5–3B. The relational data base can be used to search both files by the key "product" and create a new third file to represent sales (Figure 5–3C). In other words, we have used the available

FIELDS

RECORDS

NAME	PRODUCT	QUANTITY PURCHASED
T. J. BROWN	WIDGETS	10
W. M. JONES	WHATCHAMACALLIT	225
K. F. WHITE	DO-HICKEY	46
O. P. SMITH	THINGAMABOB	75
L. B. DOE	WIDGET	14

(A) Customer File

PRODUCT	NUMBER	QUANTITY ON HAND
WIDGETS	RM-1-16	1575
WHATCHAMACALLIT	RM-7-89	22,764
DO-HICKEY	RT-4-102	886
THINGAMABOB	RM-0-27	7900

(B) Inventory File

PRODUCT	QUANTITY SOLD	QUANTITY ON HAND
WIDGETS	24	1575
WHATCHAMACALLIT	225	22,764
DO-HICKEY	46	886
THINGAMABOB	75	7900

(C) New "Sales" File

Figure 5–3. ***Relational DBMS files.***

data to create a new file or output format that lets us look at the data in different ways or to get new information from it.

Relational DBMS are powerful, but difficult to use. Usually they must be programmed in a special query language to achieve the results indicated here.

Decision Software

Another productivity tool is decision-making software. These are programs that will examine facts and figures, analyze them, and produce a decision or conclusion. However, they are not expert systems because they do not use symbolic representation and manipulation. They do not search or "reason." Instead, they implement decision-making algorithms. The result may be similar to that achieved with an expert system but in a much different way. If producing a correct decision is a major part of your problem, these programs may be a better alternative to the expert system you are considering.

Decision software helps you to solve complex problems involving several alternatives. Ordinarily, you can put weights on the various criteria to designate their priority or importance. The software then uses these weights in an algorithm to compute the outcome for each alternative. The output ranks the various alternatives by desirability. You can then "play" with the criteria weights to see how they affect the outcome. Given the output, you can make your final decision.

Decision software is most useful for really tough problems involving many choices and interrelated factors. The decision isn't obvious by just reviewing the data, but putting factor weights into the software gives you the best decision.

A decision program may be what you want. It may actually do essentially the same thing as an expert system and give you a comparable answer. But it isn't an expert system, and it certainly doesn't work the same way.

Like training and documentation, DBMS and decision software are less expensive than an expert system. These programs are already available and modestly priced. Although some work is required to use them, it is still far less than that required to create an expert system. All of these alternatives should be analyzed carefully before making the final decision to develop an expert system.

Computing the ROI

By now you have probably decided that an expert system fits your situation. The problem has met all the tests and conditions outlined earlier. Now you are ready to compute the cost of developing an expert system and estimate the savings or other monetary benefits it will produce. None of this is easy. If you've never developed an expert system before, you will be making some uneducated guesses about the time and costs. However, if you have developed software packages, your experience will be helpful.

Estimating the Benefits

To estimate the benefits to be produced by the expert system, compute a dollar value that may result from using it. For example, what time and monetary resources will be saved? Will sales be increased or will customers be retained as a result of improved employee performance?

Some factors to consider are:

1. What is the cost of lost or wasted time due to the problem?
2. What is the value of lost sales?
3. What is the value of lost materials or resources?
4. What is the impact and value of lost image, reputation, quality, trust, or reliability?
5. What are the losses due to poor morale and demotivation due to poor performance?

6. What savings might be gained by eliminating training and lost job time during training?

Estimate a total dollar value.

You may decide that it is not possible to put a monetary value on the benefits you expect to derive. That is often the case. An example might be an expert system on board a military satellite, a fighter aircraft, or tank. If such expert systems help you win battles while saving time and lives, it is probably worth the development cost. It's hard to put a value on things like this.

Development Cost Factors

Here are some factors which must be priced out in computing the total cost of development.

1. Cost of expert system development software tools
2. Time of one or more experts
3. Time of a knowledge engineer
4. Time of a programmer (may not be needed depending on qualifications of knowledge engineer)
5. Time for employees to test the software
6. Time for debugging and maintenance
7. Cost of outside consultants

A small system with several hundred rules might take three to six months to develop and require two or three people. Outside consulting assistance may also be needed. If an expert is available and a software development tool is used, the cost will probably be in the \$25,000 to \$50,000 range. The cost could easily exceed \$100,000 if the subject is complex or if this is your first system.

If personal computers are available and the domain is relatively simple, you may be able to create a suitable expert system for \$2,000 to \$5,000. To do this, find a computer literate employee who knows the job and the problem. She will be your "expert."

Next, purchase one of the low cost expert system development tools. Prices run from \$100 to \$700. All of these are rule-based development tools that require no programming knowledge. Given a little time, your "expert" will be able to write the rules and put the system into operation. Assume a week or two to learn the system and another two to four weeks to develop it. Estimate the cost of such an effort to use in your ROI calculation.

Calculate the ROI

Finally, compute the ROI. Divide the total loss value during one year by the cost to develop. If the figure is greater than one, developing a system is probably justified. You may want to amortize the cost of development over a longer period.

If the system is fairly large and solves a major long range problem, you can spread the large development expense out over the early years of usage. Just divide the total cost to develop by the number of years of amortization. Then, use that number in your ROI calculation. It will certainly be easier to justify this way.

Select a Development Tool

At this point you have no doubt made the decision to go ahead with the development of an expert system. Before you go ahead, you should decide upon a development tool, software that will help you to create the system. In its simplest form, it could be nothing more than a programming language used with the target computer. It also could be a sophisticated expert system generator or shell that greatly simplifies and speeds up the creation of an expert system because it eliminates the programming problem. In this section we will take a look at the various kinds of expert system development tools available and describe some commercial packages.

Types of Development Tools

The two basic types of expert system development tools are languages and shells. Both are options you should consider.

Languages

Languages, of course, refer to the programming languages used with computers to create new software. Expert systems have been created using almost all types of common programming languages; however, some are easier to use for this purpose than others. Expert systems have been created using BASIC, Fortran, C, Pascal, Forth, and Assembly language. Naturally, the higher level languages such as Fortran and Pascal are much easier to use, but they generate a considerable amount of code. Since the resulting programs are usually large, languages such as C and Forth are more efficient. For greatest efficiency, nothing beats assembly language for compactness of programs and high speed.

There is no reason why you should not use one of these programming languages to create your expert system. If you are an expert programmer or your organization is lucky enough to have one or more competent programmers who can use one of these languages, give serious thought to this option. Keep in mind that an expert system is highly sophisticated. Even though you may be an expert programmer or have a superior programming staff at your disposal, considerable design and debugging time will be required to achieve the result you want.

The two best language choices, of course, are LISP and Prolog. Both of these languages were designed for artificial intelligence applications and both can be used readily to construct an expert system. If you should be so lucky as to know one of these languages or have access to a programming staff that does, then this is a viable option. Otherwise, it is usually preferable to abandon the idea of using languages. Instead, consider using one of the many available expert system shells.

Shells

An expert system *shell* or generator is a special software package created specifically to help build an expert system. Similar in some respects to software packages like DBMS or spreadsheets, a shell provides a basic framework in which data or knowledge can be entered and manipulated in predefined ways.

An expert system shell does not contain a knowledge base. The only difference between one expert system and another is the content of the knowledge base. The inference engine, data base, and user interface will work with any knowledge base. You simply code the knowledge in the designated format and enter it into the knowledge base.

An expert system generator is like a shell, but it provides a somewhat more sophisticated development environment. It has built-in utilities that further simplify and speed up the development process. One of these utilities, an editor, allows you to enter knowledge in a predetermined rule format and edit it as required. Some expert system generators are actually a type of compiler. After the rules are entered with an editor, the generator compiles them into the final code the inference engine and user interface will use.

Most expert system shells and generators use the popular IF-THEN rule knowledge representation scheme. It is simple, flexible, and very popular. When you complete the knowledge engineering and design the program, the result will be a set of IF-THEN rules you will enter into the expert system generator.

There are two basic kinds of expert system generators. The first is the most straightforward. It allows you to enter rules exactly as you write them with some type of editor or word processor. The system will compile the rules into the form suitable for its inference engine. Expert system generators, however, use special rule formats. They are still IF-THEN rules, but they may require special formatting or entry procedures.

The second type of expert system generator does not require you to use the IF-THEN format. Instead, knowledge is given to the program in the form of examples set up in a matrix similar to a spreadsheet. Each column of the matrix represents an attribute or condition. Various combinations of attributes result in specific outcomes or decisions. These outcomes or decisions are listed in a separate column. The rows in the matrix correspond to all of the combinations of attributes or conditions that lead to the specific outcomes.

With this kind of expert system generator, you first decide what all of the possible outcomes or decisions will be. These decisions are made for most expert system development regardless of the development tool you use. Then, for each of these known outcomes, you generate a set of examples made up of the attributes that will cause that outcome to occur. The result is a complete matrix defining the knowledge in your expert system.

You do not have to write specific IF-THEN rules. Instead, once you have provided the information in matrix form, the system will infer the rules itself. Once the rules have been inferred and stored away in the system, you can use them to solve problems, answer questions, or make decisions within the domain. This expert system generator is easier to use than the IF-THEN type. But in any case, both types are far faster and easier to use in creating an expert system than any language, including LISP and Prolog.

Available Tools

To give you a better feel for some of the expert system development tools available, we will describe some commercial software packages for personal computers, minicomputers, and mainframes. Some of the features, characteristics, and specifications to look for in selecting a tool are explained. Finally, we provide two examples of real-world expert system development tools for the IBM Personal Computer and its compatibles.

Appendix A lists expert system generators and shells available for personal computers. Most of these packages were developed for the IBM PC and its compatibles, but some of them run on other machines, such as the Apple II and Macintosh. Most of them also use the standard IF-THEN rule format. Several of the packages, however, use the examples matrix format. The publisher of each package is given. See the list of publishers with their addresses and phone numbers in the Appendix if you wish to send for additional information on these tools. We will describe two of the tools, Insight and Expert Ease, later in this section.

Appendix B lists some of the tools available for larger computers. Most of these tools run on Digital Equipment Corporation (DEC) popular VAX minicomputers. Some of them also run on larger IBM mainframes. Many run on the special AI workstations (LISP machines made by LMI, Symbolics, Tektronix, TI and Xerox). Again, you can find the address and phone number of each publisher in the Appendix. Like the PC tools, most of them use the rules format. However, some of them also permit the use of the frame method of knowledge representation.

Tool Specifications and Features

What are some of the important characteristics, features, and specifications you should look for in evaluating tools? The most important ones are listed in Table 5–3, but let's take a more in-depth look at them here.

Operating Environment

This is a description of the computers on which the tool was designed to run. The tool will also be designed to run under one of the operating systems used for those computers.

Table 5–3. ***Important Features and Specifications of Expert Systems Development Tools***

- Operating Environment — What computer, operating system?
- Implementation Language — Language tool written in
- Knowledge Base Format — Rules or examples?
- Inference Method — Forward or backward? Decision tree algorithm?
- User Interface — Q&A, menus, windows, color, etc.
- Special Features — Links to other software, math, NLP front-end, etc.

You want to be sure that you have the correct operating system before buying the tool. Another important consideration is memory size. Most of the systems require a certain minimum amount of memory to run properly. A typical operating environment description might look something like this:

> IBM PC/XT, 2 disk drive system using the PS DOS operating system and minimum of 256K RAM.

Implementation Language

This is the language in which the tool was originally written. Although it is not necessary to know the language to use the system, it does give you some insight into how the software was created and how it might perform. Most of the better packages are implemented in structured, higher level languages such as Pascal and C. A few use BASIC or Fortran. Some of them are also implemented in LISP or require the LISP language to be resident in order to run.

Knowledge Base Format

This designates the type of expert system shell or generator. Recall that the two basic types are rules and examples. Most of the tools will use one format or the other, but the rule systems predominate.

Inference Method

When a rule system is used, inference is done by some form of chaining. When the examples method is used, a decision tree algorithm is implemented. Since most of the systems you will be dealing with use rules, your main concern will be which type of chaining to use. Recall that two basic chaining methods are used in expert systems, forward and backward. Forward chaining uses the IF parts of the rules to make a decision. Backward chaining uses the THEN parts of the rules.

Expert system generators incorporate one type of reasoning or another, but backward chaining seems to be the most popular. It is the most flexible and also the easiest to implement, but you may have a problem that better fits forward chaining. During your design phase, you should be able to determine which method best fits your problem.

If in doubt, a good default is backward chaining, which is useful for most types of problems. Some shells have both forward and backward chaining capability.

Another factor to consider in the inference engine is how to deal with uncertainty. The two most common methods are confidence or certainty factors and probability. Both systems work well in dealing with fuzzy or incomplete information. Neither method is better than the other; they both accomplish the same thing in different ways.

User Interface

The user interface communicates with the user. You will want to examine how the expert system tool gathers information from the user and presents the results. Two basic methods are used. The first is a question and answer format. The user interface presents a question which the user answers by typing in the information on the keyboard. Another system uses menus. A question is asked and multiple choices are given. The user selects the answer that best fits the question.

You may also want to look at some of the special features provided in the user interface. For example, some user interfaces incorporate *windows,* small screens of information within the main video screen on the computer. These blocks of information form different parts of the program, allowing you to see and do more than one thing at a time.

Another feature that may be useful is color. Some systems provide full color display of information. Color may help make the system faster and easier to use when solving complex problems.

Special Features

Special features are attached to the various expert system generators. It is these special features which make a package more desirable for a given application. Here are some special features to look for. First, look for special built-in languages. Some expert system generators contain a special programming language of their own which allows you to implement special procedures for your unique application.

Another special feature is the ability to link to other software. Many expert system development tools permit reference to external languages like LISP or C. They may also allow access to a DBMS or spreadsheet software. Another useful software link is a graphics package. Although expert systems usually work with screens of text, there are many situations where the presentation of related graphics would be helpful. Some tools allow linking to standard graphics packages.

Another common feature is mathematical capability. Most expert system tools cannot do mathematical computations. However, in some applications it is necessary or desirable. A package that permits mathematical operations may be just what you need to simplify or implement your own system.

Another special feature might be the availability of an accompanying natural language interface. A natural language interface, usually part of the user interface, will permit you to communicate with the system in English in a random, natural way rather than in some structured format. In some cases this feature may be built-in, in others, the natural language interface may be available as an option.

Look for many other special features and weigh them carefully before choosing a tool.

Other Considerations

There are additional considerations to keep in mind when selecting a tool. First, try to think ahead to see if the tool can be used for more than one system. If your expert system is a one-time project, you can choose a tool that is suited to that application. If you plan to develop a whole range of expert systems, you may want to try to define them ahead of time, and choose a tool that will give you the greatest flexibility.

Second, does the tool have a *run time version*? A run time version allows a user to use the expert system but not create one. It consists of the knowledge base created with the tool plus the user interface and inference engine. The run time software does not include any of the utilities or other features used for developing expert systems. If you plan to distribute multiple copies of your expert system, you will definitely need a run time package. It is not economical to distribute the entire expert system tool with each expert system. It is unnecessary and far too expensive to give the user the power to change the system or develop his own. Some vendors sell the run time package separately and require licensing for all additional expert systems that use the run time package. Some publishers charge a fee for distributing the run time software with the knowledge base you have created. Be sure to identify your distribution requirements up front. You can then determine costs for any distribution licenses and run time packages before making your final decision.

Price is another major consideration. Prices range from less than $100 to many thousands of dollars for expert system tools. The average tool sells in the $300 to $800 range.

You should also consider vendor stability. How long has the vendor been in business and what are the prospects for the future? This will give you some feel as to how the tool will be maintained. Tools are not perfect. Bugs will be found and corrected, new features will be added, and the package may otherwise be further refined, expanded, or improved. You will want to be sure that your vendor will provide ongoing updates and revisions as they become available.

Also, don't overlook customer services. Most vendors provide telephone consultation for developers. Like most software packages, expert system development tools require some learning to master. While learning the process and developing your first expert system, you will often have problems or questions. Choose a vendor with a "hot line" for getting help. Some vendors even offer newsletters.

Last but not least is the documentation. A complex software package like an expert system development tool will take some time and effort to learn. It won't be nearly as difficult and time consuming as learning a programming language such as LISP or Prolog, but you will have to invest some time in mastering the system. Good documentation will help you do this. If you have the opportunity, examine the user manuals for the system to see how good they are. Look particularly for manuals that include tutorials. These may be printed or on-disk tutorials that lead you by the hand through learning the system and creating your first expert system.

Table 5–4. *Developing a Knowledge Base with INSIGHT*

1. Load standard word processor software or text editor
2. Enter title of knowledge base
3. Enter certainty factor threshold
4. Enter all goals, hypotheses, or final outcomes
5. Enter rules using the Production Rule Language (PRL)
6. Store PRL file on a diskette
7. Load INSIGHT
8. Call up the PRL Compiler (PRGEN)
9. Enter file name
10. Compile knowledge base.
11. Store compiled knowledge base
12. Load INSIGHT and compiled knowledge base file. Run system

Typical Tools

Now let's examine in more detail some typical expert system development tools for personal computers. The two tools described here are widely used and representative of both rule and example types of expert system generators.

INSIGHT

INSIGHT is a rule-based expert system development tool for the IBM PC computer and its compatibles. It was developed by Level Five Research, Inc., of Melbourne Beach, Florida. It runs under the PC DOS/MS DOS operating system, Version 2.0 or later.

INSIGHT is available in two versions, a minimum low cost system and a larger, more powerful expanded version known as INSIGHT2.

Both the minimum and expanded versions of INSIGHT are written in the Pascal language. Both use IF-THEN rules with confidence factors. The basic inference method is backward chaining. However, the larger version also permits forward chaining and deals with uncertainty by using Bayesian probability. The user interface uses menus and multiple choice selections. Function keys eliminate the need for the user to memorize special commands. With both versions you can write expert systems with over 2,000 rules although more than the minimum of RAM given will be required for large systems such as this.

As for special features, INSIGHT2 contains a built-in Pascal-like language referred to as DBPAS. The system contains a DBPAS interpreter, a compiler, and a debugger. With this special language, the user can create and link to special subroutines to supplement the standard system. INSIGHT2 also permits linking to external software packages such as the popular dBase II/III DBMS.

A run time version of both programs is available. There is no charge for a license on programs distributed under INSIGHT, but there is under INSIGHT2.

Developing an expert system with INSIGHT is a relatively straightforward process. The twelve steps are outlined in Table 5–4. Let's take a look at each step in more detail.

Step 1 assumes that you have completed your knowledge engineering and program design. It assumes that you have created a set of rules defining your domain. INSIGHT is then used to record and edit these rules.

Load a standard word processor software package such as WordStar in the non-document mode or the built-in text editor. Then use the word processing software or text editor to create a rule file for INSIGHT in a prespecified format.

In Step 2, enter the title of the knowledge base.

In Step 3, enter a *threshold value.* The threshold value is a decision reference point for the inference engine when evaluating confidence factors. It specifies the lowest acceptable percentage of confidence necessary for INSIGHT to reach a conclusion on a particular rule. The threshold is a number between zero and one hundred. A zero value indicates the rule is 100% false, while 100 represents complete confidence that it is true. A threshold value of 50 means the rule could be either true or false, and that you are not sure. For your expert system you will select a threshold to compare the rules against. For example, you might set a threshold value of 60. If INSIGHT examines a rule and finds the confidence factor in the rule is greater than or equal to a specified threshold value, INSIGHT will fire the rule.

In Step 4, enter all of the goals or final outcomes of the expert system. To create any expert system, particularly those that use backward chaining, you must list all possible outputs or answers the system is capable of giving. For example, if you are developing an expert system to recommend buying a specific car based on your own driving needs and budget, you would list all of the cars the system could possibly recommend based on the input data you give it.

In Step 5, you begin entering the rules you have developed. You will do this using a special format, defined by a special production rule language (PRL) built into INSIGHT. The language is extremely easy to use. It is simply a specially formatted version of the standard IF-THEN rule format you have seen before. Some examples of rules used in INSIGHT are given below.

```
RULE  Eczema symptoms
IF    The patient's skin itches
AND   The skin is very dry
AND   There is a red rash present
THEN  The patient has eczema CONFIDENCE 80

RULE  For a diamond
IF    The hardness of the stone = 10
THEN  The stone is a diamond CONFIDENCE 100
ELSE  The stone is a diamond CONFIDENCE 0
AND   The stone will not scratch a diamond
```

Note: in each line a capitalized key word designates the entry. The first line, RULE, gives the name of the rule and tells what the rule will decide. There are also the standard IF and THEN portions of the rule. AND is used where multiple conditions can be given. Finally, a confidence factor is given on the THEN line. Use a number between zero and 100 to express the confidence you have in the outcome.

Also, note that production rule language permits the use of an ELSE line. This allows you to implement an IF-THEN-ELSE scenario. If the premise part of the rule is not correct, then the conclusion will not be true. And if it is not true then perhaps the ELSE portion is true. With this format, you can minimize the number of rules in the expert system. When an ELSE statement is not available, separate rules have to be used to conclude each piece of the information being represented.

In step 6, you store your production rule language file on a diskette. In step 7, you load the INSIGHT software. In step 8, you call up the PRL compiler called PRGEN for production rule generator. In step 9, PRGEN asks for the file name, and you enter the name of your rule base. In step 10, PRGEN compiles the knowledge base into the final code that will be used by the inference engine. In step 11, you store the compiled knowledge base.

Finally, in step 12, you load INSIGHT which is the name of the run time portion of the system. You will give it the name of the knowledge base file and the system is then ready for the user.

EXPERT EASE

EXPERT EASE is one of the oldest expert system development tools available for personal computers. In fact, it was the first tool available for IBM PCs and compatibles. It is based on an original design known as the Analog Concept Learning System (ACLS) developed by Donald Michie at the University of Edinburgh. EXPERT EASE is available from two sources, Expert Systems, Inc., New York City, and Human Edge Software Corp., Palo Alto, California.

EXPERT EASE is one of the easiest-to-use systems on the market. Instead of entering the data in the form of rules, examples are entered into a spreadsheet-like matrix. From these examples, the system infers rules that it then uses in answering questions and solving problems in the domain.

EXPERT EASE is designed to run on the IBM PC and its various versions. It does not require a separate operating system because the necessary run time system components are built into the program. The system uses the UCSD P-system, a somewhat less than popular operating system for the PC. EXPERT EASE was written in the Pascal language, which is a key component of the UCSD P-system.

As mentioned earlier, the knowledge base is a set of examples, each made up of various attributes and their values that define specific outcomes. From these examples, rules are inferred and then used by the inference engine to make decisions. The inference engine implements a decision tree algorithm. In combination with the user interface, the system asks the user questions, receives answers, and uses this information to search the decision tree for the best solution. The user interface provides menus to ask multiple choice questions.

The process of developing an expert system with EXPERT EASE is outlined in Table 5–5. In Steps 1 and 2, you load EXPERT EASE and clear the system. In Step 3, you set up the attributes. These are the categories of conditions or premises for which you will establish values for each example. Each attribute is given a column in A matrix. One column is also used for the final output conclusions or results.

In Step 4 you enter the various examples. Each row in the matrix is an example, and you list the values of various attributes and the final output result.

In Step 5 you ask EXPERT EASE to create rules based on your input matrix. The rule is induced and then displayed. In Step 6 you review the rule to ensure that it makes sense and that all possible conditions are covered. In Step 7 you may add new examples as required to complete the expert system or correct problems.

Table 5–5. ***Developing a Knowledge Base with EXPERT EASE***

1. Load EXPERT EASE
2. Clear system
3. Set up attributes
4. Enter attributes and results
5. Induce a decision tree (create rule)
6. Review rule. Revise as needed
7. Add new examples as required
8. Add text to explain and comment on attributes and decisions
9. Store all data on diskette
10. Load, run and test the system

In Step 8 you add text to explain and comment on the attributes and final decisions. In Step 9 you store all of this information on a diskette. Finally, in Step 10 you load the expert system and run it.

To make this procedure a little clearer, a simple example. The goal is to create a simple expert system that will suggest ways for us to spend a Sunday. We will provide examples of two input attributes, weather and family. The final output will be advice about which activity to pursue. Figure 5–4 shows the matrix we would create and enter using EXPERT EASE. You can see the recommendations made based on the input attributes. Also note the rule that is inferred from the matrix. The colons in the rule

Example program: SUNDAY

Matrix format:

ATTRIBUTES		EXPERT ADVICE
WEATHER	FAMILY	CONCLUSION
raining	yes	museum
raining	no	museum
sunny	yes	beach
sunny	no	fishing

Induced rules:

IF the weather is raining
THEN go to the museum

IF the weather is sunny
AND the family is with you
THEN go to the beach

IF the weather is sunny
AND the family is not with you
THEN go fishing

Internal format: WEATHER

raining: museum
sunny: family
yes: beach
no: fishing

Figure 5–4. ***Knowledge format of EXPERT EASE.***

define the node points in the decision tree. You can see how the system can reach a conclusion when you give it input for various values of weather and family.

Knowledge Engineering

Now the real work of building an expert system begins. The starting point is to acquire the domain knowledge from one or more experts. You may tap other sources such as books and manuals, but in most cases, the knowledge will come from an individual who is highly experienced in the field of interest. Gathering and organizing the knowledge into a form appropriate for an expert system is the job of the knowledge engineer.

Knowledge Engineers

A knowledge engineer is a unique individual. That person is not an expert in the domain of the expert system, but is capable of understanding the domain and learning the problem-solving process within it.

A knowledge engineer knows and understands expert systems and can take knowledge in its various forms and convert it into rules or other suitable representation forms. The knowledge engineer knows how to use the various expert system development tools and may, in fact, be a competent programmer in one of the AI languages.

The knowledge engineer also has excellent interviewing and problem-solving skills. The knowledge engineer uses these to extract the knowledge from the experts, then compiles it into its final form.

Knowledge engineers are scarce, but they are absolutely essential to the creation of an expert system. This is particularly true of medium-to-large systems that cover a lot of ground. It is sometimes possible to create small systems for personal computers without a knowledge engineer, but for larger systems, a knowledge engineer is a must to ensure success.

Now let's take a look at the way a knowledge engineer goes about gathering the knowledge for an expert system.

Documentation Sources

For some small systems you may be able to find all the knowledge needed in existing documentation. It could come from textbooks, but most likely it will come from special publications related to the domain. These may be user guides, training manuals, interoffice communications, or articles. Your first job should be to collect as much of this related information as possible. It will provide not only background matter on the domain, but may provide a portion of the material for the knowledge base as well.

For example, assume you are going to build a small expert system to help an employee screen credit applications. Certain criteria have been set up for determining whether or not to grant credit to an applicant. Those seeking credit will fill out a form and submit it for consideration. The idea is to take basic information from this form and weigh it against the criteria to make a final judgment. Should credit be granted, what level of credit, or should credit be denied? The system would weigh an individual's annual income, home ownership status, number of years on the job, number of years residence, other financial obligations, and a variety of additional factors. This information is given to the expert system and the output will be a decision based on company policy.

Such knowledge can come from an individual, of course, but in this case it is most likely available in a memo or policies and procedures manual. At some time, the exact criteria and process of weighing new applications was determined. It is obviously documented somewhere. The job of the knowledge engineer is to ferret it out and use it as the knowledge base for this small expert system.

Ask those experts doing the job what their sources of information or reference are. Most of the time these individuals work strictly from their own knowledge and experience, but sometimes they have printed reference materials to consult for difficult or unusual problems.

Once you have accumulated as much of the information as you can find, use it to learn the kind of problems the experts must solve and the knowledge they must have to solve these problems. You may be lucky enough to find all you need in the documentation, but if not, you will be prepared to take the next step. That next step is to find an expert.

Definitions of an Expert

> *One who knows enough to tell others how to . . . but is too smart to try it himself.*
>
> HENRY C. BYCE

> *An expert person is any person with an ordinary knowledge of a subject who carries an attache case and is more than 50 miles away from home.*
>
> SOURCE UNKNOWN

> *An expert is a person who does not have to think, he knows.*
>
> FRANK LLOYD WRIGHT

Acquiring the Knowledge from an Expert

The best knowledge for an expert system comes from one or more experts in the domain. Your first job is to find one expert who is qualified to act as your source. In some cases the expertise may be extremely rare and lie within only one person. In other cases, you may have to search for the expert. The best way to do this is to ask around and find out who is doing the job now. Very quickly you will find that others will be able to tell you who the experts are in certain areas. In most cases you will find that the expert is one of the busiest and one of the most highly regarded individuals in the organization. This is usually the individual the organization can least afford to lose. Further, this individual is in great demand, and your main problem may simply be in scheduling the expert to work with you.

To qualify the expert you have identified, you should have an initial interview and determine not only if the individual has the knowledge you need, but also perhaps more important, to determine if the individual is willing to work with you. While most experts will not necessarily be hostile to the idea of your extracting their precious knowledge, they may be somewhat reluctant. Experts gain their knowledge over a long period of time with considerable education and experience. Most experts realize they have valuable knowledge and want to protect it. They want to use it for their own personal benefit as well as for the benefit of their employer. They may attempt to protect that knowledge for security purposes. No one likes to think they may be cloned or replaced by a computer program.

If you encounter resistance, your job is to sell the idea to the expert. You must make the expert want to share the knowledge for the good of the cause. Play upon the expert's conscience and solicit help as part of the "team." Experts may not be required to participate in the development of the expert system because it is not part of their regular job. On the other hand, a directive may come from above that encourages the expert to work on the project. You should be able to find an expert who is willing to participate in the project.

If all else fails, look for another expert. A hostile and uncooperative expert will do a poor job, and the resulting product may be inadequate. Try to find someone else willing to work on the project. Consider replacing that individual with two or more others whose combined knowledge may be equal to that of the expert. Working with multiple experts is much more difficult and time consuming, but it is one way to get the job done. On some very large projects, you may have no choice but to use multiple experts to acquire all of the knowledge you need.

The secret to working with multiple experts is to keep them separated. During the knowledge extraction process, work with them on a one-to-one basis. Don't bring your entire panel of experts together all at once and try to interview them. They may all be experts, but in most cases they will have different knowledge and experiences even though they may solve the same kinds of problems. Their problem-solving approaches may vary considerably, and this could result in considerable conflict and confusion. You will determine these differences during individual interviews, and it will be up to you to decide which information or approaches are the best.

When you are using multiple experts, appoint one of these as the chief expert or knowledge "czar" to whom you will go for all final decisions. If there are obvious conflicts or differences, this one individual can help you resolve them.

With your expert or experts in hand, you can now begin interviewing. Obviously, for a medium-to-large expert system, one interview is not going to be enough. In fact, the knowledge engineering process generally will take many weeks or months. You will be conducting a series of interviews with the expert as you define the scope of knowledge, identify the kinds of problems being solved, and determine the knowledge and approaches required to solve them.

In the initial interviews you will define all the possible outcomes or solutions. These will be the expert system outputs the user will be seeking. With this information in hand, you can work backwards to identify all of the kinds of problems that crop up that can be solved by these outputs.

Keep in mind that your job is to extract the knowledge to build the knowledge base using IF-THEN rules, frames, or other knowledge representation scheme. Since production rules are used in expert systems, attempt to extract the knowledge in such a way that it will help you create IF-THEN rules represent the knowledge.

Interviews with the expert will take on several different forms. One possible form is a question and answer session. Prior to the interview, prepare a set of questions designed to elicit responses related to the domain. During the questioning, take notes about the expert's answers. Naturally, the answers may lead to additional spontaneous questions and perhaps the elimination of some of the originally planned questions. You should be flexible enough to allow the discussion to move in the direction the expert takes it. Just remember to get back on track at some point.

Another approach is to present the expert with one or more problems during the interview, and simply have the expert talk through approaches to the solution. Given the problem, what does the expert think and do to solve the problem? Try to get at the thought process to determine what information is required to solve the problem and how that information is related to knowledge the expert has. There is usually a specific sequence of information processing and problem solving.

It is typically a good idea to record your session. The expert's time is valuable and you do not want to have to repeat an interview or follow up what was said. Get the entire interview on tape and have it transcribed so you can use it for reference.

The important thing to remember in interviewing an expert is that most experts do not truly fully understand how they go about solving problems. In fact, it has been said that the better the experts, the less they know about their actual problem-solving process. Superior experts have years of experience and in-depth knowledge about the domain, and the problem-solving process is a natural, integrated thing that is difficult to discover. The danger in interviewing experts is that you will force them to think of the problem-solving process they use. They probably don't understand it themselves, but they will attempt to give you some approach or sequence. Naturally, you should accept it, but examine it skeptically. You must discover whether the experts' knowledge and problem-solving process works for others once it is converted into a rule-based expert system.

Continue interviews until you are fully satisfied that you have all the information necessary to build a system. All of the necessary knowledge should be recorded in some form.

In some cases, it may be possible to observe an expert at work in an actual problem-solving situation. It is highly desirable to do this. In some cases you may be able to observe without interrupting or interfering. In other cases, you may work with the expert, asking questions as the process continues. With your knowledge collection complete, you are ready to begin designing the expert system.

> *. . . building your power as an expert, that is, developing mastery of information that will satisfy individual and organizational needs, is a growing path to success.*
>
> THE PRYOR REPORT

Designing the System

Once you have acquired the knowledge from the experts, you must organize it, make some sense out of it, and ultimately convert it into IF-THEN rules that you will enter using the development tool. Conversion of all that knowledge into rules is complex and demanding. There is no one approach or procedure to use. Often, the nature of the knowledge will dictate how it can be organized and formatted, but the approach can vary widely from one subject to another.

There are some common procedures that will help you to organize your knowledge base. All of them may not apply, but you can try them out and use what works best for you. In the following sections we describe some of these procedures.

Identify the Outcomes

One of your first steps is identify all of the possible solutions or answers your expert system will give. What are all the output recommendations that the system will give to a user? In almost every case you will know what these answers are or you can derive them. You should have determined these outcomes during the knowledge engineering process. If you did not do this, now is the time to make a list of them.

Once you have come up with a comprehensive list of your outcomes, you also may want to add a set of notes or comments to each one. Most expert system development tools have provisions for providing supplementary notes or explanatory text to each output answer. Some tools have a built-in explanation system that will allow the user to ask why a particular output was obtained. These supplementary comments will make it easier for the user to understand why a particular outcome was derived.

With this step out of the way, you can almost begin writing rules. In fact, in some simple expert systems, you will simply write one rule whose THEN portion is one of the desired outcomes. This may be all you have to do to complete your system.

However, in most situations, the domain is not that simple. There may be numerous other paths or alternative ways to reach a particular outcome. If those can be identified, additional rules may be written. Each rule leads to the identification of other rules.

Identify the Inputs

Identify and list all of the facts, figures, and other information that the expert system will need to answer the question or solve the problem. What information will the user have to give to the expert system to reach a conclusion? All expert systems need a starting point, and this begins when the expert system asks the user for specific data. This data will be used by the rules to start the search process. Usually you will recognize the requested bits of information. Make a list of these as this information will form the IF portions of the rules you are going to create.

Looking at the input data to be acquired from the user, you will be able to construct rules that will lead directly to the outcome rules or to any intermediate rule you may have constructed. As you can see, by simply identifying the inputs and outputs, you may have done all that is necessary to write the rules for the system.

Create an Outline

You may find that your system is too large and complex to begin writing rules directly from the inputs and outputs. If so, an outline may help you to organize the information and break it down into smaller segments. Everyone knows how to create an outline with headings and subheadings. During the knowledge engineering process, you may have created such an outline. If not, now is the time to organize the information into separate divisions and subdivisions. An outline is nothing more than a hierarchy of the knowledge you have acquired.

To take this one step farther, you may wish to create a block diagram of your outline. Instead of creating a word outline, create a picture outline with an organization chart or pyramid format. Such a chart will help you to visualize the information and show how various parts of it are related.

Develop a Flow Chart

When the knowledge involves procedures, it is sometimes useful to create a flow chart. A flow chart is a block diagram-like visual aid that shows the various steps in any procedure. Each step is a box showing a particular action or function. These are linked together by arrows to show the sequence. Flow charts also include a decision block which is generally represented by a diamond. The decision block usually asks a question which can be answered by yes or no. This shows the decision-making process in any procedure when alternate courses of action are possible.

You probably made flow charts when you were learning basic programming techniques. Although a flow chart may not fit all expert system applications, it may help you understand and organize the knowledge for your particular expert system.

Develop a Decision Tree

Recall that most artificial intelligence programs, including expert systems, are basically nothing more than a decision tree. Sometimes by using your outline or the inputs and outcomes, you can construct a tree of the knowledge. This is particularly helpful on small systems, and it may be helpful in understanding portions of larger systems. A tree will show the relationship between the various pieces of knowledge and the way they are linked together. This information, in turn, will help you to create rules and link them together. In most instances, you will find that the nodes in a tree correspond to rules in the knowledge base. The tree is a visual aid to further help you organize and understand the knowledge you have acquired.

Develop a Matrix

One of the most helpful ways to organize knowledge is to create a matrix similar to that used in spreadsheets. The matrix will consist of rows and columns showing the

PREMISES OR ATTRIBUTES				OUTCOMES
PRICE RANGE	GAS MILEAGE	No. DOORS	No. ADULTS	CAR TO BUY
$18,000 TO $22,000	17-23 MPG	2	4	BMW 325e
$14,000 TO $17,000	16-26 MPG	4	4	PONTIAC 6000 STE

Rule derived from matrix:

IF the desired price range is $18,000 to $22,000
AND the desired gas mileage is 17 to 23 mpg
AND the number of doors required is 4
AND the number of adults to be seated is 4
THEN buy BMW 325e

Figure 5–5. ***Using a matrix to organize the domain knowledge.***

parts of the knowledge base and how they are related to one another. The matrix is similar to the format we discussed earlier. Such a matrix is shown in Figure 5–5.

Note that on the far right-hand side of the matrix, a column is created to show all of the possible expert system outcomes or answers. Other columns list attributes which give conditions, premises, or antecedents that lead to the outcomes listed. You may find only one set of conditions that leads to one of the possible outputs. In other cases, you may find two or more different sets of combinations that lead to that output result. You can see that a particular output result may be listed more than once in the output column. In this example, we are attempting to create an expert system that will recommend buying a specific car based on input conditions selected by a prospective customer.

You should be able to organize almost any kind of knowledge using this method. It is also an excellent visual aid in helping you to understand the relationship between all the various factors.

Once you have constructed a matrix, you can write rules almost directly from it. The columns forming the attributes and conditions become the IF portions of your rules while the output statements become the THEN portions. Of course, you may have to construct intermediate rules, but the matrix will give you the largest part of your knowledge base.

Write the Rule Base

All of the organizing, manipulation, and visualizing of the knowledge you did in the previous steps should prepare you to begin writing your IF-THEN rules. By the process of outlining, diagramming, and building a matrix, you have probably subdivided the knowledge into chunks small enough to use in individual rules.

A good way to begin is to take a small subdivision of the expert system and write the complete set of rules for it. Usually, the knowledge base will have several possible outcomes that are related to one another. Take these and write the set of rules that leads to these outcomes. Dividing the task into segments will make the rule writing process much easier.

If you are using confidence factors or probability, don't forget to enter these as you write the rules. If uncertainty is a part of the decision-making process, you must identify this during the knowledge engineering phase. Usually the expert will be able to give you close estimates or actual numbers about probability or uncertainty. Once you have written a rule, you want to check these figures with the expert to be sure you are on target.

Build a Prototype

Once the rules have been written, you should immediately enter them using the expert system development tool. Your goal is to build a prototype as quickly as possible to test your system. If you have subdivided the system and built only a portion of it, you can put it together quickly using the development tool and try it out. Most tools will let you build a piece of the system and test it without having to create the entire system.

Once you have got a prototype running, you will do some testing yourself, but the real proof of its validity will come by trying it out with an expert. The expert who helped develop the system is an excellent judge of the result.

For an additional objective opinion, try out the prototype on one or more other experts. With their feedback, you will be able to make necessary changes and adjustments.

If the prototype you have constructed is large enough to be useful, then also try it out on one or more potential users of the system. They will be able to tell you whether the system is answering their questions or solving their problems.

This testing will probably lead to changes and additions. Continue building the prototype until the system is completed.

> *A shoemaker makes a good shoe because he makes nothing else.*
>
> EMERSON

Testing and Debugging the System

If you have tested the various segments of the prototype and made the resulting changes, your final system is probably in pretty good shape. Once the complete system has been developed, you are ready for thorough testing. This should be done on actual users, those who will be on the front lines using it. Only in this way can you determine whether the expert system does solve the problems for which it was constructed.

Test the system thoroughly. Users should attempt to work through as many different kinds of problems as possible to test all the different paths within the system. The users will, of course, keep track of the problems they have and the deficiencies they uncover. These will be reported to the knowledge engineer who will make necessary adjustments. Testing will also identify performance problems that will need debugging.

The testing phase is designed to validate the expert system to ensure that it fulfills its original goals. It will probably be an iterative process where the system is used and tested, then modified and debugged, then again tested and debugged. The process may continue until a highly refined final product has been created.

Maintaining the System

Once your expert system has been tested, debugged, and put into final form, it will go into regular use. However, its development does not end there. Most domains are dynamic and new knowledge must be added constantly. Different situations will occur which the system must be able to accommodate. When you create an expert system, you should go into the project knowing that it will be an ongoing development process, generally known as maintenance. As the knowledge changes and as the user's situation develops, the expert system will have to deal with it.

Maintenance is easy with an expert system development tool. Usually you will need to add new rules, delete old rules, or modify rules as required. Using the editing process built into the system, such changes can be made quickly and easily. The main challenge is identifying what new knowledge needs to be added. The signal will come from users. The system may not be solving all problems or may be solving them inadequately. In any case, in consultation with the user and an expert, new rules can be formulated to solve the problem.

As new rules are added, test the system again. The testing process will not have to be exhaustive because you know the system works. However, users should attempt to elicit responses based on the new knowledge to verify its correctness and validity. When you add new rules, you may have to drop or rewrite older rules to eliminate the conflicts.

Learning to Develop an Expert System

It is difficult to learn how to develop an expert system from a book or even a seminar or course. You learn to develop expert systems by actually creating one. The guidelines in this chapter will point you in the right direction, but as soon as possible you should attempt to become involved in an actual development project.

You might volunteer to be part of an expert system development project within your own organization. If none is underway, propose one. Another approach is to take it upon yourself to develop a small expert system just for the experience. There is probably some subject area in which you are an expert yourself. If you are not, you could pick a subject in which you are interested and learn that area to get expert system development experience. You may be able to find an expert willing to work with you if your project is small enough and does not involve a tremendous amount of time and effort.

If you have a personal computer, buy one of the development tools. It doesn't have to be one of the big, fancy ones. You can learn the concept with a small, inexpensive one. Outline a project, then simply follow the steps and procedures described in this chapter. It is amazing how much you will learn by going through the process yourself. It is certainly recommended that you do this before becoming involved with a larger, more complex project.

Another good way to learn expert system development is to work with someone who has already been through the process. You're lucky if you know such a person who will guide you. You will be doing some of the work yourself, but you will have the advantage of being able to tap the knowledge and experience of the person who has done it before.

> *Integrity without knowledge is weak and useless, and knowledge without integrity is dangerous and dreadful.*
>
> SAMUEL JOHNSON

An Example Expert System

To give you a better feel for the process of creating an expert system, we will present a brief example here. It is a simple domain, so you can study it in some depth.

The purpose of this expert system is to identify sea creatures. Given some facts about a creature, the system can tell you what it is. This system can identify eleven different creatures. They are whale, porpoise, dolphin, shark, flounder, salmon, crab, shrimp, scallop, oyster, and clam. All of the expertise for this system came from a set of encyclopedias and a book or two on sea animals. An expert might have been a marine biologist if a larger, more complex system were being developed.

We know what all of the outcomes are. These are the eleven sea creatures identified earlier. Based on the research, these eleven creatures can be divided into four classes or categories: cetacean, fish, crustacean, and bivalve mollusk. The breakdown looks like this in outline form:

1.0 The creature is a cetacean
- 1.1 The creature is a whale
- 1.2 The creature is a porpoise
- 1.3 The creature is a dolphin

2.0 The creature is a fish
- 2.1 The creature is a shark
- 2.2 The creature is a flounder
- 2.3 The creature is a salmon

CLASS	LENGTH	FIN	NOSE	LIVES	MOUTH	TEETH	OUTCOME
CETACEAN	25 ft.	—	—	—	—	—	WHALE
CETACEAN	6 ft.	TOP VERTICAL	SHORT, BLUNT	NEAR COAST	—	—	PORPOISE
CETACEAN	6 ft.	TOP VERTICAL	LONG, BEAK-LIKE	AT SEA	—	—	DOLPHIN
FISH	—	TOP TRIANGULAR	—	—	UNDERSIDE OF HEAD	SEVERAL ROWS	SHARK

Figure 5–6. ***A portion of a sea creature matrix.***

3.0 The creature is a crustacean
- 3.1 The creature is a crab
- 3.2 The creature is a shrimp

4.0 The creature is a bivalve mollusk
- 4.1 The creature is a scallop
- 4.2 The creature is an oyster
- 4.3 The creature is a clam

As you can see, an outline is a good way to organize the knowledge and to get a feel for how the rules might develop.

A detailed matrix could also have been created. Figure 5–6 shows what a portion of it might look like.

The rules can be derived from the outline or matrix. There is one rule for each of the four types or classes of creatures (cetacean, fish, crustacean, bivalve mollusk) and one rule for each creature. The complete rule base follows.

Sea Creature Rule Base

1. IF The creature has a backbone
   AND The creature has a horizontal tail
   AND The creature has a blow hole for breathing
   AND The creature is warm-blooded
   AND The creature's young are born alive
   AND The creature's young are nursed with mother's milk
   THEN The creature is a cetacean
2. IF The creature is a cetacean
   AND The creature is longer than 25 feet
   THEN The creature is a whale
3. IF The creature is a cetacean
   AND The creature is approximately 6 feet long
   AND The creature has vertical top fin
   AND The creature has short blunt snout
   AND The creature lives near the coast
   THEN The creature is a porpoise

4.	IF	The creature is a cetacean
	AND	The creature is approximately 6 feet long
	AND	The creature has vertical top fin
	AND	The creature has long beak-like nose
	AND	The creature lives at sea
	THEN	The creature is a dolphin
5.	IF	The creature has a backbone
	AND	The creature has a vertical fin
	AND	The creature breathes through gills
	THEN	The creature is a fish
6.	IF	The creature is a fish
	AND	The creature has a triangular top fin
	AND	The creature has a mouth on the underside of its head
	AND	The creature has several rows of teeth
	THEN	The creature is a shark
7.	IF	The creature is a fish
	AND	The creature has two eyes on one side of its head
	AND	The creature lives on the bottom of the sea
	THEN	The creature is a flounder
8.	IF	The creature is a fish
	AND	The creature lives in the waters of the N. Pacific
	AND	The creature spawns in fresh water rivers in Spring
	THEN	The creature is a salmon
9.	IF	The creature has no backbone
	AND	The creature has eyes on stalks
	AND	The creature has five pairs of legs
	AND	The creature has a shell that serves as a skeleton
	AND	The creature's young hatch from eggs
	THEN	The creature is a crustacean
10.	IF	The creature is a crustacean
	AND	The creature has a single, hard, jointed shell
	AND	The creature has two claws
	THEN	The creature is a crab
11.	IF	The creature is a crustacean
	AND	The creature has no claws
	AND	The creature has a soft shell
	THEN	The creature is a shrimp
12.	IF	The creature has two shells
	AND	The creature has a wedge-shaped foot
	THEN	The creature is a bivalve mollusk
13.	IF	The creature is a bivalve mollusk
	AND	The creature has eyes rimming its shell
	AND	The creature roams the sea
	THEN	The creature is a scallop

```
14. IF    The creature is a bivalve mollusk
    AND   The creature's shell is an irregular oval shape
    AND   The creature lives in beds on the bottom of the sea
    THEN  The creature is an oyster
15. IF    The creature is a bivalve mollusk
    AND   The creature has a siphon for eating and waste
    AND   The creature has a smooth circular shell
    AND   The creature lives in beds on the bottom of the sea
    THEN  The creature is a clam
```

Read through the rules and match them to the outline given earlier. Also, note how rules 2, 3, 4, and 6 are derived from the matrix in Figure 5–6.

These rules would be entered into a shell in a special format. A file will be created. Then the system can be run.

Figure 5–7 shows how a typical run might look. The first (A) is an introductory screen. The second (B) shows the actual dialogue between the user and the expert system. The system asks a series of questions that are answered by typing true or false. The lower case t's and f's after each question are the user inputs.

If we assume this is a backward chaining system that uses the rule base given earlier, here's how it works.

(A)

```
Welcome to the Sea Creature Identification Program.
The knowledge base contains 15 rules which will be used to
deduce one of the following 11 hypotheses:
     CREATURE IS A WHALE
     CREATURE IS A PORPOISE
     CREATURE IS A DOLPHIN
     CREATURE IS A SHARK
     CREATURE IS A FLOUNDER
     CREATURE IS A SALMON
     CREATURE IS A CRAB
     CREATURE IS A SHRIMP
     CREATURE IS A SCALLOP
     CREATURE IS A CLAM
     CREATURE IS A OYSTER
```

(B)

```
Answer the following questions with T(true), F(false), or W(why).

True or False?: CREATURE HAS A BACKBONE? t
True or False?: CREATURE BREATHES THROUGH A BLOW HOLE? f
True or False?: CREATURE BREATHES THROUGH GILLS? t
True or False?: CREATURE HAS A VERTICAL TAIL FIN? t
RULE 5 deduces that the CREATURE IS A FISH
True or False?: CREATURE HAS A TRIANGULAR VERTICAL FIN? t
True or False?: CREATURE HAS MOUTH ON UNDERSIDE OF HEAD? t
True or False?: CREATURE HAS SEVERAL ROWS OF TEETH? t
RULE 6 deduces that the CREATURE IS A SHARK
Final conclusion is CREATURE IS A SHARK.

Rerun or Quit (R OR Q)?
```

Figure 5–7. ***A typical run of the sea creature program.***

The inference engine retrieves one of the hypotheses. Since whale is given first, it starts there. It then starts trying to find data that supports the whale hypothesis. In the rule for whale (rule 2), the system first attempts to determine if we know if the creature is a cetacean. That fact is not in the data base, so it chains back to rule 1 whose conclusion is cetacean. Then, it starts asking questions based on the premises in rule 1. Does the creature have a backbone? The user says true.

Next, it asks if the creature breathes through a blow hole. The user says false. This automatically disqualifies rule 1 so the system abandons the cetacean/whale line of reasoning. This eliminates porpoise and dolphin. The system goes on to the next hypothesis, in this case shark. Rule 6 is examined. The first condition asks if the creature is a fish. This is not known, so the inference engine chains backward to rule 5. It now asks fish questions. Does the creature breathe through gills? The user says true. It also asks about a vertical fin. Again the user answers true. At this point, the inference engine concludes that the creature is a fish and rule 5 fires. All of the premises are met. Note that we established earlier in the run that the creature had a backbone. The system didn't ask that question again as the answer was still in the data base.

Now, the system asks questions based on the premises in rule 6. The user answers true to the questions about fin, mouth, and teeth, so rule 6 fires and the system concludes that the creature is a shark.

Key Points

- Developing an advice-giving, problem-solving expert system is a costly and time consuming process that is more difficult than creating other kinds of software.
- The ten steps of developing an expert system are:

    1. Identify the problem and need
    2. Determine the suitability of the problem
    3. Consider the alternatives
    4. Compute the ROI
    5. Select a development tool
    6. Perform the knowledge engineering
    7. Design the system
    8. Complete the development
    9. Test and debug the system
    10. Maintain the system

- Not all problems lend themselves to an expert solution. An in-depth analysis of the problem and need should be done to determine if a source of knowledge is a valid solution.

- There are nine major problem categories that fit expert systems. They are:
  1. Control
  2. Debugging
  3. Design
  4. Diagnosis
  5. Instruction
  6. Interpretation
  7. Planning
  8. Prediction
  9. Repair

- Nine other factors that help determine the suitability of a problem for an expert system are:
  1. Requires human expertise
  2. Has high payoff
  3. No common sense required
  4. Focuses on narrow subject
  5. No physical solution required
  6. Moderately difficult
  7. Can be solved with knowledge
  8. Has minimum number of solutions
  9. Experts are available

- Alternatives to an expert system should be considered. These options include training, documentation (manuals and job aids), DBMS, decision software and traditional algorithmic software.
- To justify the development of an expert system, the return on investment (ROI) should be high. The value of the solution should be worth more than the cost to develop.
- Expert systems can be created by programming in conventional or AI languages or using a software tool that eliminates programming.
- If conventional languages are used, Pascal and C are preferred. LISP and Prolog can both be used to create an expert program.
- Software tools are referred to as expert system shells or generators. They include an inference engine, a user interface, and an empty knowledge base to be filled by the developer.
- Typical expert system development tool specifications include: operating environment (computer and OS), implementation language, knowledge base format, inference method, user interface, links to other software, math capability, license considerations, documentation, and price.
- The key step in developing an expert system is knowledge engineering, the

extraction of the heuristic knowledge from the experts and organizing it into useable form.

- In designing an expert system, all possible outcomes or solutions must be identified.
- Methods of organizing knowledge include outlines, flow charts, decision trees, and matrices.
- Most expert systems and development tools use production (IF-THEN) rule form of knowledge representation.
- A prototype of a portion of the expert system should be built as soon as possible to test the concept.
- The finished expert system should be validated by trying it out on users and other experts and using their feedback to make appropriate changes.
- Expert systems are dynamic. As the knowledge grows or changes, so should the system. Therefore, all expert systems must be maintained to keep them up to date and useful.
- The best way to learn to create an expert system is to actually develop one yourself.

6

Natural Language Processing and Voice Recognition

Language is the dress of thought.

SAMUEL JOHNSON

Next to expert systems, natural language processing is the second largest application for artificial intelligence. Natural language processing (NLP) refers to artificial intelligence methods of communicating with a computer in English or whatever language you may speak. Today, we communicate with a computer through special codes or languages. To tell a computer what to do, we type in terse commands by keyboard or enter programs in a special language designed for creating software. In responding to a user, the computer outputs symbols or short cryptic notes of information or direction. An error message is a good example.

To use a computer properly, you must learn the commands, languages, and jargon. This usually takes considerable time and practice. It is the main reason why computers have been called unfriendly. Menus and icons with pointing devices like mice, light pens, and touch screens help, of course, but they are not perfectly natural.

Many problems could be minimized or even eliminated if we could communicate with the computer in our own language. No special commands or languages would have to be learned or used. We would simply type in directions, instructions, or information in any convenient form. The computer would be smart enough to interpret the input regardless of its format. An alternative would be to give the computer verbal instructions. Instead of using a keyboard to enter commands and programs, we would use a microphone. This ease of use could increase human productivity.

Natural language processing can also help us to cope with information overload. Books and other printed sources, television, radio, and human conversation bombard us daily. There is so much information available to us that we have no good way to absorb it all and use it. As a result, a lot of good information goes to waste.

Information overload is frustrating and wasteful, but there are ways to deal with it. Once information is collected, it can be sorted, categorized, and otherwise organized to provide access to it. The information may be put into a data base management system or even an expert system. The information may be converted to knowledge and conveniently made available.

Data base management systems and expert systems both provide a means of conveniently accessing information and knowledge, but difficult computer techniques often must be used. Special query languages are required to obtain information from a data base. Most expert systems have a less than optimum user interface. In both cases, natural language processing will make such systems much easier to use.

You may be wondering why natural language processing systems are categorized as AI. The answer is that they are simply another form of knowledge-based system. To understand a natural language inquiry, a computer must have knowledge to analyze, then interpret the input. It must understand grammar and the definitions of words. AI techniques are used to represent the internal knowledge and process the inputs. Classic search and pattern-matching techniques are used along with the knowledge to provide understanding. Once the computer understands the input, it can take the desired action.

In addition to natural language understanding, there is also natural language generation. Once the computer takes action, it will usually provide some output. In most cases it is desirable to provide that output in natural language. For that reason, the computer must be able to generate appropriate natural language, and the easiest way to do this is to provide "canned" sentences, phrases, paragraphs, or other outputs. When a particular input is detected, an appropriate output response is accessed and delivered. More sophisticated techniques for generating natural language output are also available.

In this chapter we are going to talk about natural language processing software, the programs that understand and generate natural language inputs and outputs. We will also cover the practical applications of such software.

Finally, we will also consider voice recognition systems, combinations of hardware and AI software that translate human voice input into electrical signals. The signals are in turn translated into digital data that a computer can process and understand.

The Vocabulary of Natural Language

Before we go any farther, let's take a minute to explain some of the terminology we will be using in this chapter. For starters, just what is a language? Then there are terms like linguistics, grammar, and lexicon which you should be familiar with. We will also get into a discussion of syntax, semantics, and context. To keep your head from swimming later on, let's get all of these terms straight right now.

Language

A language is a system for communications. It embodies both verbal and written expression to help us communicate our thoughts and feelings. Language uses a wide range of sounds, signs, and symbols to create words, sentences, paragraphs, and other written information. Whether written or spoken, language is the medium we use for expressing and organizing what we know, think, and feel.

Most natural languages are not deliberately invented or designed. They evolved over the centuries as human beings learned to communicate with one another. In fact, most languages continue to evolve as society changes, as new technological developments occur, and as changes in customs dictate.

There are also formal as opposed to natural languages. Formal languages are artificial or contrived languages deliberately developed for a special purpose. A good example is a computer language. If used properly, the language will permit a limited form of communications between man and computer.

Linguistics

Linguistics is the study of how languages are structured and used. A linguist, for example, is a person who specializes in the study of languages. It is also a person who may speak or use more than one language fluently.

Linguists conduct research to organize all of the symbols, words, phrases, rules, and procedures of a language in an effort to record what it is and how it should be used.

Vocabulary and Lexicon

A vocabulary is all of the words and phrases used in a particular language. As part of the study of language, linguists identify all of the commonly used words and phrases and organize them into a *lexicon.* A lexicon is nothing more than a dictionary that lists all of the words of a language alphabetically. A dictionary specifies the correct spelling and punctuation of the words and gives their definitions and pronunciation. A *glossary* is a subset of a dictionary which defines words, terms, or phrases in a special field of interest.

The vocabulary defines all the words used and understood by all those people using a particular language. But knowing the various words and what they mean is only part of a language. We must know how to assemble these words into complete thoughts.

Grammar, Syntax, and Semantics

The system of rules for putting words together to form complete sentences and thoughts is called *grammar.* Grammar is composed of two basic parts: syntax and semantics.

Syntax refers to the way in which words are assembled to form phrases and sentences. It is that branch of grammar that deals with the mixing and sequencing of different kinds of words in the language such as nouns, verbs, adjectives, and so on. Syntax is a method of putting words in a specific order so they will have the correct form according to the language.

Semantics refers to meaning in language. It is the study of relationships between words and the way they are assembled to represent a particular thought. Semantics provides us with ways of analyzing and interpreting what is being said. Just keep in mind that meaning is also a function of syntax. The way words are used and ordered very much determines the meaning of the combination.

Context and Pragmatics

We usually speak or write in complete sentences. Each sentence expresses one complete thought. We then string the sentences together forming a paragraph to convey a particular idea. As a whole, the paragraph makes sense. But if we pull one sentence out of the paragraph and look at it in isolation, its meaning may not be fully understood. We say that the sentence is out of context.

Context refers to the complete idea or thought surrounding any sentence in a paragraph. Together, all the sentences add up and make sense. Alone, each sentence contains only a piece of the whole and is often subject to interpretation. No interpretation is needed when the sentences are looked at together.

Context clarifies meaning. It explains circumstances and relationships. Therefore, it is an important part of language and understanding.

Pragmatics refers to what people really mean by what they say or write. Very often, we say or write one thing but mean another. You may ask what time it is, but you really mean am I late for the meeting. Pragmatics tries to get at the true meaning or feeling.

Both context and pragmatics play a major role in understanding. It is one thing to communicate but another to know the real meaning of the message. Context and pragmatics fill in the gaps often left by syntax and semantics.

How Natural Language Processing Programs Work

Just how does a computer analyze natural language inputs, understand them, and then take an appropriate action? The purpose of this section is to answer that question.

Presently, two major techniques are widely used in natural language processing programs. These are key word search, and syntactical and semantic analysis. A third type, conceptual dependency, will not be covered here. We will take a look at each of these to give you a taste of how a computer program can understand input text. You will clearly see both the power and weaknesses of these techniques.

Before we begin, let's get one thing straight. The natural language input to a computer will come from the user by way of the keyboard. In all of the examples here, it is assumed that the natural language input will come from the keyboard.

The keyboard, of course, generates codes representing the various input characters, such as letters, numbers, punctuation marks, spaces, and special symbols. These characters are stored away in an input buffer, a part of memory set aside for input text. It is this string of characters stored in memory that our natural language processing programs will analyze and attempt to understand.

Key Word Analysis

The first natural language understanding programs used key word analysis. In this process, the NLP program searches through an input sentence looking for key words or phrases. The program is able to identify or "knows" only selected words and phrases. Once a key word or phrase is recognized, the program responds with specific "canned" responses.

Alternately, the program may actually construct a response based on a partial reply coupled with the key word or selected phrases from the input. The program recognizes very specific inputs which it uses to construct an output response or initiate some other action.

Figure 6–1 shows a flow chart of the basic procedures that a key word NLP program uses to understand input sentences. The flow chart uses standard symbols: a rectangle represents some particular processing action carried out by a subroutine or segment of the program. The diamond symbol represents a decision point with yes and no responses. Let's work through the flow chart to be sure you understand how key word processing works.

The program usually starts by displaying a message on the screen to elicit some input response from the user. The message may simply state that the program is ready to receive input. It could give you more personalized messages such as "What can I do for you?" "Tell me your problem," or "What are your instructions?" You input a message. Your response is accepted by the program and stored in an input buffer.

Next, the program scans the input text searching for a key word. The program can tell where one word ends and another begins by looking for spaces and punctuation marks. As each word is identified, it is used in a pattern-matching processing which compares it to a list of pre-stored words and phrases. Every word or phrase that you want the program to be able to recognize must be pre-stored as part of the program.

Since you want the program to be able to respond to random natural language input, a considerable number of words will have to be stored if you wish to recognize the input text. For example, if you want the program to be able to recognize a specific word, you will also need to store variations or synonyms for that word. For example, a key word may be father. But since people call their fathers by many other names, you should include additional key words such as Dad, Daddy, Poppa, Pa, the Old Man, and so on.

Each word in the input text string is matched against those in the key word directory stored in the program. The diamond element in the flow chart labeled "keyword found?" has two output paths, depending upon the outcome of this search. The first possibility is that no key word is located. If that is the case, the program is set up to respond with one or more stock messages. Some typical examples are "I don't understand," "Please rephrase your message," or some other output that will cause the user to enter a new or different message which contains a key word. This process may continue for several iterations until an appropriate word is recognized.

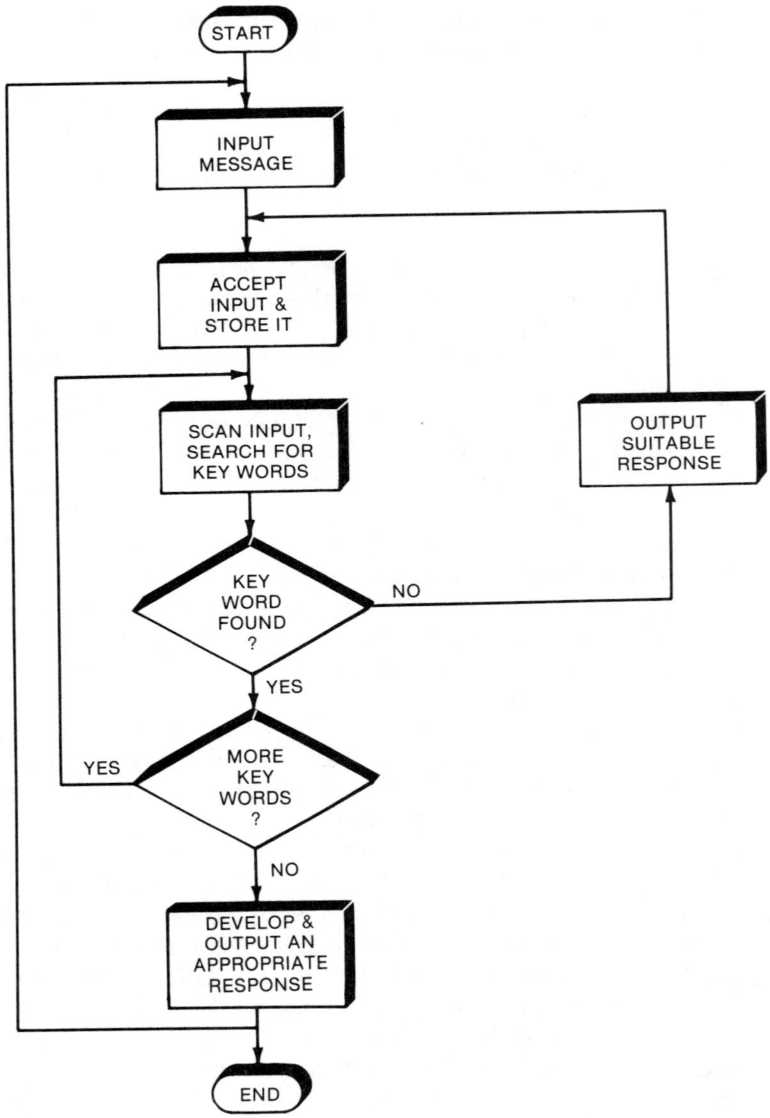

Figure 6–1. ***The process of key word analysis.***

If a key word is located, it is flagged or marked so that it can be used to select an appropriate "canned" response or can be used in an assembled response. But before that is done, the input text string is continually scanned until all possible key words are found. For example, the second diamond in Figure 6–1 asks the question "more key words?" If yes, the search continues. There may be several key words in the input. The program continues to scan all of the words in the input string to match against those in the key word directory.

If no more key words are found, the next step occurs. An appropriate output response is selected or developed and sent to the user. There are several different ways in which this is done. The simplest method, of course, is by simply relating the key word to a specific standard response stored in the program. The key word triggers the use of that response. The program branches to a subroutine where that particular response is stored, and it is outputted to the user.

In other cases, some additional processing may take place to develop, at least partially, the output response. For example, a portion of the input text, be it a word or phrase, might be remembered by the program and then combined with a preprogrammed portion to form a complete response. In another situation, selected key words will be recognized so that some special processing takes place. The words "I" or "me," for instance, are recognized in the input string and this signals the program to respond with the word "you." The user may input something like "I want to know more about computers." The NLP program recognizes the "I" and knows to include a "you" in the response, such as "Why do you want to know more about computers?" As you can imagine, there are all kinds of possibilities here depending on what the key words are and what output messages are appropriate.

To give you an even better feel for how key word matching programs work, let's take a look at a real world example. One of the most widely known and discussed key word matching programs is called ELIZA. ELIZA was written by Professor Joseph Weizenbaum of MIT back in the mid-1960s. It was not written to demonstrate natural language processing. Instead, its purpose was to show how computers could be used to exhibit a certain amount of intelligence but without really any true understanding. Weizenbaum, who is not a proponent of artificial intelligence, wrote the program to demonstrate that through the use of what are basically tricks, a computer can appear to be doing intelligent things.

While he made his point, Weizenbaum also created one of the most talked about programs ever developed. He showed what has proved to be a very effective natural language processing technique that is still widely used.

ELIZA is named after the Eliza Doolittle of *Pygmalian* and My Fair Lady fame. The program itself is designed to act like a nondirective psychiatrist. Such psychiatrists ask you to tell them about your problem, then respond occasionally to draw you out. The idea is that you will talk yourself through the problem to a solution or decision. Such psychiatrists are trained not to make judgments or suggestions, nor do they answer questions directly. The technique was developed by psychologist Carl Rogers many years ago and has been used effectively by psychiatrists since then.

The program has been written in both BASIC and LISP and is available for many different computers. Many spin-offs or variations of this program have been created.

To see what the program is like, refer to Figure 6–2. The computer's responses are in upper case letters. The program opens by having you state your problem. Of course, you can respond with almost anything. Read through the basic conversation in Figure 6–2, then let's talk about it.

This is a listing of a real conversation. This example shows the power of ELIZA in creating the illusion of a real dialogue, but it also shows the weaknesses.

The first weakness appears several lines down with the response, "Well, it is not my problem exclusively . . ." ELIZA thinks the problem is "exclusively."

Later on, things get a bit muddy with the statement "Well, sure, but not AI." The response is "earlier you said your problem." It is clear that the program doesn't really understand.

HOW DO YOU DO.
PLEASE TELL ME YOUR PROBLEM.

My problem is artificial intelligence.
YOUR PROBLEM IS ARTIFICIAL INTELLIGENCE — THAT'S INTERESTING.

Well actually, the real problem is a sub-field of artificial intelligence called natural language.
I AM NOT SURE I UNDERSTAND YOU FULLY.

That is the problem, getting a program to understand.
PLEASE GO ON.

How can I get a program to comprehend what I tell it in plain English?
WHY DO YOU ASK?

That is the source of my problem.
WHY DO YOU SAY YOUR PROBLEM?

Well, it is not my problem exclusively, but I still have it.
DOES THE FACT THAT YOUR PROBLEM EXCLUSIVELY SUGGEST ANYTHING ELSE TO YOU?

Not at all.
DOES THAT HAVE ANYTHING TO DO WITH THE FACT THAT YOUR PROBLEM IS ARTIFICIAL INTELLIGENCE

It sure does.
WHAT DOES THAT SUGGEST TO YOU?

If I understood AI well enough, I wouldn't have such a problem with natural language understanding.
DO YOU THINK ITS LIKELY THAT YOU UNDERSTOOD AI WELL ENOUGH?

No.
WHY NOT?

It is a tough subject.
YOU SEEM TO HAVE AVOIDED SPEAKING OF YOUR PARENTS ALTOGETHER.

What the devil do my parents have to do with anything?
IS IT IMPORTANT TO YOU THAT YOUR PARENTS HAVE TO DO WITH ANYTHING?

Well sure, but not AI.
EARLIER YOU SAID YOUR PROBLEM.

Yes.
YOU SEEM QUITE POSITIVE.

I'm not following you.
IS IT BECAUSE YOU ARE NOT FOLLOWING I THAT YOU CAME TO ME?

Say what?
DOES THAT QUESTION INTEREST YOU?

This whole thing is getting ridiculous.
DO YOU FEEL STRONGLY ABOUT DISCUSSING SUCH THINGS?

I'm getting tired of your wimpy response.
HOW LONG HAVE YOU BEEN GETTING TIRED OF MY WIMPY RESPONSES?

Figure 6–2. ***A real conversation***

Further along in the conversation, the statement, "I'm wasting my valusble time with you" is made. Note that ELIZA picks up and repeats the spelling error in "valusble," giving away its ignorance.

Nevertheless, ELIZA gives a good account of itself and displays a bit of wit and humor as well.

ELIZA uses a sophisticated form of key word matching. The stored responses have been cleverly worded and carefully matched to the key words. For example, if you should happen to state that your problem is with your mother, father, sister, or brother, ELIZA will respond with something like "Tell me more about your family."

As for some typical canned responses, consider those that are outputted when you respond with the words yes or no. If you type "yes" in answer to a question, the program might respond with "You seem quite positive." If you input a "no," the program may respond with "You are being a bit negative." For the input term "yes," ELIZA can respond with four possible outputs. In addition to the one mentioned above, it may also answer with "Are you sure?" "I see," and "I understand." For very common key words such as yes and no, the program contains multiple responses to avoid delivering the same reply each time. This not only provides some variety, but also creates a better illusion of understanding. The program cycles through the list of the alternative responses and keeps track of which one was last, so a new one can be given the next time the key word is recognized. A random number selection of stock phrases could also be used.

```
For the last few minutes.
BUT YOUR PROBLEM EXCLUSIVELY.

It is not mine exclusively as I said before.
WHY DO YOU NEED TO TELL ME IT IS NOT MINE EXCLUSIVELY AS YOU
SAID BEFORE?

Just as a friendly reminder.
HOW IMPORTANT IS THAT TO YOU?

I'm wasting my valusble time with you.  Goodbye.
YOUR VALUSBLE TIME WITH I — THAT'S INTERESTING.

Good bye again.
LET'S DISCUSS FURTHER WHY YOUR PARENTS HAVE TO DO WITH
ANYTHING.

Now wait a minute.
I AM NOT SURE I UNDERSTAND YOU FULLY.

Dummy. . . .
PLEASE GO ON.

Idiot. . .
WHAT DOES THAT SUGGEST TO YOU?

What we have here is a failure to understand.
WHAT IS IT YOU REALLY WANT TO KNOW?

What time is it?
I NOTICE THAT YOU HAVEN'T DISCUSSED SEX AT ALL.
```

with ELIZA.

If more than one key word is recognized in an input statement, an appropriate output response will be chosen according to a certain priority structure set up within the program. Some key words are considered by the program to be more important than others. The response to your input will be triggered by the key word with the highest priority.

Constructed responses take the form of a stored statement with one or more blanks before the key words or phrases can be inserted once they are identified. The stored portion may be something like "Tell me more about your ______." Your input sentence might have been "My boss is giving me trouble." The program recognizes the key word "boss," extracts it, and uses it to fill in the blank to provide an output that says "Tell me more about your boss."

If the program does not identify a key word in the input sentence, it simply outputs one of several possible noncommittal replies. The output may be something like "I'm not sure I understand you fully" or "Please go on."

Of course, ELIZA knows all the little tricks to make you think it really does understand, such as replacing the "I" in your input response with a "you" in its own response. In addition, ELIZA has some special tricks to give you the impression that it is intelligently analyzing your statements and responding to them. For example, ELIZA can store a brief word or phrase from one of your input statements and use it later. As an example, you might have stated earlier that your problem was your inability to afford a Mercedes. Later, during your conversation, when the subject or context may have changed, ELIZA will use that phrase in a statement such as this: "Does that have anything to do with the fact that you cannot afford a Mercedes?" It will do this if no key word is recognized. Such a response is clever, because it seems to prove that the program does have some intelligence because it did remember a previous part of the conversation and relate it back to you at another time. Many times the output expression seems meaningful regardless of what the previous discourse might have been.

ELIZA is an excellent demonstration of how key word matching can be used. However, it is not perfect. It often gives meaningless responses, and there are numerous ways that you can trick it. But for the most part, it is a remarkable demonstration of how a "stupid" program can give the illusion of intelligence. With just a few simple programming tricks, ELIZA makes you feel as though you are carrying on an intelligent conversation with a psychiatrist.

But while key word matching programs are not perfect, they can be extremely useful. Even though the program doesn't really understand what you say, it can use its bag of tricks to make you think that it does. And this, in effect, often results in a useful result. For example, some natural language front-ends for other computer programs, such as data base management systems, use key word matching. The aim is not so much perfection as it is some valuable outcome.

One important point about key word matching programs is the size of their vocabularies. The vocabulary is made up of all of the key words and phrases which the program can identify. Most natural language understanding programs implemented with this technique have a limited vocabulary. It is limited by the program itself and in some cases by the amount of memory the computer may have. But typically, the vocabulary is limited because of the application. Most natural language interfaces, for example, are customized to a particular piece of software. The number of key words they can identify is deliberately limited to those associated with the other program and the related subject matter. As a result of the limited vocabulary, the number of appropriately stored responses or actions is also limited. It would be difficult to construct a general purpose natural language understanding program using key words, because the vocabulary would simply be too large. Further, even if sufficient storage space were available, the search time would be extremely long, making the computer's response sluggish if not downright slow. The best approach is to limit the subject and customize the natural language interface to the application.

> *Grammar is the logic of speech, even as logic is the grammar of reason.*
>
> TRENCH

Syntactical and Semantic Analysis

While key word pattern matching is a widely used natural language technique, its usefulness is restricted because it simply cannot deal with the large variations in language that naturally occur. For that reason, AI researchers have looked for and developed more sophisticated ways of analyzing an input sentence and extracting meaning from it.

The most obvious and straightforward approach to the problem is to perform a detailed analysis of the syntax and semantics of an input statement. In this way, the exact structure of an input sentence and its meaning can be determined. Of course, this is easier said than done. Even sophisticated systems for analyzing the syntax and semantics fall short of the job, because there are too many words with multiple meanings and an enormous number of ways to put those words together to form sentences. Yet, natural language processing systems which do a detailed analysis of syntax and semantics do a far better job than key word matchers, particularly if their application is restricted to a narrow domain. Today, most natural language systems use the syntax and semantic analysis approach. The processes are varied and complex, but we will show you the basic procedures here.

Basic Language Units

Before we get into the step-by-step details of natural language processors, let's take a look at the individual units of the input we have to work with. First, the basic unit of the English language is the sentence. A sentence expresses a complete thought, asks a question, gives a command, or makes an exclamation. The sentence, of course, is made up of individual units known as words. The words have meaning and when they are linked together in various ways, their relationships represent ideas, thoughts, and visual images.

The individual words, besides having a meaning of their own, also fall into various categories known as parts of speech. As you recall from your English language classes, there are eight different parts of speech including nouns, pronouns, verbs, adjectives, adverbs, prepositions, conjunctions, and interjections. Every word is classified as one of these parts of speech.

The English language is tricky, however, because a word may have more than one meaning and can be classified as more than one kind of part of speech. A good example is the word "saw." It can be a noun meaning a cutting tool. Or it can be a verb meaning "did see." The true meaning of a word depends upon how it is used in the sentence; that is, how it is related to the other words. Words like this cause considerable difficulty for computer programs that attempt to analyze sentences and extract meaning.

Naturally there is a complete system within the language that describes how the various parts of speech are to be put together to form complete sentences. These arrangements or structures are stated by specific rules and collectively are known as grammar. We won't attempt to define the full scope of grammar here as you probably already know a lot of it anyway. However, it must be said that a complete proper sentence is generally made up of two specific parts, a subject and a predicate. The subject, also referred to as a noun phrase, identifies a person, object, or thing that is the main focus of the sentence. The predicate, or verb phrase, states some action that the subject takes.

Of course, there are many variations of the noun phrase and verb phrase as you shall see. Each can contain not only the basic noun or verb, but also adjectives, adverbs, pronouns, and prepositional phrases. In any case, both the noun phrase and the verb phrase must be present to form a complete legal sentence.

Although the sentence is the basic building block of language, we often communicate in incomplete sentences. Natural language processors are primarily designed to recognize complete sentences, but they must also deal with partial inputs. This phenomenon of using sentence fragments, short phrases, or even single words in a conversation is known as ellipsis. Such partial sentences are acceptable and effective. We understand them because their meaning is inferred from the context of conversation. Ellipsis causes the natural language processing software to be even more complex.

Morphemes

To analyze an input sentence, the software first breaks down the sentence into individual words. The program scans the input stream looking for spaces and punctuation marks to identify the individual words. But syntactical and semantic analyzers often go one step farther. They may divide the input word into smaller units called *morphemes.* A morpheme is the smallest unit of language. A morpheme may be the word itself, in which case it is called a free morpheme. For example, the word computer is also a morpheme. On the other hand, computers is made up of two morphemes, the basic or root word itself, "computer," and the "-s" added to the end which shows a plural. The -s is a type of morpheme called a bound morpheme. Bound morphemes are usually prefixes and suffixes that are used on the root word to modify its meaning. A typical prefix may be the morpheme un- while typical suffixes might be -ed or -ing. There are many other variations. By subdividing words like this, it is much easier to analyze the word and tell how it is being used.

A Natural Language Understanding System

Figure 6–3 shows a simplified block diagram of the major elements in a natural language processing program. The five major elements are the parser, the lexicon, the under-

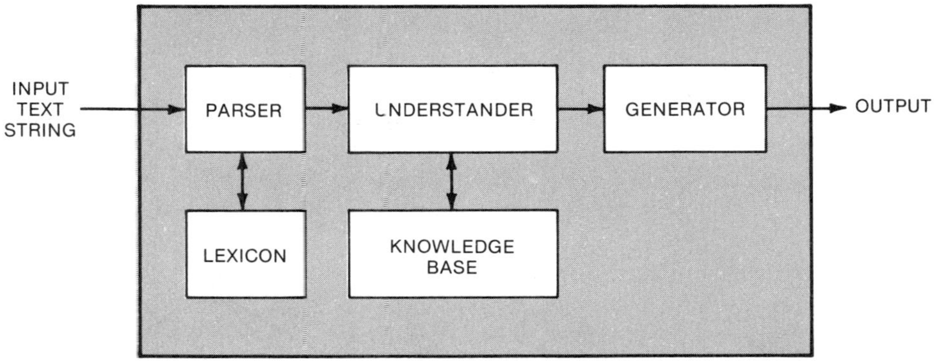

Figure 6–3. ***General block diagram of a natural language understanding program of the syntax/semantic analysis type.***

stander, the knowledge base, and the generator. Let's look at each of these major elements in detail.

The Parser

The key element in a natural language system is the *parser.* The parser is a piece of software that analyzes the input sentence syntactically. Each word is identified and its part of speech identified. The parser then maps the words into a structure called a parse tree. The parse tree shows the meanings of all of the words and how they are assembled.

The entire parsing processing is analogous to the process of diagramming sentences which you may have learned in an English class. The parser identifies the noun phrase and verb phrase and further breaks them down into other elements. This syntactical analysis is the first step toward trying to extract meaning from the sentence.

Recall that a sentence (S) is made up of a subject or noun phrase (NP) and a predicate or verb phrase (VP). We show this as:

$$S = NP + VP$$

The noun phrase could be a single noun, but it usually breaks down further into several additional parts of speech, such as an article (ART) or determiner (D) like "a," "this," or an adjective (ADJ) or two and the main noun. We show it like this.

$$NP = D + ADJ + N$$

The noun phrase may even have a prepositional phrase (PP) made up of a preposition (P) such as "of" or "with" and another determiner and noun.

$$PP = P + D + N$$

The verb phrase (VP) is made up of the verb (V) and often the object of the verb, which is usually another noun (N) and its determiner (D). A prepositional phrase (PP) may also be associated with the verb phrase. It might be represented as:

$$VP = V + D + N + PP$$

Of course, there are many other variations.

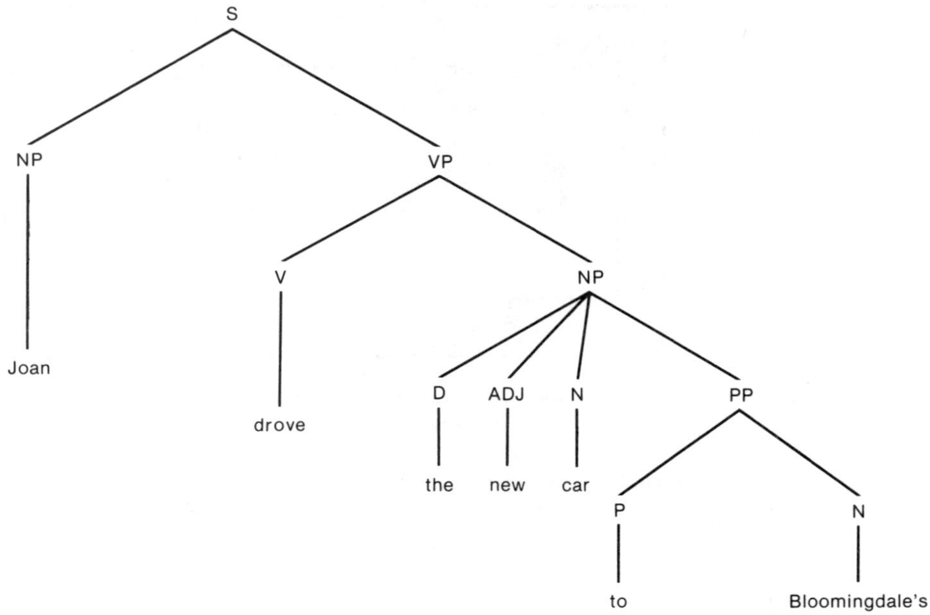

Figure 6–4. ***A parse tree example.***

The job of the parser is to examine each word in a sentence and create the parse tree that identifies all the words and puts them together in the right way. An example is illustrated in Figure 6–4. Here the sentence "Joan drove the new car to Bloomingdale's" is divided into its various parts. The parser begins by examining the word "Joan." This is found to be a woman's name which is a noun. Next, the word "drove" is examined. This is revealed to be a verb. Then the word "the" appears to the parser. This is identified as a determiner. This process is continued as the parse tree is built.

The most popular method of parsing is the *augmented transition network* (ATN). An ATN is a software emulation of a finite state machine which has discrete states or nodes that are linked by arcs. The arcs represent conditions that must be met to move from one state to the next.

A simple ATN is shown in Figure 6–5. This ATN is used to parse a noun phrase made up of a determiner (or article), one or more adjectives, and a noun. The start state is A1. To get to A2, the ATN looks for a determiner. It tests the first word to see if it is an article, such as "a," "the" or "this." Assume we are parsing the phrase "the long, black car." The ATN looks "the" up in the lexicon and determines that it is indeed a determiner. The test for a determiner succeeds, so we move to the next state, A2.

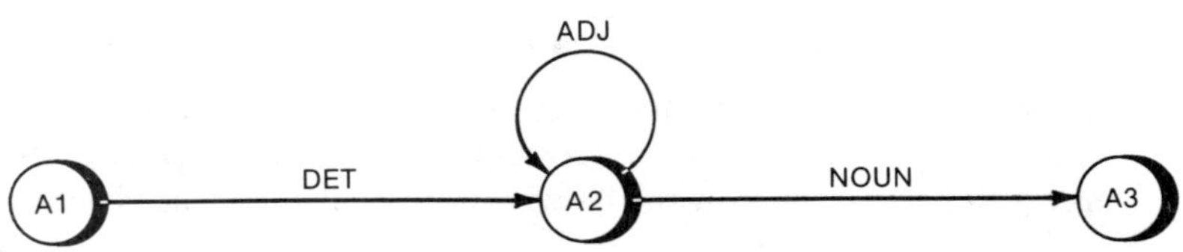

Figure 6–5. ***An augmented transition network (ATN) for parsing a noun phrase.***

Now the ATN looks at the next word in the sentence testing for an adjective. It finds "long," and the test succeeds. But the ATN must be designed to look for more than one adjective so it does not change states. It simply loops back looking for another adjective. It finds "black." It looks again at "car." "Car" is not an adjective so the test finally fails.

Now the ATN looks for a noun, and it finds "car" so we move to the final state, A3. The phrase is then parsed. This simple ATN attaches to or references other ATNs to parse larger sentences or different types of sentences. It builds a data structure in memory that identifies all the words and their grammatical relationships.

The Lexicon

The parser works closely with the lexicon in doing the syntactical analysis. The lexicon contains all of the words that the program is capable of recognizing.

The lexicon also contains the correct spelling of each word and also designates its part of speech. For words that can have more than one meaning, the lexicon lists all of the various meanings permitted by the system. For instance, consider the word "can." "Can" might be a verb indicating ability. It can also be a noun referring to a container. One of the ways to get around the problem of determining how the word is really used is to limit the lexicon entries to only those terms which are permitted by the system. If all possible combinations must be used, then the system must have some built-in segment which further determines how the word is used. Typically, this means that the word must first be related to other words in the sentence to determine its meaning. The more sophisticated NLP programs have such a capability.

Some parsers perform a morpheme analysis. They look at each input word and further subdivide it into its individual morphemes. The lexicon contains the various morphemes. In this way, a more precise meaning can be determined. Other natural language processing systems do not perform morpheme analysis, but instead store all possible variations of the root word. The overall result is basically the same.

The parser and the lexicon work together to pick apart a sentence and then create the parse tree, a new data structure which helps to get at the real meaning of the sentence. But even though the various parts of speech have been identified and the sentence has been fully analyzed syntactically, the computer still does not understand it. As a result, the need for semantic analysis is necessary.

In operation, the parser is largely a pattern matcher. Once the individual word has been identified, the parser searches through the lexicon comparing each input word with all of the words stored there. If a match is found, the word is put aside along with the other lexical information, such as part of speech and meaning. The parser then goes on to analyze additional words and ultimately builds the parse tree.

During this process, the parser can also take care of general housekeeping activities such as misspelled words. Users will frequently misspell words. They may not know the spelling or they make typing errors when they key the input sentence in. Because of this, most parsers have search routines to recognize spelling errors. Usually, the spelling errors are typos and represent discrepancies in only one or two letters. The parser attempts to match the input word as closely as possible to those existing in the lexicon. The procedure may be to flag the misspelled word, notify the user, and ask for clarification.

Once the parse tree has been constructed, the system is ready for semantic analysis to obtain further meaning.

The Understander and Knowledge Base

Semantic analysis is the function of the understander block in Figure 6–3. The understander works in conjunction with the knowledge base to determine what the sentence means.

In order to determine what is meant by an input sentence, the system must know things about words and how they are put together to form meaningful statements. The knowledge base is the primary means of understanding what has been said. As you already know, there are many different ways to implement a knowledge base. Production rules, semantic networks, frames, and scripts are all common methods used in implementing natural language knowledge bases.

The purpose of the understander is to use the parse tree to reference the knowledge base. The understander may answer a question using the knowledge base. If the input sentence is a statement, the understander will determine meaning by looking up words and phrases in the knowledge base. Rules might be fired, frames or scripts referenced, or semantic nets searched. The understander can also draw inferences from the input statement. Many English sentences do not tell the whole story directly, but we are able to infer the meaning from our general knowledge. This is also the case with more sophisticated natural language understanding systems.

The Generator

The *generator* uses the understood input to create a useable output. The understander creates another data structure which represents the meaning and understanding of the sentence and stores it in memory. That data structure can then be used to initiate additional action. If the NLP is part of an interface or front-end, the data structure will be used to create special codes to control another piece of software. It may give the software commands to initiate some action. In a DBMS, the generator would write a program in a query language to begin a search for specific information. In other systems, the action may be the generation of an output response such as a sentence or question.

In its simplest form, the natural language generator feeds standard pre-stored output responses to the user based on the meaning extracted from the input. However, more sophisticated generators will construct an original response from scratch.

In the model for a natural language processing system shown in Figure 6–3, we have used individual blocks to show the elements of the system and how they work together. They have described the system as first performing the syntactical analysis and then the semantic analysis. In practice, there are systems that work this way. However, through much research and experimentation it has been found that systems which combine the syntactical and semantic analysis have superior performance. In other words, as the syntax is being determined, semantic analysis also is being done.

This helps to minimize ambiguity. Such integrated systems may have all of the blocks shown in Figure 6–3, but they are linked to communicate with one another on a word-by-word basis. In this way, the input statement is better understood and processing often takes place faster.

> *Language is called the garment of thought: however, it should rather be, language is the flesh-garment, the body of thought.*
>
> THOMAS CARLYLE

Applications of Natural Language Processing

We have already mentioned several common applications for NLP programs. These include natural language interfaces to other software packages and language translation. Now let's take a closer look at these important uses plus some other NLP applications. The value of an AI technique is directly proportional to its usefulness, and NLP ranks way up there with expert systems in high end user value.

Natural Language Interfaces

By far the most predominant use of NLP is in interfaces of "front-ends" for other software packages. Such interfaces are used to simplify and improve the communications between the applications program and the user. Many programs are complex and difficult to use. They require learning a special language or set of commands. This takes a lot of time and effort and frequently puts off the user. As a result, the software is not used to the full extent of its capabilities. A natural language front-end helps overcome these problems.

The natural language front-end allows the user to operate the applications program with natural language. No special commands have to be learned. Once users understand the basic function of the applications program, they can use everyday language to tap it. Even the most novice users can take advantage of the applications software.

Natural language front-ends make the software transparent to the user. Because users do not have to learn or worry about special languages or procedures, they can focus on the job, not the process of getting it done. This will permit computer illiterate managers, executives, and other busy people to use the computer. Further, NLP will help open up the corporate mainframe data base to users other than data processing programmers.

Although natural language front-ends are being created for a wide variety of applications programs, their most common use is with data base management systems (DBMS). Data base management systems store and retrieve huge files of data. These files may be customer profiles, inventory items, or simply a variety of facts and figures. The easy part of using a DBMS is creating the files. The information to be stored is divided up into individual "chunks" generally known as records. Many records are used to create files. Further, many different kinds of files are combined to form the entire data base. While creating the data base may be time consuming, it is not difficult. The difficulty arises in getting at and using the information stored there.

To access the information, the DBMS must be given instructions to tell it what kind of information to access. Different operations may have to be performed to access the information, including searching and sorting. Some editing is also required to put the information into the final desired output format. For example, if you wanted to tap a customer data base and access all of the individuals whose last name is Smith and output them in zip code numerical order, you would have to have some way to tell the DBMS to do this. This is usually accomplished with a special language called a query language. It is made up of special commands and instructions that are listed sequentially to form a program that will access the data you want in format you want. This makes most DBMSs hard to use. The users who want and need the data do not have the expertise to create the program to get at the data. As a result, a programmer or some other computer oriented person must do the job. This certainly limits the usefulness of the data base.

Today many DBMS software packages include a natural language front-end or offer one as an option. As a result, virtually anyone can sit in front of a computer and tap the data base simply by keying in the details of what he or she wants out. For example, to get the information mentioned earlier, all the user would have to type is:

"List all the customers named Smith in zip code order."

INTELLECT

One of the oldest and most widely used natural language front-ends is INTELLECT, a product of Artificial Intelligence Corporation. INTELLECT is a complete natural language interface for large mainframe computers, designed primarily to be used with DBMS that operate in the IBM operating system environment.

In addition to being able to access data in a DBMS, INTELLECT allows the user to create data bases using natural language. The built-in lexicon may be modified to fit a particular application. A lexicon editor allows the user to build and maintain special dictionaries for special uses. Unique words and their meanings or synonyms can be added to the lexicon. In this way, you can customize INTELLECT to the application.

In some cases, a natural language front-end attaches directly to the data base. The natural language interface also can generate code in one of the numerous query languages used to access information in a DBMS. INTELLECT, for example, is available in a configuration which uses FOCUS, a query language for large DBMS. INTELLECT allows the user to enter natural English statements and then converts them into the command structure of FOCUS which, in turn, accesses the desired data.

As an example of how INTELLECT might work, assume that a data base has been created to keep track of the sales information on a company's products. The DBMS knows how many of the different kinds of products are sold each month in each of the sales regions. It also keeps track of monthly sales by individual salespeople. With all of this information on tap, a sales manager can access information quickly to get a picture of what is selling and what is not, who is performing and who is not. Such a DBMS can be very useful in finding problems and correcting them.

On the other hand, a sales manager is probably the last person in the organization you might expect to be computer literate. Few sales managers know query language programs and, therefore, they will have difficulty accessing this kind of information without a considerable amount of help. But with a natural language front-end, the information can be tapped quickly.

For example, the sales manager could sit down at a terminal and key in the following message:

"What are the sales of all products for February?"

The natural language front-end converts this into the code that will access that information. But there are some real subtleties in the inquiry. First, while the input states the month of the sales, it does not state the year. The sales manager obviously means the current year and, therefore, the computer must be set up to anticipate this. Otherwise, it may simply come back to the user with a question asking what year.

This inquiry also assumes that the program knows which products the company makes. Again, large sophisticated systems have no problem in dealing with such information. Smaller less sophisticated systems, however, would simply ask which products the user wants to know about.

Once these preliminaries are out of the way, the computer will display the desired information. It might look something like this:

Sales for February 1986

Widgets 14,522

Whatchamacallits 7,918

Whizbangs 22,683

The sales manager may then make another inquiry such as:

"Which sales region sold the most widgets?"

Again, the interface has to assume several things. It must know which sales regions exist. In this case, assume that the country is divided into east, central, and western sales areas. The computer then looks up the sales for each of these regions on widgets and prints out the information:

East Coast:

Widgets 6,580

Another inquiry might be:

"Which salesperson in the central region generated the most sales of whizbangs?"

Again the computer would search for the information and present it:

Herb Jones

Whizbangs 1,974

With an NLP front-end, a totally untrained computer user can sit down and access information with a few inquiries entered in "hunt and peck" form. It's not hard to see that such natural language interfaces will make computers far more attractive to many more people.

While INTELLECT is probably the best selling natural language interface for large mainframes, several other software companies offer such systems. Another system for large mainframes is EXPLORER developed by Cognitive Systems. EXPLORER is a natural language front-end that is specifically customized to the data base and the application. Other large software companies such as Cullinet also offer natural language front-ends.

Themis

Natural language front-ends are, of course, also available for minicomputers. Typical of these is Themis offered by Frey Associates, Inc., for Digital Equipment Corporation's VAX family of minicomputers. The system is designed to interface with DEC DBMS/32 data base software. Versions are also available to work with Data General's minicomputers which use Oracle, a relational DBMS for DG systems. Like most natural language front-ends, they come with a basic vocabulary which can be added to or otherwise modified to better match the interface to the system and application.

Natural language front-ends are also available for DBMS that run on personal computers. Most of these are designed to work with DBMS systems for the IBM Personal Computer and its compatibles. Let's take a closer look at several of them.

Clout

An example of such a system is Clout by Microrim. Clout is a front-end designed to be used with Microrim's popular R:Base 4000 and 5000 relational DBMS. It comes with a basic dictionary of 300 commonly used terms for accessing data and specifying relationships. The user can add up to 500 additional terms. Clout makes it extremely easy to tap the information in the data base.

For instance, a user may want to look at some customer files. By using natural language, he can ask questions such as:

> "How much does John F. Smith owe in his account?" "What was the date of the last purchase by Mary C. Jones?" "What did she buy?"

The natural language front-end can easily go into the data base and find this information.

Clout is a very effective personal computer front-end. However, it does work only with Microrim's DBMS. Further, it is strictly for use in retrieving data from the data base. It cannot be used for creating new data bases.

SAVVY

One of the oldest natural language front-ends for a personal computer data base is SAVVY. Originally developed as part of a DBMS for the Apple computer system, the

SAVVY system is a combination of both hardware and software. A special board using a Z80 microprocessor plus some special ROM chips and a RAM are plugged into the Apple II computer. Then combined with the software, natural language inquiries can be made on the DBMS. SAVVY is a product of Excalibur Technologies of Albuquerque, NM. It is also available for the IBM PC.

SAVVY is a DBMS with an unusual form of natural language front-end. Instead of implementing the standard parsing techniques, SAVVY uses a unique pattern recognition algorithm. SAVVY looks at strings of input bits and attempts to determine if it has ever seen anything like them before. The pattern matching algorithm is adaptive. In other words, it learns from the user. The more input you give the system, the more it learns specific words, phrases, and patterns. This algorithm searches for matches that are close to the input inquiries. Even if input words are misspelled, it retrieves the correct information and correct answers are given.

While SAVVY is a portion of Excalibur's own special DBMS, a unique version is available for use with other applications software packages.

NaturalLink

Another natural language front-end with a unique format is Texas Instruments' NaturalLink. This front-end is menu driven. You don't even have to key in your own inquiry statements. Instead, NaturalLink already contains all of the acceptable words and phrases you can use in a valid inquiry. These word and phrase choices are displayed in windows on the screen. At the very top of the screen is the beginning phrase: "I want to . . ." By using the arrow keys, you can move a cursor around to highlight the desired words or phrases that express the inquiry you wish to make. Once the highlighted term is entered, it is automatically added to the beginning sentence. In this way, you build a query sentence that tells NaturalLink exactly what you want to do.

NaturalLink is designed to be used as a front-end to a number of popular applications programs. These, of course, include DBMS, but also popular spreadsheets, word processing packages, operating systems, and other programs. Facilities are included so that NaturalLink can be built and optimized for a specific application program. NaturalLink runs on Texas Instruments' own personal computers as well as the popular IBM PC and its compatibles.

Q&A and Paradox

A major trend in natural language interfaces is to build them in to the applications program rather than making them extra cost add-ons. Two recent examples of this are the data base managers, Q&A from Symantec Corporation and Paradox by Ansa Software. Both contain built-in natural language interfaces which may be called upon if desired.

Q&A is a basic file manager which contains modules for building files, accessing the files, and generating an output report in a specific format. It also contains the natural language front-end called "The Intelligent Assistant." The Intelligent Assistant or IA parses common English input questions and converts them into queries which the file manager can understand. A built-in 600-word vocabulary provides the lexical information for understanding the input query. Like Clout and some other kinds of natural language interfaces, the IA in Q&A, may not understand your inquiry immediately if you use an input word or phrase that is not in the built-in dictionary. In this case, Q&A will come back to you and ask you to try again. To get closer to a successful input statement, you rephrase your query using synonyms or different terms. Eventually, the front-end will understand and access the information you want.

A unique feature of Q&A is that it paraphrases your input request to ensure that it fully understands what you want. Using the sales example given earlier, you may request the following:

"Show the total 1985 sales for the Central Region"

Q&A's Intelligent Assistant may come back with an inquiry that looks like this:

SHALL I DO THE FOLLOWING?
CREATE A REPORT SHOWING THE AMOUNT OF SALES FOR THE CENTRAL REGION IN 1985?
YES - CONTINUE   NO - CANCEL REQUEST

Paraphrasing verifies what you want to do. If it is correct, simply type Y for yes and the data access will be completed. A no answer will cancel the request, and then you may change it or rephrase it.

The primary disadvantage of the Q&A system is that it is not a relational data base. For that reason, it cannot initiate queries for multiple information items that are contained in separate files. It can only access information in one file at a time. Relational data bases, on the other hand, permit several files to be open at a time to access multiple data items. For example, if the sales for widgets is in a separate file from whizbangs, Q&A could not answer the question, "State the total sales of widgets and whizbangs." However, you can get the same information by asking for the sales in separate inquiries.

Paradox is a relational DBMS that uses an AI-like technique called query by example (QBE) to access data. Instead of writing a program in Paradox's query language, a user can simply view a template that is a model of the way data is stored, then "check off" the desired information. Using the template as a guide, Paradox looks up, then displays the data.

Other Uses

While natural language front-ends for DBMS are the most common use of NLP, other popular software packages are expected to incorporate front-ends eventually. Spreadsheets, for example, would be easier to use if a natural language interface were available. Already such packages are available. An example is HAL for Human Access Language, a product of GNP Development Corporation. It is designed to interface with the popular Lotus 1-2-3 spreadsheet. It allows 1-2-3 users to carry out the various program functions by simply typing in English language commands.

Natural language front-ends for operating systems are another possibility. Already such a program has been created using artificial intelligence techniques for the UNIX operating system. UNIX is a multi-user, multi-tasking operating system used mostly on larger minicomputers. However, versions, like XENIX, are available for the larger personal computers. UNIX, an operating system originally developed by AT&T, is one of the most powerful and useful available. However, it is somewhat difficult to use because of its complex command structure. A natural language front-end called UNIX Consultant has been developed that allows users to ask in English how to go about accomplishing specific actions in UNIX. For instance, to delete a file in the UNIX operating system, the user must type "rm" followed by the file name. If you don't know how to do this, you may simply ask in English, "How do I eliminate a file?" UNIX Consultant will come back with an answer to your question. While the program itself doesn't automatically implement the function, it tells you how to do it.

Already several universal front-ends have been created. Typical of these are TI's NaturalLink described earlier. Its menu driven format is extremely flexible and adaptable to all kinds of applications programs.

While natural language processing is nowhere near perfect, its level of development is high enough to provide a certain degree of usefulness. It is becoming more widely used every day. This is a major trend in applications software and you can expect to see it continue to grow. As natural language processing research develops, further additions and improvements will be made.

Disadvantages

The advantages and benefits of NLP are relatively clear, but there are some disadvantages. First, NLP adds cost and complexity to any system. The natural language front-end can cost upwards of $50,000 on large mainframe systems. Minicomputer front-ends are much less expensive but will still cost in the $10,000 to $25,000 range for a major system. Natural language interfaces for personal computers sell in the $100 to $300 range if they are not built in. Integrated NLP systems add cost to the software regardless of its form.

These systems also take up additional memory space. As a result, the computers on which they run must have more RAM than would be needed to run the applications program alone.

Another disadvantage of a natural language interface is that it usually takes more time to access the data than other methods do. When standard commands or query languages are used to access information in a DBMS, an experienced programmer can get to the information quickly with a few simple key strokes. Commands are very short mnemonics which tell the DBMS or query language what to do. To get the information using natural language, a complete sentence has to be typed. In many cases multiple sentences have to be typed. Sometimes these questions may not be immediately accepted, and must be rephrased and keyed in again. All of this, of course, takes time. Then, the interface itself must interpret the question or sentence. It must search for key words, parse, activate knowledge base or otherwise go through gyrations to get to the data. While most front-ends are reasonably fast, some are sluggish at best.

The excessive access time may or may not be a disadvantage. With today's systems, increased access time is the price one must pay for making that access easier and available to anyone.

Language Translation

One of the earliest proposed computer applications was language translation. The language barrier has always been a problem in dealing with people from other countries. Further, a language barrier also exists between human beings and machines. NLP is being used to break down those language barriers.

Natural Language to Natural Language

Many people would like to be able to read the publications of other countries. Wide availability of general translations does not exist, and early computer scientists proposed the computer as a solution to the problem. In the late 1950s and early 1960s, language translation became a major computer project. It was heavily funded by the government, and the goal was to create a system that would translate Russian into English.

As you may recall, Russia launched the first satellite, Sputnik, back in 1957. The great concern was that Russia was far ahead of the U.S. technically and that massive programs should be instituted to correct this condition. Major funding programs were created to increase engineering and scientific education. It was felt that by making the Russian technical literature available to U.S. scientists and engineers, advancements could be expedited. As a result, the computer language translation project was highly regarded.

This early translation system did nothing more than a word-for-word substitution. The translator looked up the Russian words in the input string, extracted their English language equivalent from the dictionary and made the substitution. Other minor adjustments were made to correct for the differences in word sequencing, no other major changes were made.

The quality of such translations was incredibly poor. Typically less than 50% of the translation was valid. The system simply could not deal with the wide variations in word meanings or the nuances and subtleties of language. Many of the translations were not only worthless, but hilarious. After considerable expense and effort, these early language translation programs were abandoned. For many years, no major language translation efforts were made. Yet basic research did continue.

Today, language translation has been reborn. With the sophisticated techniques of natural language programs, it is now possible to perform highly reliable translations of excellent quality. These language translation systems use the parsing systems described earlier. By analyzing the syntax and semantics of the sentence, translation accuracies of 80% or more can be achieved. With some pre-editing to simplify complicated sentence structures, accuracies of 90% or more can be achieved. Further improvements can be made by taking and having a human translator polish the machine translation.

Today there are many companies in the business strictly for performing computer language translations. Translations are possible in most of the European languages, Arabic, and Japanese to and from English. NLP is speeding up the translation process and, in many cases, costs less than human translators. While some of the translations are still rough, they are in most cases acceptable simply because they are better than no translation at all.

One of the most interesting approaches to language translation is the concept of creating a special intermediate language generally referred to as an *interlingua*. The interlingua is an artificial language that contains symbols, rules, syntax, and logic so that any language can be converted to it. Using the interlingua, all translations would convert one language into the interlingua which would then be retranslated into the final target language. While such an interlingua has been used on a small scale, no one has yet developed an artificial language broad enough and useful enough to be used with all natural languages. There are such wide variations from one language to the other that it is difficult to construct the interlingua. No one knows enough about the various languages to be able to develop a useful interlingua. For now it remains a concept that may one day be implemented.

Machine Language to Machine Language

If natural language processing techniques can be used to convert one natural language to another, then presumably they can also be used to convert one computer language to another. This is, in fact, the case. Artificial intelligence techniques based on natural language processing are now being applied widely to translation between different programming languages.

One of the problems that has plagued software development from the beginning is the inability to use a program written for one machine on another computer. This problem has its origin in the languages used by the two machines. In most cases, the languages are unique to the machines, thereby making the software unique to the machines. It is not possible to transport the software from one computer to another. This problem has led to considerable duplication of effort and unnecessary software costs. There is an enormous waste of good software and a lot of "re-inventing the wheel" going on because of the lack of transportability.

During the development of higher level programming languages, some effort was made to standardize languages. Considerable effort was made, for example, with Fortran and Cobol. Yet, despite these standardization efforts, many different dialects of these languages exist. Total transportability is still not possible. However, the conversion of one dialect of Fortran to another dialect of Fortran is easier than converting between different languages. Still the effort is considerable. Most programmers find that it is easier to write new software.

To make software more widely available, it would be desirable to have a standard language which all computers could understand. However, this is not the case. Many different languages are available and programmers are free to choose the one they like best or that best fits the application. As a result, the lack of transportability and its resulting inefficiency continue.

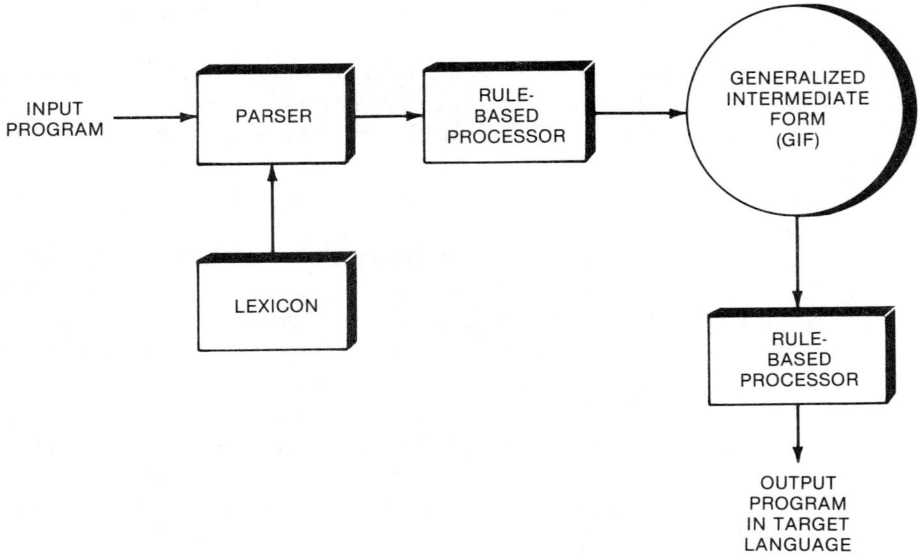

Figure 6–6. ***Block diagram of a computer language translation system.***

As the programmer shortage grows more acute and as software development costs rise, the transportability problem becomes more of an issue. Some solution is needed. This is particularly true with very large systems such as those used in the government and the military. Software developed for an older system must be totally rewritten and debugged when the computer system is upgraded to the newer, larger, and faster models. The costs of the conversion are unacceptable in some cases. This is the reason why so many government installations continue to use their very old computers. They simply cannot justify the expense of converting the software to use on a newer machine.

Several companies are now developing special artificial intelligence-based software that will perform automatic language translation. Similar forms of automated translators perform conversions from one dialect of a language to another. Systems are now available for Fortran, Cobol, and PL/1.

The more common conversion need is between two different languages. Numerous AI programs are being developed to make such translations. Two of the main target output languages are Ada and C. Both of these are modern, advanced languages which are widely used in new software. Ada, for example, is a flexible language developed by the Department of Defense in an effort to standardize software for military applications. While most new software will be written in the Ada language, the considerable existing base of software will have to be converted. Using automated NLP-like translators will save considerable time and effort.

Both Ada and C are essentially standardized languages. Although variations exist, there are fewer dialects and minimal differences between the two. For this reason, converting software to these two languages makes the programs easier to transport to a wider range of computers.

Automatic computer language translators use essentially the same techniques used in natural language understanding programs. Figure 6–6 shows a block diagram of a typical system. As in other natural language systems, the parser decomposes the input statements of a language into its basic elements producing a parse tree. Of course, the parser contains a built-in lexicon that recognizes various input terms. The parse tree is then translated into another format known as the generalized intermediate form (GIF) by a rule based processor. This is an expert system-like program that translates the parse tree made up of the input language instructions and commands and converts them to the GIF. The GIF is like an interlingua into which any language can be converted and vice versa.

Next, the GIF form drives another rule based processor which effectively translates the GIF representation into the lines of code in the target language.

Software translators are a relatively new concept and only a few have been developed. However, these have proven remarkably successful. As development continues, the process will be refined and new techniques will be uncovered. The result will be faster, easier, and lower cost translations between the various languages. This should make software available for a wider range of computers and should greatly reduce software development expenses.

Grammar Analysis

Another application of natural language processing is grammar analysis. This is done with a special NLP program to convert poor writing to acceptable writing. Written communications in business are extremely important, but the quality of written business documents is generally poor. Even though we spend years of school learning English, grammar, spelling, and word usage, many of us still write poorly. Special grammar analyzer programs can be used to process such communications and improve them.

To use a grammar analyzer, the user keys in a paragraph, memo, report, or other written document. The grammar analyzer takes over and performs a wide variety of functions. First, it checks spelling. Like most natural language processing programs, the grammar analyzer contains a rather large dictionary. In this case, the dictionary has to be unusually large to analyze a wide range of business and technical communications.

In addition to checking spelling, the grammar analyzer looks for commonly misused words and phrases. It also analyzes unnecessarily long phrases and makes suggestions for shortening them to one word that means the same thing. For example, it might shorten the phrase "in view of the fact that" to the single word "since." The analyzer also checks for subject and verb agreement, split infinitives, and sexist phrases. Even the punctuation is checked.

Some grammar analyzing programs can determine reading level. Reading levels correspond to school grade levels. For example, text with a reading level of 8th grade is easier to read and comprehend than text at the 12th grade level.

The reading level is generally computed by one of several formulas, which uses the number of words per sentence and the number of multisyllabic words used in the sentence. The shorter the sentence and the fewer multisyllabic words used, the easier the text is to read. The grammar analyzer counts the words and syllables in a block of text and computes the reading level. This allows you to make adjustments, if reading level is important.

Some grammar analyzers also fully analyze each sentence, breaking each word down into its part of speech and showing the relationships to one another. This is an easy job as they all create a parse tree which does this anyway. The grammar analyzer, in effect, diagrams the sentence for you. This allows a better representation of the sentence and more thorough analysis.

Perhaps the largest and most well known grammar analyzer is Writer's Workbench. This system was originally developed at Bell Telephone Laboratories and is available for computer systems running the UNIX operating system. Writer's Workbench has been refined over the years and does an excellent job of improving writing.

IBM has a similar system known as EPISTLE. Like the Writer's Workbench, it does in-depth analysis of each sentence in the text and provides most of the functions mentioned earlier. Presently, EPISTLE is still in its experimental and development stages, but a practical real-world product is expected in the future.

There are also several smaller grammar analyzers available for personal computers. Naturally, they do not perform many functions. They do not have as large a dictionary and as a result are more limited. But nevertheless, they are useful for some applications.

Grammar analyzers will not eliminate the need to take English grammar in school. But they will in general help to improve the quality of business writing. When they become more widely available, they will be useful in catching gross grammatical errors which can embarrass the writer and have serious detrimental effects upon the reader. Readers who know grammar and can catch such errors will usually be turned off by the poor usage. This can result in the loss of a sale or have a negative impact on the writer's original purpose.

Abstracting

Another application of natural language processing is abstracting. This is basically the process of reading a block of text and summarizing the key points.

Abstracting programs could be of major help in solving or at least minimizing the effect of the information glut. For example, magazine articles could be fed to the abstracting system for a concise summary. Such an NLP program could reduce a 4-page article to a paragraph that concisely sums up the main points and facts. The abstracting program will boil the input down into a brief statement communicating all the key information.

Such abstracting programs have already been created and tested on a small scale. Systems have been designed to read newspaper articles and summarize them into a short paragraph. In addition to being able to read and understand the article, the program must contain sophisticated text generation software that can paraphrase the information.

The main problem with such programs is that to be useful over a wide range of subjects, they must have an enormous dictionary of input terms and a massive knowledge base. If the programs are constrained to specific subjects or fields, the abstracting process can be carried out successfully. It will be years before a general purpose abstracting program will be available. Yet such a program will make our lives easier as it will allow us to assimilate a lot more information in less time.

> *The goal is not to make humans computer-literate; it is to make computers human-literate.*
>
> INFOWORLD

Speech Recognition

Another artificial intelligence application related to natural language processing is called speech or voice recognition. It is the process of having the computer recognize normal human speech. When a speech recognition system is combined with a natural language processing system, the result is an overall system that not only recognizes voice input but also understands it.

While a tremendous amount of communications takes place by the written word, it is only a fraction of our daily communications by voice. Not only is this type of communication more natural for us, it is also faster. The average human speaking speed is approximately 150 words per minute. This is approximately twice as fast as an average typist.

One of the major benefits of voice input on a computer is that it prevents diversion of the eyes and hands. Typing in data on a keyboard keeps the hands and the eyes busy. But with voice input, the eyes and the hands can concentrate on other activities. There are some computer applications where this advantage is major.

In this section we are going to take a look at how speech recognition is accomplished in a computer. One of the most complex and difficult functions to implement, it is a combination of sophisticated electronic hardware and a computer capable of running advanced artificial intelligence software.

Applications of Speech Recognition

With a voice recognition system, you can speak commands and input data. For example, today if you want to examine the list of files on drive B in your personal computer, you would type the command DIR B: to call up a list of all the files on the disk in drive B. At that point you can determine which file you want to use. With a speech recognition system, you could achieve the same result by speaking into a microphone something like, "Show me the files on drive B."

Given a more advanced system, you would be able to enter a letter into your word processor by dictating it. Once the letter was entered, you could use the normal word processing editing functions to make changes and additions. In a similar application, you might enter or retrieve records in a DBMS or provide number values to a spreadsheet by simply speaking them. While such systems are not yet available, it won't be long before they are. Voice recognition systems are more limited today but still useful in some applications.

While voice input is now practical reality for computers, most users are still more comfortable with standard keyboard entry. Despite the fact that speech is our primary method of communications, we have grown used to communicating with computers via a keyboard. Few individuals are comfortable speaking into a microphone to use the computer. People feel self-conscious about talking to a machine. Although most people speak easily over the telephone, they become uncomfortable and tongue-tied when there is an automatic answering machine on the other end of the line. In the same way, many individuals are too self-conscious or embarrassed to use a dictating machine. Many feel that it is abnormal to "speak to yourself." While such discomforts can be overcome, it does not appear likely there will be a mass changeover from keyboard to voice input in the typical office environment. Perhaps that is good. In the average, there would be considerable confusion and interference with multiple individuals speaking to their computers simultaneously.

As it turns out, there aren't too many applications in the office where it is absolutely necessary or even that desirable to have voice input to a computer. Yet it is now available if desired. Further, there are many other applications besides normal office use where voice input is not only desirable but greatly improves productivity.

Earlier we said one of the main benefits of speech input is that it frees the user's hands and eyes for other purposes. Consider a situation where a computer controls various machines and processes in a factory. Users of such systems are frequently occupied with observing the process and manually handling materials or controlling other machines. In such cases, it is inconvenient to type commands to perform control functions on the computer. If a speech recognition system is used, the user can concentrate on observation and manual operations, yet still control the machinery by voice input commands.

Consider the situation where conveyor belts are used to transport goods from one place to another. During this process, a human operator may be examining or otherwise handling the objects being moved. It may be convenient to simply say "Stop" rather than to push a button or type in a command on a computer to stop the conveyor belt. The movement of the conveyor belt could easily be restarted by simply saying "Start." Other machines can be controlled in a similar way. Commands such as forward, backward, up, or down might be used.

Some airlines use voice control systems to sort baggage by destination. The baggage handler may put the luggage on a main conveyor belt, then state the name of the destination city into a microphone. The appropriate piece of luggage is then routed to the correct place by another belt.

Inventory control is another excellent application. In taking inventory, users must have their hands and eyes free to deal with the objects being counted. Voice input permits the object to be identified and counted verbally. This saves considerable time over keyboarding.

A major application of speech processing is in military systems. Voice control of weapons is an example. Again, any time that a user's hands and eyes must be free to perform other activities, speech recognition is of benefit. In combat, soldiers or sailors need all the help they can get.

Jet fighter pilots have their hands full flying the plane, yet on most military aircraft today there are a number of computers which must be given commands and data. Often a second person must be on-board to handle such operations. But now, with reliable speech recognition equipment, pilots can give commands and information to the computers by simply speaking into their microphones.

Speech recognition systems are also ideal for any application where voice rather than a keyboard is normally used. For instance, voice recognition equipment can be used on computers for making airline and hotel reservations. A user would call up the airline reservation service and simply state a particular need to the computer. You could make a reservation, cancel a reservation, or make inquiries about schedules.

Speech recognition would also make large data bases available by telephone. You would simply call up the data base, state the desired information, and it would be provided to you by telephone. A voice synthesizer converts the binary output data into a verbal response.

To date, voice recognition systems have not been widely used with computers. The primary reason is that such systems have been limited, unreliable, and costly. But today, through a combination of technology breakthroughs, speech recognition systems are overcoming these deficiencies. They are now a practical alternative for many limited applications. While not perfect, their performance is excellent if their use is focused or constrained. Further developments are expected to bring additional improvement.

Classifying Speech Recognizers

Speech recognizers are classified in several different ways. First, there are systems that recognize individual words and others that recognize continuous speech. Second, those systems are further classified as either speaker dependent or speaker independent. Let's see what we mean by these terms.

Word Recognizers

A word recognizer, as its title implies, is a speech recognition system that identifies individual words. Such systems are capable of recognizing only a small vocabulary of single words or possibly simple phrases. To give commands or data to a computer using one of these systems, you must state the input information in clearly definable single words given one after another. There should be definite spaces between the words; they should not be run together.

Creating the hardware and software that will recognize human speech is difficult. The first practical speech recognizers were of the word recognition type. Early pioneering systems were even simpler in that they recognized only individual letters of the alphabet and numbers. Today, the majority of word recognition systems are word recognizers. Most of them have a better than 95% recognition accuracy.

Continuous Speech Recognizers

These speech recognition units, of course, recognize a continuous flow of words. You can speak to them in complete sentences, and your input will be recognized and understood. Continuous speech recognizers are far more difficult to build. The difficulty lies in separating one word from another in a continuous phrase or sentence. When we speak, most of the words slur together in one continuous stream. It is difficult for such a system to know where one word ends and another begins. Far more sophisticated and complex techniques must be used to deal with continuous speech.

Today there are very few practical continuous speech systems in use. Most of them are research and experimental systems made on very large and expensive computers. Many of them do not even operate on real time. That is, the information spoken is not recognized instantly as it is with word recognition systems. It may take many minutes for only a few seconds of speech to be analyzed and understood. Yet, progress is being made. There are some practical continuous speech recognition systems now on the market with extremely limited vocabularies.

Speaker Dependent

A speaker dependent system means that the system has been customized to the voice of a particular individual. Because there is such wide variation in speech quality from one person to another, it is difficult to build electronic and computer systems that will recognize anyone's voice. By limiting the system to the voice of one person, the system is not only simpler but also more reliable.

Speaker Independent

Speaker independent systems, of course, mean that anyone can use the system. The speech recognizer is designed to be as versatile as possible so that even though voice characteristics may vary widely from one speaker to another, the system can recognize them. Most speaker independent systems are incredibly complex and costly. They also have very limited vocabularies.

How Speech Recognition Systems Work

All types of speech recognition systems use the same basic techniques. The voice input to the microphone produces an analog speech signal. This speech signal is then converted into binary words compatible with a digital computer by an analog-to-digital converter. The binary version of the input voice is then stored in the system and compared to previously stored binary representations of words and phrases. The computer searches through the previously stored speech patterns and compares them one at a time to the current speech input. When a match occurs, recognition is achieved. Once recognition

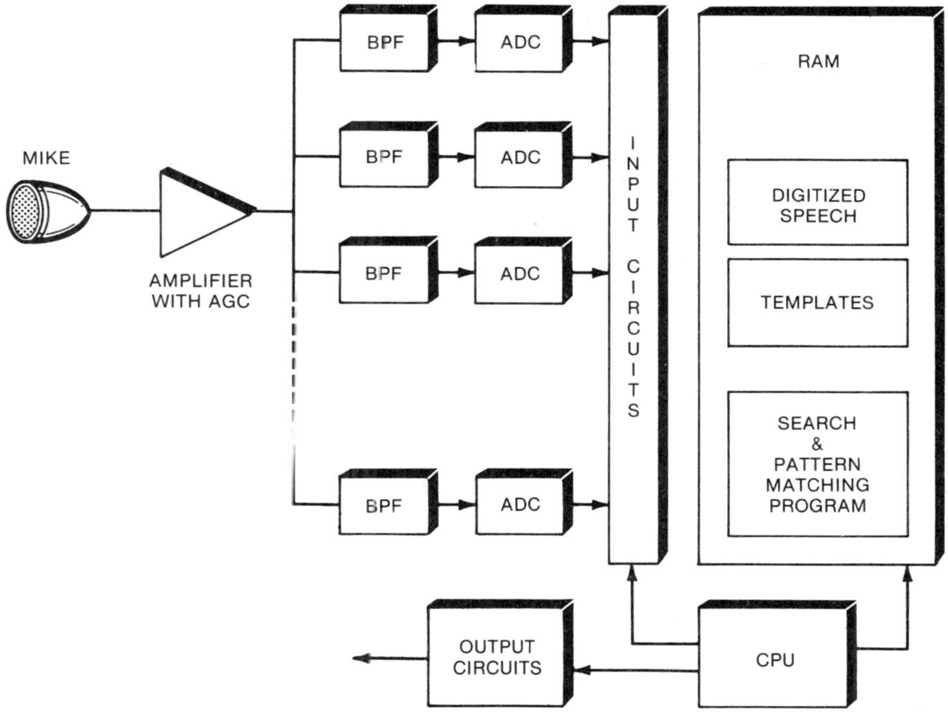

Figure 6–7. *A speaker dependent word recognition speech recognizer.*

is achieved, the spoken word in binary form is then written on a video screen or passed along to a natural language understanding processor for additional analysis.

A Typical Word Recognizer

Now let's be a little more specific by looking in more detail at a typical speaker dependent word recognizer. Refer to the Figure 6–7. The voice input is applied to a microphone. The microphone can be the kind that is attached to a stand that sits on a desk. Alternately it can be attached to a small extension on a headset. In any case, the electrical analog signal from the microphone is fed to an amplifier where it is increased in level. The amplifier will contain some kind of automatic gain control (AGC) to provide an output signal in a specific voltage range even though the input signal may vary from weak to loud or anything between.

The analog signal representing a spoken word is a complex waveform that contains many individual frequencies. It may look something like that shown in Figure 6–8. Such complex waveforms are made of signals of individual frequencies of various amplitudes and phase relationships combined. The way to recognize the spoken word is to break that complex input signal into its component parts. This is usually done with a set of filters. A filter is an electronic circuit that passes or rejects frequencies in a certain range. In speech recognition equipment, bandpass filters (BPF) are used. These filters pass frequencies only in a certain frequency range. All others are rejected. In

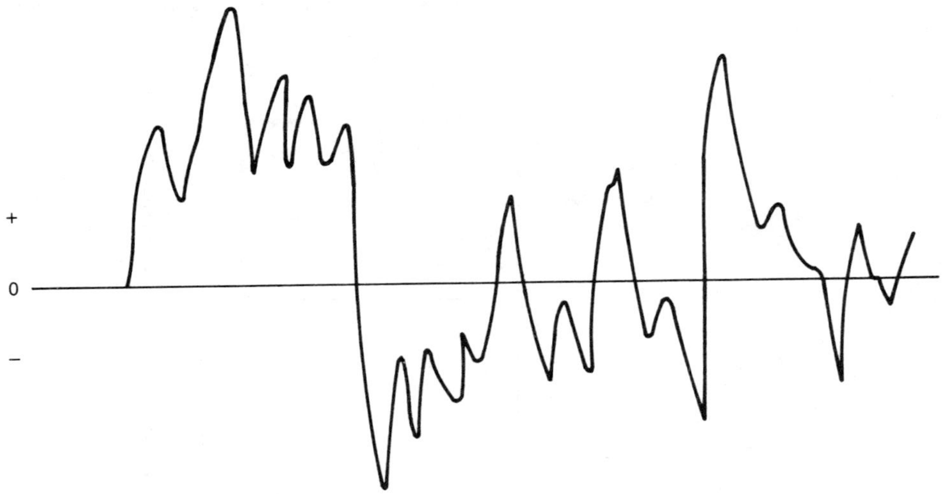

Figure 6–8. ***An AC analog signal representing a spoken word.***

some simple systems, a minimum of three filters is used to pass the low, medium, and high frequency components of the input signal. In more complex systems, as many as 16 to 32 filters are used. Of course, the more filters used, the more precise the analysis of the signal and, therefore, the higher probability of accurate recognition.

The filters themselves can be implemented in a variety of ways. In early systems standard inductor-capacitor filters were used. Active filters using operational amplifiers with resistor-capacitor feedback networks have also been used. Today, however, switched capacitor digital filters are widely used, simply because they can be implemented in integrated circuit form. They are smaller and less expensive than other types of filters.

The filter outputs are then fed to analog-to-digital converters (ADC). The analog signals are thus translated into digital words. The analog-to-digital converter samples the filter outputs many times per second. Each sample represents a different amplitude of the signal as shown in Figure 6–9. Evenly spaced vertical lines designate the amplitude of the audio filter output at the instant of sampling. Each value is then converted to a binary number proportional to the amplitude of the sample. The ADCs feed input

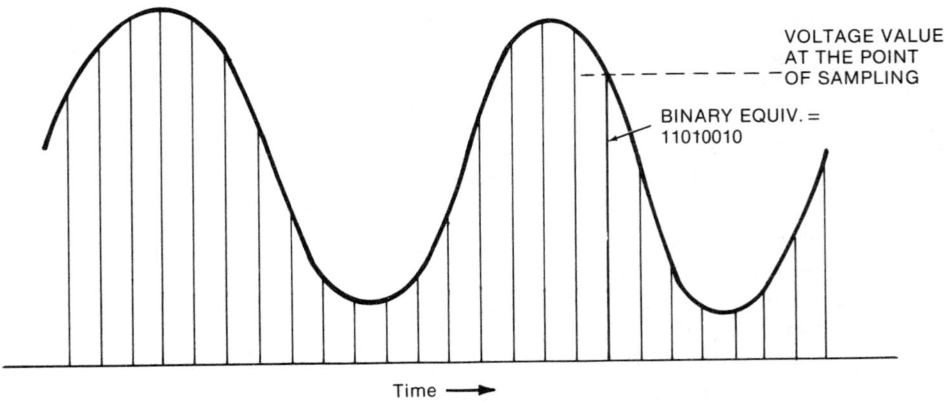

Figure 6–9. ***How filter outputs are sampled and converted to binary form by an ADC.***

circuits controlled by the CPU. All of the digital values are stored in a buffer area in a large random access memory (RAM). This digital information represents the spoken word. The central processing unit (CPU) may now access the information in the RAM and process it further.

In speaker dependent word recognition systems, the computer must first be taught to recognize the input words of a particular speaker. This process is referred to as training or enrollment. The speaker planning to use the system is asked to speak all of the words he plans to use so that they may be recorded by the system. As each word is stated, it is processed by the filters and analog-to-digital converters. The binary representation of each of these words becomes a template or standard against which future spoken words will be compared. The templates for each of the words are retained in memory. Some systems require that the speaker say each word multiple times so that multiple templates of the same word are created. Then, a special processing program generates the final template which is an average of the multiple inputs.

Once all the templates are stored away, the system can go into its active mode. Now it will recognize the spoken words. As each word is spoken, it is processed and its binary equivalent stored in RAM. Then the computer goes to work. A search routine begins looking through the templates comparing them to the binary input pattern. As you can imagine, even in speaker dependent systems rarely is the input word said exactly the same way each time. There will be slight variations in amplitude or loudness of the signal. Further, the pronunciation of the word may take more or less time. The word may also be said at a different pitch, meaning with a higher or lower frequency. In any case, even if the word is said as closely as possible each time, there will be variations. For that reason, there will never be a perfect match between the binary input word and the template. The search and pattern matching program, therefore, is designed to look for the "best fit." The pattern-matching process uses statistical techniques to do this.

One pattern-matching technique causes all of the values of the binary input word to be subtracted from those in the corresponding values in the template. If the values are the same, the difference will be zero. Since the values won't perfectly match, the subtraction will produce some difference or error. The smaller the error, the better the match.

Once the computer searches its memory comparing the templates to the spoken input word, at some point a best match will occur. It is at that point that the word is identified. A binary or ASCII version of that word may then be passed along to the video display or used in some other manner.

As you can see, a considerable amount of processing must take place before a word is recognized. The search process takes a considerable amount of time. Even though the CPU may be able to process at a high rate of speed, it must make many comparisons before recognition occurs. This means that very high speed processors are required.

In addition, memory sizes in word recognition systems are large. Even though a spoken word may last only a few hundred milliseconds, that will translate into many thousands of binary words stored in memory. In order for the system to have a large vocabulary, a large RAM is necessary. Various data conversion techniques have been developed to reduce the number of binary words in a template. Although this does reduce the memory requirement, it is still nevertheless significant.

It is important to point out that the RAM and CPU shown in Figure 6–7 do not belong to a general purpose computer. Instead, they are part of the speech recognition system itself. To minimize the computation burden on the computer to which the unit is attached, a dedicated RAM and CPU are used to handle the search, pattern matching, and other chores.

Continuous Speech Systems

While continuous speech systems use the same basic techniques, they are more complex yet. They normally have larger vocabularies and a higher processing speed to achieve real time recognition. The main problem in continuous recognition is that it is difficult to distinguish individual words. If the continuous speech is inputted as individual words with short pauses between them, the system will be far simpler and more reliable. A pause of 50 to 300 milliseconds is sufficient for the system to identify the beginnings and endings of adjacent words. However, if true continuous speech is to be processed, other approaches must be taken. In continuous speech, words are run together. In such cases more sophisticated processing techniques are needed.

One approach is to use phoneme rather than word analysis. A *phoneme* is the smallest recognizable unit of speech in a language. It is not a word, but a distinctive sound. A typical phoneme is the pronunciation of an individual letter or group of letters to produce a distinctive sound. A phoneme is to the spoken word what letters of the alphabet are to the written word. There are approximately 40 phonemes in the English language, and all English words are simply a continuous stream of phonemes.

Speech recognition systems using phoneme analysis contain phoneme templates stored in RAM. The input words are converted into their binary form and then matched against the phonemes in RAM. As each phoneme is recognized, it is grouped with others in an effort to form words. The resulting combinations are then matched against known words in the system. Phoneme analysis is far more difficult and time consuming, but produces superior results in continuous speech systems.

Another approach used in continuous speech systems is to attempt to predict which word will come after another. In certain systems where the input possibilities are limited, it is possible to anticipate the input and store many different variations of it. Once the first word in the speech is identified, the system goes along to predict which one of several words may follow next. This in turn leads to a prediction of the next word in sequence and so on. In this way, the entire input statement can be identified.

Because of the complexity of continuous speech techniques, it will be some time yet before general purpose real time systems will be available. More research plus some technology breakthroughs will be required to create useable systems. Today, a few very limited continuous speech systems are available. But word recognition units dominate because they are reliable and modestly priced.

Key Points

- Natural language refers to the system we use in verbal or written communications with others, such as English or German.

- A language is a system of symbols and rules which we use to express our ideas, thoughts, and feelings.
- Most communication with computers is difficult because it takes place via special artificial or formal languages made up of un-English-like commands, symbols, and procedures.
- Computers are easier to use and more useful if we use natural language in dealing with them.
- Special artificial intelligence techniques known as natural language processing (NLP) have been developed to allow man-machine communications to take place in man's natural language.
- The main objective of an NLP program is to "understand" the input and initiate some action.
- A common type of NLP program uses key word analysis. The input words are scanned and matched against internally stored "known" words. Identification of a key word causes some action to be taken.
- ELIZA, an early and very famous key word matching program, acts like a Rogerian psychiatrist.
- The most powerful NLP programs perform a syntactical and semantic analysis on an input sentence.
- The syntax or grammar of the sentence is determined by a program called a parser that breaks the sentence into its various parts of speech. The parser works in conjunction with a lexicon or dictionary of known words.
- The meaning of the parsed sentence is determined by semantic analysis. This is done by referencing a knowledge base that makes sense out of the various words.
- Some NLP programs contain a text generator that outputs "canned" statements or develops original replies in response to the natural language input. Sometimes the generator develops special codes to drive other software.
- The main application of NLP is in interfaces or front-ends to other software. These interfaces let anyone command a computer using natural language rather than a special language. This makes computers easier to use.
- The major use of natural language front-ends is on data base management systems (DBMS). However, they can be adapted to any other type of software as well.
- Natural language add-on interfaces are available for mainframes, minicomputers, and personal computers. The trend is to build the NLP program into the software.
- A major application of NLP is language translation, converting one natural language to another, thereby helping to overcome language barriers.
- Translators are also available to convert one computer language into another. This allows programs to be more transportable.
- Grammar analysis is another NLP use. Grammar analyzers examine input text to correct spelling and punctuation errors and to identify grammatical problems for the purpose of improving the quality of written documents.

- NLP is also used in abstracting articles or other documents. The result is a concise summary of the key points.
- Speech or voice recognition is the process of converting verbal inputs into electronic signals that a computer can understand.
- Most computer input is done by keyboard. Voice input has some advantages in that it frees a user's eyes and hands for other chores.
- Speech recognizers take the analog voice input, filter it and convert it into binary patterns that are stored in memory. These are matched against prestored templates.
- Most speech recognizers only understand single words and are customized to a specific application. Continuous speech recognizers with limited vocabularies are also available.

7

Computer Vision

Among the blind, the one-eyed man is king.

ANONYMOUS

In the previous chapters, you have seen how the various AI techniques are used to simulate the thinking and reasoning process. But as you know, the human brain does more than just pure thinking and reasoning. It is the central interpreter for all of our senses. The brain must have inputs about its surroundings to control the body. Our senses provide those inputs.

As you know, there are five basic senses: sight, hearing, smell, taste, and touch. Of all these senses, our sight is probably the most valuable. Our eyes provide more input than virtually all the other senses combined. Hearing is our second most important sense. You have already seen in the previous chapter how computer hearing is implemented. In this chapter, we cover artificial sight: the computer becomes a seeing machine. Today's computer vision systems are crude compared to real human sight, but they are performing many useful functions.

The Computer Vision Process

A computer mimics human sight in four basic steps. These are image acquisition, image processing, image analysis, and image understanding. Let's consider each of these steps in more detail.

Image Acquisition

Image acquisition translates visual information into a format that can be further manipulated by the brain. For starters then, a computer vision system needs an eye. In most computer vision systems, that eye is a TV camera. The camera translates a scene or image into electrical signals. These signals can be translated into binary numbers which the computer can work with.

The output of the television camera is an analog signal whose frequency and amplitude represent the brightness detail in a scene. The camera observes a scene a line at a time, scanning and dividing it into hundreds of fine horizontal lines. Each line creates an analog signal whose amplitude represents the brightness changes along that line.

Digital computers cannot deal with analog signals. For that reason, an analog-to-digital converter is required. The analog- to-digital converter (ADC) converts the analog signal representing one line of information into a stream of many binary numbers. These are stored in a memory and become the raw data which the computer will process.

Image Processing

The next stage of computer vision involves some initial manipulation of the binary data. Image processing helps improve the quality of the image to analyze and comprehend it more efficiently. Image processing improves the signal-to-noise ratio. The signal, of course, is information representing objects in the image. Noise is any interference, flaw, or aberration that obscures the objects. Through various computational means, it is possible to improve the signal-to-noise ratio. For example, the contrast in a scene can be improved. Flaws, such as unwanted reflections, can be removed. The process is somewhat akin to retouching a photograph to improve its quality. Once the image has been cleaned up and enhanced, it is ready for analysis.

Image Analysis

Image analysis explores the scene to determine what is there. A computer program begins looking through the numbers that represent the visual information to identify specific features and characteristics. More specifically, the image analysis program looks for edges and boundaries. An edge, of course, is formed between an object and its background or between two specific objects. These boundaries or edges are identifiable because of different brightness levels on either side of the boundary. The computer produces a simple line drawing of all of the objects in the scene, just as an artist would draw outlines of all the objects.

Image analysis also looks for textures and shadings between lines. Both are useful in future processing to help identify the scene.

At this point, a considerable amount of computer processing has taken place. Yet, objects still have not been identified and the scene is not yet understood. However, the processing has prepared the image for that major step.

Image Comprehension

The final step in the computer vision process is understanding, by identifying specific objects and their relationship. This portion of the computer vision process employs

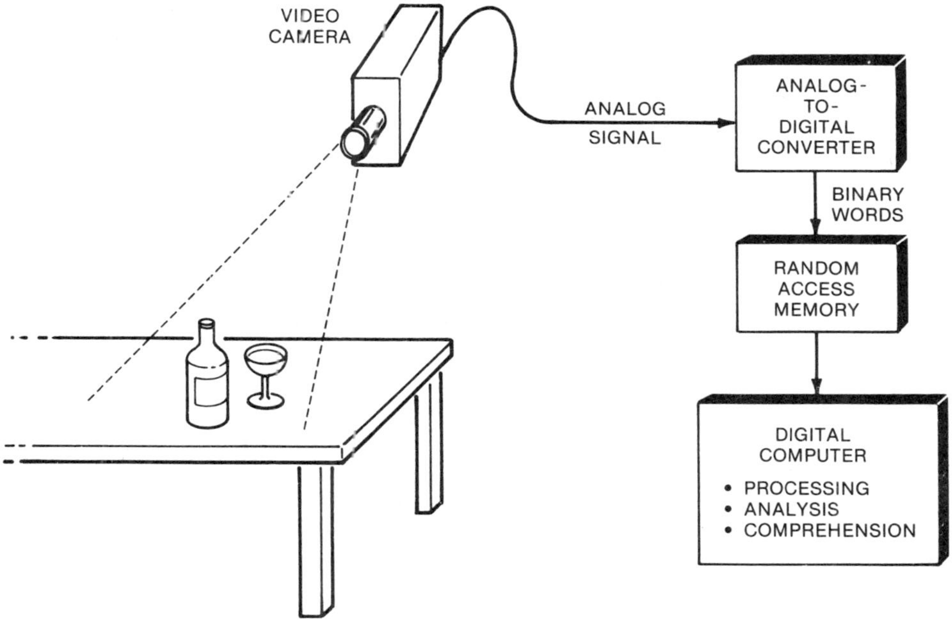

Figure 7–1. ***Image acquisition.***

artificial intelligence techniques. The previous steps of image processing and analysis were done with algorithms. Now, symbolic processing will be used to understand the scene.

Understanding what is in a scene requires template matching. The computer is preprogrammed with prestored binary images or templates that represent specific objects. Using a search program and pattern-matching techniques, the computer looks through the binary information representing the scene and compares it to the various templates. When a match occurs, an object is identified. This template matching process continues until all of the information in the scene has been analyzed and all of the objects have been identified. The computer then knows what is being viewed.

Now that you understand the process involved in computer vision, let's expand upon each of these four major steps.

Image Acquisition

As mentioned earlier, a TV camera translates the scene to be analyzed into signals. These analog signals are then translated into binary form by an analog-to-digital converter. The binary numbers are stored in RAM, then processed by the computer. Figure 7–1 illustrates the concept.

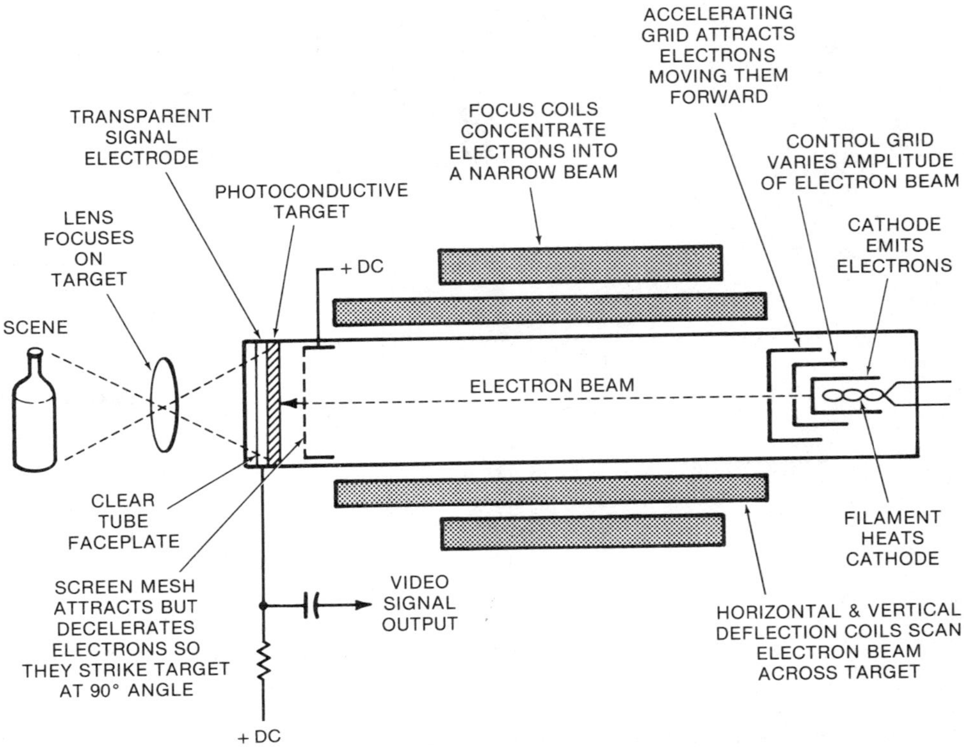

Figure 7–2. ***Vidicon tube.***

Video Cameras

The two devices most commonly used in computer vision cameras to convert light into an electrical signal are the vidicon tube and a CCD array. The vidicon tube has been around for many years and is still the primary device used in commercial television cameras. However, for computer vision systems, charged coupled devices (CCD's) are far more widely used. These semiconductor devices offer smaller size, greater light sensitivity, and lower power operation than vidicons. However, since both the vidicon and the CCD are still used, we will discuss both of them here.

Vidicon Tubes

Figure 7–2 shows a simplified drawing of a vidicon tube. The key component in this tube is in the photoconductive target on the left. The lens focuses the scene to be viewed on the target, and the target stores the scene in the form of an electrical charge. The electrical conductivity of the target varies with the amount of light absorbed. Where there is minimum light, the material has a high electrical resistance. The points on the target with considerable light have a lower resistance.

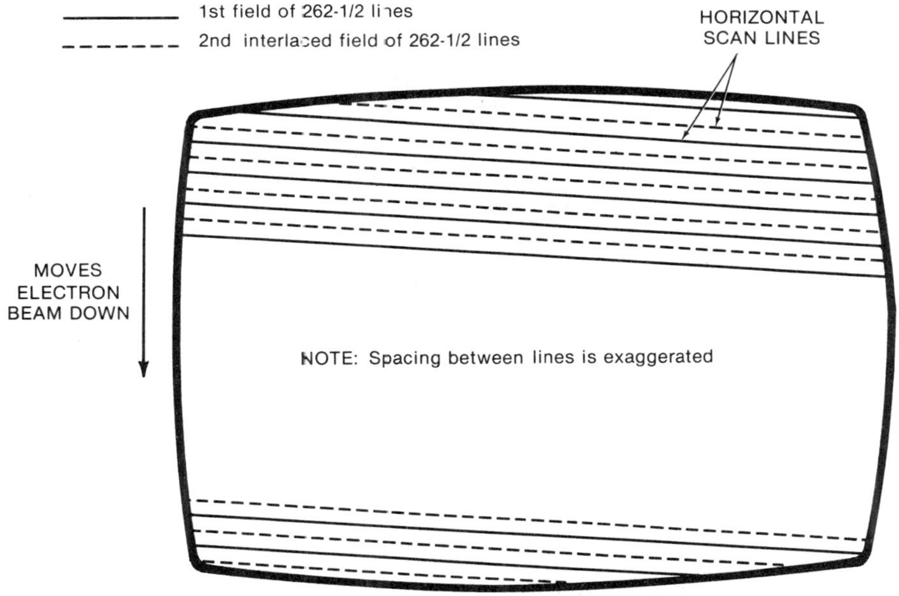

Figure 7–3. ***Interlaced scanning of the target.***

The remainder of the tube consists of an electron gun with surrounding magnetic coils. The cathode of the electron gun generates a stream of electrons focused into a narrow beam to strike the inside of the target. Other magnetic coils surround the vidicon tube to produce horizontal and vertical deflection of the electron beam. Signals applied to these coils cause the electron beam to scan from left to right and top to bottom across the inside of the target. This causes a current to flow between the target and the transparent signal electrode. This current is proportional to the light amplitude. This is the video output signal.

Numerous methods are used for scanning the target, but most systems use the standard NTSC pattern of 525 total scanning lines. Figure 7–3 illustrates the concept. As the electron beam scans the target, an electrical signal is generated. The varying amplitude in the signal represents brightness variation along one of the scan lines. As soon as one line is scanned, the vertical deflection signals move the electron beam a small distance farther down, and another horizontal scan line is developed. Special synchronization pulses designate the beginning and end of each horizontally scanned line. The signal thus developed appears as shown in Figure 7–4. The horizontal sync pulse is approximately 5 microseconds wide and occurs at a frequency of 15,750 Hz.

The total number of horizontal scanning lines is 525, but the way in which the target is scanned is unusual. In effect, the scanning takes place as two separate fields of 262½ lines, each occurring every 1/60th of a second. The scan lines of the two fields are interlaced to produce a completely scanned image every 1/30th of a second. Of the 525 total lines, only about 480 of them are actually designated to the scene itself. The remaining 22½ lines per field occur but are not seen. This provides time for the electron beam to retrace from bottom to top. Special sync pulses included in this interval keep the lines properly synchronized and meshed.

The electrical output signal shown in Figure 7–4 has an approximate voltage range of .7 volts (black) to 1.5 volts (white). Voltage levels between these two values,

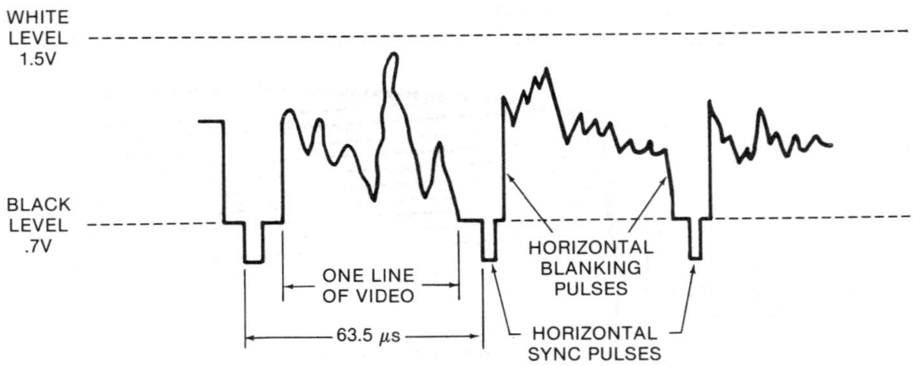

Figure 7–4. ***The video signal with sync pulses.***

of course, represent varying shades of gray. The analog video signal between the sync pulses represents the light intensity variations on one scan line. It is this voltage that will be fed to the analog-to-digital converter for translation into binary numbers.

Charge Coupled Devices

A CCD is a light sensitive integrated circuit designed to convert a rectangular visual image into a video electrical signal. A lens system focuses the scene onto a photoconductive substrate such as silicon. This device absorbs the light and stores it as a charge on thousands of tiny square or rectangular capacitors. See Figure 7–5. The silicon forms a single common plate for all of these capacitors. The other plates are individual tiny metal electrodes separated from the silicon photoconductor by a thin layer of silicon dioxide insulator. Light falling on the substrate causes the capacitors to charge and discharge to a level depending upon the intensity of the light striking the substrate directly below the tiny capacitive plates.

To "read" the scene, voltages are applied to the capacitor electrodes in sequence from right to left. As the control voltage is applied, the capacitor is discharged and an analog signal is transferred to the common silicon substrate.

The tiny capacitive cells in the CCD are arranged in a rectangular or square array. Typical array sizes are 64 × 64, 244 × 190, 488 × 380, and 512 × 512. Figure 7–6 shows a segment of a CCD array. The larger the number of capacitive storage cells, the greater the resolution. High resolution means good definition of detail.

The output signal from the CCD varies from approximately 0 to 1 volt, with the two extremes representing black and white respectively. Interlace scanning is not used. Instead, each row of the CCD matrix is scanned in turn. Each row in the matrix, of course, represents one scan line of the scene focused on the light sensitive array.

CCD video cameras are preferred for computer vision. They are small, highly sensitive, and very reliable. They are also more rugged than the delicate vidicon tubes, and they do not require a filament voltage or the high voltage required by the vidicon. Their light weight and low power consumption makes them extremely small and portable. These units are also less expensive than vidicon cameras.

One final important point should be made. Both vidicon and the CCD cameras produce a black and white analog video signal output. These cameras do not recognize

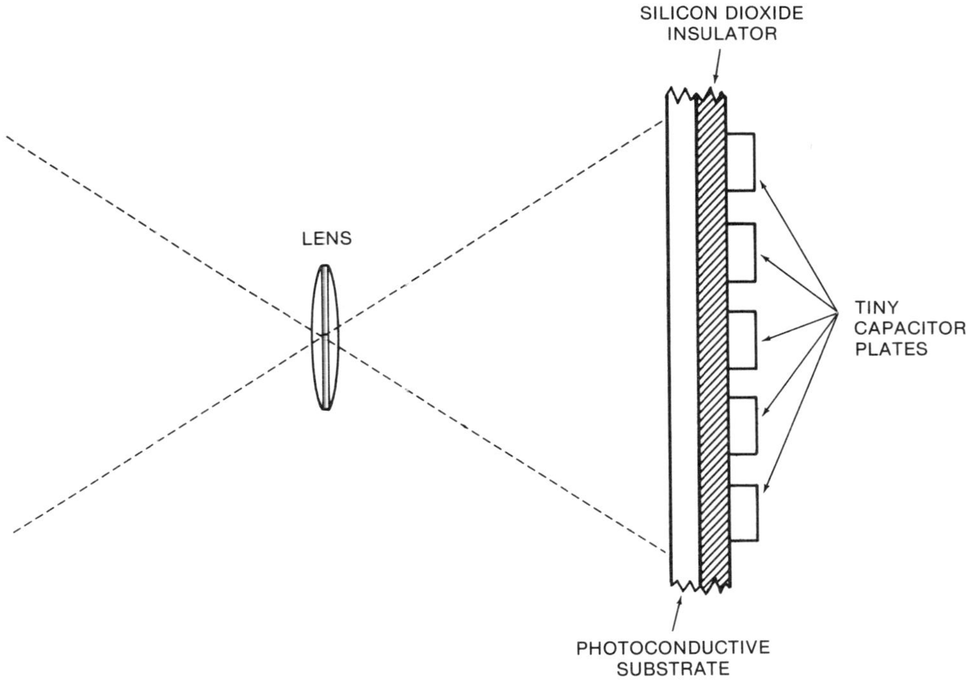

Figure 7–5. ***Cross section of a CCD IC.***

color and generate an output signal that represents gray levels between black and white. All computer vision systems are black and white. Color systems can be created, of course, but they are far more complex and expensive. Yet color adds information that makes it easier for a computer to recognize shapes, objects, background, and other characteristics of the scene. Because they are so complex and rare, color computer vision systems will not be discussed here.

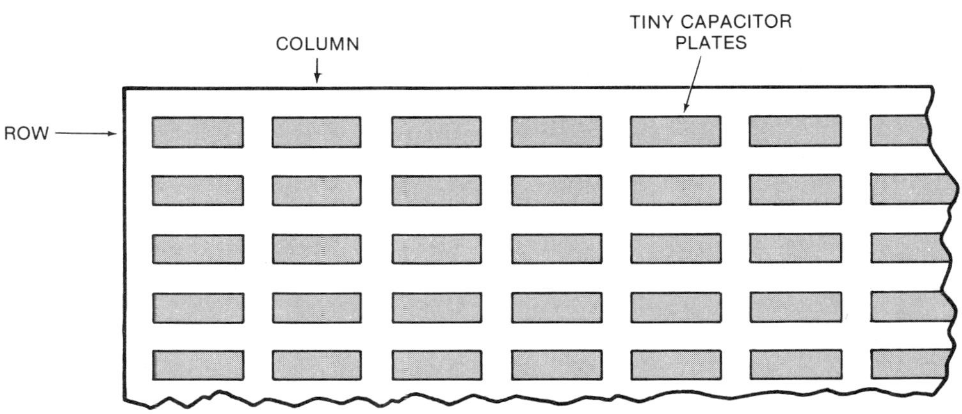

Figure 7–6. ***Segment of CCD matrix.***

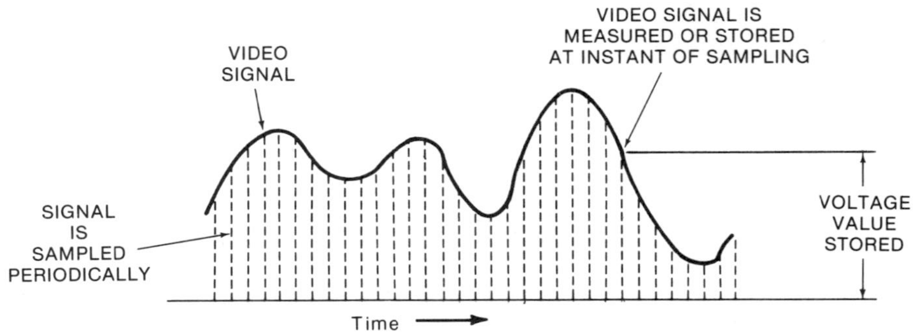

Figure 7–7. ***Sampling a video signal.***

The eye of the master will do more work than both his hands.

BENJAMIN FRANKLIN

Analog-to-Digital Conversion

The video output signal from the camera is fed to an analog-to-digital converter (ADC). The ADC then periodically samples the analog signal and converts the amplitude into a parallel binary number. This sampling process is shown in Figure 7–7. The sampling is usually done by a circuit called a track/store or sample/hold (S/H) amplifier. See Figure 7–8. As the analog signal is applied to the input of the S/H amplifier, a digital clock signal occurring at a fixed rate drives an FET switch in the sample/hold amplifier. During its sample state, the FET conducts and the output of the S/H amplifier is the same as the analog input. The charge on the capacitor follows the input voltage value. When the binary control signal switches states, the FET is cut off and the amplifier stores or holds the value of the analog input signal at the instant the FET cuts off.

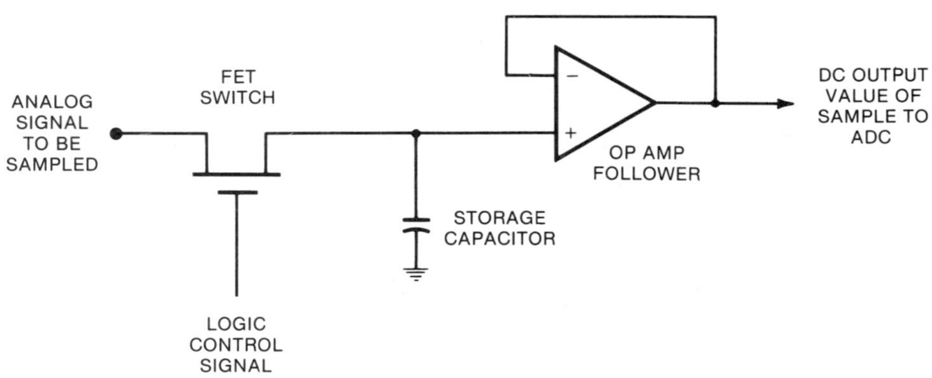

Figure 7–8. ***A sample/hold amplifier.***

That analog voltage level is stored as a charge on a capacitor. The output of the S/H amplifier is then a fixed DC voltage. This signal is then fed to the ADC. The ADC performs a conversion operation and outputs a binary number whose value is proportional to the amplitude of the analog signal.

Many different methods are used to produce analog-to-digital conversion: the counter feedback method, the dual slope method, and the successive approximations method. However, none of these are used in video ADC applications. Instead, special high speed parallel or flash converters are used. These are the only ADCs fast enough to digitize the high frequency video signals.

The light intensities of a single scan line in a scene change at a rapid rate and vary over a wide range of dark to light values. The result is an analog output signal whose frequency varies over a wide range. For some scenes, the output signal may be extremely low audio frequencies, but scenes with considerable detail and wide ranges of light intensities can have an output frequency as high as several MHz. To provide an accurate digital representation of these high frequency signals, the video signal must be sampled at a high rate of speed. The minimum sampling rate is two samples per cycle of the highest input frequency. However, faster sampling is more desirable to provide better definition. In most computer vision systems, a single scan line is sampled 200 to 500 times per line. A scan line takes approximately 60 microseconds to occur. This means that the ADC sampling rate should be approximately once every 120 to 300 nanoseconds. For each sample, the ADC outputs an 8–bit binary number whose value is proportional to the light intensity.

Pixels

Each time the video signal is sampled by the ADC, we say that a pixel has been created. A *pixel* is the value of light intensity at one particular point on a scan line. A pixel, therefore, is a small element into which each scan line is broken. Each scan line will contain approximately 200 to 500 pixels. These samples, then, give a fairly accurate representation of line intensity variation across the scan line. Naturally, the more pixels per line, the higher the definition. In any case, the pixel is a point of light that is, in effect, some shade of gray. That shade of gray is designated by a particular binary number.

The number of output bits in the ADC determines the total number of gray levels to be represented. In some low definition systems, a 4-bit output is satisfactory. With 4 bits, 16 possible gray levels can be represented, i.e., 0000 for black and 1111 for white. For higher definition systems, more bits are used. Eight- and 6-bit ADCs are common. Eight-bit ADCs are more popular today as they provide 256 individual gray levels, providing extremely fine detail. Further, 8 bits is a standard word size widely used in digital computers. An 8-bit word is referred to as a byte and most digital computers are capable of processing at the byte level.

By sampling the video signal we are converting each scan line into dots of light of varying gray levels. The effect is to represent the entire scene by a matrix of pixels as shown in Figure 7–9. Each pixel represents a light value occurring during the sampling process.

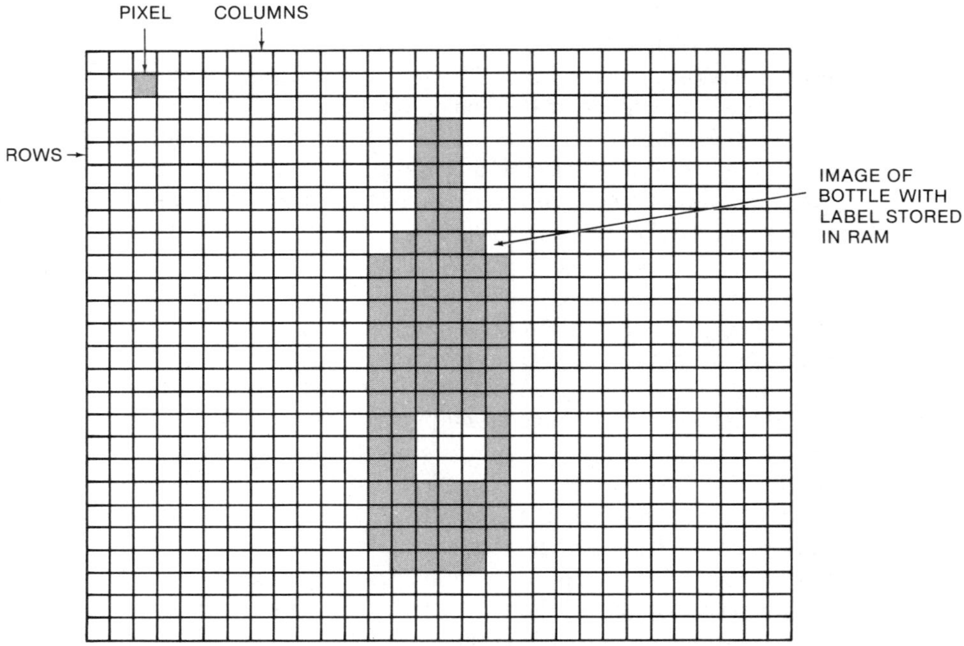

Figure 7–9. ***All scenes are represented as rows and columns of pixels of varying gray shades.***

RAM

Each pixel is represented by an 8-bit binary number that is stored in a large random access memory (RAM). Semiconductor RAM chips are used in these memories. Their storage access time must be extremely fast to accept the high speed output from the ADC. The memory must be very large to store the many pixel bytes that make up a scene. For example, if a 512 × 512 CCD is used, the scene will contain 512 × 512 = 262,144 pixels. This means that a RAM capable of storing 262,144 (256K where 1K = 1024) bytes.

In most computer vision systems, this RAM is separate from the RAM used in the computer. It is usually called a buffer RAM or frame buffer, where frame refers to the digitized scene. Image storage requirements are demanding, as you can see, and this burden is not put on the computer. Computer vision systems have their own dedicated RAM.

At this point, the computer has stored in its memory a digital representation of a scene to be analyzed and understood. Once this binary image of the scene is in memory, the computer can take over and perform many different operations on the scene to enhance it, analyze it, translate it into different forms, and to ultimately comprehend what is there.

Monitors

Most computer vision systems also include a *video monitor,* a TV set without the channel tuning mechanism, for viewing the scene the camera sees. Its main component is a cathode ray tube whose electron beam scans across the phosporous face converting electron beam intensity into light variations. It is useful for the operator of a computer vision system to know exactly what the camera sees and what the computer has stored in its memory. One easy way to do this is to feed the video signal from the output of the camera directly into the video monitor. This lets the operator point the camera, focus it, or otherwise make adjustments so it will show exactly what is wanted.

Some computer vision systems also allow you to translate the binary image stored in RAM back into video for display on the monitor. This is done by feeding the binary numbers one at a time to a digital-to-analog converter (DAC). A DAC is the reverse of an ADC in that it takes binary numbers and converts them into an analog output. Each binary input value produces a specific fixed DC output value. If the values are fed quickly to the DAC, its output changes in discrete increments or steps and recreates an approximation of the analog output signal that was originally digitized. All of the bytes of pixel information from one line are fed to the ADC to the DAC to recreate the analog signal representing one scan line. At the end of the line, a sync pulse is created to cause the electron beam in the CRT to sweep back and begin a new horizontal line. Then the sequence of pixel bytes representing the next scan line are outputted to the DAC and then the monitor. In this way, the scanning process of the camera is recreated and the digitized scene is displayed.

If the sampling rate is very high, the scene displayed on the monitor will be a fairly accurate re-creation of the original input. However, if the sampling rate is low, the picture quality and definition will not be as good. The conversion process distorts the scene but depending upon the application, it is usually acceptable. Figure 7–10 shows a complete diagram of the vision system hardware.

3D to 2D

Video cameras do not see in 3D. What we get is a two-dimensional representation of anything the camera looks at. We see the accurate height and width of our subjects, but the missing dimension is depth or perspective. Without depth information, it is difficult to determine the distance between the camera and the objects being viewed. Further, it is difficult to determine the distances between different objects in the scene. All of this is important information that helps lead to a better understanding of the scene.

A more direct approach to overcoming this problem is to more accurately emulate the human vision system. We are able to perceive depth for one reason, we have two eyes. As a result, the brain gets two similar but slightly different images of a scene because of the spacing between our eyes. These differences in the scene allow the brain to perform a type of "triangularization" that gives us the ability to sense depth and mentally measure distances from ourselves to objects and distances between objects.

To sense depth in a computer vision system, the answer is to use two cameras. This produces binocular or stereo vision which permits depth to be determined.

In 3D vision systems, the same scene is viewed by two cameras as shown in

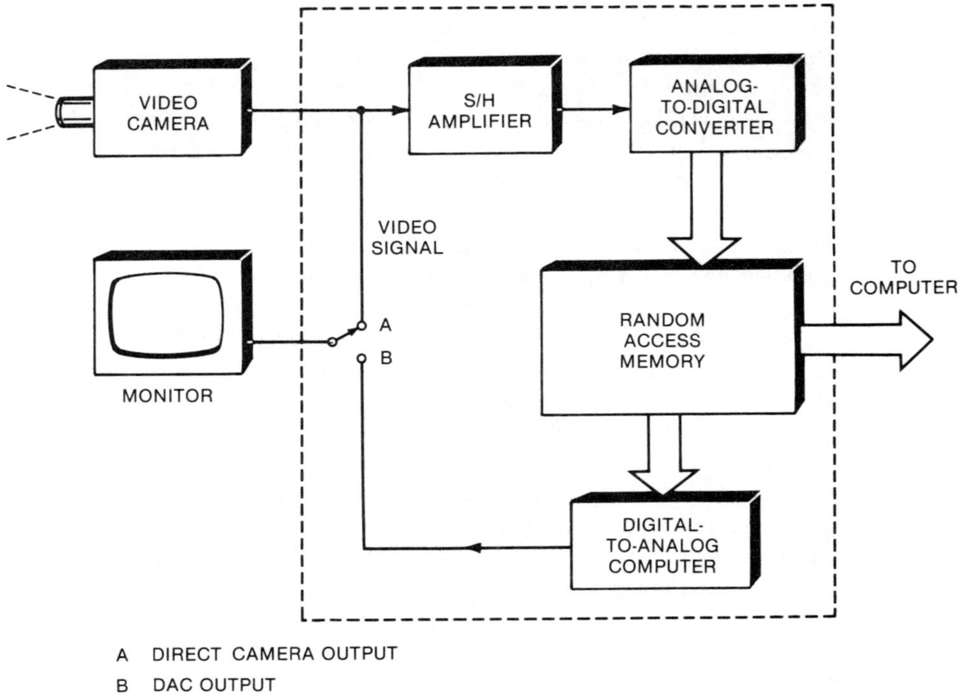

Figure 7–10. ***A computer vision system.***

Figure 7–11. The cameras are usually located at fixed and known distances apart. The scenes from the two cameras are then digitized and stored in memory. Once objects in the scene have been identified, the computer can perform various mathematical operations to help compute the distances to objects and between objects.

Because extra camera and conversion equipment are needed as well as a significant amount of additional memory, 3D computer vision systems are incredibly complex and expensive. The additional software to process the data is also an expense. As a result, few 3D vision systems are used. Only in extremely critical situations can they be justified. Most computer vision systems accept the two dimensional representation and learn to work with it or around it.

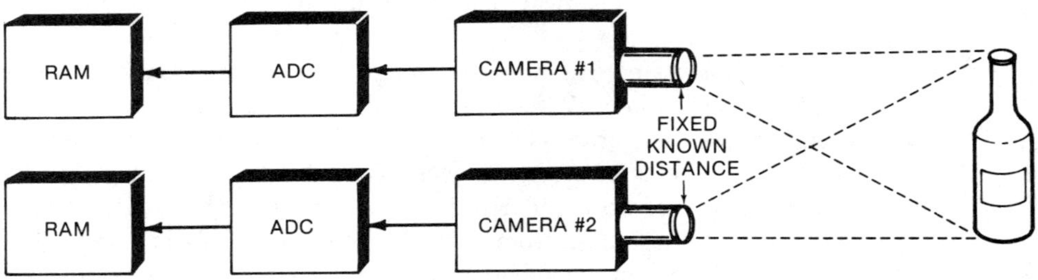

Figure 7–11. ***Stereo or binocular vision with two cameras.***

The eyes believe themselves; the ears believe other people.

OLD GERMAN PROVERB

Image Processing

With the binary version of the scene stored in memory, image processing can now begin. Image processing, also known as image enhancement, is the process of improving the quality of the image. Anything that can be done to make the image clearer will simplify analysis and lead to improved understanding.

From the very instant the light reflected from a scene enters a computer vision system, it is distorted and misrepresented by system imperfections. For instance, the camera lens produces some distortion. Inconsistencies in target area of the vidicon or CCD will produce uneven light intensities. Non-linearities in the scanning process can also introduce distortion. Finally, the imperfect process of analog-to-digital conversion introduces further misrepresentations.

There can be other problems as well. Extremely low light levels can produce a scene which is difficult for the camera to see. The camera itself may not be sensitive enough to clearly capture the fine definition in the scene. The same is true for scenes with excessive brilliance. The camera can go into overload and produce distortions.

Another problem is noise. In an electrical sense, noise is unwanted additions which obscure the desired signal. These may be unusual reflections caused by the texture on the surfaces of the objects being viewed. Noise shows up as "snow" or a salt and pepper background that obscures features in the scene.

Regardless of the source of the degradation of the signal, processing techniques can be used to eliminate or minimize these problems. In fact, many processing techniques are designed to enhance the desired features while ignoring the noise and distortion. This process is known as image enhancement.

Preprocessing

Before image enhancement occurs, some preprocessing can take place to improve the scene. First, optical filtering can be used. Filters can be attached to the lens to control the amount of light, its color, and the contrast of the various objects in the scene. Second, many computer vision systems operate in a controlled environment where it is possible not only to control illumination level, but to position light sources or the objects to be viewed for maximum visibility and comprehension. When a computer vision system is set up, the camera is pointed toward the scene and it is monitored on a video screen. Camera position, objects to be viewed, and, of course, the lighting can be adjusted to help the computer to interpret the scene.

Now let's take a look at some of the ways that the computer can process the binary image stored in memory.

Noise Reduction

Image averaging helps to eliminate noise and distortion. In this process, the vision system captures sequential views of the scene and then averages them. Minor variations may occur in the scene. For example, if the light position changes or if the object moves, the reflections from the various objects in the scene will move. In fact, deliberate movement of the light source sometimes is done simply to provide a different view of the same objects to give the computer more different points to average. As the light source moves, shadows and reflections from the surfaces change. Since this noise is random, averaging it reduces it to a very low level.

In any case, the averaging process takes several views of the scene and stores them in memory. Naturally, the memory must be extremely large to accomplish this. Corresponding pixels in the various binary images are averaged by adding them and dividing by the number of pixels averaged. The result is a composite scene that usually has better clarity.

Gray Scale Modification

Another processing technique is to lighten or darken the scene. This is called *gray scale modification.* Suppose the brightness level of a pixel is represented by an 8-bit binary number where 0 (00000000) represents black and 255 (11111111) represents maximum white. All numerical values in between represent some intermediate shade of gray.

If the scene is very dark, all of the pixels will have low values. One way to process the image is to lighten it up by adding a fixed value to each pixel. The relationship between adjacent pixels is not changed, but the effect is to cause the whole scene to be lightened.

Of course, the opposite operation can also be performed. A very bright scene will have very high pixel values. A fixed value can be subtracted from each pixel value to darken the scene.

Contrast improvement is one type of gray scale modification. Contrast is the range between the darkest and lightest points in an image. Fine detail shows up best when there is high contrast between adjacent pixels. However, the colors of adjacent objects, the intensity or position of the light, and system distortions can obscure edges and boundaries because there is insufficient contrast. In such cases, the contrast can be improved by processing.

This can be done by identifying a range of pixel intensity values to emphasize or stretch. In other words, upper and lower threshold values are set, and any pixel falling in this range would be modified.

Depending on the kind of enhancement needed, modification is done by adding, subtracting, multiplying, or dividing pixel values by a constant. A fixed value could be added to all pixels within a specific range, or the value might be multiplied by a constant. A constant might be subtracted from pixels within another threshold range to make them darker. The effect is to lighten some pixels and darken others. This stretches or improves the contrast to show the fine detail in the scene. What was previously difficult

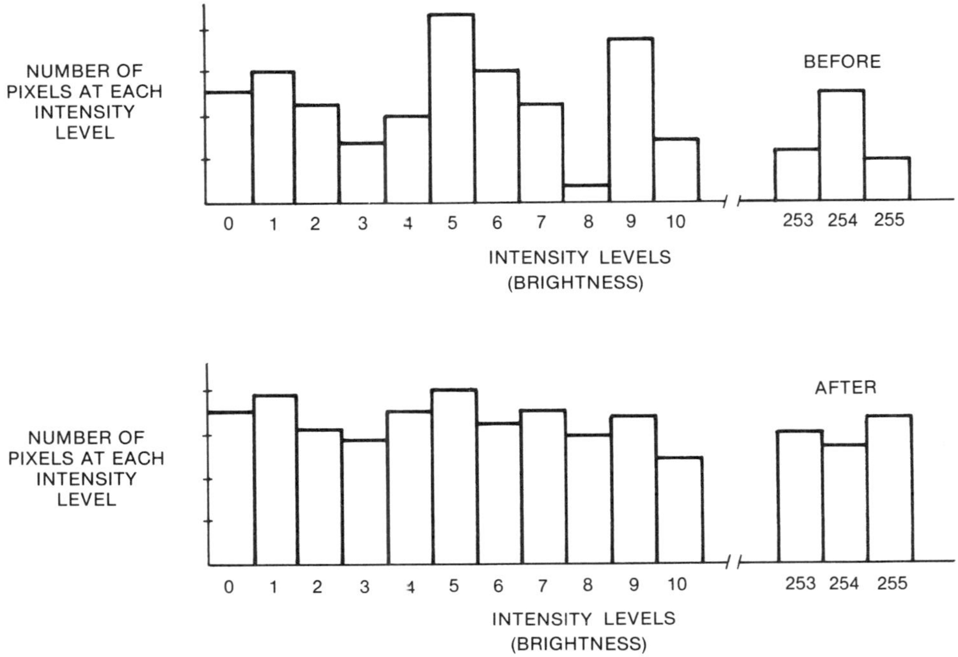

Figure 7–12. ***Histogram flattening to improve detail.***

to see becomes emphasized and thereby much easier to pick out. The resulting scene takes on a somewhat eerie, unnatural look with enhancement, but the features become more distinct.

Histogram Flattening

Another technique that helps improve some images is known as *histogram flattening.* A histogram is a vertical bar chart used to plot statistical information. A histogram can be constructed of the binary image by counting the number of times that each distinct gray level occurs. The result might look like the chart shown in Figure 7–12. With this histogram constructed in memory, a program can determine if there are excessive high or low values. For example, one analysis may discover an unusually high number of very bright or very dark levels. If certain intensity values occur widely throughout the scene, histogram flattening can reduce them. Brightness values which occur only occasionally can be increased.

Again, this process is done by setting threshold levels to divide the total pixel brightness range into blocks of brightness values. Histogram flattening then identifies pixel values within the various ranges and assigns each pixel within that range a new common intensity value. The result, of course, is that the range of intensity values in the scene is greatly reduced. It is as if an A-to-D converter with lower resolution was used. Some loss of information occurs.

Histogram flattening sharpens images by highlighting rare intensity values that occur at boundaries or edges. The more common intensity values which occur over large regions of equal intensity are de-emphasized. In any case, it is a useful technique for attempting to improve the detail in an image before analysis.

Other Applications of Image Processing

As you can imagine, the processing on a binary image can take many forms. Because the computer can perform virtually any mathematical operation, the pixels in a scene can be manipulated in a variety of ways. Besides addition, subtraction, multiplication, and division, pixel processing techniques include calculus functions like differentiation. A whole range of schemes have been developed to improve the quality of a signal.

Image enhancement is a subfield specialty of computer science. You may have seen real life examples of image enhancement. Pictures of the planets received from the spacecraft Voyager have been processed and enhanced in a variety of ways to improve contrast and clarity. The result has been astonishingly good detail.

Picture processing is also used in medicine. The CAT scan uses image processing. CAT stands for *computer assisted tomography.* A series of x-ray images of cross sections of the human body are taken sequentially as the body is passed through the system. The x-ray images are then converted to binary format and processed mathematically to give an incredibly detailed, three-dimensional view of the body and its organs.

Image processing is also used in radar and sonar. Radio signals reflected from a target are received and converted into binary numbers. These are subjected to mathematical processing to improve clarity, definition, and identification of the target. Sonar signals, sound reflections from an underwater target, are digitized and processed to identify the target.

Once we have processed and enhanced our scene, we have a new binary image of it stored in memory. The scene is now ready for image analysis.

Vision: the art of seeing things invisible.

JONATHAN SWIFT

Image Analysis

Up to this point we have been generally vague in describing the scene. It could be an outdoor landscape, an aerial photograph, a human face, or a toy block. *Image analysis* begins the process of locating and defining the various objects in the scene. The artificial intelligence process then attempts to determine what the objects are.

Image analysis is accomplished by identifying regions and boundaries, or edges. Edges represent boundaries where two surfaces come together. They also identify the

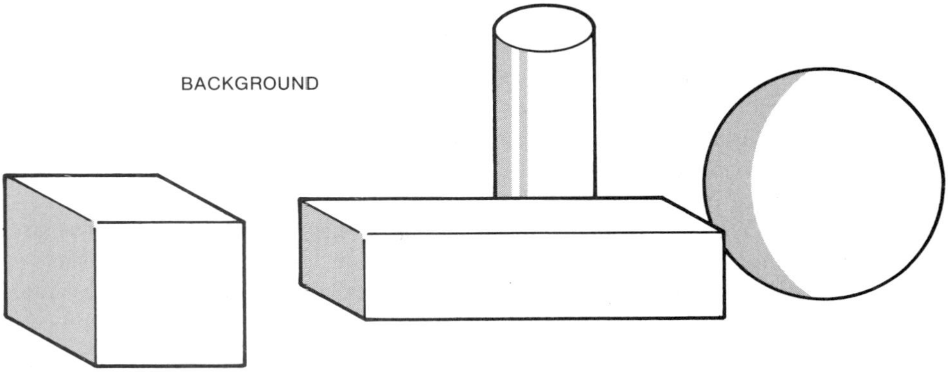

Figure 7–13. ***Examples of edges and boundaries.***

interface between two different surfaces or between an object and a background. An edge is also formed between two objects when one is in front or back of another. The line between an object and its shadow, and the outline of the shadow itself form edges. Examples of these are given in Figure 7–13. The first step, therefore, in image analysis is to locate all of these edges and boundaries.

Edges and *regions* or surfaces completely define the scene. Regions are large, flat areas of an object or scene that have the same intensity value and occur between the various edges and boundary lines. Various mathematical techniques have been developed for detecting edges and surfaces, and these form the core of image analysis.

Surface Smoothing

Surfaces are easy to identify because they are relatively uniform in light intensity. Adjacent pixels within the surface will have equal values or values very close to one another. The values may change gradually over the surface due to shadows or shading caused by the positioning of the light source.

Surfaces are often smoothed out to remove irregularities or shading before edge detection beyond. This surface smoothing is usually done by replacing each pixel value with a new value. The new value is the average of the values of the original pixels. This averaging process causes the shading of the surface to become more uniform. It blurs an image to remove small variations and make the surfaces more consistent. The smoothing or blurring process does not affect the ability of the computer to detect edges.

Edge Detection

After surface smoothing, the computer begins looking for edges or *edge detection.* A program in the computer scans through all of the binary numbers representing pixels to determine which of those pixels fall on the boundary between two surfaces. It does this by comparing the intensity of adjacent pixels. For example, the value of one pixel will be subtracted from the value of an adjacent pixel, and the numerical value will be noted. If the difference is very small, the two pixels are probably part of a large surface area. A large difference, on the other hand, indicates an edge or boundary. An extremely large variation of brightness from one pixel to another is a signal to the computer that an edge has been detected.

The edge detection program has to know in advance just how large a difference is going to be considered as edge recognition. Therefore, some threshold value is usually established beforehand. If the difference falls below this threshold value, then adjacent pixels are determined to be part of a surface region. If the difference in pixel values is above the threshold, an edge is said to be detected.

Edge detection generally takes place by having the computer edge detector look at a small group of adjacent pixels in both the horizontal and vertical directions. In other words, it "looks" through a "window" at a small square of pixels. The size of this window may be anything from approximately 2 × 2 to 15 × 15 pixels in size. The reason for examining more than two adjacent pixels is to get a better fix on the size and location of an edge. The edge itself may be more than one pixel wide. Edges may also be "fuzzy" due to lighting and noise which may cause a gradual transition from one surface to another. However, by looking at several pixels or at each side of a given pixel, better determination can be made.

The window also allows us to look in several directions rather than in a single horizontal or vertical direction. Comparing two adjacent pixels may produce no variation in the horizontal direction, but a significant difference may be noted in the vertical direction. The windowing process produces less ambiguity in detecting edges. The size of the window is a trade-off between good noise immunity obtained with a large window and good sensitivity to definition obtained with a small window.

When the boundaries of all the objects in the scene have been identified, a line drawing of the scene can be created. A new version of the scene is created showing just the black outlines of all of the objects on a white background. This line drawing is referred to as a *primal sketch.*

It is this primal sketch that completes the analysis process. The comprehension part of the computer vision program will use the outline drawing to make a final identification of the various objects.

> *And finds, with keen, discriminating sight, black's not so black—nor white so very white.*
>
> George Canning

Image Comprehension

Up to this point in the computer vision process, a lot of computation has taken place. Yet, none of it is what you could really call AI. Even though an image has been acquired, enhanced, and analyzed, the computer still does not know what the scene means. The computer is not aware of the contents of the scene, what objects are represented, and how they are related to one another. The final stage of computer vision then is to give the computer some knowledge about the things it may see in a scene. Object shapes and some kind of AI search and pattern matching program will enable the computer to examine the incoming scene and compare it to those objects in the knowledge base. The computer should be able to identify the objects there and thus understand what it sees.

As you might suspect, a considerable amount of research has gone into the comprehension process of computer vision. It is not an easy process. It is complicated by the fact that a three-dimensional scene is converted into two-dimensional format. It is from this two-dimensional view that the computer must ascertain the existence of three-dimensional objects. However, some computer vision applications do involve what we could call two-dimensional scenes. In such cases, a simple template-matching technique can be used to pick out specific object shapes. The template, which is stored in memory, is an outline or silhouette of an object that it knows. The comparison process that takes place during search and pattern matching can produce identification.

Template Matching

Template matching compares a model of a known object stored as a binary image in the computer to the binary image of the scene being viewed. The basis of comparison is the primal sketch. Both the scene and the template are stored as primal sketches. The comparison is usually done on a pixel-by-pixel basis. Corresponding pixels in the two images are, for example, subtracted from one another to obtain a difference value. If the difference is zero, a match occurs; they are the same. Very small difference numbers produce a reasonably close match. High difference figures, of course, indicate wide disparity. Various statistical calculations can also be made to determine just how close the match is between the template and the input scene.

It is difficult to match a known shape to a viewed shape because the template stored in memory is fixed in size and orientation. Chances are the template has a different size and position in the scene. Therefore, to cause a match or near match to occur, the template object must be manipulated. Various processing techniques can be used to scale or increase or decrease the size of the template to more closely match the size of the object in the scene. In addition, other mathematical routines can be used to rotate or tilt the template to better approximate the orientation of the object in the scene.

You may perform many of these calculations before obtaining a good approximation. After each reorientation or scaling of the template, a new comparison is made. If the object bears any resemblance to the template, a reasonable match will be found eventually. It is at that point that the system "understands." It can then state with reasonable certainty that it has viewed a particular shape or object.

On the other hand, the template matching process may not produce a match and the image comprehension program may simply move on to another template shape. In fact, the knowledge base for this computer vision system may be an entire set of templates of various shapes. The process is continued until an object is identified or no match occurs.

If no match occurs, the computer cannot understand the scene. It cannot recognize things it does not know about. If the template is not in the computer, that object can never be identified. Of course, that is one of the main limitations of computer vision systems.

While template matching is a simple and crude process, it is a useful one. It is, in fact, the basis of most industrial machine vision systems. In manufacturing applications, the scene can be tightly controlled and the objects to be identified can be defined very clearly. Under such circumstances, computer vision systems can view and identify objects with near 100% accuracy.

Other Techniques

While template matching is a widely used and highly successful technique, there are other methods of image understanding. The process still involves search and pattern matching, but at a different level. For example, instead of storing entire objects or shapes as templates, the computer can store bits and pieces of objects in its knowledge base. At the lowest level, the computer may store a line segment which it then manipulates and attempts to match it against lines in the primal sketch. It could do the same with squares and rectangles or circles and ellipses.

A considerable amount of research in computer vision has dealt with what is generally called the *blocks world.* A blocks world is a contrived environment where multiple blocks of different geometric shapes are used as objects to form a scene to be identified. Colored cubes, rectangles, cylinders, pyramids, triangles, and other blocks are stacked or placed adjacent to one another to form a limited controlled environment. The camera of a computer vision system is then focused on this assembly of blocks to acquire, process, and analyze the scene. The primal sketch is used as the basis for attempting to understand what is in the blocks world. But instead of looking for complete patterns or objects, the computer begins to look for identifying pieces. In a blocks world where all of the blocks are made of straight lines, it is easy to determine that all of these lines will come together in a few easily recognized formats. A line is formed between the edge of an object and the background, and between adjoining surfaces of an object. A line also is formed where two separate objects touch, overlap, or appear one behind another.

In addition, these lines form vertexes. That is, many of the lines come together to form a point. Lines form an L, a fork, an arrowhead, or a T. These various vertex possibilities are illustrated in Figure 7–14. Each of these is represented in the knowledge base of the computer. Several other types are shown in Figure 7–15. The illustrations in Figure 7–15 show how a computer, knowing the types of vertexes, can misjudge a scene. The arrowhead or peak of the pyramid shown in Figure 7–15B could be mistaken for the corner of a square.

In Figure 7–15C, the computer could have a difficult time determining if this were (1) the picture of a cube with a small cube cut out of one corner, or (2) a small cube sitting in the corner where three larger planes form a corner of two walls and a floor.

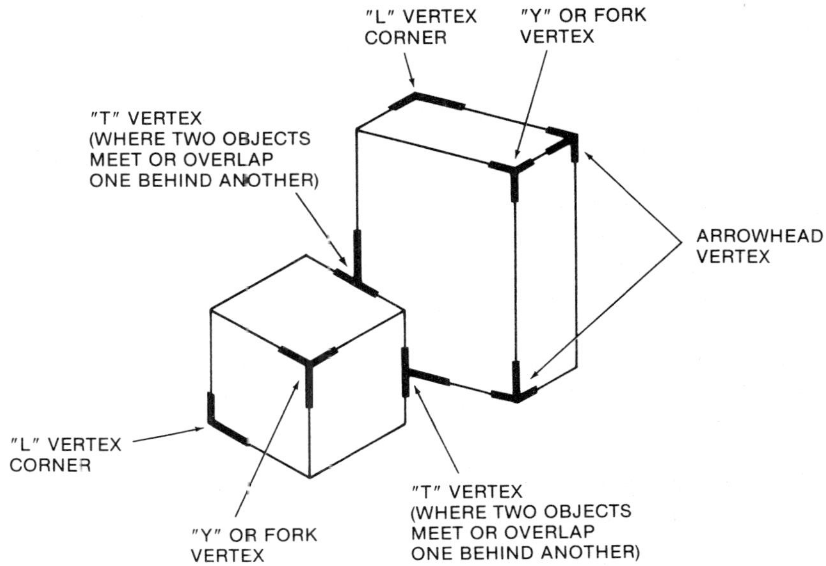

Figure 7–14. ***Types of vertexes that form functions between objects in a scene.***

The computer must be given additional knowledge to help it discriminate. For example, in Figure 7–15C, the "Y" vertex will determine which of the two representations described above is correct. If the vertex is concave, or indented inward, the first description is correct. If that vertex is convex, or pointing outward, the second description is correct. Systems have been invented to determine whether a line or vertex is concave or convex.

The search process attempts to locate vertexes in the primal sketch and match them with the various vertex models stored in memory. When a match occurs, the computer knows that it has identified a particular type of vertex and that certain surfaces

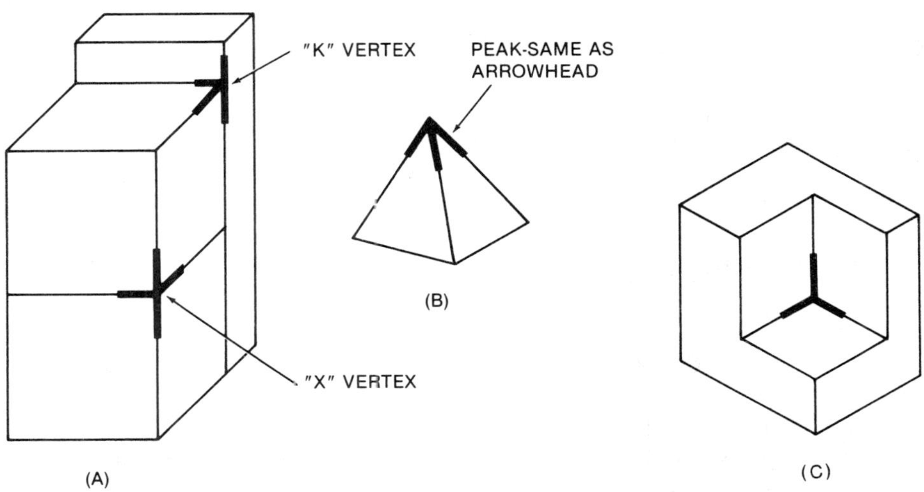

Figure 7–15. ***Other types of vertexes.***

and shapes are associated with it.

The computer goes about looking for all of the various vertexes and junctions and slowly but surely builds up a complete picture of what is being represented. At some point, sufficient information becomes available so the computer can say that it has identified a cube, a rectangle, a pyramid, or whatever. Rules stored in the knowledge base state facts about the vertexes and what they mean. In this way, the computer can decide what it has "seen."

Identifying objects in a simple blocks world is relatively easy. Identification is usually 100%. However, when we move out into the real world and attempt to identify outdoor scenes or even indoor scenes, the comprehension problem becomes incredibly difficult. In fact, few computer vision systems have been built that are even capable of such scene understanding. The reason for this is that most scenes, whether they be outdoor or indoor, contain an incredible number of different objects. In a room, for example, there may be a personal computer on a desk. There may be a printer, a typewriter, a telephone, books, and many other objects. There may be pictures on the wall, hanging plants, chairs, and even people. The primal sketch is very complex. Picking out the various objects in the scene is difficult.

Moving outside further complicates the process. Some things like buildings, cars, trucks, and airplanes are relatively easy to identify. People are somewhat more difficult, and objects such as trees, bushes and animals are very difficult. Anything with a curved or irregular surface is difficult to pick out.

For these reasons, computer vision systems have limited application. They work best in controlled environments where the scenes they view are relatively simple and contain only a few objects. As research continues in this field, more sophisticated techniques will be developed to deal with more complex scenes.

That out of sight is out of mind.

ARTHUR HUGE CLOUGH

Applications of Computer Vision

Let's zero in on the most common computer vision applications.

Machine Vision

The biggest application of computer vision is machine vision. Machine vision refers to the use of computer vision equipment and techniques with manufacturing processes usually carried out by some type of machine.

The purpose of machine vision in manufacturing applications is to replace people in some tasks and to help speed up or simplify the manufacturing process in others. Replacing people is a common objective, not because they are incapable or incompetent.

For some applications, particularly highly repetitive and boring tasks, a machine does a better job. Once the people get bored, they tend to miss details or otherwise botch the manufacturing process. Human beings get tired and make mistakes, machines don't.

Giving vision to the machine can automate its manufacturing process. Giving the machine some information about the materials it is handling or the component it is making allows it to perform completely unattended or to do most of its work with little or no human intervention. Machine vision systems greatly improve productivity, quality, and the cost and time of manufacture.

The nice thing about computer vision systems is that they operate in a controlled environment. The objects to be viewed are generally well known, and highly accurate descriptions of them can be programmed into the knowledge base. The conditions under which the objects are viewed can be carefully controlled. Camera positioning and lighting can be optimized to ensure positive identification of objects.

One way to make a template for such computer vision systems is to take the object to be identified, point the camera at it, and capture one complete frame. This frame then becomes the template. Because the template is prepared under exact conditions in which the objects must be identified, highly accurate matching can be obtained.

Machine vision systems can identify and inspect physical objects. The system may look at a collection of various parts and identify each by its shape. Once the parts are identified, they may be sorted, moved to another location, discarded or otherwise used.

Computer vision systems are becoming very popular in quality control applications. Here the camera looks at a particular object to determine if it has been made correctly. Computer vision systems are good at correcting assembly errors or faults. For example, computer vision systems are widely used in printed circuit board inspection. A correctly manufactured board can be viewed initially and an image captured for use as the template. It can then be compared to other boards to determine if components are in the right place, if solder joints have been made, or if any shorts, scratches, or breaks occur.

Robot Vision

One of the major applications of computer vision is with robots. Robots, you will recall, are machines that have been programmed to perform some physical manipulation. They are not smart because they cannot think for themselves. However, when attached to a computer with an artificial intelligence program, they do take on more intelligent characteristics. But to be truly intelligent, a robot must have sight. This sight provides feedback that allows it to adjust its operation to fit varying conditions. Computer vision, therefore, helps make robots intelligent. We will discuss this in more detail in the next chapter.

Key Points

- Computer vision is that field of artificial intelligence devoted to mimicking human sight and visual understanding with hardware and software.

- The computer vision process involves four steps: image acquisition, image processing, image analysis, and image comprehension.
- Image acquisition is the process of capturing a scene or picture electronically and converting it into a format compatible with the computer.
- A video camera is the main tool used for image acquisition. Cameras use either vidicon tubes or charge coupled devices (CCDs) to translate light into electrical (video) signals. CCD cameras are the most popular. Black and white cameras are used.
- A CCD is a semiconductor array that translates light into electrical charges. CCDs are smaller, lighter, more rugged, and more reliable than vidicon tubes.
- An analog-to-digital converter (ADC) changes the analog video signal into a sequence of binary numbers whose values represent light intensity levels. These are stored in a memory. An 8-bit ADC that can represent 256 gray levels between white and black is the most common. Each binary number is called a pixel.
- The number of pixels in the converted scene determines the resolution of the image. The greater the number of pixels, the finer the representation of detail. A typical resolution is 512×512 pixels.
- Huge RAMs are needed to store high resolution scenes. They are referred to as frame buffers.
- The stored binary image is a two-dimensional representation of a three-dimensional scene.
- Image processing refers to the enhancement of the stored image to improve quality and help ensure proper analysis and interpretation.
- Image processing includes correcting distortions, improving contrast, changing the gray scale, and reducing noise.
- Some image processing can be done optically with lenses, filters, and proper illumination prior to scene acquisition.
- Most image processing is done by the computer by performing various calculations on each pixel in the scene.
- Image analysis is the process of having the computer determine the content of the scene by defining and locating objects and areas.
- Computer image analysis is done by detecting edges or recognizing boundaries between objects and their background or other objects. This is done by comparing the values of adjacent pixels. Solid areas or regions are also identified.
- During image analysis, the computer develops a primal sketch, a high contrast outline drawing of all the objects and regions.
- Image acquisition, processing, and analysis are not AI-based activities. However, the fourth and final step in computer vision, image understanding, is.
- Image understanding or comprehension involves search and pattern-matching techniques to identify objects in the scene and their relationship to one another.

- Picking out objects is done by template matching, comparing a known template or silhouette of an object stored in the computer with objects in the scene.
- Computer vision is most widely used in manufacturing operations. Systems used in this way are called machine vision systems.
- Other applications for computer vision include robot sight and analysis or aerial/satellite photographs.

8

Robotics and AI

He that invents a machine augments the power of man and the wellbeing of mankind.

Henry Ward Beecher

From the beginning of time, we have been inventing machines that help us do our work faster and easier. As our knowledge of science, mathematics, and the technologies grew, we invented increasingly complex machines. The machines not only speeded up and simplified our work, but also allowed us to mass produce items with great precision.

For the most part, we work in conjunction with a machine to perform the work. Machines are just devices that help to multiply our capabilities. However, at some point in our development, we decided that it was possible to produce machines that could totally replace us, at least in some jobs. In fact, it was sometimes possible to create a machine which turned raw materials into the finished product without human intervention. This process is called automation.

The principles of automation stimulated the thought process and eventually the idea of a more flexible or universal machine began to emerge. Instead of creating a special machine designed to do only a few operations well, why not create a general purpose machine that could perform many of the physical functions of human beings? Thus the idea of a robot was conceived.

A robot, of course, is a machine that attempts to duplicate one or more physical capabilities of a person. Just as AI attempts to mimic the human brain, a robot attempts to mimic human manipulative capability. The two ideas go hand in hand.

A robot, regardless of its sophistication and capabilities, is still basically a dumb machine. It cannot think, reason, solve problems, or make decisions. If it is to perform some function, it must be told specifically what to do. Electromechanical control systems put the robot through its physical paces according to a predetermined program of operations.

Such preprogrammed robots are useful, but they are greatly limited in the kinds of things they can do. They can replace us for only special tasks which can be repeated again and again. In other words, the robot cannot adjust to its environment. It cannot deal with changes or deviations. It will blindly go about what it has been programmed to do regardless of problems or varying conditions.

Robots are still operated by simple electromechanical control systems. However, more and more robots are being controlled by computer. They have at last been given a brain. Although robots are not really smarter, at least the computers provide flexibility of control. The robot can be reprogrammed to meet changing conditions or new applications. Special robotics programming languages have been developed for these control computers to make it easy for human beings to specify the operations to be performed and their sequence.

With computer control, a robot becomes far more useful. Its operation can be changed to fit new jobs by simply creating a new program. Nevertheless, robots are still limited in their application, because they still cannot think. However, the days of the dumb machine have come to an end. AI techniques give the robot's computer the ability to think, reason, and make decisions on its own.

If a robot is to be able to adapt to changes in its work, it must be able to sense those changes. Sensors must be used with the work process to provide feedback signals to the computer. These feedback signals tell the computer what's going on. They allow it to reason and cause the robot to adapt to its situation.

Computer vision systems are the primary sensory input for advanced robots. Giving a robot the sense of sight lets it go about tasks in nearly a fully automated and flexible way. Other kinds of sensors, such as pressure sensors, are also used to provide additional inputs to the control computer.

In this chapter we are going to show how artificial intelligence techniques and feedback sensors make robots smarter and more useful. We will begin with a quickie review of the field of robotics. Then we will show how artificial intelligence techniques based on sensory input can give robots the smarts to operate on their own in a variety of environments. Finally, we will conclude with a discussion of some of the applications of intelligent robots.

Just What Is a Robot?

Just what is it that you think of when you hear the word robot? If you are like most of us, you probably think of an electromechanical machine designed to mimic as closely as possible both the physical and mental attributes of a human being. The robot you imagine probably looks like a machine but is shaped as much as possible to resemble a person. You have seen many variations of such creations in TV programs and movies and read about them in science fiction stories. Robots of this type are referred to as androids.

Androids and Cyborgs

Androids are synthetic human beings with mechanical limbs and electronic brains. You will also hear this type of robot called a humanoid. Good examples of androids are R2-D2 and CP30 of *Star Wars* fame.

Another term that you will often hear associated with robotics is *cyborg.* A cyborg is a human being which has been supplemented by some type of electromechanical device. A cyborg uses robot-like parts to correct a physical deficiency or to enhance mental or physical capabilities. Such human beings are partially robotic. A person with some kind of prosthetic is a cyborg.

Despite continuing advances in the field of robotics, we are still nowhere near capable of producing an android that accurately duplicates a human being. It is certainly not likely that we will do so in our lifetime and maybe then not even within another century. Many expect that we will never be able to produce a fully electromechanical duplicate of ourselves.

Nevertheless, the future will bring us closer to producing a truly useful android. When we do, we will have an incredibly flexible tool to do our work. Androids will be able to do our dirty work and fight our wars.

The Laws of Robotics

If we are ever able to produce such androids, we should make sure they are positive influences in our society. Isaac Asimov, in *I Robot*,[2] wrote that all androids should follow the three laws of robotics. These laws are:

1. A robot may not injure a human being or, through inaction, allow a human to be harmed.
2. A robot must obey orders given by humans except when that conflicts with the first law.
3. A robot must protect its own existence unless that conflicts with the first or second laws.

These laws could certainly put our minds at ease. However, human nature being what it is, it is suspected that robots also will be constructed for all the wrong reasons. Most books, movies, and TV shows are based on such incidences.

But right now, we really don't have to worry. Robots as they exist in our real world are nothing more than simple mechanical manipulators. They only simulate a fraction of total human capabilities, yet they are incredibly useful. For many years in the future, these are the robots we will develop and increasingly put to use improving our productivity and replacing humans in critical or dangerous environments.

The Real Definition

Many attempts have been made to define the term robot, but the best definition is probably the one that has emerged from the manufacturers and users of industrial robots. Their definition of an industrial robot is:

> A robot is a reprogrammable, multi-functional, manipulator designed to move material, parts, tools, or other specialized devices through various programmed motions for the performance of a variety of tasks.

[2]Asimov, Isaac. 1950. *I, Robot.* Garden City: Doubleday & Co., Inc.

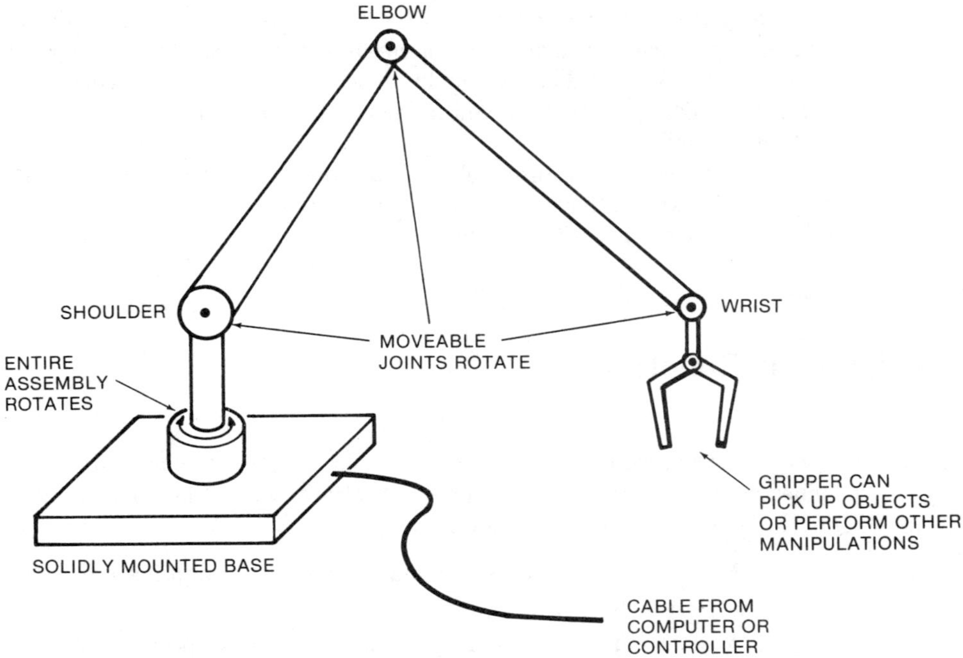

Figure 8–1. ***A typical industrial robotic arm.***

Types of Industrial Robots

You will find two basic types of robots in industry. The first type is the fixed but moveable arm. The second type is generally referred to as a mobile robot. Let's consider these types in more detail before going on.

Fixed Arm

The most predominant type of industrial robot is the fixed but moveable arm. An example is shown in Figure 8–1. These robots are mounted on a base in a single location near where it will perform its work. It is generally secured to a cement floor with heavy bolts or is mounted on a table or other work surface so that it cannot move. The materials it will handle are nearby. From there, the robot arm moves up and down, back and forth, in and out, and in whatever way it is programmed.

In some special applications, the robot arm can be moveable. For example, it may be mounted on rails so that it can slide along a production line. Even in such cases, the amount of movement is limited. However, the ability to move the robot precisely on a fixed guide allows it more flexibility in doing its job.

Mobile Robots

A mobile robot is capable of moving around. Such robots are generally manipulator arms mounted on a small vehicle-like structure with wheels or bulldozer-like tracks. Other methods of propulsion may also be used in special circumstances. For example, robots with legs have been invented to provide greater mobility in difficult terrain. Underwater robots require a propulsion motor and control fins for exploration and retrieval work under water.

Regardless of the type of movement implemented, mobile robots must have a propulsion system. Usually, this propulsion system is one or more electric motors that run on battery power.

A mobile robot can go where the work is and position itself to get the job done. Mobile robots are excellent for replacing humans in hazardous environments. The robot can be sent instead of the human into nuclear power plants, polluted mines, beneath the sea, and into outer space. Mobile robots can be used in fire fighting and bomb disposal.

Most mobile robots are operator controlled by means of a long cable. In some cases, they are radio controlled. The operator usually can see the robot performing the task but is located remotely for safety purposes. Sensors on the robot can also provide some feedback.

In environments where the operator cannot see the work, the robot itself must send back signals which tell its location, position, and status. TV cameras are normally used for such feedback. With the visual information provided, an operator using radio control can operate the robot as required.

Some mobile robots are capable of performing on their own. An example is a security robot that roams around a building at night looking for intruders or sensing undesirable conditions, such as fire.

An example of a mobile robot is Heathkit's HERO I, shown in Figure 8–2, which can be programmed for security and other applications, although its primary application is education and entertainment.

> *As machines get to be more like men, men will come to be more like machines.*
>
> JOSEPH WOOD KRUTCH

Why Use Robots?

There are three main justifications for robots. These are to improve productivity, to replace humans in hazardous environments, and improve our economic situation.

Productivity Improvement

Business and industry are very concerned about the productivity of its workers. The more work that can be turned out in the least amount of time the greater will be the profit of the company.

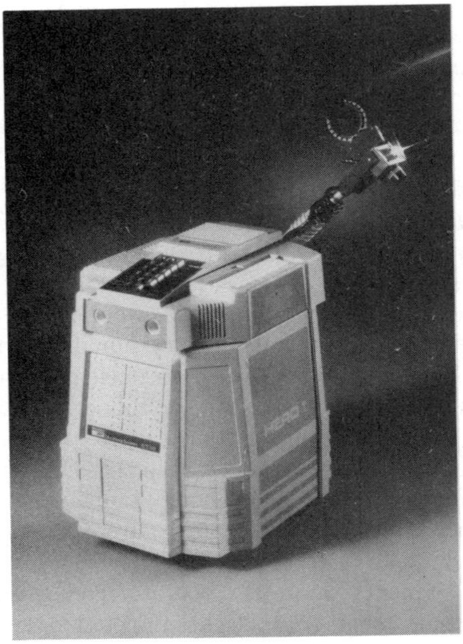

Figure 8–2. ***A mobile robot. (Courtesy Heath Co.)***

High productivity is hard to maintain. It can be achieved in short spurts, but sustaining it over a long period of time is difficult. Humans get tired or bored or sick. We take vacations and coffee breaks. Humans get mad, talk to their co-workers, and otherwise slow down the work.

The robot simply does not exhibit any of these problems. The robot works tirelessly, never having to take breaks or time off the job. They are not affected by emotional work situations or demotivational actions. They simply grind away day after day doing their job.

Robots are particularly good in assembly line jobs where the same actions are performed time and time again. If a robot is used in such jobs, the work output usually improves. Not only will the robot be able to do the work faster, but it will not get tired and make mistakes.

Replacing Humans in Hazardous Jobs

There are many jobs in industry that are just plain dangerous for human beings. Workers are exposed to hazardous materials including sharp, heavy metal pieces, elevated temperatures, toxic chemicals, and high noise levels.

While safety precautions are taken in such hazardous environments, accidents occur and humans are injured or killed.

Any place that a robot can handle the dangerous materials or survive in the less than desirable working conditions, it should be used. Not only will productivity increase, but also human injuries and all the attendant suffering, expense, and waste will be eliminated.

Robots also save money. While there are major capital costs in purchasing robots and integrating them into the workplace, that high cost is eventually repaid. Over the long term, the work simply costs less than paying a human to do it.

> *On mechanical slavery, on the slavery of the machine, the future of the world depends.*
>
> OSCAR WILDE

What Robots Do

As you can imagine, there are a variety of different tasks that robots can perform. Let's take a look at some of their more common functions.

Welding

The most frequent application of robotic arms in manufacturing is welding. Here, the arms are set up along a production line conveyor. As various components are put into place, robotic arms move in and make spot welds at predetermined locations. Today most auto bodies and frames are made using robot welders.

Welding is a dangerous activity, and it requires intense concentration and skill over a long period of time. Further, the locations of many welds require humans to physically maneuver into difficult positions.

The robot arm can position itself precisely and make the weld at the designated spot. It also can do it faster and more consistently without endangering the human.

Materials Handling

Materials, components, and assemblies can be transferred from one place to another using a robot arm. Such arms are generally referred to as "pick and place" robots.

A robot arm is used for loading or unloading. Parts on a vehicle or conveyor may be transferred to another location. Manufactured goods may be loaded upon a vehicle for transportation elsewhere.

The robot arm is also handy for moving components from a work surface to a conveyor belt or vice versa. Some robot arms can look through an assembly of parts and pick out a specific one, pick it up, and move it to another place. Such operations are sometimes called bin picking.

Assembly

In many manufacturing applications, robots actually perform the assembly of some machine or device. Individual components are picked up by the arm and put together in a proper sequence to form the device. A common application is "stuffing" printed circuit boards. Special robots pick up the integrated circuits, transistors, resistors, capacitors, and other components, bend the leads and insert them into printed circuit boards. The boards are then automatically transferred to a flow soldering machine where the final assembly operation takes place.

Spraying

Another widely used application is spraying. At the end of the robot arm, a special nozzle connected to a hose and a source of liquid is used to spray components during the manufacturing process. The most common form of spraying, of course, is painting. The robot arm can be programmed to move precisely to provide an even coat of paint to even the most unusually shaped objects in a very short period of time. The amount of paint can be controlled precisely.

Robots also can spray other chemicals to prevent rust or corrosion. Oil might be sprayed for lubrication purposes. And there are many other examples.

In most spraying applications, the environment is extremely hazardous. Humans must be physically protected so their bodies do not become coated with the paint or other liquid. Goggles and breathing filters are particularly important. It is senseless to use humans in these applications when robots can perform the job faster, better, and more consistently without risk to the human.

Other Operations

There are so many special applications in manufacturing that it is difficult to cover them all. But with the proper attachment at the end of the robotic arm, an incredible variety of operations can be performed. Screwing or tightening functions are an example. Riveting is another example. Other types of robot arms may be used for pouring operations. In most cases, special tools are attached to the end of the robot arm to perform specific operations.

Men have become tools of their tools.

HENRY DAVID THOREAU

How Industrial Robots Work

To give you a better feel for the importance of artificial intelligence in future robots, you should have an understanding of how current industrial robots operate. In this section we will give you a brief overview of the main components of a robot and explain how they work together.

Components of a Robot

The typical industrial robot consists of four major components: the manipulator arm, the end effector, the actuator, and the controller. Now, let's discuss each in detail.

Manipulator Arm

The manipulator arm is generally made to resemble or work like the arm of a human. It often has a shoulder joint, an elbow, and a wrist. The arm may rotate or slide for further flexibility. However, there are a variety of ways that manipulator arms can be made. Five basic types are used in industry.

The five types of robot arms are illustrated in Figures 8–3 through 8–6. Their names reflect the method in which they access any given point within the space defined by their reach.

The simplest arm shown in Figure 8–3 is based on Cartesian or rectangular coordinates. The idea is to move the end effector of the arm to a given location in space to perform some function. This point in space is defined by the X, Y, and Z axes of a rectangular coordinate system. The robot arm may move from right to left, up and down, and forward or backward. As the arm moves in the three possible directions within its limits in each direction, it traces out a cube-shaped work space. The end effector, of course, can be positioned anywhere inside the cube.

Another variation of the manipulator arm uses cylindrical coordinates as illustrated in Figure 8–4. Instead of simply moving back and forth from left to right, the entire arm assembly can rotate 360 degrees. The remainder of the arm can also move up and down and forward and backwards. In doing so, it will trace out a cylindrical work space with a hole in the center where the arm mechanism sits. Instead of having an X axis, this robot uses rotation. The position of the arm is determined by an angle from some reference point along with the Y and Z coordinates.

The spherical or polar coordinates system is another variation. It is illustrated in Figure 8–5. The vertical or Y component is replaced by another joint referred to as a shoulder joint. Vertical motion is achieved by rotation in this joint. Again, the entire arm can turn 360 degrees and the arm itself can move in and out (the Z axis). This arrangement traces out a work space that is a portion of a sphere.

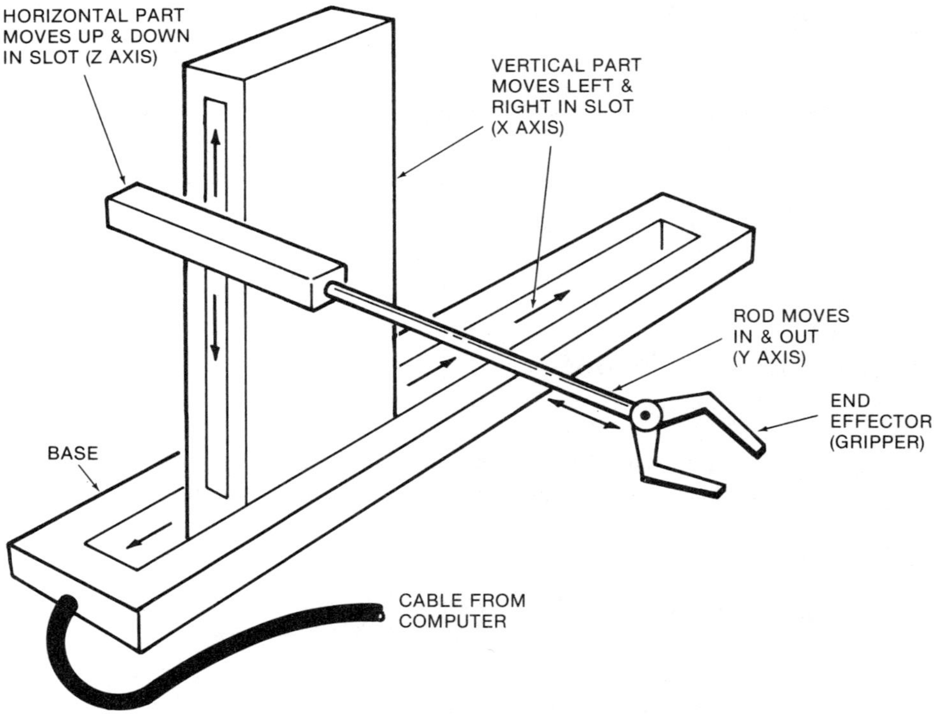

Figure 8–3. ***Rectangular or Cartesian coordinate arm.***

A fourth type of arm is known as the articulated or jointed spherical coordinate. This was illustrated in Figure 8–1. Like the spherical or polar coordinate system, it can rotate 360 degrees. However, in addition to having a shoulder joint, it also has elbow and wrist joints. This gives the arm greater flexibility of movement and, as a result, it can trace out a larger portion of a sphere. This type of arm is the most widely used in industry because of its great flexibility.

A fifth type of arm is illustrated in Figure 8–6. It is known as the selective compliance assembly robot arm (SCARA). Its basic work space is a cylinder. However, that cylinder is derived in an unusual manner. Like most of the other arms, it can rotate 360 degrees. However, it has an elbow joint that moves horizontally rather than vertically. This permits it to fold in on itself in either direction. A vertical element at the end of the arm can move up and down providing the Y axis. Arms of this type are sometimes used in high speed assembly work, such as putting together electronic equipment.

End Effector

The end effector attaches to the end of the arm. It is the device which performs the designated operation. An almost unlimited number of variations are possible. Most end effectors are specially designed for the job to be done.

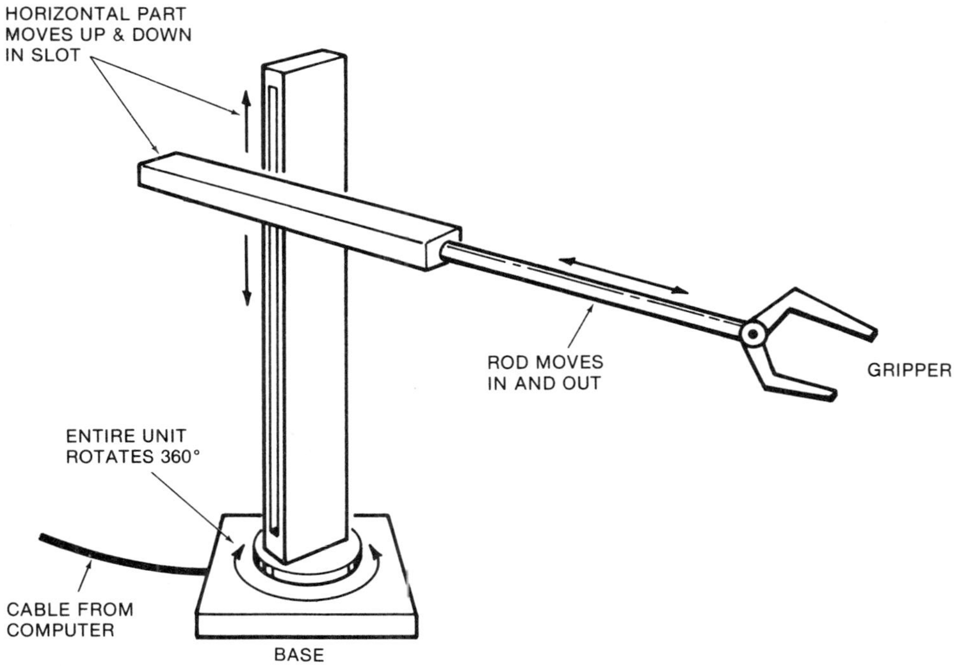

Figure 8–4. ***Cylindrical coordinate arm.***

One of the most popular types of end effectors is a *gripper.* In its simplest form, the gripper is a pincher-type assembly that simulates a thumb and one finger. This allows the robot to be able to pick up objects within a certain size limitation. More sophisticated assemblies use three or more "fingers" to provide added flexibility.

Other methods also permit end effectors to pick objects up. For example, they may use a sticky substance to adhere to an object in order to lift it. Other end effectors use a suction hose arrangement for picking up light objects.

The effector is usually mounted at the wrist of the arm and provides several additional movements referred to as wrist articulation. This is illustrated in Figure 8–7. The wrist can rotate, swivel up and down and back and forth. Once the arm has been positioned, these three additional wrist movements can provide additional flexibility in positioning the end effector for its work.

All of the methods of moving the arm and the wrist are classified by the degrees of freedom they possess. The term "degrees of freedom" refers to the number of axes about which parts of the robot arm can move. As you saw in Figures 8–3 through 8–6, the arms have three degrees of freedom. With the wrist articulation, three additional axes are achieved. This provides six degrees of freedom which permits excellent positioning flexibility.

Actuator

The *actuator* is also referred to as the power source. This is the basic source of energy for moving the arm, controlling the joints, and operating the end effector. Three basic types of power sources are used: electric, hydraulic, and pneumatic.

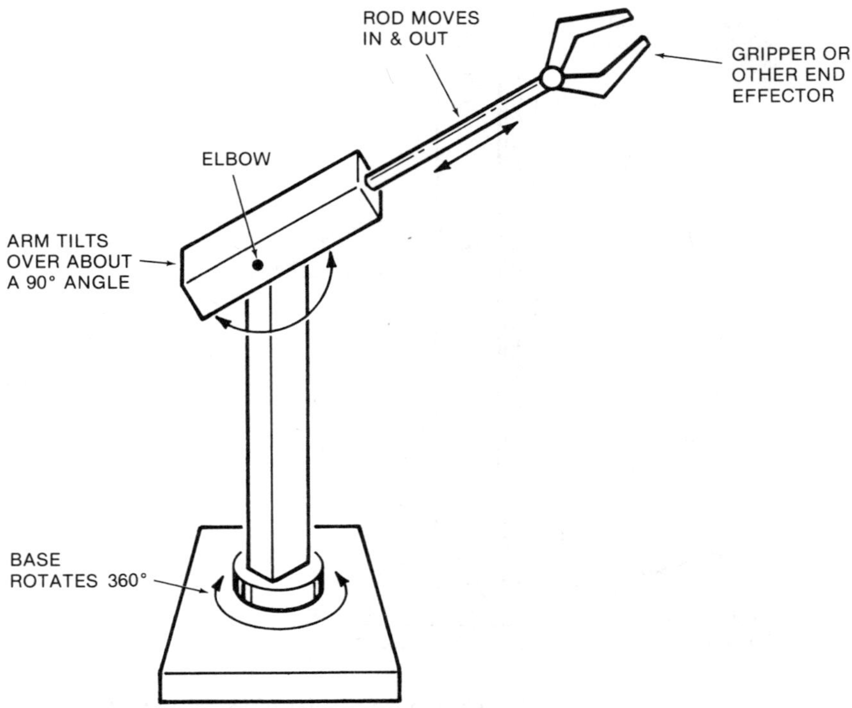

Figure 8–5. ***Spherical or polar coordinate arm.***

Electric actuators are AC or DC motors that provide rotation or joint movement. These are used in combination with mechanical assemblies such as gears or pulleys to make the basic movements. There is usually one motor per joint.

A high percentage of robotic arms use electric motor drive. Silent and powerful, motors can be conveniently controlled by electronic circuits. Continuous and stepper motors are used.

Another commonly used power source is a hydraulic system consisting of a pump which puts a liquid such as oil under pressure. By use of valves and other mechanisms, this pressurized liquid can control all of the arm motion. Hydraulic systems are extremely powerful. They are capable of lifting far greater weights than electrical systems and are, therefore, used in applications requiring maximum strength and durability. Sometimes you will find electrical and hydraulic elements combined in an arm.

A few robotic arms use a pneumatic system for power. Compressed air is forced through lines to cause movement. Pneumatic systems are weak and are used for only very light duty work.

Controller

The fourth major component in a robotic system is the controller. This is the instrumentation that sends signals to the power source to move the robot arm to a specific position and to actuate the end effector.

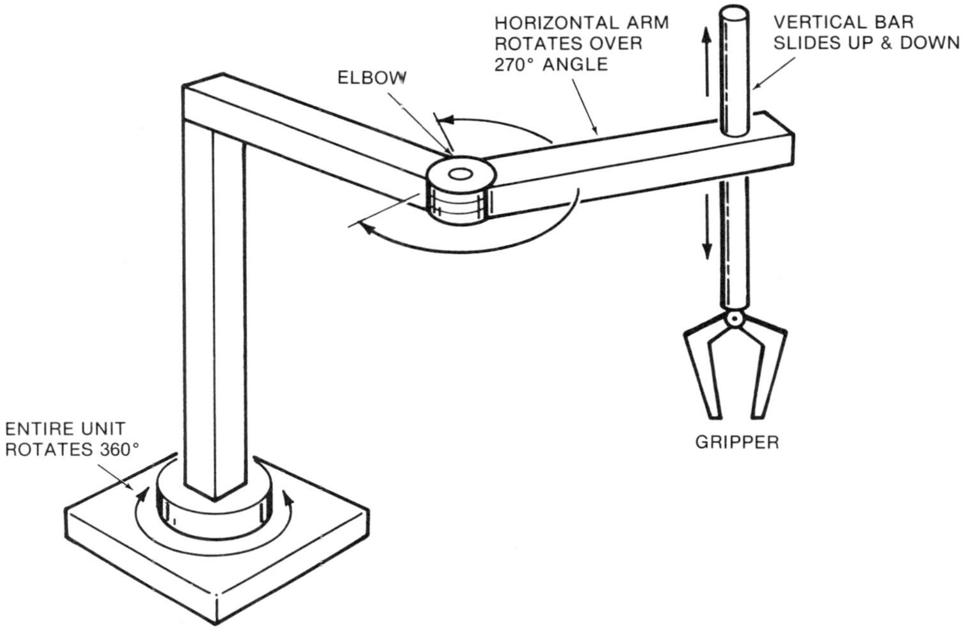

Figure 8–6. ***Selective compliance assembly robot arm (SCARA).***

Controllers are electronic circuits. They can be a special purpose programmable controller which gives the robot arm a sequence of movement instructions and actions. The most flexible kind of controller, of course, is a general purpose digital computer which allows the arm to be reprogrammed for a wide variety of applications.

The simplest form of control system is an open loop controller. Open loop means that no feedback from the arm itself is used to determine its position. Instead, the controller moves the arm until it hits mechanical stops at selected points.

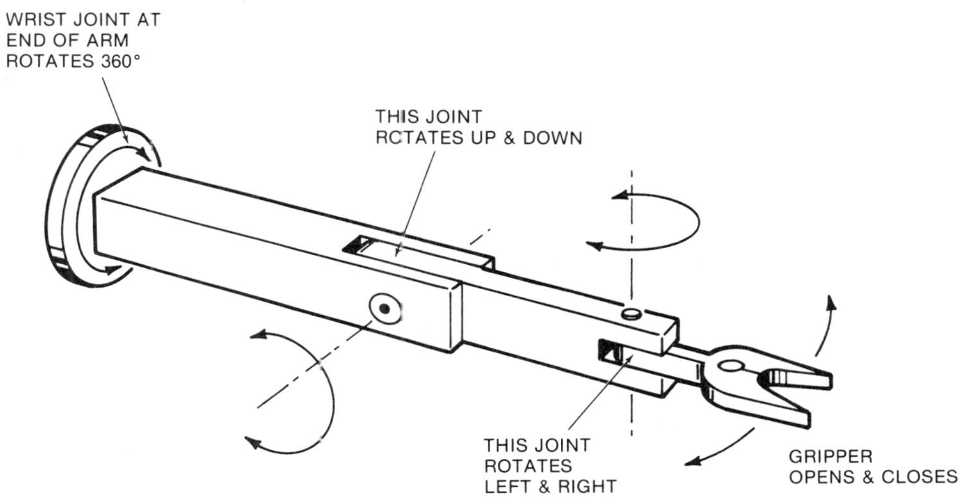

Figure 8–7. ***Wrist articulation for flexible end effector movement.***

As an example, an open loop controller sends a series of pulses to stepper motors in the various joints of the robot. A controller may count the number of pulses sent to determine how far to move each portion of the arm. Once the correct number of pulses have been sent, the arm is in the desired position. Then the action to actuate the end effector is taken.

Such robot arms are often called point-to-point systems. Also called pick-and-place robots, these machines generally move between two fixed points. They may pick up an object at one point and move it to another point and repeat this back and forth process continuously. Although such robots can perform only simple tasks, there are many applications for them in industry. For example, an arm may be needed to pick up a component on an assembly line and deposit it in another location for storage or processing.

The most sophisticated kind of controllers use *servomechanisms.* These feedback control systems provide greater control over the robot arm and its positioning.

The servo-controlled arms use feedback sensors to send signals back to the controller giving information on the position of the joints. The position sensor may be a potentiometer that generates an analog voltage or an optical coded disk which sends back a binary number that designates position. The servomechanism in the controller uses such feedback signals to determine where the arm is and when it reaches the desired position.

In addition, the controller can specifically tell the arm how to move. In open loop pick-and-place or point-to-point robot arms, the programmer of the robot really has no control over the position of the arm between the two points it can access. However, when servo control is used, a sequence of points can be programmed to move the arm from one place to another. These intermediate points can be precisely controlled. In some applications, the robot arm works in the restricted space. It cannot swing and move in and out in any way it wants to. With a servo control system, the arm can be moved accurately to avoid obstacles as it moves from one place to another.

Getting the arm to do what you want it to do requires programming. In programming, the controller is given two sets of coordinates, the beginning coordinates and the ending coordinates. This will provide point-to-point operation with no intermediate control. If a particular path must be used in moving from the beginning to the ending coordinates, intermediate points can also be programmed.

Instead of direct programming, a robot arm can be "taught" how to move by simply stepping it through the actions it is supposed to take. Many robotic arms have a hand-held control box as part of the controller which allows manual positioning and actuation of the arm. An operator uses pushbuttons or levers on the control box to put the robot through the desired motions. The feedback sensors on the robot joints provide electronic signals that can be captured and stored in memory. In other words, the controller memorizes the movements it has to make as it is manually moved. From that point on, the stored sequence can be played back and the arm will make the desired movements. Such manual control greatly simplifies the task of controlling the robot and eliminates the need for complex programming.

Most modern robots use computers as controllers. Special robotic control languages have been developed to help speed up and simplify the process of telling a robot what to do, how, and when.

The future offers very little hope for those who expect that our new mechanical slaves will offer us a world in which we may rest from thinking. Help us they may, but at the cost of supreme demands upon our honesty and our intelligence. The world of the future will be an ever more demanding struggle against the limitations of our intelligence, not a comfortable hammock in which we can lie down to be waited upon by our robot slaves.

NORBERT WIENER

Intelligent Robots

The robots we have described are "dumb" machines because they cannot think or adapt to their surroundings. They simply carry out preprogrammed actions. While such robots are useful, of course, their application is naturally limited to situations where intelligence and adaptability are not required.

Robots become far more useful when they exhibit intelligence that allows them to think for themselves. But in order to have something to think about, the robot must have senses so that it can perceive what is going on around it. Once it can sense its environment, the robot can reason about its work and what is going on. With this capability, the robot can modify its actions to fit the situation.

All of the branches of AI can be applied to robotics. These techniques can come together to give the robot perception and thought. By doing so, the robot becomes far more useful. Let's see how this is done.

The Need for Intelligence

The robot arm can be flexibly positioned, but its range of movement is sometimes limited. Therefore, the work must be fed to the robot on a conveyor belt or some other mechanism. The workpiece, in many cases, must be positioned with high precision. As a result, the systems or mechanisms that bring the workpiece to the robot are often more complex and expensive than the robot itself.

The workpiece must be carefully positioned beforehand, so the end effector can be brought to the exact point before being told to do its job. The arm will move in a certain way to rest at a definite point in space. When that final point is reached, the end effector will perform some operation, such as gripping, turning, welding, or spraying. If the piece to be worked on does not appear at the right location, the robot will fail in its task. A considerable amount of effort and dollars is expended in insuring that the robot links up with the item to be processed.

We live in a random, variable, and imperfect environment. To be useful in a work situation, a robot must be able to deal with tolerance variations, disorder, errors, breakage, and other unplanned conditions. It must be able to sense and compensate for such problems. If we give the robot senses, then give it the power to think, a robot will be able to take some appropriate action even under unpredictable circumstances.

A simple example will illustrate how smart robots can cope. Assume that the function of the robot is to pick up a bolt and insert it through a hole in a metal workpiece. The bolts are in a bin next to the robot. The arm will pick up one of the bolts by its head and move the bolt toward the workpiece. The workpiece is moved to the robot on a conveyor belt. The robot arm will insert the bolt in the workpiece, let go of the bolt, and move away. The workpiece is then moved on to another location for further processing while the arm goes after the next bolt.

All this works out satisfactorily if the bolt is positioned so that the gripper can pick it up with the proper orientation. Also, the bolt will be successfully inserted into the hole if the workpiece is properly positioned on the conveyor belt. But what happens if the bolts or the workpiece are not properly oriented? The answer is fairly simple. The bolt may be picked up incorrectly, in which case it cannot be inserted into the workpiece. The operation fails. Even if the bolt is picked up successfully, the workpiece may be out of position, in which case the bolt will not be placed where it is supposed to. Again the operation fails.

If a robot has the ability to see the items it is working with, it can certainly do a better job. The robot arm would first look for the head of the bolt to grip rather than some other portion. Further, if the workpiece were slightly out of alignment with the position of the bolt, the robot would see this and move its arm to adjust the variation. When the robot gets some feedback, it can reason about variations that occur and take action to correct its own control program to get the job done.

Robot Senses

Now let's take a more detailed look at the senses that robots can be given to perceive their environment. They are the same senses that we have, namely sight, vision, touch, and smell. It is doubtful that robots will need the taste sense to be useful.

Robot Vision

Vision systems were covered in detail in Chapter 7, so we won't really go into this further here. However, we will say that sight is not only a human's most valuable sense but also a robot's. More information about the work environment can be obtained by vision than by any other means. Machine vision systems are widely available and readily adaptable to robot systems.

Giving the robot system vision is as easy as mounting a video camera so that it focuses on the workpiece. Placement of the camera is critical to give the robot the best possible view, and the position of the camera may change as needed. In some cases, two or more cameras might be necessary to provide the kind of feedback required.

To sense and determine the distance between objects, the robot will need two cameras set up for stereo vision. With two cameras, the attached computer can perform triangulation calculations to determine the distance between the workpiece and the robot arm or any other two objects.

Fortunately, in the controlled environment of a robotic system, the lighting usually can be adjusted to provide optimum perception.

Touch

The second most useful sense for a robot is touch. This sense must enable the robot to know when it has come into contact with the workpiece. Better still, is the sense of knowing how much pressure is being applied to a workpiece by the arm or end effector. A gripper will apply a fixed amount of pressure as it picks an item up. If the pressure is not great enough, the object will fall from the grip of the robot. Worse still, the pressure applied to the workpiece might be too high and cause damage.

These problems can be overcome by applying pressure transducers to the gripper to tell the control computer exactly how much force is being used. Then, it will be able to adjust that force to just the right amount to accomplish the desired objective.

Strain gauges are used on robot grippers to provide pressure feedback. They are a type of transducer whose electrical resistance varies with the pressure or stress applied to it. When connected into an electrical circuit, the strain gauge produces an analog signal proportional to the pressure. This signal is converted into binary form by an A-to-D converter and used by the computer to determine the amount of pressure being applied by the grippers. The control program will adjust the actuation devices, either increasing or decreasing pressure as required by the application.

Another kind of sensor used in robot systems is the *proximity detector.* While the proximity detector has nothing to do with touch, it does provide feedback on the position of an item relative to the arm. Proximity detectors generate an electrical signal whenever the workpiece moves within a certain distance of the transducer. The transducers use magnetic fields to determine whenever a workpiece comes within range. Using a photocell and light source, optical proximity detectors can also be used to sense the closeness of an object. Robots must know when the workpiece is coming within range, but it doesn't have to touch the workpiece to know how close it is. As soon as the workpiece is within a specified distance, the robot knows to get ready and position itself in an appropriate way.

Hearing

Hearing is not as important as vision and touch in robot systems. However, there are some situations where the ability to hear can be useful. If sounds are associated with parts of the work, it may be desirable to detect them as a way of providing additional inputs to the robot. Such feedback could come from nothing more than a simple microphone and amplifier set-up to detect some noise. In simple situations, the nature of the noise may not be important. It may be important to know that the noise occurs and at what time.

The ultimate in hearing perception, of course, is speech recognition. We covered this in Chapter 5. There is absolutely no reason why a robot cannot be given a full voice recognition system. In this way, the robot could be controlled by a human giving it instructions.

In most cases, we want our intelligent robot to be autonomous, to carry out the work function without the intervention of a human. That is why we give the robot a control program and then provide feedback so that it can do the job automatically.

On the other hand, there may be some situations where human control of the robot may be desirable. Many robot arms are provided with a control box with appropriate buttons and levers that allow a human to operate it from some remote location. In most cases, the control box is on the end of a long cable. However, don't forget, simple radio control systems can also be used.

A robot with a speech recognition system would not necessarily be autonomous, but it could still claim intelligence. A robot that can recognize human speech and then carry out actions given by the human is certainly intelligent.

The human operator might say, for instance, "Find the bolt and pick it up by the head." Using its vision, the robot would spot the bolt and its arm would move to pick up the bolt. The vision system would be able to identify the head of the bolt, and the grippers would pick it up. At this point the robot may stop, waiting for additional directions. Next, the human operator might say, "Insert the bolt in the workpiece when it comes by." The robot could then rely on its proximity detector to determine when the workpiece is in position. At that point it would begin moving to orient itself to the proper position. The vision system would focus on the workpiece and when it was oriented correctly, the arm would move and insert the bolt. Vision feedback would insure that the bolt goes into the right position.

Smell and Taste

Industrial robots do not have to smell and taste to be successful. Taste is a sense that undoubtedly will never be developed in robots, but smell might be an important consideration. Some industrial operations produce odors that may provide the feedback the robot needs to take intelligent action. A smoke detector is an example of a sensor that has a type of smell capability. There are other forms of electrical transducers that can sense gases of various kinds. These might pick up dangerous toxic odors resulting from some improper operation or malfunction. Alternately, the smell may be created as the result of some successful operation, notifying the robot that the job was completed.

Non-Human Senses

A variety of electronic transducers are available to provide additional information about the work environment. For example, temperature sensors allow hot or cold conditions to be readily detected and fed back to the computer. Other sensors can monitor the pressure in a tank, the rate of liquid flow in a pipe, the level of liquid in a container, the degree of moisture in the air, and whether or not an item is accelerating or decelerating. Depending upon the work environment and the job to be done, one or more of these sensors could be used to provide additional input to the smart robot.

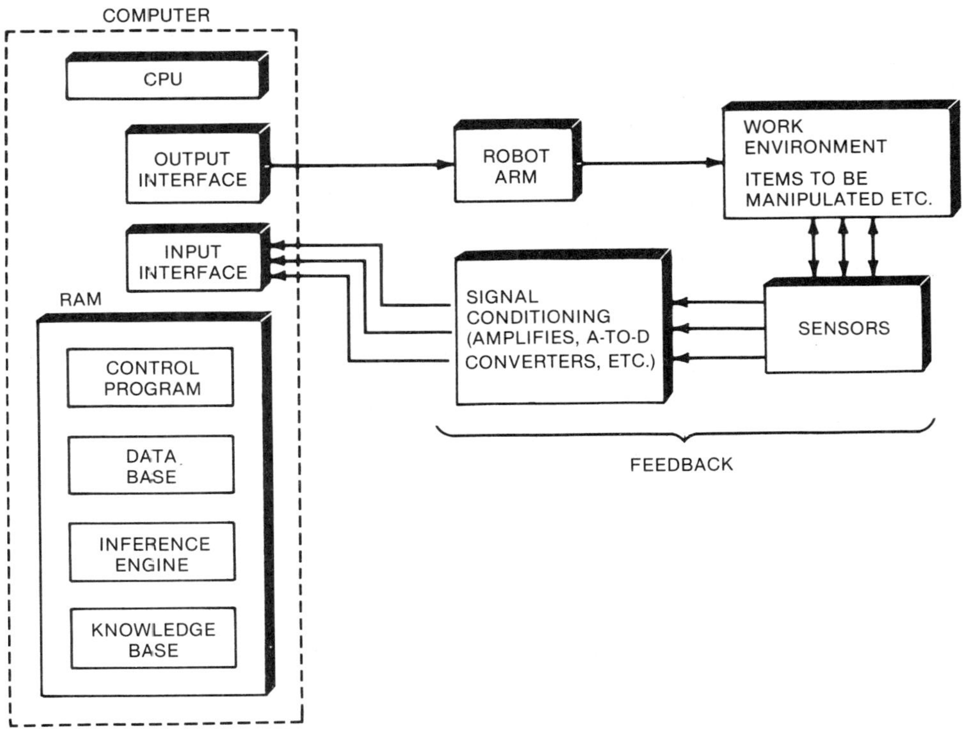

Figure 8–8. ***General block diagram of an intelligent robot.***

Perception and Intelligence

Now let's put all the pieces together and summarize what we mean by an intelligent robot. Figure 8–8 is a block diagram illustrating the main components of a smart robot. The work environment, of course, represents the objects to be manipulated. The robot arm block is self-explanatory and includes the end effector and the actuation system. The arm is driven by the computer from an output interface.

The sensors or transducers monitor various conditions in the work environment. The electrical signals they generate are conditioned by amplifiers, A-to-D converters, or other circuits to make them compatible with the computer input interface. This part of the system is the feedback.

Operation begins with sensors that monitor the environment and generate electrical signals and binary data compatible with the computer. The binary information or data base is stored in the computer's memory (RAM). This data represents feedback signals that tell the computer what's going on.

Within the computer is an inference engine that can think or reason. As in other AI systems, this inference mechanism implements a search-and-pattern matching strategy. It will use the data base information in its thought process. The data or knowledge base will contain rules, semantic networks, frames, scripts, or other representations of knowledge appropriate to the work to be done. As feedback data is analyzed, the knowledge base is referenced to make decisions. The outputs of the inferencing mechanism modify the control program, and the control program sends signals to the robot arm via the output interface. The sensors may then perceive changes that modify the data base. With new facts to consider, inference engine uses the knowledge base to make decisions about what changes to make in the control program to correct for any deviations in the work environment.

Giving the robot perception and intelligence certainly makes it adaptable. At the same time, the systems used to deliver the workpiece to the robot may not have to be as large, complex, expensive, or precise.

Better still, an intelligent robot will be able to perform in a wider range of work situations. Endowed with perception and intelligence, the robot will be more productive. Instead of making errors or not performing the work at all, the smart robot will get more work done in less time. The amount of work rejected because of errors will be far lower. When we can make the robot more nearly emulate a human, quantity and quality will increase.

Key Points

- Although AI attempts to mimic or duplicate human thought, robots attempt to emulate human physical activity.
- A robot is an electromechanical device that duplicates one or more physical functions of a human. Robots most often simulate an arm and hand.
- Robots are just dumb machines, but because they are usually computer controlled, they may be given intelligence with AI.
- Androids are synthetic humans with a human shape and limbs.
- Cyborgs are humans with some robotic limb or prosthetic device.
- Industrial robots are defined as reprogrammable multi-function manipulators.
- Most robots are fixed manipulator arms used to replace humans in manufacturing processes.
- Mobile robots provide a wider range of capabilities than fixed robots; they can propel themselves to the work.
- Most robots work more productively than humans doing the same job.
- Robots are better at repetitive, boring, manual tasks than humans. They can work longer periods without relief and make fewer errors.
- Robots are ideal for replacing humans on dangerous jobs or in hazardous environments.
- Robots often do a job not only faster and more reliably but also cheaper than humans. This makes them economically justifiable.
- The most common robot function is welding. Other popular robot applications are materials handling, assembly, and spraying.
- Robotic arms rotate and have moveable joints (shoulder, elbow, wrists) so they can move to any position within a given range. Various coordinate

systems are used to describe their position and define the scope of the work area.

- The robot arm is moved by electric motors or by hydraulic or pneumatic actuating mechanisms.
- The work of a robot arm is done by the "hand" or end effector. The end effector is a tool that grasps, welds, sprays or manipulates. Many end effectors are custom designed for the job.
- Robot arms are controlled by simple limit switches or by feedback servomechanisms. Programmable step controllers are also used.
- The trend is to operate robots from computers so their operation can be "tweaked" to optimize performance or changed completely to meet a different need.
- Special robot programming languages have been created to help simplify robot computer programming.
- Intelligent robots that think for themselves, reason, and make decisions are becoming practical and more widely used.
- Robots are more powerful, productive, flexible, and useful if they can reason for themselves.
- To be intelligent, a robot must have senses such as sight, hearing, feel, or smell. Transducers that detect pressure, light, temperature, liquid level, and other physical characteristics give robots the inputs about their work and environment. These sensors let them adapt to random, unpredictable, and imperfect surroundings and deal with unexpected events.
- The most commonly used sensor is a machine vision system with a TV camera.
- The computers controlling the robot use AI programs with a knowledge base and an inferencing system that give them the intelligence to operate independently and deal with widely varying situations successfully.

9

AI Programming in LISP

list: An item-by-item printed or written entry of persons or things, often arranged in a particular order, and usually of a specified nature or category

AMERICAN HERITAGE DICTIONARY

Since AI is software, someone must code the desired program in an available programming language. As we have already mentioned, AI programs can be written in any programming language. Assembly language, Fortran, BASIC, Pascal, C, Forth, and even Cobol, PL/1, Algol, and Snobol have been used. However, when a conventional language is used to create an AI program, the languages most often used are Pascal, C, and Forth.

A number of special AI programming languages have been developed, but the most popular and widely used of these is LISP, an acronym for LIST Processing. LISP is a symbolic processing language that represents information in lists. Objects such as people, things, or events are represented by names or symbols and their relationship is expressed by linking them together in a data structure called a list. LISP also includes procedures or functions which operate on the lists to perform a wide variety of operations. LISP can also perform basic arithmetic operations, but it is not optimized for such applications. LISP is an unusual language, particularly if you originally learned and are familiar with more conventional programming languages. However, it is relatively easy to learn and use. It is by far the most important and widely used AI programming language. If you plan to do any serious, in-depth AI work, you most certainly will need to learn and use LISP.

This chapter is designed to introduce you to this important programming language. It is a primer that shows how LISP operates and is used. In the next chapter, we will discuss the other popular AI programming language Prolog.

Some LISP Background

LISP is one of the oldest higher level programming languages. Developed in the late 1950s by John McCarthy at MIT, its first full implementation on a commercial basis occurred in the early 1960s. Since then, it has evolved and developed in many directions.

Higher Level Languages

The oldest higher level programming language is Fortran, developed by IBM in the early 1950s. Its first commercial implementation appeared in 1954. Fortran, a shorthand way of saying Formula Translation, was developed primarily to speed up and simplify mathematical calculations. It is still the most widely favored language for scientific and engineering computing. Like LISP, Fortran has survived for well over a quarter of a century, primarily because it has been continually developed and refined.

Lower level languages refer to the machine and assembly languages normally associated with a specific computer. Machine language represents data and instructions in binary code (or its hexadecimal equivalent). Programming in machine language is time consuming and error prone. It is rarely done. Machine language programming was replaced by assembly language programming which uses symbolic representation of data and instructions. Assemblers speed up and simplify writing programs for a particular computer. However, considerable knowledge of the computer's operation and architecture is required to use assembly language successfully.

Higher level languages are designed for individuals who do not want or need to know the architecture and operation of the computer. Applications or problem oriented, they are designed to facilitate the creation of programs in some particular field of interest. A system of syntax and procedures uses algorithms to solve a wide range of problems without having to know how the computer operates.

Dialects and Standards

LISP has undergone considerable changes over the years. The original LISP is generally referred to as Version 1.0. It was later refined and improved to form what is generally known as Version 1.5. Many new and different dialects of the LISP language have been created by starting with Version 1.5. There are many "spin-offs" and variations. Today, LISP is available for most popular mainframes, minicomputers, and personal computers.

Dialects

There are four general categories or dialects for the LISP language. One of these, MacLISP, was developed at MIT, and many different versions of it are available.

Another major dialect of LISP is InterLISP. It was developed primarily at Bolt, Beranek & Newman, Inc., and Xerox Palo Alto Research Labs. Like MacLISP, InterLISP has numerous variations. Both MacLISP and InterLISP or their variations are widely implemented on special AI development workstations called LISP machines.

Another lesser known LISP is Portable Standard LISP developed at the University of Utah. This was an attempt to standardize one particular dialect, but like the other dialects of LISP, it did not emerge as the standard in the marketplace. Nevertheless, Portable Standard LISP has been used on a variety of machines.

Finally, there is Common LISP. This is an attempt by a national committee of U.S. computer scientists to come up with a dialect of LISP that everyone will agree to and use. Common LISP is a new version of MacLISP. It has also been greatly influenced by the Zeta LISP dialect as well as InterLISP and some minor dialects. It is just now becoming widely available. Whether it will indeed become "the" standard remains to be seen. Nevertheless, it is a valiant attempt to create a happy medium that will help stabilize the language and make it more portable, consistent, and efficient.

Standards

A standard LISP is highly desirable to create programs that are portable. When creating AI software using LISP it is desirable to be able to transfer the program to any computer running LISP. That is not possible now because of the wide variations in the various dialects. While most versions of LISP share a common subset of features and characteristics, each has its own unique syntax, features, and extensions. When these special features are used in programming, they do not translate from one machine to another. In order to use the program, some conversion process must be used which usually entails significant reprogramming.

As interest in AI grows, considerable effort will be expended in writing new programs in LISP and other languages. There is great concern throughout the industry about the lack of standardization and thus the inability to transport programs written for one machine to other machines. This is a particular concern in the military. When old computers are replaced by new computers, it is desirable to transfer the software directly from the old machine to the new machine without reprogramming. DARPA, the Defense Advanced Research Projects Agency, a division of the Department of Defense, supports the Common LISP effort. It is hoped at some point that a formal Common LISP standard will emerge to solve many of the problems created by the multitude of dialects now used. Appendix C gives you a feel for the variety of LISPs available.

> *A new project to develop an American National Standard for the Lisp programming language is being prepared for the X3 Accredited Standards Committee (of ANSI). At the same time, a proposal to develop an international standard Lisp has been submitted for forwarding to the International Standards Organization to coordinate with international efforts.*
>
> GOVERNMENT COMPUTER NEWS
> MAY, 9, 1986

How LISP Works

The remainder of this chapter is devoted to specific details of LISP programming and application, but let's take a brief look at how LISP works. To do this, first consider how other programming languages work.

For example, in assembly language, a program contains a sequence of instructions that implement some algorithm. The algorithm is implemented by using the various computer instructions in the proper order. The computer then sequentially fetches and executes these instructions to carry out the specified algorithm.

Most higher level programs operate in basically the same way. An algorithm is chosen or developed to carry out a desired operation. Then declarations, statements, and commands are given. In Fortran and BASIC, the declarations generally define the variables and arrays to be used in the computation. Then statements using the variables and arrays are given. These statements express operations to be carried out on the data. You are familiar with statements like PRINT, READ, and GOTO. Mathematical operations such as add, subtract, multiply and divide can also be stated. Programs to implement the algorithms are formed by writing a sequence of statements to perform the desired operation. The language converts these various statements into individual machine instructions that are executed to perform the desired operation.

LISP operates in a different way. LISP operates on words called *atoms.* Atoms can be numbers but more often are symbolic names for some object, place, or event. These atoms are grouped together to form lists. LISP then manipulates these lists to carry out the desired operation.

Instead of using statements and commands, LISP uses procedures or functions to operate on the data. A *procedure function* is an operation that is applied to the atoms and lists. An example is the arithmetic procedures: add, subtract, multiply, and divide. LISP also includes question-answering procedures called predicates. Predicates look at a symbol and determine whether it is true or false. Typically, a procedure appears as the first element in a list. It tells the program what to do with the items in the list. Most LISPs contain built-in predefined procedures called *primitives* which can be used to perform most operations. However, LISP is unique in that the programming can easily define new procedure functions using the basic primitives.

The basic operation of LISP is to read the procedure, evaluate it, and print out the result. This read-evaluate-print cycle is repeated again and again on each procedure until the desired processing takes place.

Another feature common to LISP is *recursion.* Recursion means that a function can refer to or call itself. A function is said to be recursive if it refers to itself in its definition. Recursion is a very powerful concept that greatly simplifies some programs and allows many special operations to be implemented. Recursion can sometimes be substituted for iteration, generally implemented with a loop in other programming languages. We will talk more about recursion and iteration later, but for now, it is important to note that recursion is a key feature of LISP and extremely important in implementing AI programs.

Interpreters and Compilers

Higher level languages may be implemented as either compilers or interpreters. A compiler is a special computer program that takes the original source program (consisting of lines of declarations and statements) and converts it into a machine code object program the computer can execute. To use a compiler, you first write the program and enter it into the computer. This is usually done using a text editor or even a standard word processing package. The program file created is known as the source

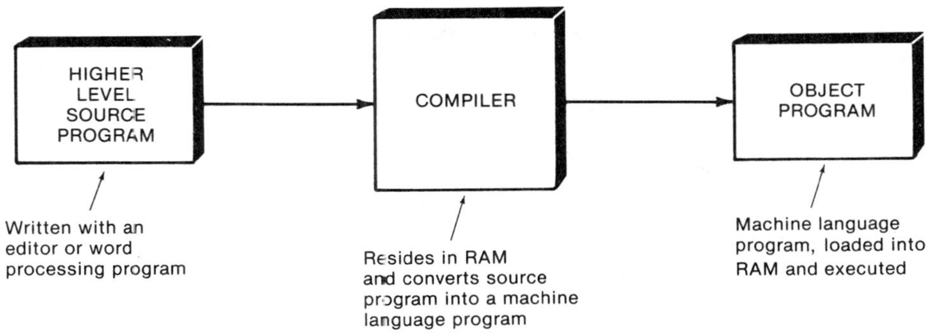

Figure 9–1. *A compiler.*

program, and it becomes the input to the compiler. The compiler then works its way through the input source program and creates machine code instructions the computer can use. The program thus created is known as the object program. See Figure 9–1. The machine code object program can now be stored on a disk, then loaded into RAM and executed.

Compilers are generally the preferred type of translation program because they produce the fastest executable code. However, if problems occur or mistakes are made in the programming process, it is a time-consuming and difficult problem to go back and make the correction, recompile the program, and execute it again. This process may be necessary several times before the final program runs properly.

An interpreter, on the other hand, is entirely interactive. In an interpreter, the machine code to implement the various statements and commands in the language are prestored, usually in RAM or sometimes in ROM. The interpreter has to be co-resident with the program to be executed. As with the compiler, the original program is written in the higher level language and entered into the computer. The interpreter then looks at each line of code in the program, then references routines in the interpreter which executes them. This idea is illustrated in Figure 9–2.

Interpreters operate much slower than compiler-developed programs. This is a considerable disadvantage in some applications. However, the trade-off is interaction. No compilation is required; and, therefore, if problems are encountered or bugs detected, they can be corrected immediately and the program re-executed with a minimum of complexity.

LISP was originally developed as an interpreter, and for a long time it was the only interpreted higher level language available. Today the most commonly used interpreted language is BASIC, which is a feature on most personal computers. Most versions of LISP are still of the interpreted variety. However, LISP compilers have also been created. LISP compilers are able to create shorter, faster programs for applications requiring higher performance. In the marketplace today, the most popular versions of LISPs are those for which both interpreted and compiled versions are available.

LISP Machines

While most LISPs are interpreters or compilers that run on some general purpose mainframe, minicomputer, or personal computer, LISP is also available in a very special

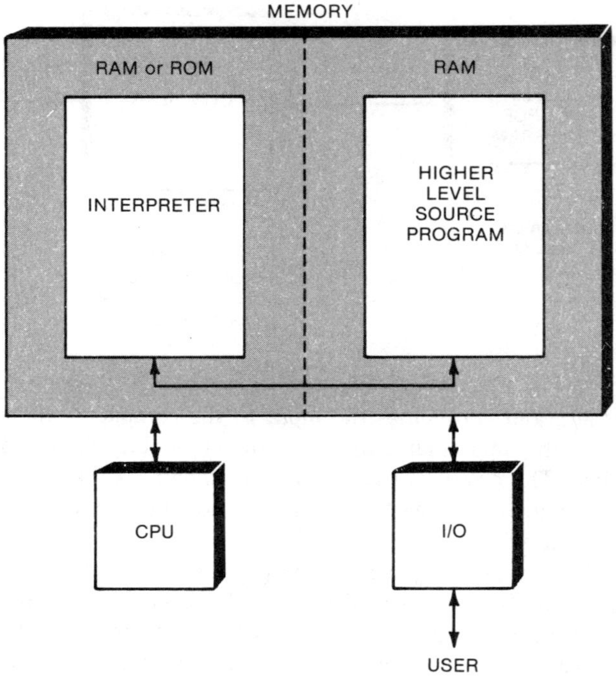

Figure 9–2. *An interpreter.*

hardware format. A unique category of AI computer known as a LISP machine has been developed specifically to create and run LISP programs. In fact, the basic LISP functions and capabilities are preprogrammed into the LISP machine, usually in microcode stored in a ROM. Most LISP machines use some version of either MacLISP or InterLISP plus many other utility programs such as editors and debuggers, which greatly speed up and simplify the creation of LISP programs. While most LISP machines can run other programming languages, they are usually dedicated to the LISP function because they are optimized for that application. We will talk more about these special computers in Chapter 11.

Atoms and Lists

The purpose of a digital computer is to process data. The LISP language processes or manipulates data, although the types of data and the way it can be processed are somewhat different from more conventional programming languages. In this section we want to take a look at the way the LISP programming language represents data. In a later section, we will discuss the functions or procedures that LISP uses to process this data.

Atoms

The basic data element in LISP is an atom, a single word or number that represents some object or value. Atoms are the smallest data element in LISP and cannot be subdivided.

There are two basic types of atoms, numbers and symbols. Let's consider each type in more detail.

Numbers

Numbers, as you would expect, are simply numerical values. Almost any number qualifies as a LISP atom. Both integer (whole number) and real (floating point or decimal) values are acceptable to most LISPs. Numbers may also be either positive or negative. Listed below are some of the kinds of numbers that are valid in LISP.

1986

.00015

48.3

−27

Symbols

Symbols are words that represent people, places, or things. Symbols can be actual names or words that mean something or they can be contrived combinations of various characters. Further, symbols can be a combination of both letters and numbers, although a symbol cannot begin with a number. These combinations are referred to as alphanumeric symbols.

Listed below are representative examples of the symbol that can be used in LISP. As you can see, the possibilities are enormous.

FRIEND JOAN

XYZ ANIMAL-TYPES

JK36 ALLOWED-COLORS

Note that characters like the hyphen and dash can be used within an atomic symbol to replace spaces, which are not allowed.

Lists

While the atom is the basic data element in the LISP programming language, nothing really meaningful can be done with individual atoms. Further, LISP does not process individual numbers or symbols. For practical processing to occur, a number of atoms must be assembled to form a list, a sequence of multiple atoms grouped together. An example of a list is shown below:

(CAR TRUCK AIRPLANE MOTORCYCLE SHIP)

Note that a list is designated with parentheses. Inside the list are individual atoms. These are also referred to as elements of the list. Note that the atoms are separated from one another by a single space. Note also that the list contains atoms that usually have something in common. In this case, the list is of objects of transportation.

Several other examples of valid lists are illustrated below.

(T U V W X Y Z)

(red gold purple white)

(Bud Ann Janet Mark John Sally)

(A1 G2 B4 C6 I8)

(19 27.1 83 50 46.9)

In these examples, all of the elements of the list are atoms. It is also possible for a list to be an element of another list. The following example shows how a list can be made up of atoms and other lists.

(A(B C D)(E F)(G H I)(J K)

The example below shows how a list is made up of multiple lists. That is, each element in this list is also a list.

((M N)(O P)(Q R)(S T))

Lists can be part of lists which may be part of other lists. The example below shows an example. Such multiple lists are said to be "nested."

((U V W)((M N O)((D E F)(A B C))(P R S T))

It is important in creating and using lists that you keep track of the number of parentheses used in the various expressions. Whenever you have an open parenthesis, you must also have a corresponding closed parenthesis to formally complete or balance the expression. If a list is not properly enclosed with the correct number of parentheses, LISP will not process it correctly. So take care to count your opening and closing parenthesis whenever you are entering a list.

Note that we have referred to a list as an expression. You will often hear this term applied to lists when LISP programs are discussed. Individual atoms can also be referred to as expressions. You will also hear the term S-expressions used to refer to lists. The "S" refers to symbolic.

When typing in lists on the computer, the lists do not have to be all on one line. In fact, it is sometimes easier to enter lists in such a way that each element is on a separate line. In this way, the individual list elements are easier to pick out and recognize. Two formats can be used. In the example below, each list element is written on a separate line but is indented from the others.

```
((M N)
  (O P)
    (Q R)
      (S T))
```

Lists can also be created by simply putting each element on a separate line, one below the other, as shown in the example below.

((IBM)

(Apple)

(DEC)

(Compaq))

Note that even though each element is on a separate line, the use of the parentheses is the same as if the list were written in one continuous string on a single line.

The Empty List

It is also possible to have what is known as an empty list, one that does not have any elements. It is simply written as a pair of parentheses:

()

The empty list can be an element in a larger list, or it may stand by itself.

The empty list is also referred to as NIL. The empty list () may be used interchangeably with the expression NIL. We will explain more about the empty list later.

Representing Lists inside the Computer

So far we have shown how lists are typed into the computer and how they appear on the video screen or in a printout. But this is certainly not how they appear to the computer hardware. It may give you a better feel for how a computer processes a LISP program if you understand how the various lists are actually constructed or represented within the computer.

Lists are represented inside the computer as chains of elements known as *CONS* cells. A CONS cell is a two-part structure consisting of two addresses. One address points to the element of the list it represents, while the second address points to the next element in the list. A CONS cell is usually illustrated as shown in Figure 9–3. Each element of a list is associated with one CONS cell. A group of these CONS cells linked together represent the entire list. An example of this is shown in Figure 9–4.

All data in a computer is stored in memory, made up of individual storage locations for binary words. Each of these words is associated with or identified by a number called an address. The address is the numerical location of a particular data word in the memory. For example, a typical memory consists of many hundreds of thousands of bytes of data. A byte contains 8 bits. Usually numbers, letters, and other symbols are represented by the ASCII or other code. These are 7- or 8-bit binary representations for these various characters. Each character is stored in an individual memory location. An atom might consist of the three letters "red." Each of these characters would be stored as a byte in a sequential memory location. The address of the first character "r" would represent the pointer in the first or left side of the CONS cell representing that atom, which we can assume is an element of a list.

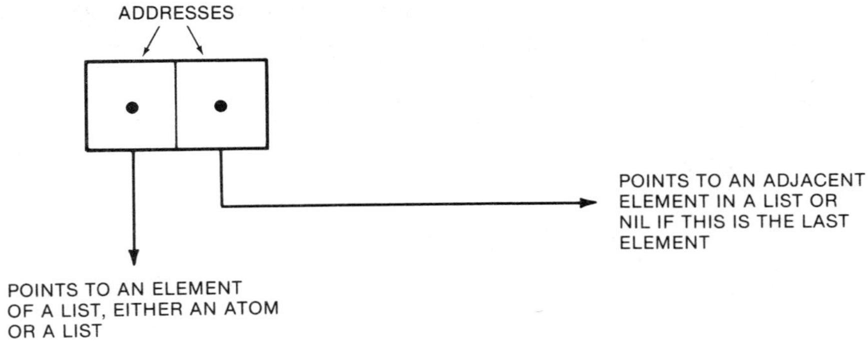

Figure 9–3. *A CONS cell.*

The other address in the CONS cell points to the memory location where the first character of the next element is stored. This might be a "b" as in blue, another element in the list.

In the example of Figure 9–4, each element of the list is an individual atom. Let's look at an example of a CONS cell representation of a list containing a list. An example of this is shown in Figure 9–5.

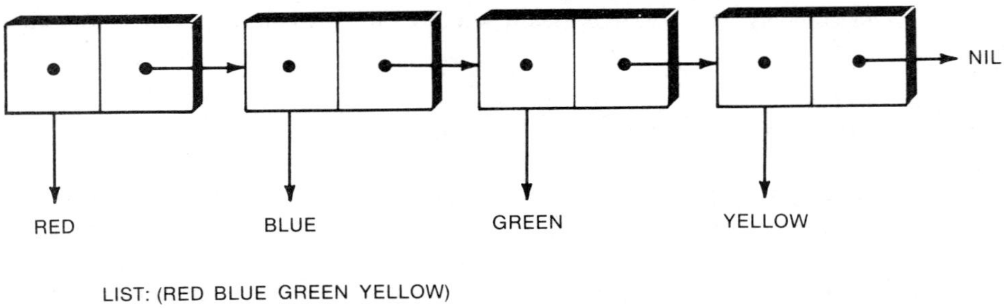

Figure 9–4. *A CONS cell representation of a list.*

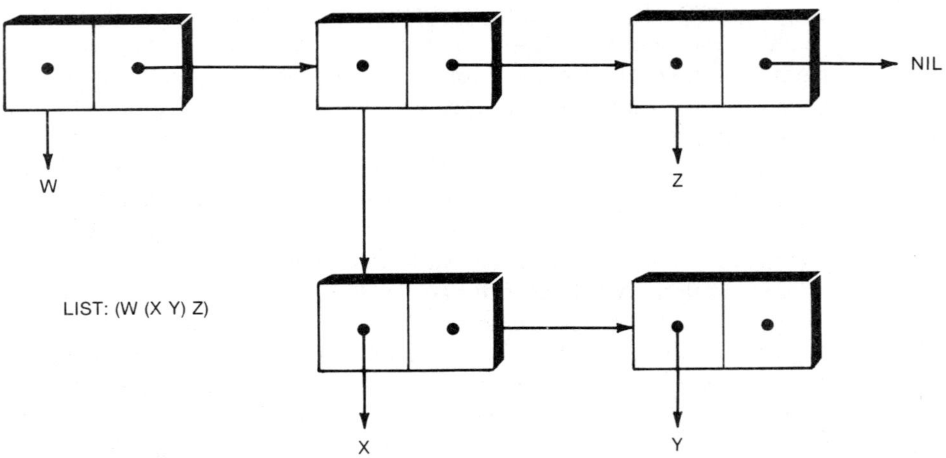

Figure 9–5. *A CONS cell representation showing a list within a list.*

In using LISP, you won't have to worry about CONS cells, but it may help you visualize how the data is stored and used.

Functions, Procedures, and Primitives

Atoms represent numbers or symbols and are used collectively to form lists. Lists can also be formed with other lists and atoms. The atoms and lists are referred to as symbolic *expressions* or simply expressions. An expression is called a form if it is designed to be evaluated. Remember, the basic processing procedure of LISP is to read an expression, analyze or evaluate it, and print the result.

In this section we want to look at that evaluation process. Expressions are operated upon by procedures or functions. A procedure is a description of how data is to be processed in LISP. The terms procedure and function are often used interchangeably, but more precisely, a function computes a value based on its arguments. Therefore, all functions are procedures. But not all procedures are functions.

LISP comes with a complete set of predefined procedures a programmer can use to evaluate lists. This basic set of procedures is referred to as *primitives.* Although the set of primitives supplied with a LISP programming language is broad and flexible, there is always something you want to do not provided for by primitives. LISP permits you to define your own unique functions or procedures. You simply make them up out of the basic primitives, give them a name, and call them whenever you need them. Because you can create your own procedures, LISP is said to be extensible. As the programmer, you can literally make up and use your own processing procedures.

Finally, if we combine a group of procedures that performs various operations in some sequence, we create a program. The program uses an algorithm that defines the procedures to be used and in what order. LISP will evaluate the procedures one at a time as it executes the program.

The Basic Primitives

All versions of LISP come with a set of basic primitives or functions, that vary considerably from one dialect of LISP to another. Also, common primitives often are named differently or are used in a different way. However, most LISPs do contain a basic subset of primitives common to virtually all LISPs. It is this basic subset of primitives that we will look at in this section. When you begin working with a specific LISP program, you will learn the primitives and other features unique to that language.

Arithmetic Primitives

We will begin by looking at the arithmetic primitives used to perform mathematical operations. LISP is not the best language for heavy mathematical operations, but it can do a creditable job. Like most other programming languages, it can perform the four basic arithmetic operations: add, subtract, multiply, and divide. Some special primitives include square root, add one, subtract one, negate, and so on.

The basic format for a mathematical primitive, or for any LISP procedure for that matter, is shown below:

```
(Procedure Argument1 Argument2 . . . )
```

In this expression, the procedure is given first. This is a word or symbol that specifies the operation to take place. The following elements of the expression are referred to as *arguments.* Arguments are nothing more than the numbers, symbols, or lists to be operated upon by the procedure. Of course, this expression is enclosed in parentheses.

Now let's take some real examples. Below we show how to do addition with LISP.

```
(+ 2.34 7.59)
```

Whenever you type this expression into LISP, it will immediately evaluate it and return the answer, 9.93. It looks at the first element of the list or expression, sees the plus sign, and knows that addition is called for. The two numbers to be added are given as the next two elements of the list or expression. The addition is performed and the sum is immediately typed out.

The first thing to note here is that most mathematical primitives work with only two arguments. That is, the primitive can deal with only two numbers at a time. If you want to add a sequence of numbers, you will need to make a running total. Add the first two numbers together, then the third number to the subtotal, then the fourth number to the subtotal, and so on. For example, this expression would add 2, 4, 6, and 8.

```
(+2 (+4(+6 8)))
```

Second, some LISPs call for putting the procedure or primitive outside the parenthesis as shown below:

```
+(2.34 7.59)
```

When you begin using a particular dialect of LISP, the instruction manual will tell you the correct format to use.

Third, some LISPs also use names for the mathematical functions instead of a special character. For example, addition may be specified by the words ADD or PLUS. The expression to add two numbers with such a format may look like:

```
(PLUS 2.34 7.59)
```

Subtraction of two numbers is performed as illustrated below:

```
(− 8.6 1.1)
7.5
```

Some LISPs use the primitive DIFFERENCE or just DIF instead of the minus sign. Note that the minuend is the first argument while the subtrahend is the second argument. When you key in the above expression, LISP evaluates it immediately and returns the difference.

The example below shows how LISP does multiplication:

```
(* −4.9 2.3)
−11.27
```

Some LISPs use the word TIMES to express multiplication instead of the asterisk. Note also that LISP can deal with negative numbers.

An example of division is shown below:

```
(/ 4.9 .7)
7.0
```

You will also see the term QUOTIENT used instead of the slash to specify division in LISP.

In all of these examples we used real or floating point numbers; that is, those using decimal fractions. Some earlier, simple LISPs can work only with integers or whole numbers. This may be a handicap if you are doing a lot of math. When only integer arithmetic is used, division sometimes produces incorrect results. This happens when the division does not turn out even. Consider the expression below:

```
(/ 7 3)
3
```

With integer division, dividing 7 by 2 does not produce the desired 3.5. Instead it produces only 3. Some LISPs allow you to corect for this by having a primitive called REMAINDER. REMAINDER does the same thing as division in that it divides the first number by the second but gives the remainder instead of the quotient.

```
(/ 7 3)
1
```

Of course, all of these basic math operations may be combined to compute more complex expressions. The example below shows how this is done. Work it out yourself to be sure you understand the process.

```
(−7 ( / (* 6 8)(+ 3 9)))
3
```

The standard way of expressing the problem is $7-(6\times 8)(3+9)$.

Keep in mind that although we know this is a mathematical computation, LISP sees the expression only as a list. It evaluates that list as it does all others.

Most LISPs will perform a variety of other mathematical primitives. Some of the more common ones are summarized in Table 9–1. Before starting to use any version of LISP, familiarize yourself with the available primitives and how they work.

Predicates

Predicates are a special class of procedures that answer questions about an argument and respond with either true or false. Some predicates require only one argument while others take two.

For example, there are predicates that determine whether an expression is a number, a symbol, an atom, or a list. Occasionally, the program needs to know what it is dealing with and such predicates can tell it.

Table 9–1. *Other Arithmetic Primitives*

1. ABS	Computes the absolute value (ABS - 6.4) 6.4 (ABS 6.4) 6.4
2. EXPT	Raises the first argument to the power of the second argument (EXPT 2 4) 16
3. MAX	Finds the largest number in a list of arguments (MAX 2 9 14 3 17 8) 17
4. MIN	Finds the smallest number in a list of arguments (MIN 2 9 14 3 17 8) 2
5. SQRT	Finds the square root of a number (SQRT 4096) 64

The predicate NUMBERP determines if an expression is a number. Two examples are given below:

```
(NUMBERP 17)
T
(NUMBERP GAL)
NIL
```

In the first case, the argument is the number 17, therefore, the predicate returns the value T which means true or yes, 17 is a number. In the second case, the argument GAL, of course, is not a number but a symbol. LISP responds with the designation NIL, which means no or false.

ATOM is a predicate that determines whether an expression is an atom. Two examples are given below.

```
(ATOM RED)
T
(ATOM RED BLUE GREEN YELLOW)
NIL
```

Here the predicate ATOM determines that the symbol RED is an atom. In the second case it asks if the expression in parentheses is an atom, in which case it answers NIL. The expression, of course, is a five-element list.

The predicate LISTP does essentially the same thing, as you can see from the examples below:

(LISTP RED)
NIL
(LISTP RED BLUE YELLOW)
T

Some kinds of predicates indicate something about the value of a number. Such predicates are ZEROP, ODDP, EVENP.

The two examples below show how ZEROP works:

(ZEROP 4)
NIL
(ZEROP 0)
T

In the first case, we ask LISP if the number 4 is zero. Of course, it is not so it returns with NIL indicating false. In the second case, 0 is zero and the response is T.

ODDP and EVENP designate whether a number is odd or even.

(ODDP 7)
T
(EVENP 7)
NIL

Some predicates require two arguments. An example is the widely used predicate EQUAL. EQUAL compares two expressions, either atoms or lists, to see if they are the same. If they are identical, then the EQUAL predicate returns T. Otherwise, it responds with NIL. The examples below show this operation.

(EQUAL (A1 A2)(A1 A2))
T
(EQUAL (A1 A2)(B1 B3))
NIL
(EQUAL 14 24)
NIL

EQUAL can be used to implement a simple form of pattern matching.

Two other widely used predicates are LESSP and GREATERP. These two predicates determine whether one number is less than or greater than another. The examples below show how they work:

(GREATERP 7 5)
T
(GREATERP 3 5)
NIL
(LESSP 2 9)
T
(LESSP 8 3)
NIL

Table 9–2. ***Other Predicates—NOT and NULL***

1. NOT	Returns either T or NIL depending on argument (NOT T) NIL (NOT NIL) T
2. NULL	Checks to see if argument is an empty list-same as NOT (NULL ()) T (NULL T) NIL

In some LISPs, the characters > and < will be used instead of GREATERP or LESSP respectively.

There are numerous predicates in other LISPs. We won't try to cover them all here, but some of the more common ones are described briefly in Table 9–2.

Assembling and Disassembling Lists

Most of the operations in a LISP program involve creating new lists, modifying existing lists, and looking for or extracting parts of lists. A number of procedures or primitives are available within LISP to do this. Five of the most common are: CAR, CDR, APPEND, CONS, and LIST. Let's take a look at each of these in more detail. All of these procedures are designed to operate on lists.

Using the CAR primitive to evaluate a list causes the first element in that list to be returned. A simple example is given below.

```
(CAR '( W X Y Z)))
W
```

Here the primitive CAR operates on a list (W X Y Z). The single quote mark will be explained shortly, but for now, just ignore it. The CAR function on the list gives us the first element of the list, in this case, W.

Another example using a list of lists is given below:

```
(CAR ' ((A B C)(D E F)(G H I)))
(A B C)
```

The CDR primitive produces the complement of the CAR primitive. That is, CDR (pronounced cud-er or could-er) returns all the rest of the elements of a list except the first one. Using the two examples given above, you can see how CDR works.

```
(CDR '( W X Y Z))
(X Y Z)
(CDR ' ((A B C)(D E F)(G H I)))
((D E F)(G H I))
```

Using these two procedures in various combinations, you can search out and select virtually any element of any list regardless of the depth of nesting.

For example, the expression below shows how it is possible to extract the second element of a list.

(CAR (CDR' (W X Y Z)))

X

Again note the single quote mark in this expression. The purpose of this quote mark is to tell LISP what part of the expression to evaluate and what part to ignore. The single quote (actually an apostrophe) separates the procedure from the data that is to be evaluated. If we did not provide the quote mark above, for example, LISP would start at the innermost list and attempt to evaluate the expression there. Here, it would start with (W X Y Z). In this example, it would first assume that W was some procedure attached to the remaining elements of the list. The result would be that since W is not a primitive, an error message would be given and computation would cease. Here, the quote mark says that (W X Y Z) is simply a list to be operated upon by the CDR first and CAR second.

You can see in this example that the CDR function is performed first and causes (X Y Z) to be returned. The CAR procedure then uses this and extracts the first element, in this case X.

Just to be sure you understand the concept of the single quote, let's change its position and see the result. Let's assume that the expression is changed to put the quote mark directly after CAR instead of after CDR, resulting in the expression:

(CAR '(CDR (W X Y Z)))

This tells the CAR function to operate on the list (CDR (W X Y Z)). It says to extract the first element of that list, which in this case is CDR. The placement of the quote effectively ignores CDR as a procedure and simply assumes it is the first element of a list.

In some forms of LISP you will see the actual word QUOTE used instead of the apostrophe symbol.

Some additional examples combining CAR and CDR are given below. Work your way through them to be sure you understand how each evaluation is arrived at.

(CAR (CDR (CDR' ((A B)(J K)(T U)(R S)))))

(T U)

The right most CDR works on the list first, returning ((J K)(T U)(R S)). The next CDR gives us ((T U)(R S)). Final CAR produces (T U). The third element of the list was selected.

(CDR (CAR' (RED YELLOW BLUE GREEN)))

ERROR

Here the CAR produces RED. But CDR cannot operate on atoms alone. CAR and CDR operate only on lists.

Most LISPs use a shorthand procedure to represent multiple combined CAR and CDR primitives. Instead of writing the complete primitive CAR or CDR each time, a single primitive of the form C--R, C---R, or C----R is used. Here each dash can be a capital A representing CAR, or a capital D signifying CDR. To show how this works, consider our previous example and its equivalent as shown below:

(CAR (CDR '(W X Y Z))) is equivalent to (CADR '(W X Y Z))

The important thing to note when dealing with a composite procedure such as this is that the capital A's and capital D's work on the list in reverse order. In other words, as you are evaluating an expression using the composite form, start with the capital A or capital D directly to the left of the last R and then work backwards, right to left, in sequence on the list performing either a CAR for A or CDR for D. The expression below illustrates this point.

```
(CDAR ' ((RED YELLOW)(BLUE GREEN)(SILVER GOLD)))
(YELLOW)
```

The CAR function works first here to give the list (RED YELLOW). The CDR function works next to produce YELLOW.

The CAR and CDR primitives disassemble or take apart lists so that we can get to individual elements. Other primitives are used to construct or modify lists. These include APPEND, CONS, and LIST.

The APPEND primitive combines the elements of two lists to form a larger list. It takes the elements of the two lists and runs them together one after another. The example below illustrates this point.

```
(APPEND ' (S T U V) '(W X Y Z))
(S T U V W X Y Z)
```

Note that you have to have a single quote ahead of each list you wish to append.

The CONS primitive adds a new element to the front of an existing list. When you use the CONS primitive to state the element to be added, either an atom or a list, you also show the list to which it is to be added. When CONS is evaluated, the result will be the new expression that shows up as the first element of a longer list made up of the previous list. The example below shows how this is done:

```
(CONS 'V '(W X Y Z))
(V W X Y Z)
```

With CONS you can build new lists from scratch or modify existing lists. Several more examples are given below. Be sure to work your way through them to understand how they work.

```
(CONS '(J K L) '((M N)(O P Q)(R S)))
((J K L)(M N)(O P Q)(R S))
(CONS 'RED '(BLUE))
(RED BLUE)
```

The LIST primitive also allows you to build lists from scratch. It takes the argument that it is given and creates a new list with each of the arguments as an element of that new list. The example below shows how this works:

Table 9–3. *Other Primitives for Working with Lists*

1. LENGTH	Returns the number of elements in a list (LENGTH '(W X Y Z)) 4 (LENGTH 'J K) (L M) (N O))) 3
2. REVERSE	Reverses the order of a list (REVERSE' (W X Y Z)) (Z Y X W)
3. LAST	Returns the last element in a list (LAST '(W X Y Z)) Z

```
(LIST '(S T U V) '(W X Y Z))
((S T U V) (W X Y Z))
```

Another example of LIST is given below to ensure that you understand the concept.

```
(LIST '(BLACK) '(GRAY) '(WHITE))
((BLACK)(GRAY)(WHITE))
```

Some other procedures used in working with lists are described briefly in Table 9–3.

Assigning Values

All programming languages have a means of assigning values to a *variable*. Most programs contain quantities known as variables. A variable may assume any one of a number of different values. Usually we designate the variables by symbol names, such as a letter of the alphabet, a word, or an alphanumeric designation. Some examples of variables are A, X, TEST, Z3. In order to perform a computation involving variables, the program must know what the value of the variable is. Variables are assigned values in some programming languages by stating in mathematical or algebraic form just what the value is. For example, in some programming languages you can set the variable X equal to the value 7 with the simple statement X = 7. In the BASIC language, the LET statement does the same thing. For example, to set the variable J to the value 48 you write the statement LET J = 48.

In LISP, variables are assigned values by using the SETQ primitive to bind a variable to a particular value. The parameters for the SETQ procedure are the variable name and the value to which it is to be set. Here's an example of SETQ:

```
(SETQ X 86)
```

Whenever you type this in on the computer, LISP will evaluate the procedure and return the value to which X is assigned. In this case, the value is 86. Now, whenever you use X in a procedure, the value 86 will be used when the expression is evaluated. For example:

```
(SETQ X 14)
14
(SETQ Y 23)
23
(+ X Y)
37
```

Here's another example of SETQ using a symbolic value:

```
(SETQ LF 'WRITER)
```

Here you are assigning the variable LF the value of WRITER. Note that you have to use the single quote ahead of the assigned value. You didn't have to do this in the first example because no quote is required when numerical values are used. When the above expression is typed in, LISP will evaluate it and return the assigned value, or for this example, WRITER.

You can also use SETQ to bind a list to a variable name. An example is shown below:

```
(SETQ PRIMARY-COLORS '(RED BLUE GREEN))
```

Here you are assigning the variable PRIMARY-COLORS the value of the list (RED BLUE GREEN). Again note the single quote before the value, which in this case is a list.

Note that in the variable name we used a hyphen between the words PRIMARY and COLORS. We cannot use a variable name of two or more words. LISP looks for a single variable name. It determines where one word leaves off and another begins by looking for a space. If we leave a space, LISP will misinterpret our intent. To overcome this problem, we make the variable name PRIMARY COLORS into one word by using a hyphen instead of a space between the two words. You can also use a dash, such as PRIMARY-COLORS. In this way you can use two or more words in a variable name. The benefit of this is that variables can be given names that are more descriptive and more meaningful than using single letters of the alphabet or some cryptic mnemonic. For example, we could have used PC for primary colors but it would not be as meaningful. If you wanted to create a variable designated RETURN ON INVESTMENT, you could use initials, ROI. However, to be more literal, you could also use the expression RETURN-ON-INVESTMENT.

Once you have assigned a value to a variable using the SETQ primitive, the LISP program will use that value any time it encounters the variable in another procedure. For that reason, you must use the SETQ primitives at the beginning of the program to assign the values for variables to be used in the program. Once this is done, you can write the remaining procedures that actually perform the desired operations.

Here are some examples based on the previously defined list PRIMARY-COLORS:

(REVERSE 'PRIMARY-COLORS)
(GREEN BLUE RED)
(CDR 'PRIMARY-COLORS)
(BLUE GREEN)

If you want the variable to change as the result of some computation, you will need to use the SETQ function again within another expression to change its value.

Creating Your Own Functions

All LISPs have a built-in set of features or functions called primitives. These are the basic building blocks which you use to create programs to process data. These primitives are comparable to the computer instructions in assembly language or the statements and commands in higher level programming languages. However, in creating a program, regardless of the language used, there are always some things you want to do that are not defined by individual instructions, statements, or commands. This is also true of LISP. Many times the processing you wish to perform is not available as a primitive. In this case, you must create your own.

LISP provides the define function or DEFUN procedure to create new procedures or functions by using the existing primitives. This process is similar to creating a subroutine in another language. For example, in many computers, multiplication is not available as a single instruction. Instead, a subroutine has to be written using existing instructions that will cause multiplication to be carried out. This subroutine will then be called when multiplication is desired.

While all LISPs will let you define your own procedures, not all of them call the procedure DEFUN. In other LISPs it may be called DE, DEF, or DEFINE. But regardless of what the procedure is named, the entire process is usually referred to as *procedure abstraction.* All that means is that you can build new procedures by simply combining existing primitives.

Let's look at a couple of examples to illustrate this concept. Suppose your application required the repeated calculation of the cube of a variable. Recall that the cube of a number is that number multiplied by itself three times. For example, the cube of the number 2 is 2 × 2 × 2 = 8. Instead of writing out a procedure multiplying the number by itself three times each time you wish to determine the cube, you can create a new function called CUBE. To do this, you will write the expression shown below:

(DEFUN CUBE (X) (*X(*X X)))

Take a look at this expression and we will analyze it for you. First, the primitive DEFUN designates what this expression will do. Next is the word CUBE. In defining a function the second term that you enter is some symbolic name for the new procedure that you are creating. Whenever you want to use your new function, you will use it at the beginning of an expression just as you would a primitive. Next, you will give the variable names to be used in the new function in parentheses. In this case, our variable is X so we list it in parentheses as shown. Finally, in parentheses at the end of the expression you write the body of the new procedure which, in this case, is a computation. To multiply the variable X by itself three times requires the expression shown. The inside set of parentheses calls for multiplying X by itself. Remember that only two parameters or arguments are permitted in any LISP mathematic operation. Once X is multiplied by itself, it must again be multiplied by X to create the cube. This is done with another asterisk X and enclosed in parentheses.

Whenever you type in the above expression in LISP, it will be evaluated and LISP will return the name of the new procedure, in this case CUBE.

Now you can use your newly created procedure. All you have to do is type in the new procedure name with a value for the variable and the computation will be completed automatically. An example of this is shown below:

```
(CUBE 3)
27
```

Here's another example to be sure that you get the idea. Suppose you wished to define a procedure that computed the speed in miles per hour (MPH) if you are given the speed value in kilometers per hour (KPH). You can compute the speed in miles per hour by dividing the speed in kilometers per hour by the constant 1.6. Using this information, you can define a new procedure called MPH. This is done below:

```
(DEFUN MPH(KPH) (/ KPH 1.6))
```

Typing this in on the computer will cause LISP to evaluate it and return the name of the new procedure MPH. To use the new procedure all you do is give the new procedure name along with the value you wish to convert. Suppose you wanted to know the MPH equivalent of 100 KPH. You would type in the following on the computer:

```
(MPH 100)
62.5
```

Here's another example using symbols rather than numbers:

```
(DEFUN OPENING-LINE (NAME) (LIST 'HELLO NAME
'WHAT'S YOUR 'SIGN?))
```

Looking at this you can see that we have defined a new procedure that generates the list HELLO NAME WHAT'S YOUR SIGN? Whenever you now give the new procedure OPENING-LINE to LISP, it will evaluate it and generate the above expression. However, to work properly, you must give it a specific name. This you can do by using the SETQ procedures described earlier.

```
(SETQ NAME'JOAN)
```

Here you are assigning the value JOAN to the variable NAME. Do this before evaluating your new OPENING-LINE procedure.

Now you can try your new procedure. Simply type:

```
(OPENING-LINE NAME)
```

and the result will be:

```
(HELLO JOAN WHAT'S YOUR SIGN?)
```

Defining new procedures is the heart of LISP programming. In implementing an algorithm, you break the process down into the smallest segments and write a new procedure for each. Then you link them all together to form the final program.

Error Messages

Whenever you type in an expression that LISP does not understand or allow, you will get an error message. All LISPs examine what you have typed in and try to evaluate it. But if you do not use the correct syntax and procedures, LISP will balk.

However, although it cannot evaluate what you have given it, LISP will at least give you some feedback. This feedback is a short error message that attempts to tell you, in a general way, what you did wrong. Here are a few representative examples:

```
(FAST RULE)
UNDEFINED FUNCTION: FAST
```

There is no primitive FAST and FAST has not been previously defined.

```
(X   3.14159)
UNBOUND VARIABLE: X
```

Here X is not assigned a value so the evaluation cannot take place.

All LISPs document their error messages so you can look up their meaning in an appendix if you cannot figure out what is meant.

Decision Making

All programming languages have some built-in facility for making decisions. Almost all programs contain some means for evaluating the results of computations or other processing actions and making a decision based on that information. In this way, the programmer can create programs that perform some processing functions automatically and can change their direction or course of action based on conditions resulting from computation or processing.

LISP includes special procedures that allow it to make decisions. These procedures are referred to as *conditionals.* While conventional languages such as BASIC and Fortran have conditionals such as IF or IF-THEN, LISP has its COND primitive. The COND primitive has the basic format shown below:

```
(COND (cond1 action1)
      (cond2 action2)
      (cond3 action3)

      (condN actionN))
```

The COND form consists of a number of lists called *clauses,* each containing a condition and a corresponding action. The condition is a test; the action part is something to be evaluated. If the condition part of the clause is true, COND evaluates the action portion of the clause and returns an appropriate value.

Table 9–4. *Representation of the IF Conditional Procedure*

The IF primitive has the form:

```
(IF TEST CONDITION TRUE CONDITION FALSE)
```

The test is a predicate that evaluates some expression and returns either T or NIL. If it returns T, the condition true part is evaluated. Here's an example:

```
(IF (EVENP 27) 'NUMBER IS EVEN 'NUMBER IS ODD)
  NUMBER IS ODD
```

When COND is executed, it searches through the various clauses evaluating the conditional part of each clause. It does this until one is found whose value is true or non-NIL. It then evaluates the action or result portion of the clause and returns its value. If the condition evaluates to false or NIL, COND ignores the action part of the clause and moves on to examine the condition or test part of the next clause listed. If none of the clauses test true, COND returns NIL.

Several examples of COND are given below to show you the basic idea.

```
(DEFUN FEVER (TEMP)
(COND ((EQUAL TEMP 98.6) 'NORMAL)
((GREATERP TEMP 98.6) 'TAKE-ASPIRIN))
```

Here we define a new function called FEVER that has the symbol TEMP as an argument. This new function uses COND to determine if the temperature of a patient is equal to or greater than 98.6 degrees. The first COND clause uses the predicate EQUAL to determine if the temperature is 98.6. If it is, the action part of the clause is evaluated. In this case, the word "normal" is printed. This is a non-NIL result.

If the temperature is not equal to 98.6, the action part of the first clause is ignored and the next clause is examined.

The predicate GREATERP (or >) checks to see if TEMP is greater than 98.6. If it is, the action part is evaluated causing TAKE-ASPIRIN to be printed out. If TEMP is not greater than 98.6, COND concludes NIL.

An important point to note here is that predicates are often used as the conditional part of COND.

Here's another example:

```
(DEFUN REST (L)

(COND ((LISTP L)(CDR L))
(ATOM L) 'SYMBOL))
```

This code defines a function REST with variable L. The predicate LISTP checks to see if L is a list. If it is, it uses the CDR to give us all but the first of the list or the "rest" of the list. If L is not a list, it is an atom, in which case, symbol is printed out.

Another conditional procedure in some LISPs is IF. It is described briefly in Table 9–4.

Iteration and Recursion

Most programming languages, including LISP, support operations called iteration and recursion. In fact, the process of recursion, because it is so easily implemented in LISP, is one of the major benefits of using LISP languages in some applications. In this section, we want to take a look at these two important operations and how they are implemented in LISP.

Iteration

Iteration is the process of repeating some operation over and over again. We do this by constructing a program loop that causes a small portion of the program code to be reiterated a certain number of times. The code is executed once, then it loops back and executes again and again until some condition is met which stops the iterative process.

While LISP can perform traditional iteration by using built-in primitives such as PROG and DO (which we won't cover here), most repetitive operations are implemented with recursion. Most pure LISP programmers wouldn't have it any other way.

Recursion

The best way to illustrate recursion is to give an example. One problem that is easy to understand is the computation of a factorial. Recall that factorial (represented by the symbol, !) is an integer (N) multiplied by all succeeding smaller integers. To show this, consider the factorial of 5.

$$5! = 5 \times 4 \times 3 \times 2 \times 1 = 120$$

The factorial of zero is one.

$$0! = 1$$

A generalized form of factorial is:

$$N!\ N(N - 1)(N - 2)(N - 3) \ldots (1)$$

It is pretty easy to write a program for computer factorials. If you were doing it in BASIC, you would use an ordinary iterative loop to reduce the value by 1 each time through the loop multiplying as you go. One way to do this is shown below:

```
INPUT N
LET F = 1
FOR X = N TO 1
LET F = F*X
```

```
NEXT X
PRINT F
```

A FOR-NEXT loop decrements X each time through the loop multiplying it by F. When X = 1, the loop terminates and F is the factorial.

Another way to show how factorial works is to express it like this:

5! = 5 x 4!

4! = 4 x 3!

3! = 3 x 2!

2! = 2 x 1!

1! = 1 x 0!

Our newly defined function will use this process. Now let's show how we would do this recursively in LISP.

As usual, we define a new function factorial.

```
(DEFUN FACTORIAL (N)
(COND ((ZEROP N) 1)
(T ([*] N(FACTORIAL (−N 1)))))
```

To use it, we do:

```
(FACTORIAL 3)
6
```

This is mainly a COND primitive with two conditions. The first checks to see if the number whose factorial is to be found (N) is zero. If zero is found it evaluates and returns the 1. (0! =1)

If N is not zero, the next condition is checked. The condition is T, meaning true, so the associated expression is evaluated. That expression multiplies N by the factorial of the number one less than N. To get that value, FACTORIAL calls itself to compute the factorial of N-1. What happens is that the first time through the computation, N gets set to 3. But no final computation occurs because FACTORIAL is called again and N is set to 2. This happens again. FACTORIAL is called a third time setting N to 1. Finally N equals zero. At this point, LISP evaluates FACTORIAL 0 to 1, then multiplies it successively by 2 and 3 finally returning the correct answer 6.

There must be a way to stop recursion. The argument must be changed in some way each time through the loop so that eventually some condition can be detected to stop the computation.

AI Applications of LISP

By now, you have at least a taste of how LISP works and how it is used. In this section, you will see how LISP is used to do basic AI operations. First, we will discuss knowledge representation and pattern-matching. Finally, we will examine the search process. As before, simple examples will be used to help you get the basic idea.

Knowledge Representation

As you saw in Chapter 2, there are lots of ways to format knowledge. Some methods included predicate logic, lists, semantic networks, rules, frames, and scripts. All of these can be implemented in LISP. The most popular formats are lists, rules, and frames. We will limit our discussion to these.

Lists

As you saw earlier, a list is a pretty good way to represent certain kinds of knowledge. A list is an ordered sequence of objects. Their order might determine their priority, importance, sequence of usage, or so on. The list obviously contains items that are related to one another in some way.

As an example, consider a list that shows the basic features of a personal computer. The name of the list might be PC. On the list might be features such as type of microprocessor, data word size, amount of RAM, and type of I/O port. Such a list might look like this:

PC

microprocessor - 8088

data word size - 8 bits

RAM - 512K

I/O - parallel

LISP has ways of creating and manipulating such lists which are referred to as property lists. These lists are made up of associated pairs of objects, the name of the item and a related value.

Each atom can have a property list associated with it. The items in the list are referred to as properties and each has a value. A property list has the basic form:

(property 1 value 1 property 2 . . . property N value N)

The property names must be symbols, but the values can be anything.

To create a property list, we use the PUT or PUTPROP primitive. Its basic form is:

(PUTPROP ATOM NAME VALUE)

Atom is the symbol (list) we are defining or creating. Name is the property name, and value, of course, is the property value. Using the personal computer list given earlier, we could add a property like this:

(PUTPROP PC MICRO 8088)

The atom or property list PC is given the property MICRO (what microprocessor used) and its value 8088. The process is repeated until all of the properties are added to the list.

Another primitive, GET, is used to retrieve the properties. Its format is:

```
(GET 'atom 'name)
```

Again, atom is the name of the property list while name is the property desired. GET returns the value of the property. Using our previous example:

```
(GET 'PC 'MICRO)
8088
```

Another primitive often used is REMPROP or REM which is used to delete a property from a property list.

Once you create the property list, you can, of course, manipulate it in various ways using standard primitives or new procedures you define. The property list is your knowledge base which you can search or use in pattern matching.

Rules

Production rules are a popular way to represent heuristic knowledge in an expert system. You can create those rules in LISP. There is no set format. One way to write a rule in LISP is shown below:

```
(Conditions Action)
```

Rules have the basic form shown above: a condition, antecedent or premises, and a corresponding action, consequent, or conclusion. The first and second parts can be implemented as lists. Here is one approach:

```
(((W)(X)(Y))(Z))
```

Here the conditions W, X and Y are each made into a list. The action Z is another list. The two are combined to form a single rule list. The rule is read, IF W AND X AND Y, THEN Z.

Another way to write a rule is:

```
(RULE name 1
  (IF (condition 1)
    (condition 2)
    .
    .
    .
(THEN (action)))
```

The rule is given a name to identify it, then the IF portion has one or more conditions or antecedents to be met. If multiple conditions are given, it is assumed that they are ANDed, that is, all must be true if the THEN portion of the rule is true. The THEN portion describes a consequent or action.

Using this format, all parts of the rule can be accessed with available primitives or separately defined special procedures. Using such procedures, a rule base can be searched using pattern matching techniques.

Frames

Recall that a frame is a type of knowledge structure that describes a specific object. The frame contains multiple slots which, in turn, contain facts, characteristics, or specifications about the object. A frame is like a property list which has multiple properties with values. The main difference is that frames usually are linked. The slot in one frame is explained or expanded in another frame, and so on. The lower level frames inherit the properties of the associated higher level frames.

A simple frame can be implemented as a property list. But more practical and, therefore, more complex frame structures can be implemented by a data structure known as *association lists.*

An association list is a variation of a standard LISP list. It is, more specifically, a list of multiple sublists. The first element in every sublist is a marker called the key. The key is a symbol that tells what the list is. It is a word that categorizes or describes what's on the list. The remaining elements of the list are the various characteristics, properties, or values.

A special primitive is included in some LISPs to deal with association lists. Called ASSOC, it has two arguments, the key and the list itself. It has the form:

(ASSOC KEY LIST)

What it does is examine an association list and look for a sublist with the designated key. It does a CAR on each list looking for the key which is the first element. If it finds the key, it returns the entire sublist. If no key is found, ASSOC returns NIL.

A frame structure can be set up using the association list idea. The resulting lists look like this:

(FRAME (SLOT 1)(SLOT 2)(SLOT 3) . . . (SLOT N))

Here, FRAME and SLOT are the names of the frame and slots.

The slots are themselves lists. They have a similar structure. Each slot is made up of features or characteristics.

(SLOT (FEATURE 1)(FEATURE 2) . . . (FEATURE N))

This can go one step farther. Each feature is also a list with values.

(FEATURE (VALUE 1)(VALUE 2) . . . (VALUE N))

You can see how ASSOC plus other primitives such as CAR and CDR can be used to sort through multiple levels of such lists to get at desired information. You can also write some special procedures comparable to PUT, GET, and REM that you can use on your frames.

Pattern-Matching

Pattern-matching is, of course, one of the key operations performed in AI programs. When combined with search techniques, pattern-matching can look for specific data items, then operate on them or perform some computation just as the result of locating them.

Pattern-matching is not a built-in LISP procedure, although it probably should be. The closest primitive to pattern-matching is the predicate EQUAL. Recall that EQUAL compares two symbols or lists and gives T (true) if they are identical and NIL if they are not. For simple pattern-matching, EQUAL may suffice. But usually, it is necessary to define your own special procedure.

Most LISP programmers end up defining a procedure that is similar to the one shown below:

```
(DEFUN MATCH (PATT DATA)
  (COND ((AND (NULL PATT)(NULL DATA)))
        ((OR (NULL PATT)(NULL DATA)) NIL)
        ((EQUAL (CAR PATT)(CAR DATA))
        (MATCH (CDR PATT)(CDR DATA)))))
```

Note that it uses recursion because it does call itself.

The procedure is called MATCH and it has two arguments, the standard pattern (PATT) against which the data input (DATA) is compared.

The first (AND) part of the COND checks to see if both lists are empty. If so, you get true. That means the procedure has matched or compared all the individual items in the pattern and data lists. This part of the procedure also stops the recursion.

If either PATT or DATA is empty and the other is not, it simply means that they do not match, that is, one has fewer elements than the other. The result is NIL. The OR part of COND does this.

Next, EQUAL extracts the first elements of PATT and DATA with CAR and compares them. If they are not the same, the whole procedure terminates with NIL. If they are alike, then the procedure calls itself to match the remainder of PATT and DATA, which are derived with CDR. The process repeats until a match is confirmed or not.

This procedure can be modified with additional COND clauses that do special matching functions. For example, we may consider a match successful if the two input lists are the same except for one or more elements. There are other possibilities.

Pattern-matchers such as this are used in all kinds of AI software. They are used in natural language parsers and the inference engines of expert systems. You will also find them in vision systems and voice recognition systems. LISP is flexible enough to permit you to construct a matcher optimized for any of these applications, including yours.

Search

Search is the process of looking through a network of nodes and arcs in an attempt to locate a specific goal. Ordinarily, we associate search with trees like that shown in Figure 9–6. The search usually starts with the root node S and then works downward using various techniques. Depth-first and breadth-first searches are popular and many

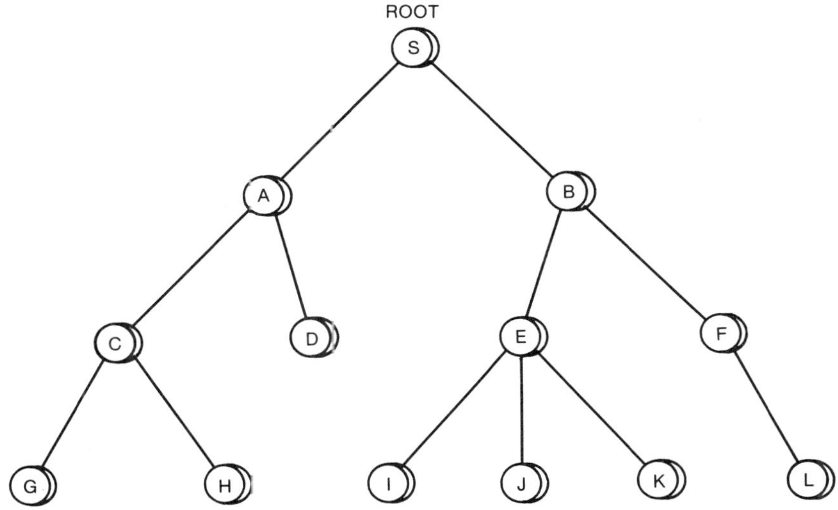

Figure 9–6. ***A search tree.***

variations with heuristics, which help shorten the search, are possible. Obviously, we can create special procedures that will search a tree. But first we have to represent that tree in LISP.

One way to represent a tree is to create a list of sublists that show the various nodes and arcs and how they are related. The tree depicted in Figure 9–6 would be expressed as follows:

```
(ROOT (A (C (G H) D))(B (E (I J K) F (L))))
```

Another, better way to represent a tree is to use property lists. In this way, each node can be matched up to its children. For example, the tree in Figure 9–6 would be created with PUT primitives as below:

```
(PUT 'ROOT 'CHILDREN 'A B))
  (PUT 'A 'CHILDREN '(C D))
    (PUT 'B 'CHILDREN '(E F))
      (PUT 'C 'CHILDREN '(G H))
        (PUT 'E 'CHILDREN '(I J K))
          (PUT 'F 'CHILDREN '(L))
```

Once you have defined the tree, you can write a procedure that will implement a depth- or breadth-first search. Defining such a function is complex so we won't try to describe it here. But basically, using COND with some form of iteration or recursion, you create a loop that examines the various paths through the tree. The EQUAL primitive inside the loops tests to see if the goal is found.

LISP in Perspective

As you have discovered in this chapter, LISP is an unusual but very powerful and flexible language. It is ideal for AI, but it has many other possibilities in data processing as well. What other language represents programs the same way it represents data (in list form)? It means you can manipulate programs as data. That's a very powerful concept with many advantages.

Further, LISP is not that hard to learn, at least not any more difficult than any other language. Once you learn to manage your single quotes (') and parentheses, you generally have it made.

LISP is still king in the AI community. If you plan any serious AI work, you must surely learn LISP as a first step. So much of the literature explains key concepts in LISP format that it is difficult to learn them without LISP. Take a course or two. And by all means, read several books on the subject. There are many good ones available. But most important, start playing with LISP. Because it is interactive, it is easy to begin by learning the primitives one simple step at a time, then working up to more complex defined functions. The only way you'll ever really learn LISP is to wade in and start programming. Get a LISP interpreter for your personal computer. There are many available, from simple public domain versions all the way up to the newer full implementations of common LISP. See the Appendix for the various sources and vendors.

Finally, learning LISP will clarify important AI concepts that are difficult to explain in text.

Key Points

- LISP is a programming language developed by John McCarthy of MIT (now at Stanford) in the late 1950s.
- LISP is considered to be the oldest programming language next to Fortran.
- LISP is short for LISt Processing.
- LISP is the most widely used AI programming language, at least in the U.S.
- The basic data structure of LISP is a list. A list is a written sequence of items that are related, given in order of importance or priority, or have some special relationship.
- Lists are a powerful but simple way to represent knowledge.
- Lists are made up of atoms or other lists separated by spaces and enclosed in parentheses.
- An atom is a number, word, or alphanumeric symbol. Examples of atoms are: F, 1938, FULL, H25.
- A list has the following form: (A B C D).
- A list of lists looks like this:

  (R (S T)(U V)(W X Y Z))
- Most LISPs are interpreters but are also available as compilers to improve speed and reduce memory requirements.

- There are dozens of different dialects of LISP. The two most popular are MacLISP and InterLISP and their various extensions.
- Common LISP is an attempt to standardize the language and make programs more portable.
- Knowledge and data represented in list form is manipulated by LISP to accomplish some useful end result.
- Atoms and lists are operated upon by procedures or functions.
- A sequence or collection of procedures forms a LISP program.
- LISP contains common built-in procedures called primitives.
- Using the supplied primitives, the programmer can easily define new procedures and functions.
- LISP can do common mathematical operations but is best at symbolic manipulation.
- Many LISP primitives and defined functions are used to assemble and disassemble lists or to select or replace specific elements in a list. Examples: the CAR primitive selects the first element in a list. CDR selects all but the first element of a list.
- New procedures are defined with the DEFUN primitive.
- LISP can make decisions among alternatives by using the COND primitive.
- Repetitive operations can be achieved with standard iteration techniques or recursion.
- Recursion is the process of defining a procedure that uses or calls itself in the process. Recursion is a powerful and often-used technique in LISP.
- Lists are a good way to represent knowledge, but LISP can easily implement production rules, frames, semantic networks, or any other scheme.
- Pattern-matching is done by creating a special matching procedure that fits the application.
- Search is accomplished by writing procedures for depth- or breadth-first tree searches.
- LISP is easy to learn and widely available on mainframes, minicomputers, and personal computers.

10

Prolog and Other AI Languages

prolog—An introduction, preface.

WEBSTER'S II NEW RIVERSIDE DICTIONARY

Although LISP is the premier AI programming language, at least in the United States, many new and different programming languages optimized for artificial intelligence applications have been developed. Of those new languages, one stands out because of its unique structure and operation. Known as Prolog, this new language is challenging LISP in some areas of AI. Unlike LISP, which has been around for over a quarter of a century, Prolog is a relatively new language that has yet to experience the evolution and refinement LISP has seen over the years. However, the use of Prolog is growing rapidly and many implementations are available. There is some speculation that it could eventually become the world's key AI language.

Most experts seem to agree that LISP will continue to dominate AI programming with Prolog gaining an easy second place position. Like conventional programming languages, LISP and Prolog will compete with one another for some applications. But in many cases, clearly one language or the other will be preferable for a given situation. Because LISP and Prolog are different in the ways they go about solving problems, they are complementary and, therefore, less competitive than other more conventional higher level languages. It is up to the programmer to choose the language of preference that best fits the application.

This chapter is a prolog to Prolog. We will introduce you to this new and unusual programming language and show you how to solve AI programs with it.

In addition, we will also introduce you briefly to some of the other programming languages that have been expressly developed for AI applications.

Some Background

LISP was invented by Professor Alain Colmerauer at the University of Aix-Marseille, France. Professor Colmerauer and his team were looking for faster, more efficient ways to create natural language processing and language translation programs. The result was a language that is suitable not only to natural language applications but also many other AI projects as well.

Prolog's name is derived from the expression "PROgramming In LOGic." Prolog is, in fact, an implementation of the processes and procedures involved in first order predicate calculus. Recall that we described predicate calculus and the basic concepts of logic programming back in Chapter 2. Predicate logic or calculus expresses facts as statements or premises. These are then used with a system of mathematical and symbolic logic to draw conclusions and make inferences. Prolog provides a means of automating that process. This makes it considerably different from other programming languages.

Procedural vs. Descriptive Languages

Programming languages can generally be classified as either procedural or descriptive. Most languages are procedural because they are used to state specifically some procedure that is to be implemented. To solve a problem, a programmer conceives of an algorithm that processes available inputs into new usable outputs. Then, using the syntax and procedures of the programming language, code is written to implement that algorithm. Various instructions, statements, or commands are written in sequence to carry out the step-by-step process of the algorithm. The computer executes the language's instructions or statements sequentially, thereby solving the problem. Languages such as BASIC, Fortran, Pascal, C, and, yes, even LISP are procedural languages.

Prolog, on the other hand, is a declarative language. It is non-procedural in that instead of describing a sequence of steps or a specific algorithm, the programmer gives Prolog known facts and relationships about a problem. Prolog takes facts which are known to be true and uses them to deduce new facts and solve the problem automatically. Prolog is problem oriented rather than solution oriented.

To program in Prolog, you give the computer a set of facts and rules describing people, places, or things and their relationships. Each of these statements, called clauses, gives a particular fact that is true. Recall that this was the process for solving problems in predicate calculus. Logical statements were made and then the rules of predicate calculus were applied to solve the problem by making deductions from the information given. Once you have stated the facts and relationships, you can ask Prolog questions to obtain new facts which Prolog gleans from the information given to it earlier.

Prolog has a built-in inference engine that performs search and pattern matching functions automatically. When you ask it a question, it will search its data base of facts and relationships looking for matches and new relationships. Prolog implements the unification and resolution functions of predicate calculus to solve problems.

Programming in Prolog is essentially the process of making assertions about objects and then querying the system about their relationships. The main job of the programmer is to obtain the necessary information about objects and their relationships and give that data to Prolog. The programmer does not have to come up with a specific step-by-step procedure that the computer must implement to solve the problem. Instead, once the programmer gives Prolog the data, Prolog will go to work using its own built-in procedures for solving the problem when the user begins asking specific questions. The secret to good programming in Prolog is sufficient quality information to create a sound data base. Prolog will determine how that data base is used to solve the problems you give it.

Prolog Standards

Despite Prolog's short life, there are already many implementations of it. Versions of Prolog are available to operate on mainframes, minicomputers, and personal computers. As a result, there are no standards. Like LISP, Prolog has undergone considerable evolution. Its early use was primarily in France and its usage quickly expanded to other European countries. England and other United Kingdom countries have also widely adopted Prolog in artificial intelligence applications. Many new versions have been developed. The British Standards Institute has attempted to create a standard composite Prolog, but many dialects still exist.

Prolog has also been adopted by the Japanese as the primary AI language for their fifth generation computer systems which are now under development. Japan's goal is to be the first to create and market the so-called fifth generation computer systems which are based on parallel processing techniques (to be discussed in Chapter 11) and artificial intelligence concepts. Most of these machines will use Prolog rather than LISP or other AI languages.

The considerable use of Prolog in Europe and the U.K. plus its adoption by the Japanese caused the United States to take a look at Prolog and give it serious consideration. Today, many U. S. companies have implemented Prolog and are beginning to use it on a broad scale.

Although no Prolog standards exist, most users in the United States have informally agreed that Prolog is the language defined in *Programming in Prolog.*[3] Virtually everyone uses this book as a Prolog tutorial and the most popular implementations follow the details of the language as described here. Clocksin and Mellish outline the University of Edinburgh (Scotland) version of Prolog. Other than this, there is no effort to produce a standard Prolog similar to the effort underway to standardize LISP by creating Common LISP.

Prolog is still growing in popularity; and, therefore, once it matures and users gain more experience with it, standardization will make more sense. Prolog has also been found suitable for creating relational data base management systems as well as the fourth generation query languages normally associated with them. Prolog has established a firm place for itself in computer programming, AI or otherwise.

Prolog Characteristics

Prolog is essentially a declarative language, but most implementations do have procedural features as well. Any language must have some procedural capability if it is to perform basic functions such as arithmetic and input/output operations. Prolog has numerous procedural capabilities depending upon which dialect is used. The combination of both procedural and declarative capabilities makes Prolog unusually powerful.

Most Prologs are interpreters, but many compiler versions are becoming available. Compiler versions produce shorter, more efficient code, and, therefore, take up less

[3]Clocksin, W. F. and Mellish, C. S. 1981. *Programming in Prolog.* New York: Springer-Verlag.

memory space and execute faster. These are important considerations in many applications.

The Benefits of Prolog

The primary benefit of Prolog is that programmers can create many artificial intelligence programs faster and easier with it. Prolog is ideal for implementing expert systems and natural language processing programs. The inference engine, pattern matching, and search procedures are already built-in. A programmer does not have to create these from scratch as he would have to do using LISP or another language. As a result, the programmer can put together these kinds of applications with much less effort. Time is saved and development costs are reduced. Further, novices and beginning programmers find Prolog relatively easy to learn, and can begin implementing expert systems and natural language programs much faster than it would take them to learn and use LISP or another programming language.

> *While Prolog has adherents in the U. S., most veteran American AI researchers are still convinced that LISP is generally superior and that the Japanese newcomers will eventually realize that too.*
>
> FORTUNE MAGAZINE,
> OCT. 29, 1984

Programming in Prolog

Writing and using a program in Prolog involves three basic steps. These are:

1. Writing facts that define objects and state their relationships.
2. Creating rules that define relationships about objects.
3. Asking specific questions about the objects and their relationships.

The first two steps describe the process of creating a Prolog data base. Step 3 shows how Prolog goes about answering our questions. In the following sections we will describe each of these three basic steps.

Entering Facts

The first step in writing a Prolog program is to create a data base of facts. What you are doing here is compiling a knowledge base that the built-in Prolog inference engine will use to answer questions, make inferences, and draw conclusions. Remember, when you are programming in Prolog, you are not writing a step-by-step procedure. Instead, you are giving the computer facts and rules about a particular subject which Prolog will use to give you an answer or reach a decision, if it can.

The facts we will enter are called clauses or statements, and they will name one or more objects and state some relationship.

The statement of a simple fact in Prolog is shown below:

```
owns (charles, buick).
```

The first word in the fact is called the predicate, and it states a relationship between the two arguments given in parenthesis. The first argument is charles and the second is buick. This simple statement when expressed in English is "Charles owns a Buick." To read a fact, simply put the predicate between the two arguments.

There are several important things to note about a predicate clause in Prolog. First, all of the words in the expression are typed in lower case letters. This includes proper names like charles and buick. A comma separates the two arguments within the parentheses and a period ends the clause. When the Prolog prompt appears on the screen, simply type in the expression and type Enter or carriage return after you type the period. The fact will be entered into Prolog's data base immediately.

To form a more complete data base, you would enter additional facts like the ones shown below:

```
owns (mary, toyota).
owns (bob, audi).
```

Another type of predicate clause has only one argument.

```
silver (buick).
```

This predicate in English simply states "The Buick is silver." The first word, the predicate, states a fact about a particular object. The argument is given in parentheses.

To expand the data base, you may want to add some additional facts:

```
red (toyota).
black (audi).
```

Although one-argument predicates are certainly valid, another way to enter them would be as shown below:

```
color (buick, silver).
color (toyota, red).
color (audi, black).
```

The single argument predicates assign colors to each of the car types, but Prolog doesn't really know what that means. You can tell Prolog about color by writing the predicates as shown immediately above. In this way, Prolog knows what color means whereas it did not before. Besides, other objects in a data base may have the same color as silver, red, and black, and Prolog would get confused if only single argument predicates were used in assigning those colors to multiple objects.

Asking Questions

With a basic data base now in memory, you can immediately begin using the data base by asking questions. The easiest kinds of questions are those that Prolog will answer with either yes or no. For example, to ask the question "Does Charles own a Buick?" you would type the expression below:

```
owns (charles, buick)?
```

Note the question mark instead of a period at the end of the clause designating a question. In some Prologs, the question mark must appear at the beginning of the clause as shown below:

```
? - owns (charles, buick).
```

Check the correct form in your Prolog reference manual before you use your system.

Prolog accepts the question and then proceeds to search its data base. It performs a pattern matching process which attempts to match predicates as well as arguments in the question to those in the data base. It searches through the various clauses in the data base one at a time in the order they were entered. If a match occurs, Prolog will answer "Yes."

Suppose you ask the following question:

```
owns (charles, bmw)?
```

Given the simple data base we described above, Prolog would search it looking for pattern matches to the predicate and arguments given in the question. It would find and match "owns" and "charles," but not "bmw." Since no match is found, Prolog would respond "No."

This brings us to a very important point. Charles may own a BMW in addition to his Buick. However, Prolog responds with the answer "No" because it cannot find the facts spelled out in its data base. If a fact is true but you have not told the data base about it, Prolog will always respond with "No." This makes it sound like the fact is not true even though it is. That's just the way Prolog works. If the fact isn't in the data base, the answer will be "No."

Here are some other yes/no questions using the data base given above:

```
color (buick, gold)?
                                   No

color (audi, black)?
                                   Yes
```

Variables

Variables are expressed in Prolog by capital letters or words that begin with capital letters. Some typical Prolog variables are Y, Car, and TREE.

By using variables, your questions can be much more flexible. That is, you can ask them in such a way that the response does not have to be yes or no. For example, you could ask the question "What does Charles own?" as shown below:

```
owns (charles, What)?
```

You could also ask the same question by substituting the variable such as X for the "What" as indicated below:

```
owns (charles, X)?
```

Here Prolog again searches the data base looking for a match to the predicates and arguments. When it encounters a variable starting with a capital letter, it will assign whatever argument it encounters to the variable name given in the question. In this case it searches the data base and finds that Charles owns a Buick, so it assigns the variable What or X the value of Buick. The answer to the above questions would be:

```
What = buick
X = buick
```

Using Conjunctions

A conjunction is the simultaneous occurrence of events. A coincidence. In grammar, it refers to a word such as "and" or "but." In Prolog, it means "and." By using a conjunction when asking questions, more interesting and complex relationships can be determined.

To illustrate this, let's ask the following questions:

```
owns (bob, x),
owns (charles, y)?
```

In this expression, the comma between the two clauses means "and." Prolog responds with:

```
x = audi
y = buick
```

You can also answer more complex questions such as, "What does Mary own that is red?" You would do this with a compound question as illustrated below:

```
owns (Mary, X) ,color (X, red)?
X = toyota
```

Note that the above question has two parts. The first part asks "What does Mary own?" while the second part asks "What it is that is red in color?" Here Prolog has to search through the data base matching up the various predicates and arguments. It finally concludes that Mary owns a Toyota which is red in color.

Entering Rules

While facts make up a large part of our data base, rules are also used. Rules are another way of expressing relationships between objects in the data base. Rules, in fact, express the dependence of a fact on one or more other facts.

Rules in Prolog are similar to the production rules discussed previously in this book. They consist of two parts, a condition and an action, or premises and a conclusion. More specifically, Prolog rules have an IF and a THEN part. IF the conditions are met, THEN the action is carried out.

Rules are entered in Prolog in a unique format. The conclusion is entered first followed by the various premises or conditions. An example will illustrate this.

Suppose that you want to enter the following rule:

```
IF      X is female
AND     X is parent of Y
THEN    X is mother of Y
```

That's the traditional form of a rule as you have seen before. In Prolog the rule would be entered as follows:

```
mother_ of(X, Y) :-
female (X),
parent (X, Y).
```

Here the conclusion or THEN portion of the rule is stated first. This is followed by a special symbol or operator which consists of a color followed by a hyphen. This special symbol means IF. The conditions or premises are stated in the next two indented lines. The comma after the first condition means AND.

The rule becomes a part of the data base. In order to use this rule, other facts about X and Y would also have to exist in the data base.

Some other parts of the data base may look like the following:

```
female (chris).
male (morgan).
female (jo).
male (pat).
parent (chris, pat).
parent (chris, jo).
parent (morgan, pat).
parent (morgan, jo).
```

With the above rule and data base, you can now ask more interesting questions. For example, you can ask if Chris is the mother of Pat. This would be done with the question:

```
mother_
"of(chris, pat)?
```

Yes.

Prolog has to search its data base to get the answer. It sees that the conditions of the rule are that Chris has to be a parent and also Chris has to be female. It does find that these two conditions are true, so it concludes that yes, Chris is the Mother of Pat.

Another question this rule will help answer is "Who is Chris the mother of?" Prolog could answer this question if keyed in in the following manner:

```
mother_ of (chris, X)?
X = pat
X = jo
```

Here, again Prolog searches the data base and determines that Chris is the female. Looking through the data base it attempts to match up the variable X to the children of Chris. In this case, it finds two answers and sets X equal to both Pat and Jo.

As you can see, rules allow you to state more complex relationships. Prolog's inference engine searches the data base and makes multiple matches that comply with the rule in order to give a correct answer. Using this data base as a starting point, you could easily add additional facts and rules describing an entire family and all of the various relationships. Then you could use the data base to find out the relationship of one person to any other person. Aunts, uncles, cousins, grandparents through marriage, and other relationships could be determined easily by simply asking questions.

The Prolog Interpreter

Before we go any farther, let's take a minute to discuss the actual operation of the Prolog interpreter. The Prolog interpreter is basically an inference engine that searches through a set of clauses, either facts or rules, and attempts to match them up to some hypothetical goal. We ask the interpreter to achieve a particular goal or prove a given hypothesis. The interpreter searches the data base trying to find evidence to support the goal. In other words, it looks at the various premises to see if they are true in an effort to reach a conclusion or prove the goal.

To give you a better feel for this process, let's take an example program and work through it. Assume that our data base is as shown below:

```
works_ for (bob, acme).
works_ for (bill, bob).
works_ for (ann, bob).
works_ for (tom, bill).
works_ for (X, Z) :- works_ for (X, Y), works_ for (Y, Z).
```

As you can see, our basic data base contains four fact statements and one rule. As an example of how to read the facts, simply put the predicate between the two arguments. For example, the fact, works_ for (bill, bob), reads Bill works for Bob. We could have also created the predicate, reports_ to. Optionally, we could have used boss_ of, which, in this case, would reverse the order of the arguments. Keep in mind that you are free to make up your own predicates and word them as you see fit. Prolog will accept anything you will give it.

Now look at the rule. Basically all this rule says is that X works for Z IF X works for Y AND Y works for Z.

What we have defined here is a simple company hierarchy where if one person is an employee for another, then that person is also an employee of a person at the next higher managerial level.

Now let's take an example. Let's attempt to prove that Tom works for Bob. We ask Prolog this by typing in the question:

works_ for (tom, bob)?

Prolog immediately goes to work in an attempt to match the goal we have set up to something in the data base. Prolog searches the data base in the order that each of the various statements are entered. It looks through the first four facts and does not find an exact match. Then, it encounters the rule.

The instant that our goal, work_ for (tom, bob), is encountered, Prolog instantiates the variables X and Z. This means that it assigns the variable X equal to Tom and the variable Z equal to Bob.

Now, Prolog looks at the conditions necessary to satisfy the rule. There are two conditions and both must be met. This is indicated by the comma between the two conditions which represents the logical conjunction AND.

Prolog again starts at the beginning of the data base and now searches it, attempting to find a match for the condition works_ for (X, Y). The first, second, and third facts do not provide a match, but the fourth one does. Here we see that works_ for (tom, bill) is selected. The reason for this is that tom matches X because X was previously instantiated to Tom when our question was asked. Variable Y has not been instantiated yet, and, therefore, it becomes instantiated to Bill as this fact is encountered. The first part of the rule is then satisfied.

Now the Prolog interpreter goes to work looking for a match for the second condition in the rule, works_ for (Y, Z). Again, Prolog goes back to the beginning of the data base to begin its search. Fact 1 does not provide a match, but fact 2 does. Since Y was instantiated to Bill, the first argument matches. The variable Z has not been instantiated yet, and, therefore, it is instantiated to Bob. The second condition in the rule is satisfied. This means that since both conditions are satisfied, our original goal has been proven to be true. Prolog prints the statement, Yes, because since Tom works for Bill and Bill works for Bob, then Tom also works for Bob.

As you learned in the discussion of expert systems, an inference engine that attempts to prove a given goal is said to use backwards chaining. That is exactly what Prolog does. It attempts to find matches to goals that we set up as questions. The Prolog interpreter is nothing more than a backwards chaining inference engine.

Backtracking

One of the most important features of the Prolog interpreter is backtracking. Backtracking is the process of attempting to satisfy goals in a conjunction statement by repeatedly going back and initiating a new search if a previous search fails. Some goals are initially set up when we ask a question with a conjunction (AND condition) in it. In order to ask the question or satisfy the goal, all parts of the statement containing the conjunction AND must be true or must match. The Prolog interpreter begins by searching for the first match. If it finds one, it then attempts to match or approve the second condition. If the first attempt fails, Prolog backtracks. That is, it starts all over again to find another set of conditions in the data base that do match. This process of backtracking continues until all the conditions are satisfied and the question is proven true. Alternately, if all of the conditions are not matched, the question is answered with NO.

Another kind of condition can occur when there is more than one rule. In other words, there may be more than one way a goal can be achieved. There may be two or more rules that will satisfy the goal. This is a logical OR situation where one rule OR another OR another will work. If one rule fails, Prolog backtracks and tries the next rule in an effort to validate the hypothesis posed by asking a question. This process continues until the goal is satisfied or failure is indicated.

A simple example of backtracking is illustrated using the data base shown below:

```
bachelors (mark) masters (john).
grad_ hrs (mark).
bachelors (jim).
grad_ hrs (jim).
masters (paul).
qualified (X) :- masters (X).
qualified (X) :- bachelors (X), grad_ hrs (X).
```

This is a simple program that decides whether or not an individual is qualified to enter a doctorate level degree program at a university. The person is qualified if he has a masters degree OR is qualified if he has a bachelors degree plus some hours of graduate work represented by the predicate grad_ hrs.

So, we can begin by asking the question:

```
qualified (jim)?
```

Prolog begins by searching the data base from the beginning. It searches through the initial set of facts not finding a match. However, a match is made to the first rule where X is instantiated to be Jim. Immediately, Prolog begins to search again, this time attempting to determine if Jim has a masters degree. Prolog searches through the facts but cannot prove that Jim has a masters degree. We see that Jim has a bachelors degree but no masters. As a result, the attempt to prove this rule fails.

Backtracking now begins again. This time it encounters the second rule. It immediately begins to attempt to prove that Jim has a bachelors degree as well as some graduate hours. Its search first determines the fact that Jim does have a bachelors degree. Next, it has found that he also has some graduate hours, therefore, the second condition is proven. The goal is satisfied. The answer to the original question becomes Yes.

Mathematics in Prolog

Like other programming languages, Prolog will do addition, subtraction, multiplication, and division. And that's about it. Prolog is not known for its calculating prowess, so if you need that, forget Prolog. There are occasions in logical symbolic computing where math operations are required. Prolog can deal with them if they are basic.

Prologs vary widely in their ability to deal with numbers. Some allow only integers (whole numbers). Others permit real or decimal numbers. Further, the number range is often restricted. Check your Prolog for these limitations.

To work with numbers, there must be some way to assign values to variables. In Prolog, this is done with the "is" operator. For example:

```
x is 15
```

assigns 15 to the variable X. Prolog responds with X = 15. In some Prologs you have to make the assignment by asking questions such as:

```
x is 15?
x = 15
y is 12?
y = 12
```

All Prologs have the following arithmetic operators: +, −, [*], /. These correspond to addition, subtraction, multiplication and division respectively. To use these, you must combine them in expressions with variables or constants and ask them as a question. Here are some examples of addition:

```
x is 9 + 4?
13
y is 15 + 27
42
```

Here's another way of using a rule:

```
sum (A<B<C) :− C is A + B.
```

You define a predicate "sum" with arguments A, B, and C. This is the sum C of A and B IF C is A + B. To solve a problem you key in:

```
sum (7, 9, C)?
C = 16
```

Now, here are some examples of subtraction:

```
J is 12 − 8?
4
K is 21 − 32?
−11
```

Multiplication in Prolog looks like this:

R is 5 [*] 8?

40

S is 10 [*] 100?

1000

Division is done this way:

T is 64/16?

4

T is 64 div 16?

Some Prologs use "div" instead of "/."

U is 9/4?

2

Note in the last case that most Prologs do integer division only. The quotient is rounded to the lowest integer. You can find the remainder by using the "mod" operator.

V is 9 mod 4?

V = 1

Finally, some Prologs also permit exponentiation. It is expressed with the operator "^." For example, 3 raised to the fourth power would be computed as:

X is 34̂?

81

There are also operators for comparing numbers or variables. Some of these are:

X = Y   equal

X > Y   greater than

X < Y   less than

X /= Y or X <> Y   not equal to

X = > Y   equal to or greater than

X + < Y   equal to or less than

Some examples follow:

5 = 5

yes

7 = 11

no

7 > 11

no

11 < 7

yes

4 /= 7

yes

Overall, arithmetic in Prolog is a pain in the neck. It is certainly easier and more intuitive in say BASIC or Fortran. But you can do it in Prolog if you have to.

logic—The art of thinking and reasoning in strict accordance with the limitations and incapacities of the human misunderstanding. The basic of logic is the syllogism, consisting of a major and a minor premise and a conclusion—thus:

Major premise: Sixty men can do a piece of work sixty times as quickly as one man.

Minor premise: One man can dig a post-hole in sixty seconds; therefore—

Conclusion: Sixty men can dig a post-hole in one second.

This may be called the syllogism arithmetical, in which, by combining logic and mathematics, we obtain a double certainty and are twice blessed.

AMBROSE BIERCE

Expert Systems in Prolog

In many ways, Prolog is an expert system with an empty knowledge base waiting for you to fill it in. In this regard, it is like the expert system shells discussed in Chapter 5. The inference engine is built-in. You supply the knowledge base of facts and rules, then build a user interface using some of the procedural programming capability and you will have a decent expert system.

Prolog is not as easy to learn and use as an expert system shell or generator, but it comes pretty close. What it lacks in ease of use it makes up for with its power and flexibility. Unlike a fixed shell, Prolog is a language you can use to optimize your expert system to the application.

You have already seen how to write rules in Prolog. That is also how you write production rules for an expert system. Do your knowledge engineering first, develop your matrix, then write the rules in their standard IF-THEN form.

Let's use a rule from the sea creature expert system described in Chapter 5 as a sample. The rule in standard format is:

IF the creature has a backbone
AND the creature has a vertical fin
AND the creature breathes through gills
THEN the creature is a fish.

We have to rearrange this information to form a valid Prolog rule. Here's what it looks like:

is_ a (Creature, fish) :-

has_ a (Creature, backbone),

has_ a (Creature, vertical fin),

breathes_ through (creature, gills).

In Prolog, the THEN statement comes first followed by the IF symbol (:-). The various premises or conditions are then listed. The comma after each signifies AND. Note that we make up our predicates as we need them. Also note that we start Creature with a capital letter since it is a variable.

Once you enter all the rules, you can turn Prolog's backward chaining inference engine loose on the knowledge base. It can then identify sea creatures given enough facts. You can use Prolog to write sequences that ask you questions if it can't find a fact. And you can use it to create special explanation sentences or paragraphs that a user can call up to justify or understand the results.

Babel; because the Lord did there confound the language of all the earth.

GENESIS XI.9

Special AI Languages

LISP and Prolog are the main languages in AI work. They are probably used in over 90% of the AI programming effort in the world. But there are some special languages that show up now and then in AI applications. They are either enhanced or modified versions of more conventional languages or unique languages that were created to deal with specific types of problems. There are many to cover, but here we will list only the most well known of this group. And we certainly won't attempt to show you even elementary programming concepts.

Most of these languages were designed to run on minicomputers such as DEC's popular VAX machines. Some of the languages will run on selected LISP machines or mainframes. Only a few are available in personal computer versions.

LISP and Prolog Combos

If LISP and Prolog are both so good for AI, then certainly a mix of the two ought to be even better, right? Well, that's what some developers have assumed, and in some cases, proven. As a result, there are several LISP and Prolog combination languages.

One example is LOGLISP, developed at Syracuse University, that integrates LISP with Prolog. Another version is Lisp/Prolog, a combination designed for the Prime 50 series of computers. It allows you to either interpret or compile. And you can intersperse

LISP and Prolog code into a single program. One language can call subroutines or portions of the other.

These combo languages almost eliminate the great LISP vs. Prolog debate that continues to occupy AI programmers. If you can't do what you want in one language, the other will handle it. It's a form of having your cake and eating it too.

Variations of this theme are languages that are extensions or improvements of either LISP or Prolog. One example is QLISP. It is basically an extension of InterLISP that incorporates a data base as well as procedures for pattern matching and backtracking that give it Prolog-like qualities.

Another combination is POPLOG, a mix of LISP, Prolog, and POP-11 available from Systems Designers Software, Inc. It can be used to create LISP and Prolog programs alone or in combination. It also includes POP-11, which is another deduction/theorem prover language like Prolog. Based on POP-2, POP-11 was designed for beginners learning AI and programming.

PLANNER, CONNIVER, POPLER, and AMORD

Many special languages are based on deduction and theorem proving concepts. Like Prolog, they implement an algorithm that tries to reach a conclusion from a set of facts or premises stored in a data base. They use a variety of techniques for representing the premises and manipulating them. Basically, they are declarative languages with some procedural elements that permit more conventional programming.

PLANNER

The earliest attempt at such a language was PLANNER conceived by Hewitt at MIT. It was never fully implemented. However, a subset called Micro-PLANNER was. The language uses a data base made up of assertions and theorems. A search and pattern matching process is used to satisfy goals. Chronological backtracking is used. Micro-PLANNER was built with LISP, and the LISP code can be mixed with PLANNER code. It is another example of one language built on top of another. That means that one language is used to construct another. That language must be present if the other is to be used.

CONNIVER

CONNIVER is similar to PLANNER in organization and operation. It was created in an attempt to improve upon the PLANNER idea. The result was a language that was simpler to use and more flexible. It provided more control structures that allowed the programmer to specify and manipulate the search process rather than accepting some fixed method. Like PLANNER, CONNIVER was built with and on top of LISP. The two could be mixed. Both PLANNER and CONNIVER were interpreters.

POPLER

POPLER is similar to PLANNER and CONNIVER, but it was written in the POP-2 language, a programming language developed at the University of Edinburgh for AI research. POP-2 combines the features of LISP and Algol to form an unusually powerful programming language. An off-shoot of POP-2 is POP-11 designed for the DEC VAX computers. POPLER can be compiled into POP-2 language for fast execution.

AMORD

AMORD is also similar to POPLER, CONNIVER, and PLANNER. It uses dependency-directed backtracking as opposed to the chronological backtracking of the others. AMORD was embedded in SCHEME, a dialect of LISP.

None of these languages was widely used. Most of these languages exist in the university/research environment. Few if any real life end user programs have been created with them.

It took Prolog, created in France and enhanced in the U.K., to make the deduction/theorem prover language concept practical.

SAIL

SAIL (Stanford Artificial Intelligence Language) is an enhanced version of Algol. Algol (short for Algorithmic language) was developed jointly in the U.S. and Europe during the 1960s. It is a general purpose programming language optimized for developing and communicating algorithms and running them efficiently on a variety of computers. It was highly standardized and thus programs were unusually portable. Algol was also widely used in teaching computer science. Algol is not used much today, but it had a major influence on language design.

SAIL was built on top of Algol. It had all of Algol's features plus it permitted a data base of facts to be constructed using "triples." A triple allows you to represent knowledge in the form of "X is a property of Y which has the value Z." The data base could be searched using pattern matching techniques.

Mainsail is an extended commercial version of SAIL available from Xidak, Inc. Its main goal is to provide complete portability of AI programs between computers. Mainsail runs on most versions of DECs minicomputers (VAX, PDP-11, TOPS, etc.).

LOGO

Most people think of kids and education when the LOGO computer language is mentioned. Although it is true that LOGO was developed to help simplify the teaching of computer concepts and programming to kids as well as adults in a school setting, it is nevertheless a very powerful programming language. And it is eminently suitable for AI applications.

LOGO is really an expanded and easier-to-use version of LISP. It was developed at MIT by Paparet. Its main feature is "turtle" graphics. LOGO can draw pictures by using a simple command structure. The pictures are traced out using a "turtle," either an on-screen prompt-like symbol or an actual external peripheral device that looks like a turtle and rolls around on wheels holding a pen drawing pictures on paper.

One of these days, LOGO will be "discovered" as a very serious and capable AI programming language. Many versions are available for personal computers.

Smalltalk

Smalltalk takes a completely different approach to programming than the list language (LISP and LOGO) or the deduction/theorem prover languages (Prolog, et.al.). Developed at Xerox's Palo Alto Research Center (PARC), Smalltalk is known as an object-based language. It is based on a language called Simula created in the 1960s in Norway.

The basic element of Smalltalk is an object (sometimes called an actor). An object is a piece of data that can be numeric or symbolic. The object also describes the valid operations that can be performed on it. Objects embody a combination of declarative and procedural knowledge.

Objects belong to a class, description, or category of one or more similar objects called *acquaintances*. Objects inherit the characteristics of other members of their class.

Programming in Smalltalk is totally unlike programming in a conventional procedural language. In a procedural language, you use commands and statements that tell how to manipulate the data. In Smalltalk, programming is done by sending messages between objects. A message is a word describing one of the operations that can be performed on an object. Objects recognize messages they can perform. When sent a message, the object carries it out on itself and generates a response.

Smalltalk's main benefit is modularity. It allows a programmer to build very small specific modules like generic subroutines that, in turn, can be used to create larger programs that do bigger and better things.

Smalltalk has not been widely available commercially. However, a version is now available from Digitalk, Inc., in Los Angeles for the IBM PC.

LOOPS and FLAVORS

Both LOOPS and FLAVORS embody the basic object-oriented programming processes of Smalltalk. LOOPS is a superset of Smalltalk. That is, LOOPS is a larger more powerful programming language that has procedure-oriented, data-oriented, and rule-oriented capabilities as well as an object-oriented element. LOOPS is implemented in InterLISP and runs on Xerox's line of LISP machines.

FLAVORS is a Smalltalk-like language that was created to run on the Symbolics and LMI LISP machines. It is built on top of LISP. Its main difference with Smalltalk is that it permits multiple inheritances across classes which is not permitted in Smalltalk.

FRL and KRL

Both FRL and KRL are frame-based programming languages. They are based on the use of frames as a knowledge representation method. They facilitate the building of frame-based expert systems and other knowledge-based AI programs.

FRL (Frame Representation Language) implements the classical frame concept conceived by Minsky at MIT. It permits slots with facets to describe objects and their relationships. It also permits inheritance.

KRL (Knowledge Representation Language) is similar to FRL and was created over the years at Stanford and Xerox PARC. It was never available commercially. Today, all of its concepts are included in LOOPS described earlier. Both FRL and KRL were implemented in LISP.

OPS5

OPS5 is a rule-based programming language developed at Carnegie Mellon University in Pittsburgh. Its basic knowledge representation scheme is production rules. It has a built-in forward chaining inference engine.

OPS5 is more than just a shell for building expert systems. It is a full language that uses rules more fully than any shell. For example, special rules may be written to change the flow of control in a program. OPS5 also allows other types of data to be represented, namely objects with attributes and values as well as vectors. Like many other AI languages, OPS5 is built with LISP. Versions of OPS5 are available for the IBM PC and Apple Macintosh.

Language Selection

There are many other AI programming languages lying around in universities and research organizations. Most of them are not available commercially. The only way to learn about them is to read the literature. Although they are interesting in an academic sense, they are not practical for real-world AI productivity. Your best bet is to stick to well-known and widely used languages you can buy commercially. Such languages are taught in colleges and seminars and documented in one or more books. LISP and Prolog certainly fall into this category. It is usually best to stick to the mainstream if you are looking for the fastest way to produce profitable results. Use the special languages only if they offer some overriding benefit or are the only way to implement your application.

By all means, don't overlook the conventional languages like Pascal, C, and Forth. This is especially true if you can program in one of these languages or have access to a programming staff that does. This will save you the time, effort, and money involved in learning a new language. However, it will probably be easier to create AI software with LISP or Prolog.

Conventional languages offer one key benefit over LISP and Prolog: the programs are smaller, occupy far less memory, and execute faster. These are major advantages that may allow you to do the job whereas a LISP or Prolog implementation may not. The C programming language is emerging as the predominant choice of programmers who have to squeeze an AI program into smaller available memory and make it execute in a reasonable time.

Key Points

- The second most popular AI programming language is Prolog.
- Prolog means PROgramming in LOGic.
- Prolog was invented in France in the 1970s, then expanded and enhanced in the U.K.
- Prolog is based on the concepts of predicate calculus.
- Prolog is a declarative language that you use to tell the computer what problem to solve with what data but not how to solve the problem. Traditional procedural languages require the programmer to conceive of an algorithm that tells how to solve the problem. Prolog solves the problem in its own unique way.
- There are no Prolog standards, but most publishers follow the Prolog guidelines established at the University of Edinburgh (Scotland) and outlined in *Programming in Logic* by Clocksin and Mellish.
- The Japanese have adopted Prolog as their main AI language and are basing the design of their fifth generation computers on it.
- Prolog was written with AI applications in mind. Therefore, developing expert systems, natural language interfaces, and other AI programs is often faster, easier, and less expensive than using conventional languages.
- Prolog is basically an empty knowledge base and a backward chaining inference engine plus assorted procedural statements.
- Programming in Prolog is the process of entering facts and rules into the knowledge base.
- A Prolog program taps the knowledge base to solve a problem by asking questions.
- Most Prologs are interpreters but compilers are also available for faster operation.

- Facts are entered as statements that show some relationship between two objects. The fact "John likes Mary" is entered as:

  likes(john, mary)

  Likes is the predicate showing the relationship between the two arguments John and Mary.
- Variables in Prolog statements are indicated by capital letters (Z, Joan, BUD).
- Other Prolog programming statements are called rules. Rules show the dependence of one fact upon others. The rule

  IF The celestial body is the satellite of a planet

  THEN It is called a moon

  is expressed as

  celestial body (moon) :-

  is_ satellite (celestial body, planet)

  The symbol :- means IF.
- The Prolog inference engine uses the facts and rules entered into the knowledge base to draw conclusions. When a question is asked, the inference engine uses backward chaining and backtracking to examine the facts and rules looking for evidence to support the hypothesis posed by the question.
- Prolog can perform basic arithmetic operations, but the language is not optimized for numerical work. Therefore, calculation is awkward.
- Prolog contains numerous procedural commands that permit the programmer to customize the program using conventional programming techniques.
- Expert systems using production rules are easy to create with Prolog as it is an empty knowledge base with an inference engine to begin with.
- Many other programming languages have been developed for AI work. Most exist only in a university or research environment. Few are commercial products.
- One type of language combines LISP and Prolog, permitting them to communicate with one another. An example is LOGLISP.
- Other declarative languages based on deduction and theorem proving like Prolog include PLANNER, micro-PLANNER, CONNIVER, POPLER, and AMORD. None are available commercially.
- LOGO, a simplified and expanded version of LISP, is widely used in education to teach computer and programming concepts. It has excellent AI applications potential. Many versions are available.
- SAIL is an enhanced version of Algol that uses a data base of "triples" to represent and reason with knowledge. A commercial version is called Mainsail.
- Smalltalk is an object-oriented programming language that uses objects and message passing to implement programs. It is highly applicable to AI.

Versions of Smalltalk called FLAVORS and LOOPS are available commercially.

- FRL and KRL are programming languages based on the frames method of knowledge representation.
- OPS5 is a programming language that incorporates production rules and a forward chaining inference engine.
- Conventional programming languages such as Pascal, C, and Forth are viable alternatives to LISP, Prolog, and other AI languages where program speed and small size are important.

11

AI Hardware and the Future of AI

Sales of LISP machines have generated most of the AI dollars to date . . . In 1985, AI software sales generated \$67 million and AI hardware sales \$125 million (65%) . . . From 1985 to 1989, however, AI software revenues will grow 61% per year . . . while AI hardware sales will increase 33% per year.

ELECTRONIC BUSINESS MAGAZINE
FEBRUARY 1, 1986

As you have seen throughout this book, AI is software. It is programming languages, special software development tools, and specific applications programs embodying AI concepts. But while our focus has been on software, the hardware is not unimportant. We have taken for granted that AI software runs on almost any computer. Although it is true that AI can be implemented on virtually the full range of computers from simple personal computers to the most sophisticated mainframes, each has its limitations. Present machines can run AI, but their usefulness is limited by their speed, memory size, and in some cases their inherent architecture. To implement larger, more sophisticated and far more useful AI programs, new, bigger, and faster computers are required.

It has long been recognized that AI programs often require special hardware traits. But little has been done about it until fairly recently. New, special computers optimized for AI, like the LISP machines, have emerged. Research and development on totally new architectures such as RISC and parallel processing has produced new computers whose AI performance is considerably improved over traditional processors. The Japanese are building their fifth generation machines which are unique in architecture and specifically optimized for knowledge based applications.

In this chapter we want to take a look at the hardware limitations of current machines and introduce you to some of the more recent developments. We will talk about supercomputers, parallel processors, RISC computers, and the Japanese fifth generation machines. We will also describe that special class of AI workstation known as the LISP machine.

Finally, to conclude this chapter, we will take a brief look at what you can expect in the future from the field of AI. Despite the fact that AI has been around for about 30 years, it is still considered to be in its infancy. This is true even in light of the fantastic developments that have occurred in the past five years. You can expect to see some incredible developments yet to come. We conclude with some scenarios and predictions.

Computer Architecture: The Old and the New

The digital computer was invented in the early 1940s to meet needs of World War II. Faster calculating machines were needed to produce projectile trajectory tables for every type of gun and cannon. The work was simply overwhelming even for huge teams of individuals who made the calculations manually. Further, the complex calculations and simulations required in the design of the atomic bomb produced a need for automatic computing machines. The first real digital computer, known as ENIAC, was developed by John Mauchly and J. Presper Eckert. Their work was expanded upon and refined by John Von Neumann at Princeton. As it turns out, von Neumann's design for a digital computer is the one that eventually became the model for all present-day digital computers. Known as von Neumann architecture or the stored program concept, this architecture proved to be ideal for performing virtually all types of computations. That concept has been refined and updated over the years. Yet still, every computer from the largest mainframe to the smallest personal computer uses some variation of that idea.

Today, the concept is still valid and it is expected that the von Neumann design will continue to be used for years to come. Further improvements are expected. However, there is considerable effort underway to find a new model or concept that will greatly improve our ability to perform computations with electronic circuits. No one single new model or concept has been discovered, but many non-von Neumann (known as the non-von architecture) approaches have been discovered and tested. The only one that has emerged is that of parallel processing with multiple CPUs. Other ideas are being explored. The goal is to come up with a new architecture that will increase computing speed many times over and make it easier to implement some kinds of computing problems which do not fit well with the serial processing von Neumann architecture. Parallel processing appears to hold the most promise. Such parallel processing computers should also greatly improve the ability of a computer to handle many types of artificial intelligence applications.

In this section we will take a look at the basic von Neumann architecture, describe its limitations, and show how improvements have been made over the years. We will also introduce special versions of von Neumann computers which greatly improve upon the concept and make AI applications possible. These include super- computers, the new RISC architecture, array processors, and, of course, the new parallel processing machines.

The von Neumann Architecture

Most of you are probably familiar with the basic architecture of a digital computer. You have seen the basic block diagram of such a machine illustrated many times. See

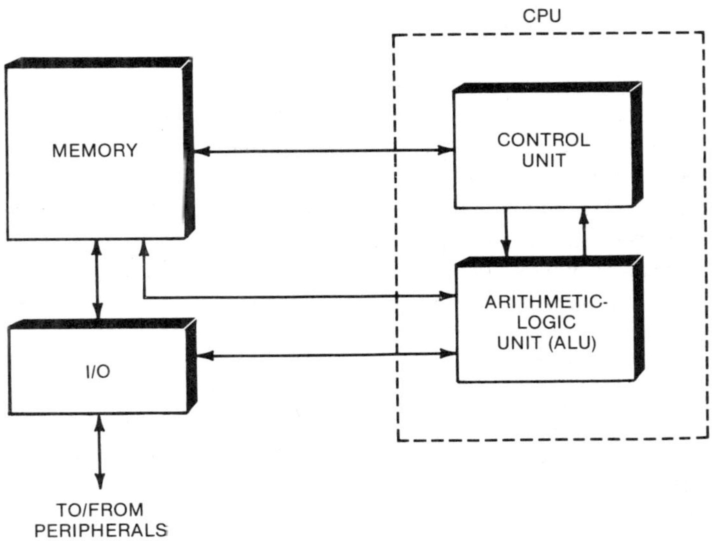

Figure 11–1. ***The basic von Neumann digital computer.***

Figure 11–1. All digital computers consist of four basic elements: the memory, the arithmetic logic unit (ALU), the control unit, and the input/output (I/O) unit. The ALU and control unit are usually considered to be one integrated component and it is generally referred to as the central processing unit (CPU). Most micro- processors are nothing more than single chip integrated circuit CPUs.

Digital computers operate on the von Neumann principle or stored program concept. Binary words, called instructions, tell the computer specific operations to perform. Instuctions specify ways of moving binary numbers into and out of the memory and between various registers in the CPU. Instructions also tell the computer to perform a variety of arithmetic and logic operations. To solve a problem on a digital computer, a step-by-step procedure called an algorithm is conceived. This algorithm is implemented by performing the step-by-step operations with the computer's instructions. The sequence of instructions implementing the algorithm, of course, is called a program. That program is stored in the digital computer's memory. It is stored as a sequence of binary instruction words in adjacent memory locations. The data to be processed is also stored in the memory. This is the stored program concept.

The problem is solved when the CPU executes the program. The control unit fetches the instructions one at a time, decodes and interprets them, and issues control signals to the ALU and other parts of the computer to carry out the specified operations. The instructions are executed sequentially one at a time as the algorithm solves the problem.

The only thing that makes this seemingly slow cumbersome process practical is that the instructions can be executed at extremely high speed. In most computers, instruction execution may take only a few microseconds and in many cases, only a few nanoseconds. Millions of instructions can be executed per second permitting what appear to be long, impossibly tedious programs to be executed in a very short period of time. To the human, some long sequential programs appear to execute instantaneously.

Computing Component Speed

Early digital computers were extremely slow. They were implemented with vacuum tubes and used both CRTs and delay lines as memory units. Some computations took many seconds and complex operations took minutes to perform. Still this was an enormous improvement over manual calculations. However, as electronic components were improved, computing speeds increased. Transistors, then integrated circuits came along and speed improved dramatically. Computing speeds went from milliseconds to microseconds to nanoseconds. New types of memory devices were created. Magnetic core memories were popular for a time but today have been totally replaced by semiconductor memories which are smaller and faster.

As larger and more complex problems are tackled, the computers required to process them adequately need to be larger and faster. Specifically, memories must be capable of storing not just hundreds of thousands of words, but many millions of instruction and data words. Further, processing speed must be increased if the computation is to be completed in a realistic period of time. Even with processing speeds of nanoseconds, large complex problems can take minutes and/or hours to complete on the largest and fastest computers.

AI applications are particularly demanding of both memory and computing speed. Computer vision and speech recognition are two applications where speed and memory size are of the utmost importance. Many types of special mathematical calculations require unusually large memories and high speed.

The memory problem is overcome simply on a brute-force scale. The idea is to produce CPUs with the capability of addressing huge amounts of memory. That's no problem, but the big hangup has been memory cost. As the semiconductor manufacturers have learned to put more and more bits of storage on a chip, memory prices have dropped considerably over the years. Today, memory is relatively inexpensive and getting cheaper as higher memory chip densities are achieved. Today, 256K bit chips are commonplace and the one megabit chip will soon be with us.

Computing speed, on the other hand, is a different problem. Faster electronic circuits are the basic solution. Today the largest and fastest computers still use bipolar transistor technology. Original machines used discrete bipolar transistors to build their logic circuits. Eventually, integrated circuits were adopted. Transistor-transistor logic (TTL) circuits have been popular for years and are still widely used. Their computing speed has been increased gradually over the years, particularly by the use of Schottky diode technology. Even faster emitter-coupled logic (ECL) circuits are available. The fastest computers today use both TTL and ECL VLSI gate arrays.

The primary problem with increasing computing speed with bipolar devices is that power consumption rises considerably. In very large computers cooling becomes a major problem. Forced air can be used in some cases, but in the largest and fastest machines, liquid cooling is required to dissipate the heat generated by circuits that produce the desired computing speeds.

While MOS circuits are used almost exclusively for memory, they have not been used in the CPUs of the larger, faster minis and mainframes. Of course, most microprocessors are made with NMOS. Microprocessors made with MOS integrated circuits are relatively slow compared to bipolar devices. But tremendous advances in NMOS technology have improved computing speeds tremendously. The newer 16 and 32 bit microprocessors are impressively fast. The newer CMOS logic circuits are extremely fast and at the same time offer the major benefit of very low power consumption. CMOS appears to be the semiconductor technology of choice for future CPUs.

Further improvements in computing speed are promised by the use of gallium arsenide (GaAs). Today, most transistors or integrated circuits are made with silicon, an excellent semiconductor material. It has been found that the combination of gallium and arsenic produces a superior semiconductor material which can make even faster transistors and integrated circuits. Already GaAs field effect transistors, called MESFETs, are being used to produce linear amplifiers in the GigaHertz region. Considerable research and development is underway to produce gallium arsenide integrated logic circuits for extremely fast computing. Gains in speed of five to ten times over silicon circuits are expected.

The speed of computation in a digital computer is determined by the propagation of the digital pulses through the various logic circuits. Every circuit has a built-in delay which results from taking a finite period of time for voltage or current level transitions to rise or fall as they pass through the various circuits. These delays are generally caused by the charging and discharging of parasitic capacitances through the various circuit resistances. The propagation delay of the fastest gates is in the hundreds of picosecond range (one picosecond is .000000000001 second) and continuous reductions are being made. With such circuits, arithmetic logic units can be designed to execute individual instructions in only a few nanoseconds. Rarely is there a complaint over the computing speed abilities of the ALU itself. After all, it is the part of the computer that does the actual processing, and its possible computing speeds are awesome.

The von Neumann Bottleneck

The problem lies not so much in the ALU computing speed as it does in the ability of the CPU to access the memory. To get the data and instruction words into and out of the CPU for computation requires a continuous stream of memory accesses. Instructions must be fetched from memory and decoded. Operands to be used in computation must be brought into the ALU registers, used in some computations, and the newly computed data stored back in memory. As it turns out, computing speed is almost entirely controlled by the ALUs memory access speed. This limitation is generally referred to as the von Neumann "bottleneck."

The bottleneck is illustrated in Figure 11–2. All von Neumann machines have this basic arrangement. Programs are sequential instructions stored in memory. Data is also stored in memory. The control unit fetches instructions, decodes them, and issues control signals to the ALU and other circuits. Data words are brought into the accumulator register in the arithmetic-logic section where computations are performed.

The simple program in the memory adds two numbers stored at addresses 252 and 253 and stores the sum back in location 254. Here's how it is done.

1. Control unit fetches first instruction (LDA 252), stores it in the instruction register, and decodes it.
2. The first instruction is executed. It says to load the accumulator register with the data word at address 252. The number 19 is retrieved from memory and put into the accumulator.

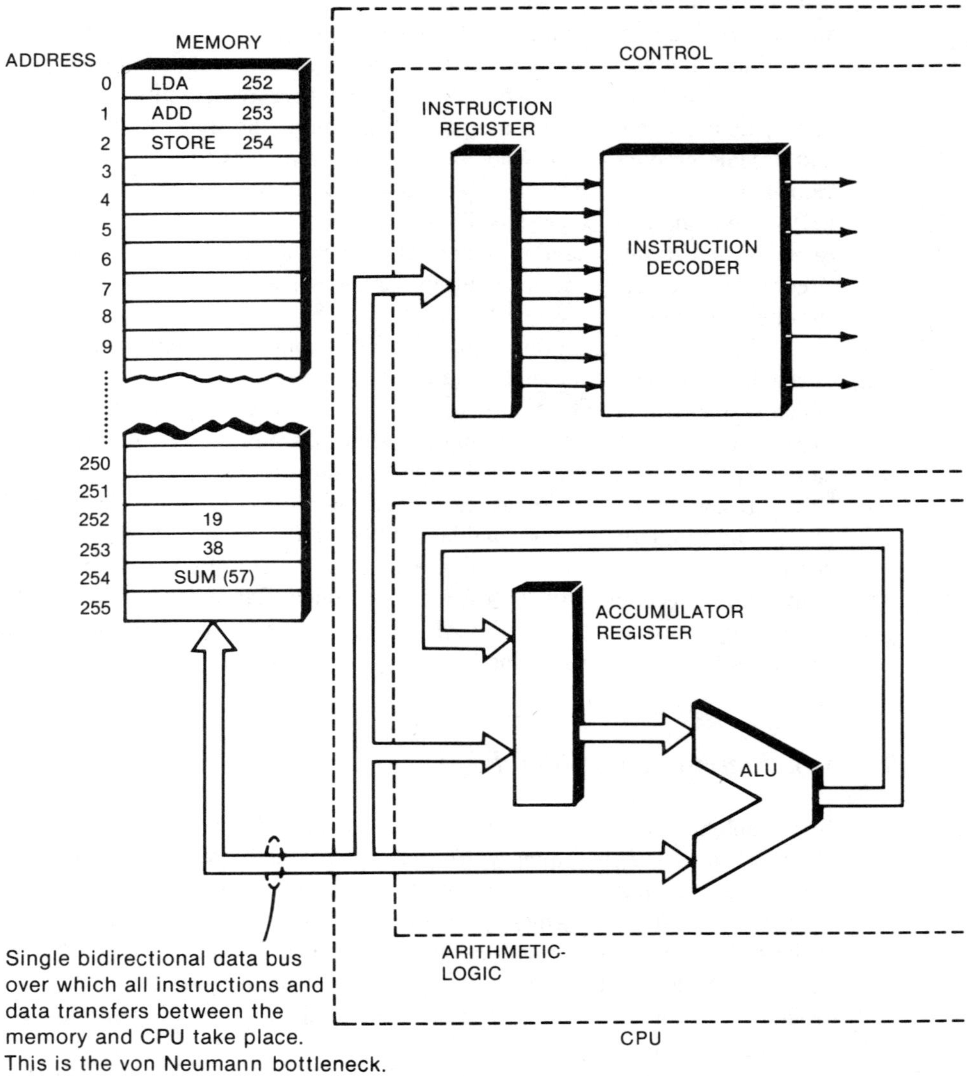

Figure 11–2. ***Illustration of the von Neumann bottleneck.***

3. The second instruction word (ADD 253) is fetched, store in the instruction register, and decoded.
4. The second instruction is executed. It says to add the number in address 253 (38) to the one in the accumulator (19). This is done and the sum (57) is stored in the accumulator.
5. The third instruction (STORE 254) is fetched, stored, and decoded.
6. The third instruction is executed. The number in the accumulator is transferred to memory location 254.

As you can see, even this simple program required six memory accesses. If each access takes 100 nanoseconds (ns) and the add operation takes 10 ns, the total execution time is 610 ns. Of that time, only 10 ns or about 1.6% is computation. The remaining 98.4% is pure memory access.

Improving computing speed then requires much faster memories. Further, it requires changes in architecture that will permit multiple simultaneous rather than single accesses to the memory. Multiple memories are another solution.

Cache Memories

Although faster memories have been developed over the years, numerous additional techniques have been devised for overcoming the memory access problem. One of these techniques is to use a small, fast, intermediate memory between the main memory and the CPU. Known as a cache memory, this small storage unit is capable of storing several thousand words. It is made of very high-speed bipolar memory chips rather than the usual slower MOS memory chips in most computers. A portion of the instructions or data from the program to be used are first loaded into the cache memory where they can be accessed very rapidly by the ALU. This greatly improves computing speed. Various techniques are used to bring the desired instruction and data words into the cache from the main memory as they are required in processing. Some machines have separate cache memories for instructions and data.

Pipelining

Another technique known as pipelining has also helped to improve computing speed in standard von Neumann architecture machines. Pipelining is the process of overlapping the fetch and execute portions of the typical CPU operation cycle. While some instructions are executing, additional instructions are being fetched and prepared for execution.

Pipelining also refers to the simultaneous performance of some operations involved in fetching and executing instructions. Most instructions consist of several clearly defined sequential steps. These steps are triggered by the computer's master clock oscillator. Pipelining allows some steps to be performed while others are being carried out. Figure 11–3 gives an example. Here each instruction consists of four equal length steps. It takes twelve clock cycles to carry them out. With pipelining the various steps are overlapped. Additional circuitry is required to do this, but the result is that it takes only six clock cycles to get the job done. Computing time is cut in half or speed is doubled.

While the basic von Neumann architecture is a limitation, computer designers over the years have made vast improvements in its performance and capabilities. It is still a viable concept, and most future digital computers will continue to use this kind of organization and operation. Further improvement in logic circuits and memories will continue to be made, keeping the von Neumann design alive and well for a long time.

Yet, the pressure is on to create new and different architectures that will produce orders of magnitude of greater computing power. This will permit the speedier solution of many special problems, among them artificial intelligence problems.

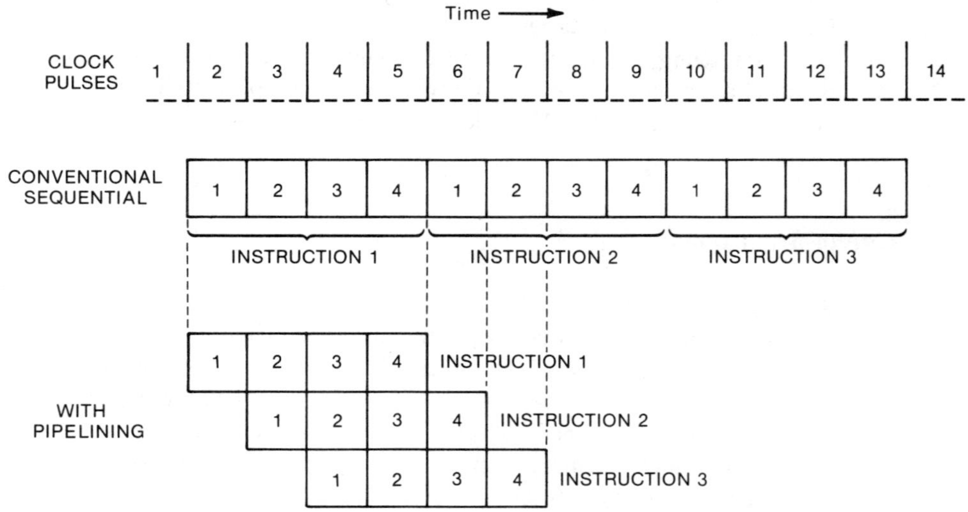

Figure 11–3. ***How pipelining improves speed.***

> *Each generation of computers has had an upper echelon—an elite group of machines that pushed the technological frontiers of the day and provided performance that far surpassed their closest rivals.*
>
> HIGH TECHNOLOGY MAGAZINE
> MAY, 1984

Supercomputers

Supercomputers are conventional von Neumann computers carried to the extreme. To achieve their exceptional high speed performance, supercomputers use leading-edge technology to push computing speeds to their maximum.

Supercomputers, of course, are the largest and most powerful computers in existence. By large we mean storage capacity. By powerful we mean computing speed. Supercomputers have the highest everything, including memory capacity, processing speed, and price. For those who require the most powerful computer available, supercomputers are it.

A supercomputer is generally defined as one with a minimum computational speed of 20 million operations per second. (See accompanying sidebar on Computing Speed Measurement.) Most supercomputers perform hundreds of millions of operations per second and already the billion operations per second barrier has been broken.

Vector and Floating Point Operations

Although speed is the primary determining factor as to whether a computer is a supercomputer or not, other factors also enter into the definition. Word size is another typical measurement. Most mainframe and minicomputers process 32-bit words, but supercomuters process 64-bit words in full parallel. In addition, supercomputers can perform not only standard scalar calculations but also vector calculations. Scalar operations are those involving only single variables. Vectors are a special type of variable which involves multiple quantities or dimensions. A vector is usually pictured as a line with an arrowhead pointing in some direction. The length of the vector represents one part of the variable, while the direction in which it is pointed represents another part of the variable. To define the direction in which the vector is pointing requires additional values. Performing mathematical operations on vectors involves many calculations.

Most data processing applications require only the use of scalar variables, but in many scientific and engineering applications, vector variables are the norm. Supercomputers can deal with vector quantities and can process all portions of the vector variables simultaneously.

Supercomputers also employ floating point representation of numbers. Most smaller computers use a fixed point representation. Floating point representation of numbers is a digital version of the popular scientific notation that represents numbers in a two-part format including a number between 1 and 10 multiplied by a factor that is some power of 10.

Some examples are:

$$.000000259 = 2.59 \times 10^{-7}$$

$$1{,}348{,}000{,}000{,}000 = 1.348 \times 10^{12}$$

Floating point representation permits a wider range of numbers to be represented. This is not necessary in standard business data processing, but in scientific and engineering applications it is essential. Floating point number representation requires considerably more hardware and processing operations. Most vectors and scalar variables in supercomputers are floating point numbers.

As for memory size, it varies considerably with the application need. However, most supercomputers contain millions of words of storage. Main RAM sizes vary from about 8 to 256 million bytes.

Speed and Heat

The processing hardware in a supercomputer is generally made with high speed bipolar emitter-coupled logic (ECL) circuits. ECL is the fastest logic available, and in its most recent form it has propagation delays of less than 1 nanosecond for a typical gate. Circuits with propagation delays in the 300 to 700-picosecond range are commonly found in supercomputers. Memories are implemented with both bipolar (TTL and ECL) RAM chips and ultra-fast MOS memory chips. Typical memory access times are 50 to 70 nanoseconds compared to hundreds of nanoseconds in conventional computers.

As for architecture, supercomputers are strictly von Neumann. However, they do use all of the tricks to improve computing speed, such as cache memories and pipelining. Supercomputers simply exploit the latest technology and refine it to the nth degree to achieve their high performance. In other words, supercomputers use sheer brute force to achieve their power.

The very high computing speeds and the large number of circuits used in a supercomputer make power consumption a real problem. The heat produced by a supercomputer's circuits would melt them if it weren't for very special cooling systems. Supercomputers long ago gave up on air cooling and today use strictly liquid cooling techniques. In some machines, pumps are used to circulate cooling liquid through special mechanical housings that carry the heat away from the circuits. In the newer computers, the entire electronic assembly is immersed in a fluorocarbon liquid to carry the heat away.

The heat problem is not just one of high power consumption that comes from using high-speed ECL circuits. It is compounded by the fact that the computer circuitry in a supercomputer is highly compacted into a small space. This is done to keep the distance between circuits as short as possible.

It takes a finite period of time for a signal to travel over a given distance. The limit, of course, is the speed of light, 186,000 miles per second. Light, or an electrical signal, can travel about one foot in a nanosecond. This means that one foot of wire has a delay of about one nanosecond. In practice, a pulse probably travels only about 9 inches in one nanosecond. With logic gate speeds already less than one nanosecond, you can see that computing speed is greatly affected by how long the interconnecting wires are. That's why supercomputer designers use every physical trick possible to shorten interconnections. The result is an assembly that forces all parts very close together. This increases computing speed, but causes massive heat build-up. Liquid cooling is the only solution.

Software

Supercomputers typically have a limited repertoire of software. They have their own proprietary operating system, although newer units are beginning to use the popular AT&T UNIX operating system or some variation of it. As for programming languages, Fortran is the mainstay. Virtually all programming for supercomputers is done in Fortran. The C language has been implemented on some machines and, of course, some work is done in assembly language.

Applications

Supercomputers are used primarily for scientific, engineering, and mathematical applications. They are widely used in analysis and design. However, one of the things they do best is simulation and modeling. This is the process of writing complex mathematical equations that describes some physical system. Then by solving the equations on the computer, the concept of the system or device can be verified before building a real-world model. Simulation saves a lot of time and money since it eliminates the need to build model after model to achieve a working finished product. Simulations let engineers design airplanes, cars, and other complex mechanical devices by simply playing with the design on the computer. Once the design has been proven and optimized, a real-world model is built.

Supercomputers also solve problems in oil field production and seismic data analysis. They are used in cryptoanalysis and weather forecasting. Such computations can be performed on conventional computers, but the amount of computing time required is often impractical. Supercomputers do the job so much faster that it makes these techniques practical.

Although supercomputers have not been used extensively for AI applications, the potential is certainly there. Their size and computing speed makes them particularly attractive for very large AI problems. Further, as supercomputers move toward the new parallel process architectures, they will become far more suitable to AI applications.

The Vendors

Who makes supercomputers? Only a handful of companies make these awesome machines. The first supercomputer, the Cray 1, was made by Cray Research, Inc. This company was started by Seymore Cray, a premier computer designer, when he left Control Data Corporation. Cray learned his trade by designing CDC's large 6600 and 7600 mainframes.

Today, Cray is the leader in the supercomputer field. There are only about 150 total supercomputers in the world, and nearly two-thirds of them are Crays.

Control Data also builds supercomputers. Their main machine is the Cyber 205. Recently an approved spin-off company of CDC, ETA Inc., has been given the goal to create the next generation of supercomputers.

IBM doesn't build supercomputers as such. However, their Sierra 3090 series just barely qualifies.

The main competition in the supercomputer field is coming from Japan. Fujitsu, Hitachi, and NEC (Nippon Electric) all have machines that stand up well to the Crays and Cybers. They are also less expensive. Most supercomputers have a price tag in the \$5 to \$15 million range.

Super-Minicomputers and Array Processors

In some special applications, supercomputer performance can be achieved by less powerful computers by adding an array processor to them. The usual combination involves either a large mainframe or a super-minicomputer, such as Digital Equipment Corporation's upper end VAX machines (Models 11/780-785 and 8600) combined with an array processor. Such a combination often produces the desired performance for considerably less money.

Super-Minis

Super-minis are the upper end scale of the minicomputer class of computing machines. These machines have 32–bit word and processing speeds in the 1 to 10 MIPS range. Although they do not qualify for supercomputer status, they are considerably faster than the average mainframe or minicomputer, and, therefore, are widely used in mathematical, scientific and engineering applications. Yet for some jobs, they are still too slow. However, by adding an array processor to them, they become a different machine.

Array Processors

An array processor is a very high speed floating point arithmetic/logic unit which attaches to an existing mainframe or minicomputer. They are also referred to as floating point processors or accelerators. An array processor uses high speed logic circuits and pipelining techniques to achieve very high speed arithmetic operations on large floating point numbers. Whenever such calculations are required, the host computer passes control to the array processor. The array processor works with the standard memory and I/O circuits of the computer while the main CPU provides control. The array processor does its high speed calculations and passes the data back to the host computer.

Like supercomputers, array processors have exceptional computing speed. They perform math operations 10 to 100 times faster than their typical host computer. Computing speeds up to several hundred million floating point operations per second can be achieved with such machines.

Computing Speed Measurement

Computing speed means a lot of different things, and there are numerous ways of expressing it. It refers to the clock frequency or period of the master timing oscillator in the computer. It refers to how fast arithmetic and logic operations are carried out. And, of course, it includes memory access times. When referring to supercomputers and parallel processing machines, speed is generally expressed in one of these ways: MIPS, FLOPS, and LIPS. MIPS means millions of instructions per second. This is the most common measure that is applicable to any computer. The dividing line between common everyday computers and high performance machines is one MIPS. The newest, largest, and fastest super minicomputers and mainframes break the one MIPS barrier. IBM's Sierra 3090 series mainframes run at 28 MIPS while DEC's newest 8600 VAX machines hit 2 MIPS. An IBM PC runs at a peak speed of about one thousand instructions per second or .001 MIPS.

Supercomputers and array processors are even faster, but the measure of their speed is usually expressed in terms of FLOPS or floating point operations per second. The speed is often quoted as mega FLOPS or MFLOPS for millions of floating point operations per second. The speed of most current supercomputers is in the 80 to 1300 MFLOPS range. A speed of 1000 MFLOPS is called one Giga FLOPS or GFLOPS. It means one billion floating point operations per second. The new supercomputers are expected to run at speeds of 4 to 5 Giga FLOPS.

Since floating point operations are more complex and require several steps more than conventional instructions, floating point speeds are lower. You can get a ballpark figure for floating point operations by dividing MIPS by 2 or 3. For example, a 12 MIPS machine would run between 4 and 6 MFLOPS.

For parallel processing machines optimized to do AI, specifically logical inference, an entirely new measure of speed has been created. Speed is expressed in terms of LIPS or logical inferences per second. It is a speed measure that tells, for example, how many Prolog rules can be instantiated per second. There are no commercial AI processors available yet, but prototype Japanese fifth generation machines have been clocked at speeds of 20,000 to 35,000 LIPS. Speeds up to 150 LIPS are achievable. The goal is a speed in the 100M to 1G LIPS range.

With massively parallel, super high speed VLSI processors, that speed may eventually be obtained.

All of these measures of speed are very general and a poor way to compare the performance of different machines. It is like the horsepower rating of a car engine. It doesn't really tell how fast a car can go as so many other factors, such as weight and wind drag, are involved. However, since there is really no other speed measure, manufacturers and users will continue to fall back on these unreliable measures.

Just keep two important facts in mind. First, the peak speed is rarely if ever achieved in practice. Depending upon the problem being solved, the speed may only be one-tenth or one-twentieth of the max.

Second, the best way to compare computing speeds of computers is to run a benchmark. This is a special program made up especially to exercise the various instructions to determine overall computation time. A real world problem to be solved on the computer also makes a good benchmark.

Reduced instruction set computers, relatively a new approach to computer architecture, increase computer performance while lowering cost.

ELECTRONICS MAGAZINE
JULY 15, 1985

Reduced Instruction Set Computer

Although the supercomputer is the ultimate attempt to improve upon the basic von Neumann architecture, another recent approach is more modest. Known as the reduced instruction set computer (RISC) architecture, the idea is to increase computing speeds and thus overcome the inherent von Neumann bottleneck limitation.

The approach in RISC architecture is to minimize the number of basic instructions the CPU can execute. Developing a RISC computer is basically that of creating a superfast minimum instruction set CPU. By reducing the number of instructions, the circuitry becomes simpler and less complex. As a result, such circuits are easier to put on an integrated circuit chip and also can have shorter propagation delays and thus higher computing speeds.

Over the years, computers including microprocessors have become far more complex. They are referred to as complex instruction set computers (CISC). They have grown not only in the bit size of the word they process, but they also have been given more capabilities in the form of many sophisticated instructions. Earlier computers used only a few instructions and more complex operations were implemented by writing appropriate software subroutines. For example, multiplication and division were almost always carried out by programs in the older computers. But today most computers, even the newer microprocessors, have built-in multiply and divide instructions. Most computers and microprocessors offer literally hundreds of different instructions to perform not only the basic add, subtract, compare, and branch operation but also those for performing macro operations.

The design of such computers has become extremely time consuming and costly. Extensive prototyping and testing is required. Figuring out how to get all the circuitry on one chip is a real challenge. Most seminconductor manufacturers have had considerable problems in bringing to market the new 32-bit microprocessors. New approaches to computer design had to be taken as the number of instructions grew larger. Most early computers featured hard-wired logic in their control sections. This was possible with few instructions, but with many instructions, the control logic became impossibly complex. Today, most computers and the larger microprocessors are implemented with microcode. (See Sidebar on Microprogramming) Microcode is special binary words stored in a microcode ROM that are fetched and read out in sequence to generate the control signals for the various computer instructions. The microcode section of a computer or microprocessor is essentially a computer within a computer. Such complexity adds size and cost as well as reducing computing speeds.

RISC architecture is an attempt to return to the simpler architectures of old in an effort to improve computing speed. The main features of a RISC CPU are described below:

Simplified Fixed Instruction Set

Most RISC CPUs have as few as 30 instructions but usually no more than 100. Tests conducted using larger conventional computers determined that most of the very complex instructions were executed infrequently. It was found that Parado's 80-20 rule applied. About 80% of the instructions were being used about 20% of the time. In other words, about 20% of the instructions were doing 80% of the processing. The instructions most often used were the basic add, subtract, compare, jump, load, and store.

Hard-Wired Control

When the instruction set is small, conventional logic can be used to wire the control section of the CPU. This eliminates the need to use the larger more expensive and slower microprogramming approach to implementing the instruction set.

One-Cycle Execution

Most RISC instructions are designed to operate in one single cycle of CPU operation. The cycle includes both the fetch and execution of the instruction which typically involves many clock cycles. By executing in a single machine cycle, high speed is assured.

Large Register Set

Another feature of RISC CPUs is their very large set of processing registers. While most CPUs have 16 to 32 registers, RISC computers typically have more than double that. By using many general purpose computing registers, considerable storage space is provided for the operands in a computation. This allows the CPU to retain operands in its registers rather than having to continually access memory which slows computing speed. Remember that memory access is the von Neumann bottleneck. In RISC machines, only the load and store instructions access memory. All other instructions perform very high speed register-to-register transfers.

RISC Implementations

Most RISC CPUs have been implemented as 32-bit single chip VLSI microprocessors. However, some discrete IC RISC processors, both Schottky TTL and ECL, have been developed. RISC machines also use cache memories and pipelining to improve speed. Computing speeds of 1 to 4 MIPS have been achieved to date. However, as the designs are improved, computing speeds from 10 to 50 MIPS are predicted. Some future designs will use GaAs circuits.

There are already several RISC computers on the market. The earliest machines were introduced by Pyramid Technologies and Ridge Computers. Hewlett-Packard's new Spectrum™ series of computers uses RISC architecture. IBM's new PC/RT™ computer uses RISC architecture. All of these are proprietary CPU designs, but off-the-shelf RISC microprocessors are expected to be available soon.

While the RISC architecture helps increase computing speed by minimizing the impact of the von Neumann bottleneck, software may be more difficult to develop. Since fewer operations are implemented with instructions, complex processing will have to be implemented with subroutines written with the basic instruction set. This may require more programming time. On the other hand, some programmers argue that the more complex instruction sets are often harder to learn and use, thereby slowing programming productivity. In any case, the RISC concept is viable and one that is providing lower cost computers with exceptional performance. RISC machines are expected to find wide application in artificial intelligence.

Microprogramming

Microprogramming is not the programming of a microcomputer. Instead, it is a technique used to implement sequential digital logic circuits. It is widely used in designing the control unit of a digital computer or microprocessor. It provides a highly organized way to replace what otherwise would be an extremely large and complex network of both combinational and sequential logic circuits.

Microprocessing is done with a circuit called a microcontroller. The heart of the microcontroller is a ROM containing many large binary words called microinstructions. Each ROM contains hundreds or even thousands of these 16 to 128 bit words. Reading these words out in sequence generates the timing pulses to control external circuits.

A simplified block diagram of a microcontroller is shown in Figure 11–4. The ROM with its built-in address decoder is driven by a counter/register. The counter is incremented by clock pulses and may be loaded externally from a multiplexer. The multiplexer selects one of several input sources including a portion of the ROM output. Here's how the microcontroller in a computer works.

First, an instruction is fetched from memory and stored in the instruction register. The instruction word is fed to the multiplexer and passed through to be loaded into the counter/register. This serves as the starting address of a sequence of microinstructions in ROM. The clock pulses increment the counter/register, thereby causing sequential microinstruction words to be read out at high speed. The words usually are loaded into an external register. The outputs of the flip flops in this register are the individual control signals that operate other logic circuits in the computer.

Each computer instruction is carried out by a short sequence of microinstructions (also called microcodes). A portion of the microinstruction word is used as an address to cause branching. The output address bits are fed to the multiplexer which passes them through to the counter/registers. This causes a jump to another portion of the ROM where other microinstructions are read out.

The benefit of microprogramming is that computer design is faster and easier. New instructions are added by creating new microcode. No additional circuits are required. Some computers contain a microcode RAM instead of or in addition to the ROM. Called a writeable control store, this RAM can be used by the programmer to create new instructions or modify existing ones to optimize performance.

Parallel processing appears to be the natural and most efficient way to solve a host of problems . . .

F. DAVID PEAT
ARTIFICIAL INTELLIGENCE,
HOW MACHINES THINK

Parallel Processors

It is generally agreed that the performance limit of conventional von Neumann architecture computers has almost been reached. Virtually all the techniques for making conventional computers faster have been explored and implemented. While some future improvements are still expected through the application of the latest technology, such as gallium arsenide semiconductors, the days of performance improvements of orders of magnitude are over. Unless some new and significantly faster circuits are discovered, von Neumann computer performance will saturate at a level not much beyond where it is now. Predictions of cryogenic, optical, and biological logic circuits offer some promise of further improvements, but these developments appear far in the future, if they occur at all.

The real solution appears to be a completely different architecture. Something that will produce the 100 to 1000 speed factor gains that many feel is necessary for real computing breakthroughs in some fields, AI included.

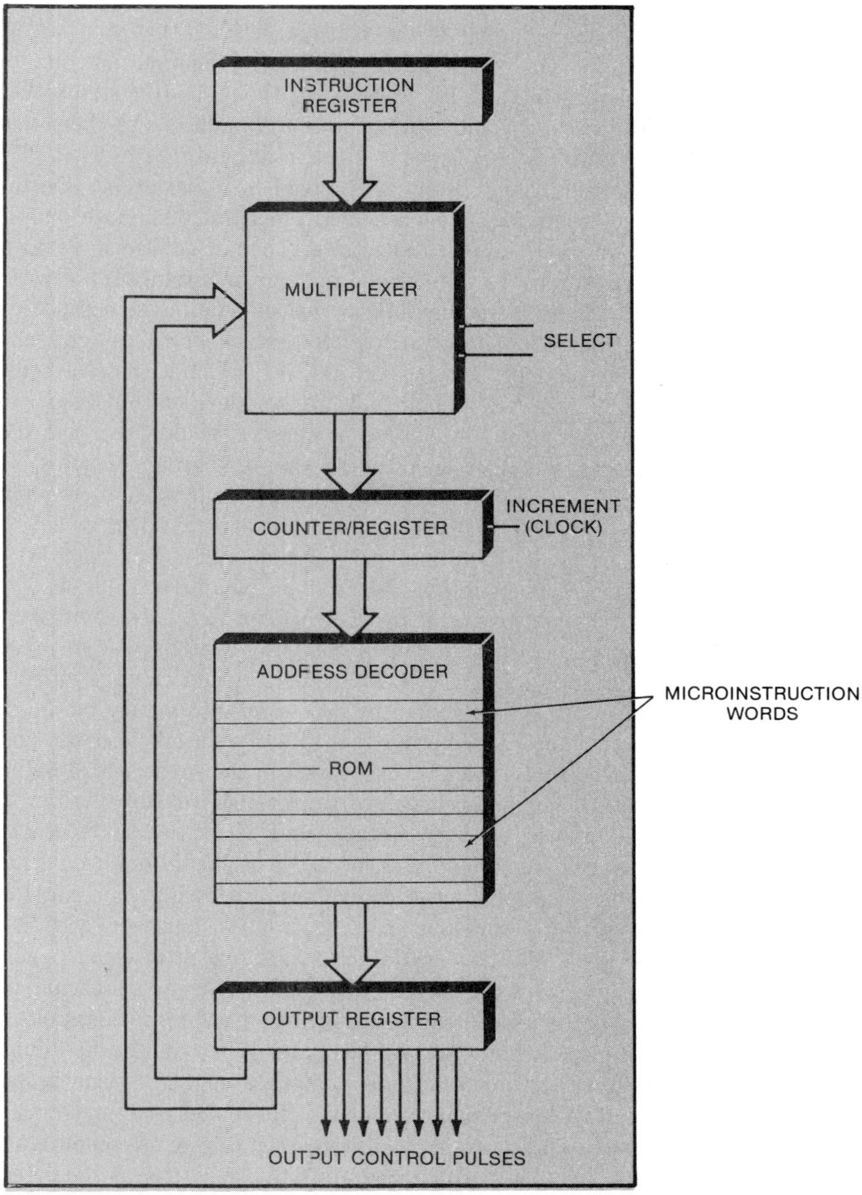

Figure 11–4. *A microcontroller.*

That new architecture already has been identified. Specifically, it involves the use of multiple CPUs and memory units. Known as parallel processing, this technique makes use of hundreds or even thousands of processors which will work on one small piece of a problem in concert. The result can be enormous increases in overall computing speed. Where a von Neumann computer must execute its program and process data sequentially, parallel computers split the program among available processors and execute all portions simultaneously.

As a simple example of this concept, assume that you had a list of 512 numbers to add together. This would be done in a von Neumann machine by first bringing two of the numbers into the CPU and adding them. To this sum would be added the next number. The process would continue until 511 additions had been made. Adding together all of the memory access times and the addition times of the CPU would give you the total computation time. Granted, it would be considerably shorter with today's high speed computers. In fact, if we assumed a modest 200 nanosecond time for each addition including a memory access, the total number of additions would probably take about 102.4 microseconds. To us it would appear instantaneous. Nevertheless, one hundred microseconds is an incredibly long period of time in the computer world.

If the same problem were given to a parallel processing machine, the computation speed could be cut significantly. Assume, for example, that you could divide the problem of adding 512 numbers among 256 processors. Each processor would add two of the numbers, producing a sum. These processors would then give their sums in pairs to 128 processors which would compute the next group of sums. These sums, in turn, would be given to 64 processors. On each computation, the number of processors required to deal with this problem would be cut in half. It would take a total of 8 such additions to achieve the total. That's 8 additions compared to 511. That represents a speed-up factor of about 64 over the von Neumann solution. That is an impressive speed gain, but even greater improvements can be achieved with some types of problems.

For example, assume that a computer was needed to process image data and extract information from it. A TV camera would capture either the real scene or a photograph of it. It would then be converted into binary by an A-to-D converter and stored in a memory. A computer then would be used to search and analyze the binary image of the scene. Typically, each pixel in the scene would be used in some form of computation. A computer may use subroutines of 100 or even 1000 instructions on each pixel. Some scenes may contain hundreds of thousands or even millions of pixels. Using a von Neumann computer, all these computations would have to be carried out serially. Even with high speed computers, processing time could be extremely long.

If a parallel processing approach is used, however, considerable gains could be made. The ideal situation would be to allot one processor to each pixel. In some low resolution systems with only a few hundred or few thousand pixels, this might be possible. The alternative approach for large pixel representations is to assign one processor to a group of say 10 or 100 pixels. What could take minutes or even hours of processing time on a conventional computer might be done in only a few seconds or less with parallel processing techniques. This makes real time image processing possible.

Overall, parallel processing is expected to give us computers that are 100 to 1000 times as fast as present supercomputers. At least, that is the potential. The good news is that this significant increase in computing speed may, in fact, be less expensive than current supercomputers. When thousands of processors are used, their actual computing speed does not have to be anywhere near as fast as the processor speeds in a supercomputer. Although processing speed is important, it is the parallel nature of the problem solving that makes the computer fast. For example, if the computing speed of a single processor is S, and N processors are used, the computing speed of the combination is $S \times N$. If one processor computes at 2 MIPS, then 100 processors should compute at 200 MIPS. In practice, however, this theoretical speed cannot be achieved.

There are already several parallel computers on the market. Many new designs are expected over the next couple of years. Parallel computers bring a whole new approach to problem solving and users are only just beginning to learn how to use them. Parallel processors don't do much for conventional data processing applications, but problems involving many clearly discernible segments will be solved faster and more efficiently with parallel computers. Many scientific and engineering computations fit this model, and, of course, many artificial intelligence applications are waiting to take advantage of this new architecture.

Parallel Architectures

The idea of parallel processing is not new, and over the years many schemes have been developed for putting together parallel processing machines. Research and debate in parallel architectures is expected to continue for years to come. There does not appear to be a best parallel architecture as many configurations have been shown to work satisfactorily.

Multiprocessing

Don't confuse multiprocessing and parallel processing. Multi-CPU computers have been around for years doing what is generally known as multiprocessing. Basically, multiprocessing is the use of two or more CPUs sharing a common memory but each running a different program. Multiprocessing means one application per processor.

On the other hand, parallel processing is the dividing of one application program among many processors. Parallel processors speed up the computation of a single job while multiprocessors handle more jobs in a given time. Multiprocessors improve productivity whereas parallel processors do one job faster.

To give you some idea of the scope of parallel architecture, let's first consider the number of processors to be used. How many is the correct number. In reality, the "right" number of processors is probably directly dependent upon the problem to be solved. In other words, how can the problem be subdivided and partitioned. How many smaller problem segments does the problem divide itself into naturally? This will vary widely with the types of problems to be solved. Each segment of the problem is assigned a processor.

Another issue is what type of processor to use. Although minicomputers, mainframes, and supercomputers still rely on unique proprietary CPU designs, most parallel computers are expected to use conventional off-the-shelf microprocessors. Today's newer microprocessors are incredibly fast and powerful. By combining hundreds or thousands of them, an extremely fast and powerful parallel computer can be easily created. Already, numerous commercial parallel machines have been developed using microprocessors such as Intel's 8086 and 80286, Motorola's 68000, and National Semiconductor's 32032. Special microprocessors have been designed especially for use in parallel architectures. An example is Inmos's Transputer. This is a 32-bit CPU with special communications circuits that make it easier to interconnect to other processors.

Another issue is how memory should be connected to the various processors. Should the multiple processors share a large common memory or should they have their own individual memories? That question has already been answered partially as most parallel designs include a significant amount of RAM with each processor. In that way, it can store instructions for its segment of the problem. However, since the various processors must share computed results to achieve a final problem solution, there must be some way to transfer results from one processor memory to another. A larger shared memory is one possibility, although the solution may lie in schemes for interconnecting memory and processors.

One of the key issues in parallel architecture is how the processors should be interconnected. One approach might be to have them share a common bus. Although this is a workable scheme for a small number of processors, bidirectional data busses allow only one processor to talk to another at a given time. Even with very high speed bus operation, overall computing speed would be limited as many processors wait for another to finish before using the bus.

Most parallel architecture involves a network structure rather than a bus. The study and design of such networks is called topology. Network configurations are referred to as topologies. There are an incredible number of different processor interconnection schemes possible. The various configurations depend upon the number of processors as well as the interconnection rationale. For example, should each processor be connected to every other processor? Some arrangements permit this. In other designs, processors are connected only to their adjacent neighbors. Still others are connected in a binary tree configuration. All of these topologies have advantages and disadvantages.

Figure 11–5 shows several different CPU networks. In A, four processors are used, each connected to all of the others. In B, eight CPUs are used, but each is connected only to its adjacent neighbor. The configuration at C also uses eight processors, but each is connected to every other CPU.

Figure 11–5D shows a six dimensional hypercube network. it consists of 64 processors, each of which is connected to its six closest neighbors. A binary tree architecture is shown in 11–5E. Each processor communicates with two lower branches and one upper level CPU.

Perhaps the most flexible arrangement of all is the lattice structure in Figure 11–5F. Here 16 CPUs can be linked to one another by switches. The switches let the programmer configure the network to the problem. In this way, the solution is optimized.

In addition to the interconnection scheme, some kind of communications protocol also must be devised. What procedures do the processors use to communicate with one another? A packet switching type of message passing system is one possibility.

There appears to be no one optimum parallel architecture. The efficiency of a given scheme is highly dependent upon the problem it is solving. For that reason, it appears that the most useful parallel processor is one that can be easily reconfigured. One forthcoming commercial machine uses 64,000 processors but permits their interconnection to be changed under program control. This allows the architecture to be adjusted to the problem for maximum efficiency.

Software

The hardware technology to make even the most sophisticated parallel computers already exists. The problem seems to be deciding upon a workable architecture and making the necessary network interconnections. The big problem in parallel computing is the software. Presently, most parallel computers are impractical simply because either no software exists or the limited amount of software makes them incredibly difficult to program. Until the software problem is solved, the promise of parallel computing will not be achieved.

Present parallel processor programming goes something like this. First, the problem should match the architecture. In other words, it must be possible to divide the problem into simultaneously executable segments. A programmer must examine the problem carefully, then make an attempt to divide it up. Then, each part of the problem is given to an individual processor. Problems which can be divided into many small segments produce what is called a fine grain processing. Problems that divide into only a small number of segments are called large grain processing problems. Problems that are basically sequential in nature do not lend themselves to parallel processing.

The division of a problem is a tricky process. The idea is to segment the problem into elements as small as possible to use a greater number of processors and multiply

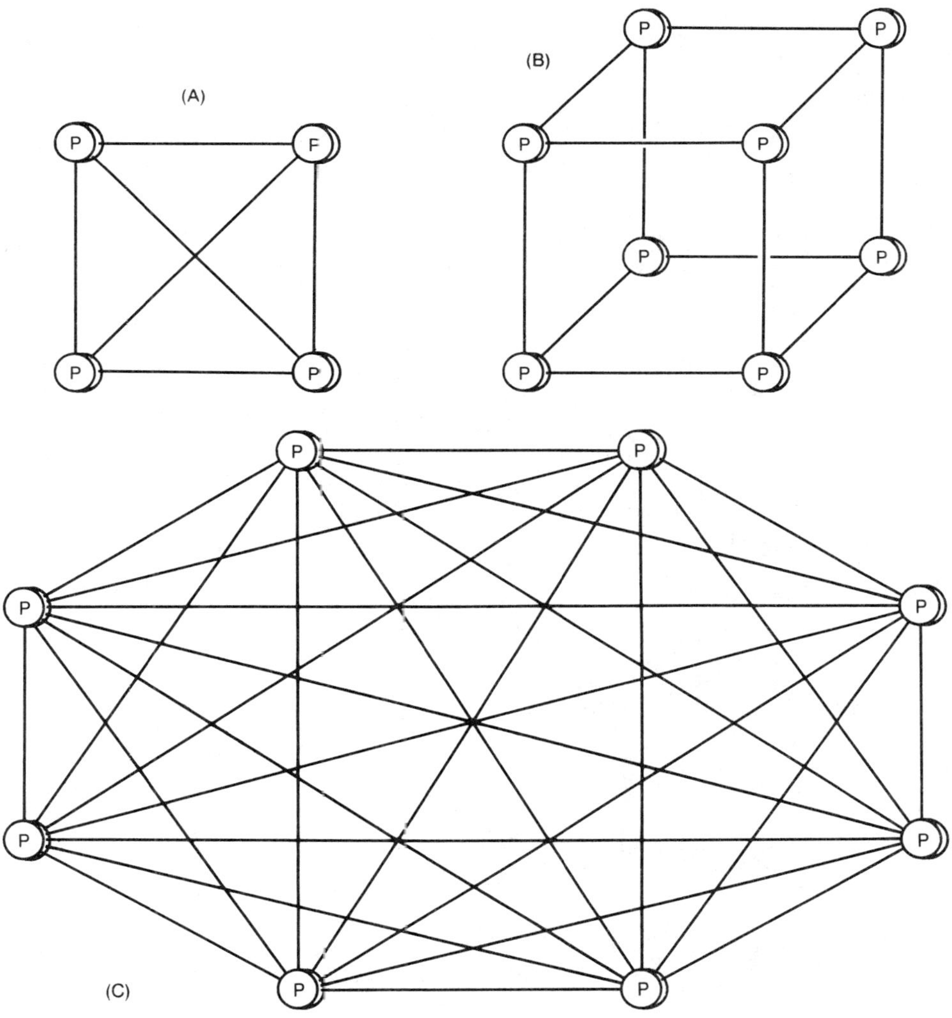

Figure 11–5. ***Different network topologies for parallel computers.***

computing speed. But as you know, all of the various portions of the problem must communicate with one another in some way. One segment of the program may need as its input a value computed by another processor. That means that one processor may have to wait for another to complete its calculation before it can begin. When there are many of these situations in a problem, computing speed slows. You want all the processors processing simultaneously and few, if any, waiting. This ideal situation can only be approached and not completely realized. Matching the problem to the architecture and then dividing it cleverly are key to the success of parallel processing.

Once a problem has been segmented, it must be coded. Although assemblers for the processors are available, most programmers prefer to work in a higher level language. Currently, there are no higher level languages for parallel processing. However, considerable work is being done in this area. One example is the development of a Fortran compiler that will automatically partition a problem as the programmer codes it in Fortran. Many believe the success of parallel processors lies in creating special higher level languages and operating systems that assist the programmer in segmenting the problem and determining the number of processors to use and how they should be

(D)

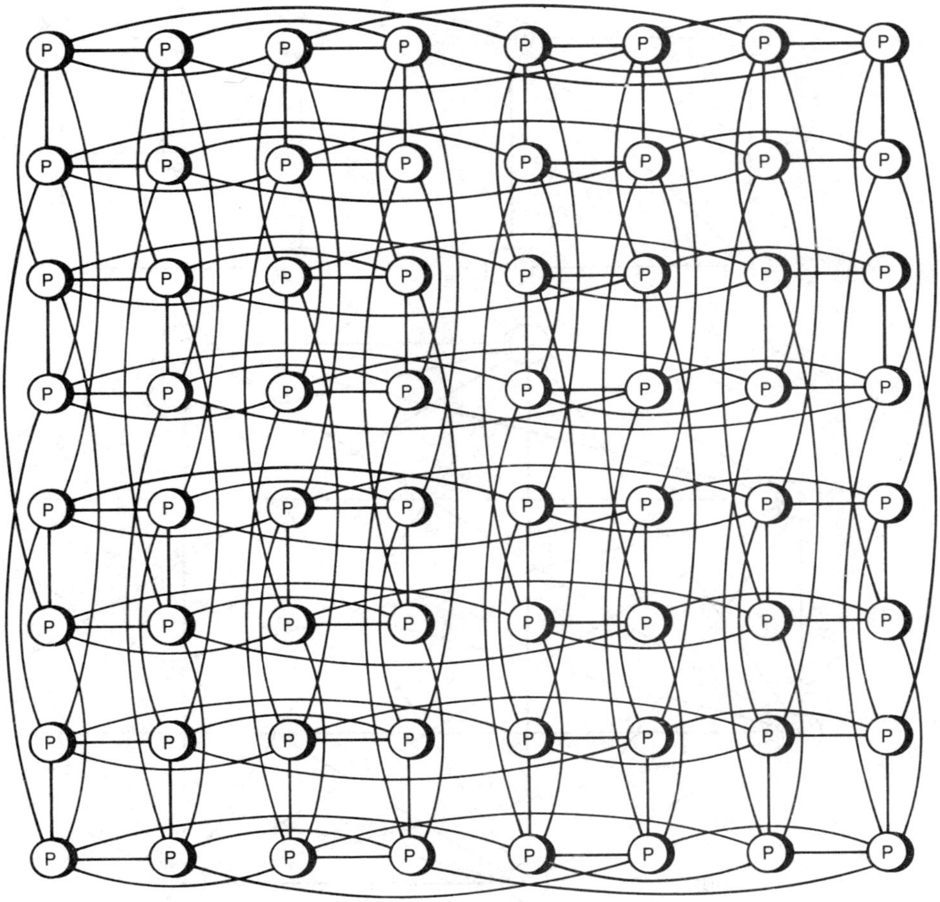

Figure 11–5 *continued*

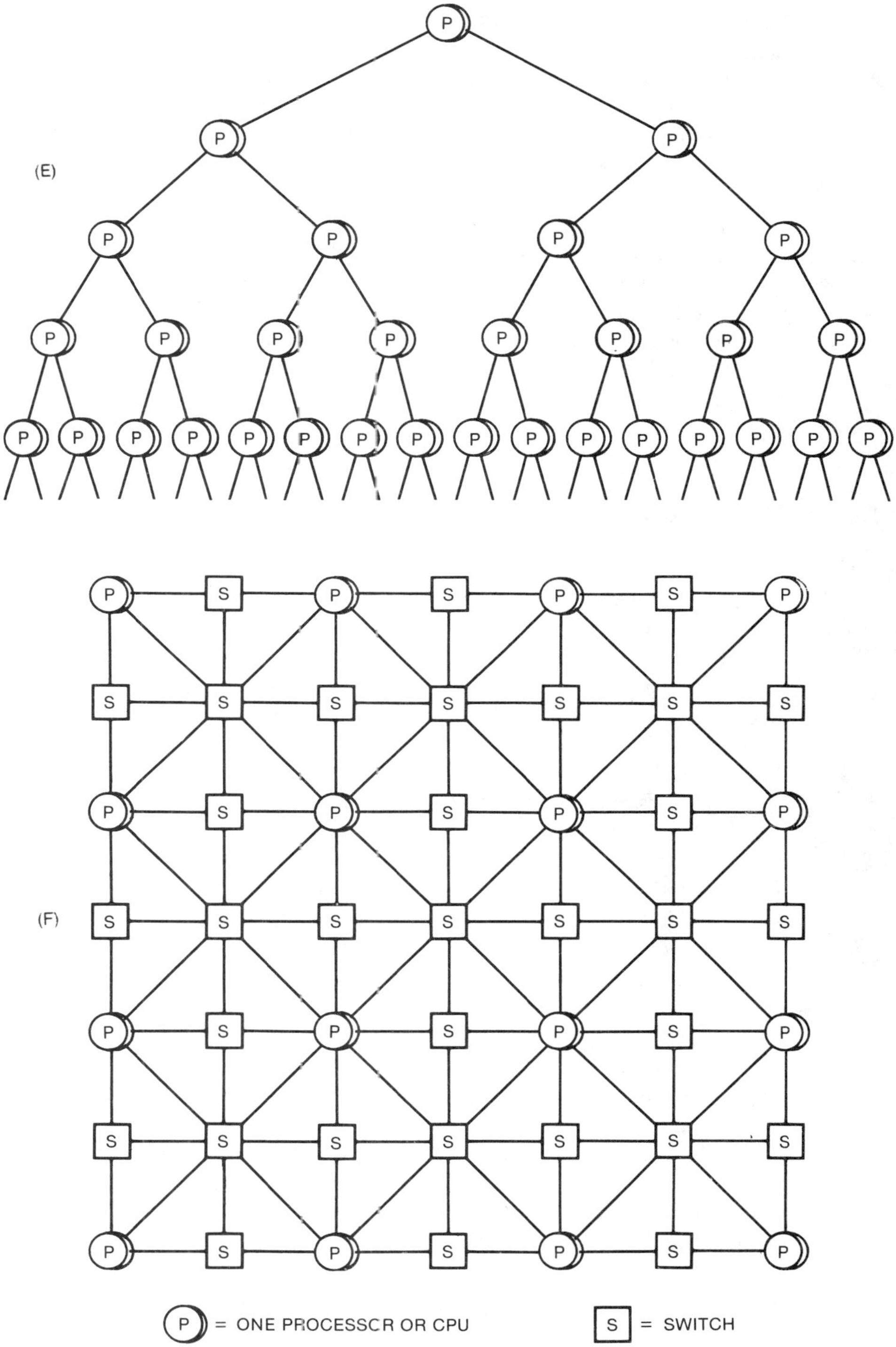

Figure 11–5 ***continued***

interconnected. Unless the programming of parallel processors is made easier, the best approach may be to stay with convenional von Neumann computers, program in the conventional way, and bear the burden of the longer processing time.

Parallel computers are here now and more will be forthcoming. Most of the current machines compete with the high end superminicomputers such as the DEC VAX 8600. By using multiple processors, comparable computing power can be obtained for considerably less money.

In the future, parallel processors will replace or supercede supercomputers. And finally, parallel computers will help implement and optimize many AI applications which are not practical on conventional machines. Consider a parallel computer running an expert system in which each rule is assigned a processor. Naturally, searches and pattern matching will take place far faster with a parallel arrangement than in a conventional machine. This makes large scale AI systems practical where they would not be on a conventional machine.

Fifth Generation Computers

Most computer scientists agree that the fifth generation of computers is under development. They are expected to emerge during the 1990s. The Japanese have a concentrated development effort going to be the first to create and market a fifth generation computer. Their effort is significant, but there is some question as to whether they will beat the U.S. computer industry or replace it as the world's computing leader. Many development efforts are underway in the United States, both independent and those funded by the government.

There is considerable development effort in the U.K. and Europe. Britain has an enormous fifth generation computing project underway. Who will win the race to have the first real fifth generation computer is anyone's guess. Most place their bet on the United States.

But just what is a fifth generation computer? Unfortunately, there is no single fully agreed upon definition. The fifth generation computer will not be defined until one is fully developed and put into use.

However, fifth generation computers will have two basic characteristics. First, they will use parallel processing techniques. Second, they will make heavy use of artificial intelligence. Don't think of fifth generation machines as the next step of improvement in supercomputers. Although supercomputers will get faster because they will incorporate parallel processing techniques, they are not likely to incorporate AI techniques. Real fifth generation machines will be both parallel and AI-based. This doesn't mean that they won't perform conventional data processing. Fifth generation machines will accommodate traditional applications but will be far more capable of solving larger complex problems and particularly those involving symbolic computing.

Special fifth generation machines may be optimized strictly for AI applications, such as expert systems and natural language. Current prototypes of Japanese fifth generation machines, in fact, are based upon predicate calculus. The Japanese have adopted Prolog and similar languages as the primary computational model. Prolog is even microcoded into many of these machines. One type of Japanese fifth generation machine may be an AI workstation that uses parallel CPUs and Prolog and is comparable to the popular LISP machines. Some designs even incorporate relational data base management systems.

As more is learned about the development and application of parallel processing machines and as the field of artificial intelligence sorts itself out, the configuration of a fifth generation computer will emerge. As with parallel processing machines, it is expected that there will be no single standard architecture. Instead, there will be considerable variation in the number of processors and how they are divided up and used. Such machines may also be optimized for specific classes of problems rather than present themselves as generic all purpose machines.

LISP Machines

A LISP machine, as we've already mentioned, is a special purpose AI computer basically dedicated to the LISP language. Also referred to as AI workstations, LISP machines are optimized for the development of AI programs using the built-in LISP language. However, LISP machines are also general purpose computers which can execute other languages as well. These include not only Prolog and other AI languages, but also conventional languages such as Fortran, Pascal, and C. Because these special computers are so dominant in AI work, we want you to understand the rationale for them and how they work.

LISP and Conventional Computers

LISP is probably one of the most demanding programming languages. It taxes even the largest and fastest mainframes and minicomputers. LISP, because of the way it links together symbols used in processing, eats up a tremendous amount of memory. Even small and medium size programs use more memory than would be required for performing the same function in Pascal or C. Large programs take even more memory and can easily swamp or overwhelm the largest of computers. When the program is executed, it may run slowly as memory accesses take time. This can cause some LISP programs to run too slowly to be useful.

On the other hand, LISP generally runs successfully on conventional computers if the program size doesn't overwhelm the machine. The new special class of super microcomputers with high speed CPUs and huge memories run LISP programs very successfully. These special computers are known as engineering workstations because they have been designed to perform scientific, engineering, and mathematical applications. They work well with LISP and other AI programs. Some of the manufacturers of these machines are DEC, Sun, and Apollo.

Although it is possible to get to use a conventional computer to develop and run LISP programs, AI developers have long wished for a special machine that would give them all the memory and speed possible to expedite their work. They have particularly wished for machines that would help them in developing large LISP programs.

Many large AI programs are developed by teams of programmers. The problem is partitioned and each programmer is given one or more segments to work on. The programming work often is done on a large minicomputer or mainframe using a time sharing operating system. This means that multiple programmers can use the system at the same time. When LISP is running on the machine, the various users take turns accessing memory and CPU. Because the computer runs at very high speeds, multiple programmers can access the machine concurrently while the CPU gives each a time slot. In this way, it looks as though the users are working simultaneously when in reality the CPU is quickly switching back and forth between users. Even with a high speed computer, the LISP burden slows down the process and often causes programmers to wait. This is an unacceptable situation as it greatly reduces programming productivity. Ideally, each programmer would have a dedicated computer. However, in most cases, this is too expensive.

The solution to problems posed by running LISP on conventional computers is solved with LISP machines. The first of these machines was introduced in the early 1980s. There are currently about a half dozen manufacturers of these special AI workstations. They easily overcome the memory and speed problems. Further, they are designed to be stand-alone individual computers rather than large minicomputers or mainframes. In this way, each programmer can have a machine. In addition, each computer is supplied not only with the LISP language, but an entire array of supportive utility programs that further speed up and simplify the programming process. In short, the LISP machine provides a total integrated environment that greatly facilitates the development of LISP programs. Programmer productivity has been said to double with LISP machines. Anyone contemplating considerable serious development of AI programs, particularly in LISP, should look at these machines as an alternative to conventional computers. Figure 11–6 shows a typical LISP machine.

Features of a LISP Machine

The basic idea for a specialized LISP machine was conceived at the Artificial Intelligence Laboratory at MIT in the mid-1970s. The concept was simulated successfully on a larger computer, and prototypes were built. Ultimately, MIT licensed the concept to two new companies created to exploit the potential of LISP machines. These two companies were Symbolics and LISP Machines, Inc. Both began building commercial LISP machine products. Their designs have already gone through two generations with the third in process.

Later, Xerox entered the LISP machine marketplace. More recently, Texas Instruments and Tektronix have joined the competition. Sperry sells a private labeled version of TI's Explorer workstation. The Japanese have developed their own LISP machine which is available through Fujitsu. Hewlett-Packard also offers an AI development system based on its 9000 series computers.

A LISP machine is generally similar in architecture to a conventional von Neumann computer. It features a memory, a CPU, and various I/O ports and peripherals. However,

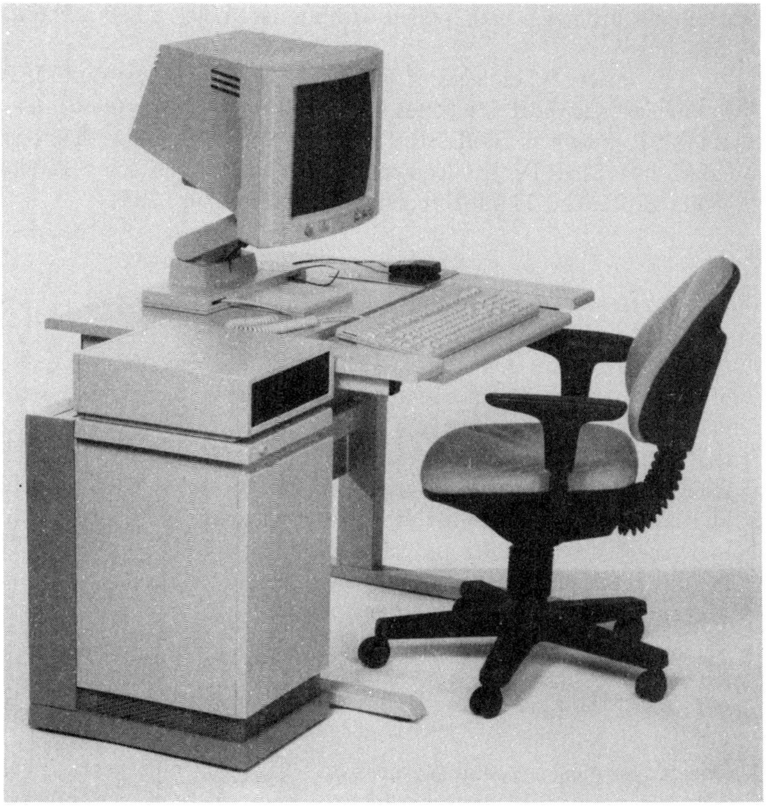

Figure 11–6. ***The TI Explorer AI workstation. (Courtesy Texas Instruments, Inc.)***

the architecture of these various components varies somewhat from more conventional machines. They have special features that optimize the development and execution of LISP programs. Let's take a look at the key features of LISP machines.

Large Word Size

All LISP machines feature a large word size. Most machines have a minimum 32-bit word while others use 36 and 40 bits. These large words permit both very large and very small numbers to be represented. It also means they can process more data faster. Special 32- to 40-bit wide CPUs are used to process these data words.

Microprogrammed Operation

Another key feature of a LISP machine is that its operation is microcoded to implement the instruction set and control functions. What's unique about a LISP machine is that the basic LISP primitives are built into the microcode. Although LISP machines do indeed have a machine code and binary microcode, these are invisible to the user. LISP machines are not even supplied with an assembler. LISP is the native language of the machine.

A variety of dialects of LISP are used in the various LISP machines. Both the Symbolics and LMI machines implement a highly refined and enhanced version of MacLISP, known as ZetaLISP. The Xerox workstations use their own version of InterLISP called InterLISP-D. The Tektronix AI workstations use a version of LISP known as Waltz LISP. The TI LISP machine uses Common LISP.

Stack Architecture

Like most modern computers, LISP machines also feature a *stack.* A stack is a area of main memory set aside for special memory operations based on a last-in first-out basis. Most CPUs feature one or more special address registers called stack pointers that are used to access the stack. Special push and pop instructions put data on the stack and retrieve it respectively. The stack is widely used for dealing with subroutines and interrupts. A stack architecture is particularly important in LISP because of the many nested operations and the ability to handle recursion. LISP machines have numerous stack pointers that allow the machine to keep track of many different levels of operations going on within other operations.

Tagged Architecture

One of the most unusual features of a LISP machine is that each word carries a *tag.* A tag is a group of bits attached to the word that give information about the word and how it can be used. Specifically, tags in LISP machine words designate a data type and differentiate between data words and address words. Anywhere from 4 to 8 bits of the basic machine words are devoted to the tag. The tag greatly facilitates the allocation of words in memory and helps to implement the CONS cell structure for linking atoms and lists. It also eliminates all of the data checking operations that must go on in other programming languages to ensure that valid opertions are performed on the right kind of data.

Large RAM

All LISP machines have incredibly large memories. Few have less than 1 megabyte of RAM and most have many megabytes. Many can directly address over 100 megabytes of RAM. Such large memories let LISP machines deal with even the largest of LISP applications programs.

Huge Mass Storage

All LISP machines also feature hard disks for mass storage of programs and data. A typical system has over 100 megabytes of storage.

Virtual Memory

In addition to its large, directly addressable memory, most LISP machines also feature *virtual memory.* Virtual memory is a process by which the CPU is fooled into thinking that its directly addressable memory is larger than it actually is. In this way, extra large programs, which take up more space than is available in directly addressable RAM, can be stored on high-speed hard disks. Built-in software permits the CPU to address this virtual memory on disk as if it were directly addressable. If a portion of the program data addressed is not in RAM, the built-in software goes out to the disk, gets it, and brings it into RAM for processing. This operation is transparent to the user. LISP machines use a kind of virtual memory known as demand paged memory which automatically goes to the disk to get one or more pages of additional program or data if called for or demanded by the CPU.

Garbage Collection

LISP machines feature a special form of memory management known as *garbage collection.* Garbage collection is also performed in LISP software that runs on conventional computers. Developing and executing LISP programs generates an enormous amount of data that is stored throughout RAM. Often this data is no longer needed. However, it lies there unused taking up valuable memory space. Garbage collection helps to reclaim large chunks of memory that are no longer used. Garbage collection is usually automatic, but can also be called up by the programmer.

Bus Architecture

Most LISP machines feature a bus architecture. Various processors, memory modules, and I/O ports communicate with one another over this 32-bit or more bus. The bus architecture gives a programmer flexibility to add new circuits and devices as they are required.

Many LISP machines permit multiple processors to share the bus. For example, several LISP processors may be placed on the bus, thereby permitting multiple users to share the machine. The multiple processors share the main memory, mass storage, and peripherals.

Some LISP machines also have more conventional processors that can be installed on the bus. For example, one LISP machine features a 68000 microprocessor that runs the UNIX operating system and the Prolog language.

Graphics Monitor

Another feature common to most LISP machines is a large, high resolution, bit-mapped black and white video monitor. Screen sizes of 17 and 19 inches are common although larger screens are available. Such huge screens are unusual in more conventional computers. The monitors are driven by graphics circuitry using bit-mapped techniques. A resolution of 800 × 1000 pixels is typical and permits use of sophisticated graphics.

Virtually all LISP machines also use windows, multiple areas on the screen where several different programs, menus, or displays can be shown simultaneously. High resolution color monitors are also available on some systems.

Mouse

Most LISP machines also use a manual input device called a mouse. The mouse moves a cursor around on the screen and allows pointing to menu choices or selected data. Click buttons on the mouse initiate the selections.

Software

Most LISP machines now are capable of running software other than LISP. With co-processors, Fortran, Pascal, C, and other conventional languages can be used. In addition, many of the LISP machines also permit programming in some object-oriented language. The LISP Machine, Inc., and Symbolics computers implement Flavors, a version of Smalltalk. The Xerox machine features Loops which includes a version of Smalltalk. The Tektronix workstation runs a version of Smalltalk.

LISP machines also include a variety of utilities and tools for building programs. These include a superior editor and a multi-feature debugger that permit rapid troubleshooting of program problems. All together, these utilities and various development tools can generally be called up immediately from the mouse or keyboard. The result is an extremely efficient and powerful programming environment.

I/O and Peripherals

LISP machines, like regular computers, also need I/O devices. Most have two or more RS-232 serial ports for connecting the usual peripherals, such as printers. Another feature is an Ethernet interface which permits connecting LISP machines in a communications network. In many software development environments, LISP machines are linked together. Developers can share programs and data as well as perform other communications functions.

Pros and Cons

Those creating large LISP programs will tell you the fastest and easiest way to create LISP programs is to use LISP machines, if you can afford them. They sell in the $50,000-$100,000 range each. That's a hefty price and usually only major LISP programming efforts can justify such expense.

The alternative, of course, is to run LISP software on a conventional machine. The software is mostly reasonably priced, and you may already have the computer.

Another gripe about LISP machines is that users of the software find the machines too expensive. This problem is being addressed by Symbolics who now offers a cheaper run-time-only machine for executing programs but not developing them.

My interest is in the future because I am going to spend the rest of my life there.

CHARLES F. KETTERING

I never think of the future. It comes soon enough.

ALBERT EINSTEIN

The Future

Since AI is only now getting some attention, we can begin to expect big gains in the future. There is more funding for AI from the government as well as the private sector. Many research and development programs are underway in universities and in profit-making companies. More individuals are entering the field. Competition from abroad is spurring us on. Finally, computer users are now aware of AI and are expecting it to help them in some way. All this adds up to the accelerated creation of new AI and knowledge-based products and applications. The future looks exciting.

But the computer scientists warn us to be conservative in our expectations. AI is a very tough subject, and practical products and uses will emerge slowly. And they may not be as exciting and glamorous as many predictions make them sound. Progress will be made, but it will be evolutionary rather than revolutionary as most computer developments turn out to be. That's really OK to most of us.

Before the 21st Century

Let's get more specific and outline some of the developments and products that are likely to occur before to the year 2000. Here are my predictions:

- Natural language front-ends will be used on more software. Most applications programs will gradually incorporate natural language interfaces to simplify their use.
- Improved foreign language translation services will become available. Computer translators will get faster and more accurate. More languages will be included. Competition will help lower costs.
- Off-the-shelf expert systems on a variety of generic topics will become available. There will be programs for mainframes, minis, and personal computers. Financial programs will be a dominant category, but an incredibly wide scope of topics will be covered. Prices will be reasonable. At last it will be possible to buy knowledge as well as information.
- Robots will get intelligence. Limited at first, gradually it will increase in scope. The applications will still be highly focused on one job.

- Voice recognition systems will get better and cheaper. They will find wide use in defense systems and factories but will be a total flop in the office. The voice-to-printer typewriter machine will still not be introduced because of vocabulary limitations and cost. This is a 21st century product.
- Computer vision systems will proliferate in industry doing simple low resolution jobs. Improvements will be made in image analysis, but it will take cheap parallel computers to make really valuable visual analysis practical.
- Many new parallel computers will be designed and introduced. These will be mainly minicomputers and mainframes with some supercomputer competition. Prices will remain high. No parallel personal computers will be offered.
- Software progress for parallel machines will be slow. But some compilers will become available using various scheduling algorithms to automatically partition large problems into many small parallel segments. The demand will intensify for more and better parallel software for the expanding number of parallel computers.
- Desktop Prolog machines similar to LISP machines will come to market. They will not be as popular as LISP machines, but they will be cheaper and better for running expert systems.
- The first commercial fifth generation computers will come into being in the mid-1990s. Both U.S. and Japanese machines will be marketed. It will be hard to tell which country introduced first as there will be an on-going debate about just what fifth generation computer is and does.
- AI software will become widely embedded in other more conventional software. Programs will incorporate AI techniques where applicable to make themselves more powerful and useful in new areas.
- Special AI hardware will be created to make special purpose AI computers. Just as microprocessors are embedded into many products and systems as dedicated controllers, so will unique AI chips become part of more powerful weapons systems, factory automation equipment, and even consumer products for superior performance. Already, Texas Instruments has developed a single chip VLSI LISP microprocessor for use in dedicated, embedded AI computers. AT&T has also already created a single chip expert system with an inference engine based on fuzzy logic and rules stored in ROM or RAM. Such developments will continue.
- Intelligent computer assisted instructional (ICAI) programs will become available on a small scale. These will test and diagnose current student knowledge, then dispense new knowledge as required to meet specific learning objectives. The systems will be large and expensive and justifiable only for critical learning applications. ICAI will not be available for personal computers.
- Computers that learn by themselves will not be commercially available. Good research progress will be made, but the techniques will not be practical because of size and cost restrictions. Commercial self-learning AI systems won't show up until the 21st Century.

- A shortage of AI computer scientists and programmers will continue, although the pressure will be relieved somewhat as more universities incorporate AI courses into their mainstream computer science programs.
- President Reagan's "Star Wars" Strategic Defense Initiative Program will continue to be funded and considerable progress will be made toward a practical system. AI will play an important part. However, a fully operational system will not be in operation before the end of the century.
- AI techniques will be used to help simplify conventional programming. As problems become larger and more complex, programmers will seek new products. AI programs to help speed up and simplify the creation of other AI programs will become available.
- A chess-playing program implemented on a massive parallel processor computer will beat everyone including grand masters, thereby leaving chess strictly to ignorant humans.
- AI will help solve a lot of truly boring problems that humans must contend with. Programs for planning, scheduling, project management, and other tedious processes will be automated, relieving us to do more productive work and thinking.

After 2001

Predictions this far in advance are too hard to make. It is possible to extrapolate the future from trends, but even then many predictions just don't come true. Further, some "out of the blue" developments occur that everyone overlooked or never heard of before. A lot of technology comes to us through pure old-fashioned serendipity.

In a broad general way it is easy to assume that AI and knowledge-based systems will be highly developed and firmly entrenched. Computers truly will be more powerful, more useful, and easier to use. We can expect to see at least one large computer similar to the HAL 9000 of movie fame ("2001") and androids approaching the capabilities of R2D2 and maybe even C3PO of the movie "Star Wars." At least these are our models, unofficial or not, and AI research work will gradually head in that direction as technology permits.

Key Points

- The operation of all digital computers is based on the stored program concept developed by mathematician John von Neumann at Princeton during the 1940s. These so-called von Neumann machines solve problems by executing a program of sequential instructions that implement a specific algorithm.

- Because problems are solved serially, one step at a time, high speed circuits are required to make them practical.
- Computing speeds have improved dramatically over the years thanks mainly to incredible developments in semiconductor technology.
- The speed limitation of computers is caused by the von Neumann "bottleneck," the need to repeatedly access memory that is slower than the computing circuits over a single bidirectional data path.
- High speed bipolar cache memories and pipelining techniques alleviate the "bottleneck" problem but do not eliminate it.
- Supercomputers are the elite of all non-Neumann machines. These ultra-powerful mainframes, used primarily in scientific and engineering calculations, exploit the latest technology to achieve maximum speed and performance.
- Most supercomputers use liquid cooled bipolar ECL logic circuits to achieve computing speeds of 80 to 1300 MFLOPS.
- A super speed minicomputer with a floating point array processor can achieve supercomputer performance on some problems at less cost than a supercomputer.
- Reduced instruction set computers (RISC) are a new approach to achieving higher performance with von Neumann architecture at lower cost.
- RISC architecture features a single, super fast, single chip VLSI microprocessor with fewer than 100 basic instructions. Other features include hard-wired rather than microcoded control and a large register set.
- The performance of all von Neumann architecture machines has nearly peaked out, although some additional speed gains can be expected by using the new, faster gallium arsenide (GaAs) semiconductor chips.
- Most computer scientists agree that future computing speed improvements will come from the use of parallel processor computers.
- Parallel computers use multiple CPUs operating simultaneously on different segments of a problem.
- Commercial parallel processing machines will be based on hundreds or even thousands of high speed microprocessors connected in one of many different network topologies. Speed gains of 100 to 1000 percent over present supercomputers are expected to be achieved.
- The main problem with parallel computers which already exist commercially is the lack of software. Currently, programmers must manually segment or partition big problems into smaller programs which can be run simultaneously on separate CPUs. New compilers that automate the segmentation process are being developed.
- Fifth generation computers will incorporate both parallel processors and AI/knowledge-based techniques. The United States and Japan are in a race to see who can introduce the first practical fifth generation machine. Commercial computers are expected in the 1990s.
- LISP machines are special AI workstations optimized for the development of AI programs in LISP.

- LISP machines feature 32- to 40-bit tagged words, LISP primitives microcoded in ROM, high speed CPUs, massive RAM, virtual memory and high resolution graphics.
- LISP machines not only run LISP programs faster but also cut development time in half because of their interactive programming environment that includes editors, debuggers, and other tools and utilities that greatly facilitate software creation.
- Computer speed is usually expressed in terms of millions of instructions per second (MIPS). Supercomputers that calculate with floating point numbers are rated in terms of millions of floating point operations per second (MFLOPS). Fifth generation computers based on logic and Prolog are rated in terms of logical inferences per second (LIPS).
- Many factors are speeding up research and development in AI. Considerable progress is expected before the year 2000. Many new commercial AI-based products are expected to make computers more powerful, more useful, and easier to use.

Appendix A: Expert System Development Tools for Personal Computers

Program	Publisher	Computer	Type
ADVISOR	Ultimate Media, Inc.	Apple II, Commodore 64	Rules
AL/X	Univ. of Edinburgh, Scotland	Apple II	Rules
CxPERT	Software Plus	IBM PC	Frames, Rules
DAISY	Lithp Systems	IBM PC	Rules, Frames, Semantic nets
ESI	Abacus Programming Corp.	IBM PC	Rules
ES/P Advisor	Expert Systems International	IBM PC	Rules
Expert Ease	Expert Systems International & Human Edge Software, Inc.	IBM PC	Examples, Matrix
Expert Edge	Human Edge Software, Inc.	IBM PC	Rules
Expert-2	Mountain View Press, Inc.	IBM PC	Rules
ExperOPS5	ExperTelligence	Apple Macintosh	Rules
Expert System	Potomac Pacific Engineering	IBM PC	Rules
Expert Systems Toolkit (EST)	Mind Path Technologies, Inc.	IBM PC	Rules
EXSYS	Exsys, Inc.	IBM PC	Rules
1st Class	Programs in Motion, Inc.	IBM PC	Rules or Examples

Appendix A: ***(cont)***

Program	Publisher	Computer	Type
GURU	Micro Data Base Systems, Inc.	IBM PC	Rules
INSIGHT	Level 5 Research	IBM PC	Rules
KDS	KDS Corp.	IBM PC	Examples
KES II	Software A&E, Inc.	IBM PC	Rules
KNOWOL	Intelligent Machine Co.	IBM PC	Rules
M.1	Teknowledge, Inc.	IBM PC	Rules
Micro Expert	McGraw-Hill	IBM PC	Rules
Micro-PS	Ashton-Tate	IBM PC	Rules
NEXPERT	Neuron Data, Inc.	IBM PC/AT	Rules
OPS5+	Artelligence, Inc.	IBM PC, Apple Macintosh	Rules
OPS/83	Production Systems Technologies, Inc.	IBM PC	Rules
Personal Consultant (Plus)	Texas Instruments	IBM PC, TI PC	Rules
Rule Master	Radian Corp.	IBM PC	Examples
SeRIES	SRI International	IBM PC	Rules
Shells	ExpertTelligence	IBM PC	Rules
TIMM	General Research Corp.	IBM PC	Examples
TOPSI	Dynamic Master Systems, Inc.	IBM PC, CP/M Machines	Rules
Turbo Expert	Thinking Software, Inc.	IBM PC	Rules
VP-Expert	Paperback Software, Inc.	IBM PC	Rules
XSYS	California Intelligence	IBM PC	Rules

Appendix B: Expert System Development Tools for Minicomputers and Mainframes

Program	Publisher	Computer	Type
ART	Inference Corp.	LMI, Symbolics, DEC VAX, TI, Xerox, LMI	Rules, Frames
HPRL	Hewlett-Packard Co.	HP, DEC VAX	Frames
IKE	LMI	LMI	Rules
KEE	Intellicorp	Xerox, Symbolics, LMI	Rules, Frames
KES	Software A&E, Inc.	TI, Symbolics	Rules
Knowledge Craft	Carnegie Group	LMI, DEC VAX	Rules
LOOPS	Xerox	Xerox	Rules (also a language)
OPS/83	Production Systems Technologies, Inc.	DEC VAX, AT&T, Apollo, Tektronix	Rules
PICON	LMI	LMI	Rules
Rule Master	Radian Corp.	DEC VAX, TI	Examples
S.1	Teknowledge, Inc.	DEC VAX, Symbolics	Rules
TIMM	General Research Corp.	IBM, Amdahl, DEC VAX, Prime	Examples

Appendix C: Dialects of LISP

Name	Publisher
BYSO LISP	Levien Instrument
Common LISP	Gold Hill Computers
DG Common LISP	Data General
ExperLISP	ExperTelligence
FranzLISP	Franz, Inc.
InterLISP-D	Xerox
IQLISP	Integral Quality
ISI-INTERLISP	Digital Equipment Corp.
Le-LISP	CRIL
LISP/VM	IBM
LISP/80	Software Toolworks
LISP/88	Norell Data Systems
MacLISP	MIT (Franz, Zeta)
Microsoft LISP	Microsoft Inc.
muLISP	Microsoft Inc., The Soft Warehouse
P-LISP	Gnosis, Inc.
PC-LISP	IOTC, Inc.
PC Scheme LISP	Texas Instruments
Portable Standard LISP	University of Utah
TLC-LISP 86	The Lisp Co.
TransLISP	Solution Systems
UNXLISP	Cybermetrics
UNXLISP-86	Automata Design Associates
UO-LISP	Northwest Computer Algorithms
VAXLISP	Digital Equipment Corp.
WaltzLISP	Pro Code International
XLISP	PC/Blue Users Group
ZetaLISP	LMI, Symbolics, Xerox

Appendix D: Glossary

The purpose of this Glossary is to familiarize you with all the unique terms and "buzzwords" associated with the field of artificial intelligence. As you are reading this book, another text, or magazine article and spot a word that you do not understand, take a minute to look it up in this glossary. Although most key words in this book are defined when they are introduced, you may forget the meaning as you are reading. Don't hesitate to look up the word for a quick refresher. Nothing is more aggravating than trying to read something you don't understand. AI concepts are relatively easy to grasp if you just know the meanings of the words.

This glossary contains primarily those terms associated with the field of artificial intelligence. Some general computer science terminology, where it is applicable to AI, is also included. But for the most part, general computer terms are not included. It is suggested that you acquire a copy of *Computer Dictionary*[4] should you need greater coverage of computer terminology.

A* An algorithm of search procedure used to determine the optimum path in a search tree problem. A form of branch and bound search technique that attempts to find the minimal path joining the start and goal nodes in a search tree by estimating the promise and value of a particular path.

algorithm A step-by-step procedure for solving a problem. A precisely defined group of rules or processes that leads to a desired output from a given set of inputs.

alpha-beta pruning Also known as alpha-beta cutoff or the alpha-beta procedure. A search technique used in limiting the size of the search tree in implementing games and other adversarial programs. A search technique that is a variation of the branch and bound method which greatly reduces the number of tree branches that must be explored and the number of static evaluations that must be accomplished in a search, thereby greatly reducing computing time. Alpha-beta pruning works by maintaining two threshold values, one representing a lower bound (alpha) and another representing the upper bound (beta).

analogical reasoning Deciding or determining the outcome of a problem by the use of analogies. A procedure for drawing conclusions about a problem by analyzing a model or analog of it.

analogy A statement that indicates how one thing is alike or similar to another. An indication of some relationship or correspondence between unlike things. An inference that assumes if two things are alike in some ways, then they must be alike in other respects.

AND/OR tree A form of graph or goal tree that shows how goals and subgoals of a problem solving processing are related using the logical AND and OR functions. A method of representing the solution of a problem that can be solved by breaking it up into a set of smaller problems.

arc The lines interconnecting nodes in a search tree or transition net.

[4]Sipple, Charles J. 1985. *Computer Dictionary*, Fourth Ed. Indianapolis: Howard W. Sams & Co.

architecture The structure, framework or organization of a computer or a program.

argument The independent variable of a function. A variable whose quantity determines the value of a function. The variables that appear in parentheses after a function or predicate name.

ARPANET A widely used communications network originally established by the Advanced Project Research Agency (now DARPA) of the U.S. Department of Defense. This worldwide communications network links hundreds of universities, research centers and government installations, allowing individuals to exchange information via electronic mail.

array A set, group, or series of numbers, terms or elements arranged in some logical or meaningful pattern. A typical array might be a set of numbers arranged in rows and columns to form a matrix.

array processor A special purpose processor used to improve computer throughput or enhance the performance of some specific algorithmic process. A stand-alone processor or sometimes a co-processor to a host computer made up of very high speed ALUs, usually for manipulating large floating point numbers. These high speed ALUs are often combined with high speed RAM to perform parallel optimized arithmetic operations on matrixes, fast Fourier transforms, and other special mathematical functions.

ART An expert systems development tool by Inference Corp.

artificial intelligence The branch of computer science devoted to the study of how computers can be used to simulate or duplicate functions of the human brain. Hardware and software techniques that make it appear as though a computer is thinking, reasoning, making decisions, storing or retrieving knowledge, solving problems, and learning.

associative memory Also called content addressable memory. A form of read/write memory where the word storage locations are identified by their content rather than by an address. Associated or content addressable memories are faster than conventional memory in performing data searches or interrogating memory to retrieve a desired element.

ATN Acronym for augmented transition network. A type of parser grammar used in natural language understanding systems. A system of nodes and arcs showing the sequence and relationships of words to be parsed, translated and understood.

atom A symbol, group of symbols, or word used to represent numbers and non-numeric objects. The smallest element used to represent values or name objects in the LISP programming language. Multiple atoms, when combined, form lists.

automatic programming The process by which a computer uses a special AI program to create another program to solve a specific problem. A technique that combines problem-solving techniques and a data base of task and programming knowledge to allow individuals to solve problems on a computer without having to write the programs themselves. The user describes the program and the computer generates the algorithm and then a program to solve the problem.

backtracking A technique used in tree searches. The process of working backward from a failed objective or an incorrect result to examine unexplored alternatives. Simply the process of backing up to a previous choice point in a computation and trying again.

backward chaining A method of reasoning that starts with the desired goal and works backward looking for facts and rules that support the desired outcome. A technique used in tree searches where a conclusion or objective is hypothesized and the system works backward to find rules that support the hypothesis. Also known as goal driven, expectations driven, or top down reasoning. Also called backward reasoning.

bang The slang term that refers to an exclamation point (!) which is used as a command terminator in the UNIX operating system.

best first A search technique using heuristics to select the most promising branches in a search tree. A technique combining breadth and depth first procedures using a heuristic function to compute the best path.

blackboard A method of organizing, presenting and communicating information. A data structure made up of all of the hypotheses generated by the system. A central communications point for various knowledge sources in an intelligence system. These multiple sources of knowledge communicate through the blackboard which is a common structure that contains the current status of the problem's solution.

blind search A general category of search technique that makes use of no knowledge or heuristics to help speed up or simplify the search process. A time consuming and arbitrary search process that attempts to exhaust all possibilities in searching rather than relying upon information which can help narrow the search.

blocks world A domain made up of bricks, blocks, pyramids, balls, and other geometric elements to be manipulated by a robot arm. A system originally designed to test and validate new natural language processing and robotics techniques. See SHRDLU.

bottom up A method of reasoning, searching or parsing that starts with an initial state in a tree or the string to be parsed and works toward the goal or solution. A data-driven approach. See forward chaining.

branch and bound A search algorithm or procedure used for finding the optimal path in a search tree. A technique that attempts to locate the shortest path in a search tree by estimating distances to the goal and eliminating redundant paths to intermediate nodes. Similar to the A* technique.

breadth first A search strategy or technique where all of the nodes on one level of the search tree are examined before any of the nodes of the next lower level. No node on a level is examined until every node at the next highest level has been examined.

C A popular higher level programming language widely used in systems and applications programming. Originally developed at AT&T's Bell Labs along with the UNIX operating system.

CAE Acronym for computer-aided engineering. The use of the computer to aid in all engineering activities, including design, sometimes using AI techniques.

CAI Acronym for computer-aided (or assisted) instruction. Using a computer to teach.

CBT Acronym for computer-based training. Same as CAI.

certainty factor A number assigned to a fact, action, relationship, etc., that indicates how likely it is to be true or happen. For example, a certainty factor of 1.0 means 100% true, 0.5 means partially true, and 0.0 means not true. Also see confidence factor.

children Successor nodes to a parent node.

Chinese room An analogy sometimes used to prove that even AI computers are not intelligent. If an English language speaking person is locked in a room with a book that explains the translation of Chinese characters into English and successfully converts unknown Chinese characters into understandable English language outputs, does this individual represent an intelligent machine? A test for intelligence similar to the Turing test.

closed world assumption A kind of default reasoning where the system assumes that if it has not been told that a particular fact is true, then it is assumed to be false. All relationships not directly stated to be true are not assumed to be true.

cognition The mental process of knowing. Having knowledge.

cognitive model A computer model or analogy of human thinking. Theories derived from psychology about the human thought process which are developed into processes which can be implemented as intelligent computer programs.

cognitive science An interdisciplinary science made up of psychologists, linguists, neurologists and computer scientists all working together to discover improved cognitive models for the purpose of understanding how humans think and how computers can be made to think like humans.

combinatorial explosion A condition or phenomena that occurs when attempting to solve large complex problems using search techniques. The condition that occurs when a large number of possible alternatives or sequences must be evaluated to find the optimum path leading to a solution or goal. The possibilities examined become too large and time consuming, thereby making them impractical for computer implementation even on large, very fast systems.

Common LISP A popular dialect of the AI programming language LISP. An attempt to agree on a common subset of LISP primitives that can be widely supported and used for the purpose of encouraging greater portability of LISP programs.

common sense The large, general and varied base of knowledge that humans possess about the way things are and how they work.

common sense reasoning A kind of decision making that permits the system to retract a conclusion in the face of new evidence. The ability of a system to revise its beliefs and decisions in light of new knowledge received or otherwise derived.

computer vision A field of AI study that seeks to duplicate human vision for use in robots or other applications. Using a TV camera or optical sensors to "see," then converting this electrical output to binary signals that can be processed by the computer for the comparison, identification and pattern-matching of input symbols or images.

conceptual dependency A system of representing meaning in and extracting meaning from written sentences that is used in some natural language processing software.

confidence factor A number or system of numbers indicating the certainty or confidence we have in a specific fact, statement or piece of evidence. The degree of truthfulness or belief we have in our information or knowledge. A method of dealing with uncertainty in production rule systems. Not the same as probability.

conflict resolution The priority ordering process an inferencing system uses to decide which rule to recognize or fire when more than one rule's IF statement(s) matches the data base.

control strategy A method of reasoning in a search space (i.e., forward or backward chaining, depth or breadth first, etc.).

CPU Acronym for central processing unit. The heart of all digital computers that carries out most of the processing functions. A combination of the arithmetic logic unit (ALU) and the control section of a digital computer. A microprocessor.

cybernetics An interdisciplinary science founded by MIT professor Norbert Wiener that focuses on the concepts of animal and/or machine systems, how these systems communicate, and how they are regulated or self-regulated. The science of control and communication in animal and machine. The basis for some artificial intelligence techniques.

DARPA Acronym for the Defense Advance Research Project Agency. A division of the Department of Defense which works on leading edge high technology weapon and information systems, and has funded considerable research in AI.

data driven A kind of inference used in tree searches. Data directed reasoning is bottom up or forward chaining.

DBMS Acronym for data base management systems. A form of general purpose computer applications program used for the storage, organization, search, manipulation, and retrieval of information stored in various records and files.

decision making software Programs using decision theory algorithms to help humans make decisions in complex situations.

decision support system A class of software used by management to help make decisions. Software used for creating mathematical models of problems to be solved, usually incorporating a spreadsheet and often using AI techniques.

deduction Coming to a conclusion by the process of reasoning. Reaching a decision through a rational or logical thought process.

deductive reasoning In logic, reasoning from the general to the specific. Conclusions follow premises. Consequent reasoning.

default reasoning A process used to overcome the problem of insufficient information or knowledge. Default reasoning uses guesses and assumptions to reach goals or decisions. Unless the system has knowledge to the contrary, these defaults are assumed to be true and will be used in determining the outcome.

default value A value given to a symbol or variable automatically if no other value is defined by the programmer or user.

demon A procedure that is automatically activated if a specific predefined state is recognized.

DENDRAL One of the first rule-based expert systems. A system used to determine the structure of an organic chemical compound using data acquired from mass spectrometers and nuclear magnetic resonance instruments.

dependencies How outcomes and decisions are related to and derived from prior knowledge and decisions.

dependency directed backtracking A technique used in tree searches to speed up and simplify the process of reaching a conclusion. The process of going back to and withdrawing only those decisions that lead to the incorrect outcome.

depth first A search procedure which explores each branch of a search tree to its full vertical length from left to right. An arbitrary search technique used when there is no heuristics or other guiding information to help limit the search. Each branch is searched for a solution and if none is found, a new vertical branch is searched to its depth, etc.

domain A field of knowledge or expertise. A problem area of interest in an AI application.

DUCK A logic programming language that works in conjunction with the LISP programming language to generate expert systems and intelligence data bases.

EL An expert system for analyzing and understanding electronic circuits.

ELIZA A program developed by MIT professor Joseph Weizenbaum that exhibits intelligence. This program simulates a psychiatrist or psychotherapist and using a natural language understanding program it allows a user to interact with the "doctor." The program is written in BASIC and is intended to be more of a game than a practical product.

embedded system AI software built into or buried in and referenced by another larger piece of algorithmic software.

EMYCIN An empty version of the widely known MYCIN expert system. The rules specific to MYCIN are removed leaving a shell, a reasoning system, and a natural language interface. By adding rules for a different problem domain, EMYCIN permits the rapid implementation of new expert systems.

environment A software development facility usually including a programming language such as LISP and other utilities or programs to make software creation faster and easier.

examples A system of attributes and outcomes arranged in a matrix and used to capture and represent certain kinds of knowledge in an expert system. Production rules are usually inferred from the examples.

ExperOPS5 A version of the popular OPS expert system development software written in LISP to run on the Apple Macintosh personal computer. Available from ExperTelligence Inc.

Expert Ease An expert system generator available from Human Edge Software Corp. and Expert Systems Inc.

Expert Edge An expert system generator available from Human Edge Software Corp.

expert system A major class of artificial intelligence software. A program consisting of a knowledge base, an inference engine or reasoning system, and a natural language user interface. The expert system embodies all of the facts, information, knowledge, and rules of thumb and other elements of expertise in a specific domain. A user may tap this expertise as an expert advisor or a consultant to solve problems or make decisions.

expert system generator A software tool designed to simplify the development of an expert system. Any program that permits the creation of an expert system without having to program all elements of it from scratch.

EXSYS A commercial expert systems generator developed by Exsys Inc.

facet A feature or attribute associated with an object in a frame. Same as slot.

fifth generation The next phase or level of development of computers. The expression used by the Japanese to refer to their program designed to achieve world supremacy in the computer business. A class of knowledge-based computers employing super high speed/parallel techniques and artificial intelligence.

fire To put into use one of the rules in a production system or knowledge-based system. To initiate the action specified by a rule if certain conditions are met. See trigger.

FLAVORS An object-oriented programming language based on Smalltalk and used in some LISP machines.

FLOPS Acronym for floating point operations per second. A term used to measure the performance of supercomputers and array processors that use floating point numbers. The usual measure is mega FLOPS or MFLOPS for millions of floating point operations per second.

forward chaining A problem-solving technique used in production and rule-based systems where conclusions are drawn or decisions are made by starting with the known facts. A search procedure or reasoning process where known facts are used to produce new facts and to reach a final conclusion. Also known as data driven or bottom up reasoning and inductive or antecedent reasoning.

fourth generation language A programming language usually specialized for a given area and designed to help facilitate the creation of applications programs. For example, a language designed to help program and use a DBMS.

frame A method of representing knowledge. An organization or collection of attributes, characteristics, or properties called slots that describe a particular object, event or action. An outline or an hierarchical structure containing slots for listing relevant facts and attributes.

Franz LISP A widely implemented dialect of the LISP programming language in which all entries (functions, commands, data, etc.) must be in lower case.

front-end A program or piece of hardware or both that serves as an interface between man and machine or program to speed up or simplify usage.

function A mathematical expression or rule showing the correspondence between two sets such that there is a unique part in one set assigned to each part in the other. The relationship or association between one item from a set with each item of another set.

fuzzy reasoning A method of dealing with inexact or imprecise information by making it of some value in determining an outcome. Techniques of avoiding complexities when dealing with subjective information or poorly understood processes. A method of determining an *adequate* solution from imprecise information.

garbage collection In the LISP programming language (and some other languages), the process of gathering and eliminating unneeded, unwanted or discarded data so as to create more memory space for further computation.

generate and test A problem-solving paradigm. A two-part search process that involves generating possible solutions and a test which evaluates, prunes, accepts or rejects solutions.

goal driven A method of reasoning that begins with the goal or conclusion and works backward through the rules and facts of a knowledge base searching for the path that will achieve the desired goal. Backward chaining.

grammar The study of language and how words are put together to form sentences. A system of structure, syntax, and semantics that make up a language for communication.

granularity A measure of how finely programs, information, or knowledge is subdivided.

HEARSAY An AI speech understanding system using blackboards for knowledge organization.

heuristic Anything that helps a human or computer to discover or learn. The use of empirical knowledge to aid in problem solving. Rules of thumb, "tricks," procedural tips and other information that help to guide, limit, and speed up the search process.

hierarchy A ranked or graded series of persons or things. A body of knowledge or information organized into successive ranks or grades. Most hierarchies can be illustrated with the use of tree graphs.

hypothesis A statement that is subject to proof or verification. A proposition used as the basis for argument, discussion or reasoning. An assumption used as the basis for action.

ICAI Intelligent Computer-Aided Instruction. Using AI techniques in a special program used for teaching with a computer.

ICOT Acronym for the Institute for New Generation Computer Technology. The organization doing the work on Japan's fifth generation computer project.

IF-THEN The form of the rules used in many AI systems and AI programs and expert systems. A conditional rule in which a certain action is taken only if some condition is satisfied. Decision-making tests that initiate an action if a specific condition is met (i.e., IF it is dark outside, THEN turn the light on).

inductive reasoning In logic, reasoning from the specific to the general. Conditional on antecedent reasoning.

inference The process of drawing a conclusion from given evidence. To reach a decision by reasoning.

inference engine That part of an expert system that actually performs the reasoning function. That part of an AI program that analyzes the information or knowledge base using rules to make decisions or reach conclusions.

information Data. Facts and figures about people, things, events, etc.

inheritance The process by which one object takes on or is assigned the characteristics of another object higher up in a hierarchy.

INSIGHT An expert system generator by Level Five Research Inc.

instantiation The process of assigning or substituting a specific value or name to a variable in a logic expression making it a particular "instance" of that variable.

instruction A computer word or number that tells a computer CPU a specific thing to do. A statement or command in a program that specifies a unique action to be taken.

INTELLECT The first commercially successful natural language interface based on AI techniques. A natural language interface for DBMS and other applications programs on mainframe and minicomputers. A product of Artificial Intelligence Incorporated, Waltham, MA.

intelligence The ability to acquire and apply knowledge through thought and reason.

interface That portion of a computer system or program that links two other portions of the system and allows them to communicate. A portion of a computer program that interacts with both the computer user and the remainder of the program or system. A go-between.

InterLISP A dialect of the LISP programming language implemented on Xerox AI workstations.

KDS An expert system generator using examples for the IBM PC. Available from KDS Corp.

KEE An expert system building tool featuring rules or frames. Available from IntelliCorp.

KES An expert system development system available from Software A&E Inc.

KIPS Acronym for knowledge information processing system. The term often given to fifth generation computers.

knowledge Understanding, awareness, or familiarity acquired through education or experience. Anything that has been learned, perceived, discovered, inferred, and understood.

knowledge base A collection of facts and figures, data, rules, inferences, and procedures organized into frames, blackboards, semantic networks, scripts, rules and other formats. The assembly of all of the information and knowledge of a specific field of interest that forms the basis for an intelligent computer system.

knowledge-based systems Expert systems and other artificial intelligence programs that use a knowledge base as their source for problem solving in a particular field of interest.

knowledge engineer A person who designs and builds expert systems. Computer science/AI specialists who acquire knowledge from all sources including human experts and organize it into a knowledge base.

knowledge engineering The process of acquiring and formatting knowledge to form a knowledge base.

knowledge representation A vocabulary and syntax of symbols and conventions used to describe and present knowledge and information. The structure and organization of information used to solve a problem.

knowledge source A body of knowledge in a specific domain relevant to solving specific classes of problems. Information that has been collected and codified and made applicable for use in an expert system.

language A system of words and symbols used for expression or communications among people. A system of instructions, commands, statements and data types used to create programs for a computer.

leaf A node having no successor.

learning Gaining knowledge, understanding or skill through education or experience. The process of improving performance by acquiring new knowledge.

LIPS Acronym for logical inferences per second. The unit of measurement of processing speed for AI and fifth generation computers.

LISP Acronym for ListProcessor. The most widely used artificial intelligence programming language. Invented by John McCarthy at MIT in the late 1950s.

LISP machine A special purpose digital computer or workstation for artificial intelligence program development where the LISP programming language is resident.

list A linear sequence of elements or objects separated by blank spaces and surrounded by parentheses. An arrangement of numbers, words, or other segments including atoms or other lists. The basic form of knowledge representation in the LISP programming language.

logic A system of reasoning based on the study of propositions and their analysis in making deductions. A system developed by philosophers and mathematicians for the process of making inferences from facts.

LOGO A programming language incorporating LISP and artificial intelligence concepts developed by Seymour Papert at MIT. A programming language designed for educational applications and to help people learn about programming and feedback.

LOOPS A multi-element programming language with rule-based, object-based, and logic-based segments. Used on Xerox AI workstations.

M.1 A commercial expert system generator developed by Teknowledge Inc. for the IBM PC.

MACLISP A major dialect of the LISP programming language developed and supported by AI researchers at MIT. It is different from other variants of LISP by its inclusion of a text editor for structure editing and a compiler.

MACSYMA An expert system used to help people solve complex applied mathematics problems. Provides fast automatic solution to complex math problems without problem solving or programming. Excellent at algebraic simplification and integration. Also works with vectors, inequalities, series, and other mathematical forms.

MCC Acronym for Microelectronics and Computer Technology Corp. A high-tech research organization in Austin, Texas, headed up by ex-Admiral Bobby Inman and funded by a consortium of U.S. electronic and computer companies. Research projects include artificial intelligence.

means-ends analysis A technique for controlling the search process. The current state and the desired goal state are defined. A procedure is selected to reduce the difference between the current state and the goal state. The result is a new state which is closer to the goal state. The process is repeated using the new state and the goal state.

menu A list of items displayed on a computer screen from which the user can select. A user friendly approach to presenting control alternatives to a user rather than have the user remember specific commands or directives which must be typed in.

meta A prefix of a term that designates a self-reference to the given term. Several examples are given below.

meta cognition Thinking about your own thought processes.

meta knowledge Knowledge about knowledge.

metaphor A figure of speech where a term, phrase, or characteristic is applied to something to which it is not truly applicable for the purpose of pointing out a similarity. Explaining one thing by likening it to or comparing it to another dissimilar thing.

meta rule A rule that describes how rules should be used.

minimax A search procedure used in implementing games. A technique for searching game trees in order to determine the best next move in a game. A limited depth first search that attempts to look ahead at the various possible moves and determines which of them will produce the maximum advantage over an opponent.

MIPS Acronym for millions of instructions per second. A unit of measurement for determining the speed performance of a computer.

modus ponens An inference rule used in propositional calculus. A rule of logic that allows us to infer a fact or truth from two other statements. For example, if sentence X is true and if sentence X implies Y is true, then we can infer that sentence Y is true.

monotonic logic A reasoning system based on rules or theorems that do not change as new rules are added or as new information is received. What is true remains true despite additions and other modifications.

MYCIN One of the earliest if not the first practical expert system. A rule-based, backward chaining expert system that helps a doctor determine the probable identity of a blood infection and helps to prescribe appropriate treatment.

natural language A language such as English used by humans in everyday conversation, reading and writing.

natural language interface That portion of an expert system or other AI computer program that allows the user to communicate with the computer using his natural language. The interface understands and interprets natural language input and generates natural language outputs.

natural language processing Getting a computer to understand natural language as language rather than as a meaningless list of letters, words or sounds. The process of extracting meaning from a natural language input.

nodes Places, goals or subgoals in a search tree. Achievable states in a state space.

nonmonotonic logic Reasoning based on rules or theorems which can change based on new input information. A kind of default reasoning.

object-oriented programming The use of statements and procedures called objects to represent knowledge and their use in writing programs by passing messages. The Smalltalk and FLAVORS languages are examples.

operating system The master control program for a computer. A collection of programs that allows the user to conveniently manipulate all facilities of the computer and to access and use various applications programs, languages, and utilities. A system for creating and maintaining computer files and automatically handling input/output routines for peripheral equipment.

OPS A rule-based programming language used to develop expert systems and other AI programs developed at Carnegie Mellon University. The most well known version is OPS5. Another is OPS/83.

paradigm An example or model.

parallel architecture New methods of creating computers that will operate faster. Computer structures that minimize or eliminate the von Neumann bottleneck associated with most digital computers. The use of multiple CPUs or other circuits to carry out simultaneous processing of multiple programs or different parts of one program for the purpose of improving performance. Computer designs which are essential to improving performance in AI applications.

parsing The process of breaking down a character string of natural language or computer language input into its component parts so that it can be more readily analyzed, interpreted or understood. The examining of natural language or computer language input to determine the function of the words or commands in the string for the purpose of determining what action to take.

path A route or course through a search tree.

pattern A diagram, plan, model or template to be followed or identified.

pattern-matching The automatic recognition or identification of figures, characters, shapes and forms according to predetermined conditions or standards. Usually the comparison of the pattern input to a stored template or standard that determines the closeness of fit.

Personal Consultant An expert system tool by Texas Instruments Inc. for the TI and IBM PCs.

pixel A picture element. The smallest part of a picture or scene as seen by a TV camera or displayed by a CRT. A dot of light.

planning systems A form of AI program that helps to determine an optimum plan to reach a given goal. A computer program that analyzes the various steps to be taken in reaching a given goal and attempts to specify a particular sequence that will lead to the successful achievement of the objective. Used for determining priorities, setting schedules, resolving time conflicts, etc.

predicate A statement about the subject of a proposition. An assertion that denotes the relationship among two or more objects or elements.

predicate calculus A formal language or logic system used to express statements about objects in a domain and their relationships. A logical system which includes rule of inference which states how symbols can be used to create a formula and how new formulas can be reduced or derived from the old formula. A system of reasoning widely used in AI programs to indicate relationships among data items.

primal sketch A two-dimensional line drawing or high contrast outline of a three-dimensional object represented in binary form for the purpose of image analysis. **primitive** A fixed or built-in function or procedure in the LISP language.

probability A number indicating the likelihood of the occurrence of a specific event. A ratio of the number of expected occurrences to the number of repetitions required to achieve the expected occurrences. Often expressed as a percentage. Used in production systems to deal with uncertainty. Not a confidence factor.

problem solving What most AI programs do. The process of answering a question, seeking a solution to a tough issue, resolving a conflict, making a decision, etc.

procedure A way of doing something. In LISP, a statement that describes a specific computational process. Also called a function.

production rule An IF-THEN rule. See rule.

production system An AI problem-solving program consisting of a set of rules, a data base to which the rules are applied, and a control strategy for using the rules on the data base. A rule-based problem-solving system that typically uses a search process.

program A sequence of computer instructions or commands that implement an algorithm to solve a problem, perform some calculation or control function. Software.

Prolog Acronym for PROgramming in LOGic. A popular AI programming language developed in France and based on the concepts of predicate calculus.

propositional calculus A form of logic system used for reasoning in which conclusions are drawn from a series of statements according to a set of rules.

PROSPECTOR An expert system that helps find ore deposits from geological input data.

pruning Various techniques used to limit the search through a knowledge base or search tree.

R1 An expert system used to configure VAX computers. See Xcon.

real time computing Processing that occurs fast enough to appear simultaneous or to keep up with other actions or operations.

reasoning The mental process of drawing conclusions from facts, observations or hypotheses. Making inferences from arguments or evidence.

recursive Any operation that is defined in terms of itself. A technique for performing a repetitive operation where the result of one repetition is usually dependent upon the result of a previous repetition. A self-referencing or self-modifying function or computer program.

resolution A method of deduction or theorem proving used in predicate calculus to draw a conclusion from a set of premises. Also a measure of fineness or detail as in a video camera or CRT.

RISC Acronym for reduced instruction set computer. A technique that trades off instruction set richness and complexity for simplicity and very high speed. A typical RISC CPU has few instructions and many registers constructed on a single VLSI chip. A typical RISC microprocessor has a 32-bit word, pipelined architecture and computing speeds of up to 10 MIPS.

robotics The science of developing and using robots, machines that are capable of performing human tasks. Robots are mechanical devices usually under the control of a computer used for automating some manufacturing function. AI techniques are widely used to make robots intelligent.

root node A node in a search tree with no predecessor. The starting node in a search tree.

rule A regulation or statement defining a particular conduct, habit or behavior. In AI, a two-part direction consisting of a condition and a consequent action. An IF-THEN rule states that if a given condition is true, then a specific action should be taken.

rule-based Any program or system that uses a set of rules to draw conclusions, make decisions and solve problems.

RuleMaster An expert system tool by Radian Corp.

rule of thumb A heuristic. A principle, technique, "trick," or method often used to simplify, speed up or otherwise facilitate some process. A technique that does not always work or that is not always accurate. A general guideline.

run time system A piece of software that permits you to run a program created with a software package but does not permit you to develop or modify programs.

S.1 An expert system generator developed by Teknowledge Inc.

scenario A summary or outline of a plot of a hypothetical situation or chain of events.

schema A data structure for knowledge representation. A method of presenting information about commonly occurring patterns of behavior. A means of organizing the data base of knowledge about a particular domain. A collection of observations, experiences, and reactions that are assumed to be always in effect. Examples of schemas are frames and scripts.

scripts A form of schema used for describing common sequences of events.

search The basic process involved in virtually all artificial intelligence applications. To explore. To examine or look over carefully in order to find something. To seek a particular object or goal.

search space Also called state space. All of the attainable states (nodes) in an AI problem defined by a search tree or graph.

search tree A graph which looks like an inverted tree and is used to illustrate the search of all of the various alternatives in a search space. A hierarchical structure showing all of the goals and subgoals (nodes) interconnected by arcs that have been discovered during the search process.

semantic Referring to the meaning, intention, or significance of a word, symbol, or expression.

semantic network A method of knowledge representation using a graph made up of nodes and arcs where the nodes represent objects, situations, concepts or entities and the arcs represent links describing the relationships between the nodes.

set A group or collection of people, things, objects or elements, such as numbers that have some common feature or which are related to one another in a special way and are generally treated as a whole.

shell A form of software interface between two programs or between the user and a program in a computer system. A framework for constructing an AI program. For example, an expert system natural language interface and inference engine but without the knowledge base which can be added in order to create an expert system for a specific domain.

SHRDLU A natural language understanding system developed by Terry Winograd as his doctoral research at MIT. A computer system driving a robot arm that manipulates toy blocks on a table according to natural language inputs. An interactive natural language understanding system for manipulating blocks in a blocks world.

simulation The process of having a computer mimic or imitate some physical or social system. A mathematical model implemented on a computer. Studying or designing a system or process by having the computer duplicate it.

skeleton A supporting structure or framework for creating an AI program. An expert system without the knowledge base. See shell.

slot A sub-element of a frame or schema. A particular characteristic, specification or definition used in forming a knowledge base. The name, definition, feature, or description of an attribute in a frame. **Smalltalk** A programming language developed at Xerox's Palo Alto Research Laboratory and useful in AI applications. Programming is viewed as a collection of objects which communicate with one another by passing messages.

Socratic method An instructional process originated by Socrates where the student learns through a one-on-one exploratory conversation of questions and answers with the teacher. A method of implementing computer-aided instruction (CAI) using AI techniques.

software A general term describing a program or collection of programs used by a digital computer. Systems programs used in controlling and programming the computer or applications programs that implement specific useful functions.

SOPHIE An intelligent computer-aided instruction (ICAI) system using AI techniques to teach students how to analyze, troubleshoot and debug electronic circuits.

speech recognition See voice recognition.

speech synthesis See voice synthesis.

supercomputer The largest and fastest computers available, typically mainframes with superior operating speed and extensive data storage capability. Computers using the latest and most advanced technology to achieve superior performance in scientific and engineering computations. Computers with a speed of at least 20 MFLOPS but often in the 100 to 2000 MFLOPS range.

syllogism Deductive reasoning from the general to the specific. A method of deductive reasoning made up of a major premise, a minor premise, and a conclusion.

symbol One thing that represents something else by convention or association. A printed sign or designation used to represent some element, quantity, quality or relationship in mathematics, logic and computer programming.

symbolic computing Using symbols to represent and manipulate facts, ideas, concepts, knowledge, and relationships rather than numbers to reason and understand.

symbolic logic A formal system for calculus where symbols are used to represent quantities and relationships for the purpose of reasoning and problem solving.

symbolic manipulation What all AI software does. Working with symbols that represent knowledge to reach a decision or solve a problem.

TEIRESIAS An ansilliary system or offshoot of the MYCIN expert system used to help the user use and interact with the system. A portion of the MYCIN expert system that explains its reasoning, justifies its conclusions or answers, and helps acquire new knowledge and modify the existing knowledge base.

template A pattern or gauge of a symbol or other object used as a standard for comparison in searches.

thinking The process of thought or reasoning. To formulate in your mind. To decide, judge, consider, and otherwise reflect upon some subject.

TIMM An expert system tool by General Research Corp.

tool A software package, such as an expert system generator, that makes it easier to create other software. Includes high level languages such as LISP and Prolog.

top down reasoning A structured method of working backward from a desired goal to determine subgoals and a path through the search tree that will yield a suitable solution to a problem. See backward chaining.

transition net See ATN.

tree A graph that resembles a tree with a root, branches and leaves. A diagram made up of nodes which represent objects, goals or subgoals interconnected by arcs which link the various nodes to form branches and leaves. A graphical system for defining a domain or search space.

tree search The process of exploring or investigating a tree graph for the purpose of solving a problem or reaching a decision.

trigger The condition that exists in a rule-based system when all of the conditions of a rule are satisfied by the current situation. See fire.

Turing Alan Turing, a British mathematician and logician, who worked at Kings College, Cambridge, and Princeton University, and is often considered to be the father of AI. (1912–1954).

Turing machine A theoretical binary computing machine that can be programmed to carry out any mathematical operation.

Turing test A form of test designed to determine if a machine has intelligence. An interrogator or examiner is separated from a person or a machine and communicates with that person or machine through a terminal. If, through a series of questions and inquiries, the examiner cannot be certain whether he is communicating with a person or a machine, then the machine is said to be intelligent or to be able to think.

unification A pattern-matching algorithm where the mathematical expressions for the patterns are manipulated by substituting specific values for variables until they are identical.

UNIX A multi-tasking, multi-user operating system developed by AT&T and widely used on mainframes, minicomputers, and microcomputers for AI research and development.

user interface That portion of a computer program that communicates with the operator. A portion of the program that accepts inputs and generates outputs using techniques such as natural language and menus. See interface and menu.

VAX A line of minicomputers made by Digital Equipment Corp. (DEC) and widely used in AI research and development.

VHSIC Acronym for very high speed integrated circuits. Special circuits used primarily in military applications for special computing functions including AI in weapons systems.

virtual memory The process of using a mass storage device, such as a hard disk, controlled by a special operating system or other software to make it appear that the CPU can directly address more words of random access read/write memory than would ordinarily be possible with standard addressing techniques.

vision See computer vision.

VLSI Acronym for very large scale integration. The term applied to integrated circuits that typically contain 1000 or more gates, flip-flops, or logic circuits of equivalent complexity. Typical circuits include 32–bit microprocessors and large customized gate arrays, both often used in AI hardware.

VMS An operating system developed by DEC using virtual memory techniques on the VAX line of computers.

voice recognition The process of having a computer or other electronic device recognize voice input from a user or operator. A system of picking up voice commands with a microphone, recognizing spoken words and converting them into digital signals which can be processed by a digital computer and used for control purposes. The front-end of a natural language understanding system.

voice synthesis The process of creating artificial speech by electronic and/or computer techniques. Having a computer generate electronic signals that appear to be a real voice at the output of a speaker.

von Neumann John von Neumann, a mathematician and computer scientist, generally credited with conceiving the idea of the stored program concept that is the basis for all digital computer operations today.

von Neumann bottleneck The problem of limited processing speed caused by the basic architecture of a von Neumann stored program machine using a single CPU which must repeatedly access memory for instructions and data. Instructions are executed one at a time and the actions they specify are carried one step at a time in sequence. Because all operations must be carried out in a serial manner by the CPU, large complex problems are processed slowly. Despite the high speeds of modern computer circuits, large complex problems are slowed down due to the need to refer to memory via a single limited port.

wff Acronym for well formed formulas. Expressions representing real world facts in propositional logic.

wisdom Knowing and understanding what is right or true. Good judgment and common sense combined with extensive learning. Having awareness and knowledge based on education and experience.

workstation A computer, sometimes of the desktop variety, generally dedicated to a specific application such as artificial intelligence program development or computer-aided design. A computer system that assists the user and improves productivity in a special field of endeavor.

XCON An expert system developed jointly by Digital Equipment Corp. and Carnegie Mellon University and used to help configure VAX computer systems. Also called R1.

ZetaLISP A major dialect of the LISP programming language typically available on special purpose AI workstations from Symbolics, Inc. and LISP Machines, Inc.

Appendix E: References

Books about AI

The following books were read and reviewed during the process of writing this book. It is not an exhaustive list, but it covers most of the mainstream AI books. In the opinion of this author, those books marked with an asterisk (*) were the most interesting, helpful, and practical.

A Comprehensive Guide to AI and Expert Systems
R. Levine, D.E. Drang, B. Edelson
McGraw-Hill, Inc., 1986

A Guide to Expert Systems *
Donald A. Waterman
Addison-Wesley Publishing Co., Inc., 1985

A Practical Guide to Designing Expert Systems
S. M. Weiss, C. A. Kulikowski
Rowman & Allanheld Publishers, 1984

Applications in Artificial Intelligence *
Edited by Stephen J. Androiole
Petrocelli Books, Inc., 1985

Applying Expert Systems in Business
Dimitris N. Chorafas
McGraw-Hill, Inc., 1987

Artificial Intelligence *
Elaine Rich
McGraw-Hill, Inc., 1983

Artificial Intelligence *
Patrick Henry Winston
Addison-Wesley Publishing Co., Inc., 1984

Artificial Intelligence A Theoretical Approach
Ranan B. Banerji
North Holland, 1980

Artificial Intelligence An Introductory Course
Alan Bundy
North Holland, 1978

Artificial Intelligence An MIT Perspective Vols. I & II
Patrick H. Winston, Richard H. Brown
MIT Press, 1979

Artificial Intelligence and Natural Man
Margaret Boden
Basic Books, Inc., 1977

Artificial Intelligence Concepts, Techniques & Applications
Yoshiaki Shirai, Jun-ichi Tsujii
John Wiley & Sons, Inc., 1984

Artificial Intelligence for Microcomputers
Mickey Williamson
Brady/Simon & Schuster Inc., 1986

Artificial Intelligence How Machines Think *
F. David Peat
Baen Books, 1985

Artificial Intelligence Projects for the Commodore 64
T. J. O'Malley
Tab Books, Inc., 1985

Artificial Intelligence, Making Machines "Think" *
Neil Graham
Tab Books, Inc., 1979

Artificial Intelligence
Reality or Fantasy?
Information Industry Association, 1984

Artificial Intelligence
The Search for the Perfect Machine
Lawrence Stevens
Hayden Book Co., 1985

Artificial Intelligence
Tools, Techniques and Applications
Tim O'Shea, Mark Eisenstadt
Harper & Row, 1984

Artificial Vision for Robots
I. Aleksander
Chapman and Hall/Methuen, 1983

Brains, Behavior & Robotics
James S. Albus
Byte/McGraw-Hill, Inc., 1981

Build Your Own Expert System
Chris Naylor
Halsted Press, 1983

Building Expert Systems
Frederick Hayes-Roth, Donald A. Waterman, Douglas B. Lenat
Addison-Wesley Publishing Co., Inc., 1983

Building Your First Expert System
Tom Nagy, Dick Gault, Monica Nagy
Ashton-Tate Publications Group, 1985

Catalogue of Artificial Intelligence Tools
Alan Bundy
Springer-Verlag, 1984

Designing and Implementing Your Own Expert System
Beverly, William Thompson
Byte/McGraw-Hill, Inc., 1985

Designing and Programming Personal Expert Systems
Carl Townsend, Dennis Foucht
Tab Books, Inc., 1986

Experiments in Artificial Intelligence
John Krutch
Howard W. Sams & Co., Inc., 1981

Expert Systems
Paul Harmon, David King
John Wiley & Sons, Inc., 1984

Expert Systems
A Practical Introduction
Peter S. Sell
Halsted Press: John Wiley & Sons, Inc., 1985

Expert Systems:
Techniques, Tools and Applications
Edited by Philip Klahr, Donald A. Waterman
Addison-Wesley Publishing Co., Inc., 1986

Exploring Artificial Intelligence on Your IBM PC (or Apple II)
Tim Hartnell
Bantam Books, Inc., 1985

Godel, Escher, Bach: An Eternal Golden Brain
Douglas R. Hofstadter
Vintage Books, 1980

Intelligent Systems
J. E. Hayes, D. Michie
Halsted Press: John Wiley & Sons, Inc., 1983

International Directory of Artificial Intelligence Companies
Artificial Intelligence Software srl (Italy)

Into the Heart of Mind
Frank Rose
Harper & Row, 1984

Introduction to Artificial Intelligence
E. Charniak, D. McDermott
Addison-Wesley Publishing Co., Inc., 1985

Introduction to Natural Language Processing
Mary Dee Harris
Reston Publishing Co., 1985

Machines Who Think
Pamela McCorduck
W. H. Freeman Co., 1979

Next Generation Computer
Edward A. Torrero
IEEE Press, 1986

Principles of Artificial Intelligence
Nils J. Nilsson
Tioga Publishing Co., 1980

Programming Expert Systems in OPS5: An Introduction to Rule-based Programming
L. Brownston, R. Farrell, E. Kant, N. Martin
Addison-Wesley Publishing Co., Inc., 1985

Rule-Based Expert Systems
Bruce G. Buchanan, Edward H. Shortliffe
Addison-Wesley Publishing Co., Inc., 1984

Supercomputers of Today and Tomorrow: The Parallel Processing Revolution
Richard A. Jenkins
Tab Books, Inc., 1986

The AI Business
Patrick H. Winston, Karen A. Prendergast
MIT Press, 1984

The Binary Brain: Artificial Intelligence in the Age of Electronics
David Ritchie
Addison-Wesley Publishing Co., Inc., 1983

The Cognitive Computer
Roger C. Schank, Peter G. Childers
Addison-Wesley Publishing Co., Inc., 1984

The Fifth Generation
Edward A. Feigenbaum, Pamela McCorduck
Addison-Wesley Publishing Co., Inc., 1981

The Handbook of Artificial Intelligence, Vols. I, II, III *
Avron Barr, Edward A. Feigenbaum, Paul Cohen
William Kaufmann, Inc., 1981

The Hitch-Hiker's Guide to Artificial Intelligence *
Richard Forsyth, Chris Naylor
Chapman and Hall/Methuen, 1985

The Micro Millenium
C. Evans
Viking Press, 1979

The Sciences of the Artificial
Herbert A. Simon
MIT Press, 1981

Understanding Artificial Intelligence
Paul Y. Gloess
Alfred Publishing Co., Inc., 1981

Understanding Artificial Intelligence
Henry C. Mischkoff
TI/Howard W. Sams & Co., 1985

VISION
David Marr
W. H. Freeman Co., 1982

Books about AI Languages

LISP

Common LISP
Guy L. Steele, Jr.
Digital Press, 1984

Learning LISP
Gnosis
Prentice-Hall, 1984

LISP *
P. O. Winston, B. K. P. Horn
Addison-Wesley Publishing Co., Inc., 1984

LISP - A Gentle Introduction to Symbolic Computing *
David S. Touretzky
Harper & Row, 1984

LISP Craft
Robert Wilensky
W. W. Norton Co., Inc., 1984

Looking at LISP
Tony Hasemer
Addison-Wesley Publishing Co., Inc., 1984

Understanding LISP
Paul Y. Gloess
Alfred Publishing Co., Inc., 1982

Prolog

Beginning Micro-Prolog
Richard Ennals
Harper & Row, 1984

Foundations of Logic Programming
J. W. Lloyd
Springer-Verlag, 1984

Implementations of Prolog
Edited by J. S. Campbell
Ellis Norwood Ltd., 1984

Logic for Problem Solving
R. Kowalski
North Holland, 1979

Logic Programming
K. L. Clark, S. A. Tarnlund
Academic Press, Inc., 1982

Programming in Prolog *
W. F. Clocksin, C. S. Mellish
Springer-Verlag, 1981

The Art of Prolog
Leon Sterling, Ehud Shapiro
MIT Press, 1986

Other Publications

AI Expert
2443 Filmore Street
Suite 500
San Francisco, CA 94115

AI Magazine (quarterly)
American Association for Artificial Intelligence
445 Burgess Drive
Menlo Park, CA 94025

AI Trends Newsletter
DM Data, Inc.
6900 East Camelback Road
Scottsdale, AZ 85251

Applied Artificial Intelligence Reporter (monthly)
ICS - University of Miami
P. O. Box 248235
Coral Gables, FL 33124

Artificial Intelligence Markets
AIM Publications, Inc.
P. O. Box 156
Natick, MA 01760

Expert Systems Journal
Learned Information
Besselsleigh Road
Abingdon, Oxford
OX136LG U.K.

Expert System Strategies
Cutter Information Corp.
1100 Massachusetts Ave.
Arlington, MA 02174-9990

Expert System User Magazine
Cromwell House
20 Bride Lane
London EC48DX U.K.

IEEE Expert (quarterly)
345 East 47th Street
New York, NY 10017

Intelligence
P. O. Box 20008
New York, NY 10025

Knowledge Engineering
Richmond Research
Box 366, Village Station
201 Varick St.
New York, NY 10014

Release 1.0
Ziff-Davis Publishing Co.
One Park Avenue
New York, NY 10016

The Artificial Intelligence Report
SRI International
3600 West Bayshore Rd.
Palo Alto, CA 94303

The Spang Robinson Report
3600 West Bayshore Rd.
Palo Alto, CA 94303

LISP Machines and AI Workstations

Hewlett-Packard Co.
3000 Hanover St.
Palo Alto, CA 94304

LISP Machines, Inc.
6033 West Century Blvd.
Los Angeles, CA 90045

Sperry Corp.
P.O. Box 2191
Princeton, NJ 08543

Symbolics, Inc.
11 Cambridge Center
Cambridge, MA 02142

Tektronix, Inc.
P. O. Box 500, Mail Stop 63635
Beaverton, OR 97077

Texas Instruments
P. O. Box 225012, Mail Station 57
Dallas, TX 75265

Xerox Special Information Systems
250 North Halstead Street
Pasadena, CA 91109

AI Software and Services

Abacus Programming Corp.
14545 Victory Blvd.
Van Nuys, CA 91411
Programming, consulting

Applied Expert Systems, Inc.
5 Cambridge Center
Cambridge, MA 02142

Artelligence, Inc.
14902 Preston Rd.
#212-252
Dallas, TX 75240
Expert system tools

Arthur Anderson
69 West Washington St.
Chicago, IL 60602

Arthur D. Little, Inc.
Acorn Park
Cambridge, MA 02142

Artificial Intelligence Corp.
100 Fifth Ave.
Waltham, MA 02254
Natural languaage processors

Bolt, Beranek & Newman, Inc.
10 Moulton St.
Cambridge, MA 02338

Brattle Research Corp.
215 First St.
Cambridge, MA 02142

Carnegie Group, Inc.
650 Commerce Court
Station Square
Pittsburgh, PA 15219
Knowledge-base tools, consulting

Chalcedony Software
5580 La Jolla Blvd.
La Jolla, CA 92137
Prolog

Cognitive Systems
234 Church St.
New Haven, CT 06510

Decision Support Software, Inc.
1300 Vincent Place
McLean, VA 22101

ExperTelligence
559 San Ysedro Rd.
Santa Barbara, CA 93108
LISP, LOGO, expert system tools

Expert Knowledge Systems, Inc.
P. O. Box 6600
McLean, VA 22106
Knowledge engineering, consulting

Expert Systems, Inc.
868 West End Ave., Suite 3A
New York, NY 10025

Expert Systems International
1150 First St.
King of Prussia, PA 19406
Prolog, expert system tools

Exsys, Inc.
P. O. Box 75158, Contract Station 14
Albuquerque, NM 87194
Expert systems tools

Franz, Inc.
6321 Thornhill Dr.
Oakland, CA 94611
LISP

General Research Corp.
7655 Old Spring Rd.
McLean, VA 22102
Expert systems tools

Gold Hill Computers
163 Harvard St.
Cambridge, MA 02139
LISP

Human Edge Software, Inc.
2445 Faber Place
Palo Alto, CA 94303
Expert systems tools

Inference Corp.
5300 W. Century Blvd. #501
Los Angeles, CA 90045
Expert systems tools

Infotym
20705 Valley Green Dr.
Cupertino, CA 95014

Intellicorp
707 Laurel St.
Menlo Park, CA 94025
Software tools

Intermetrics
733 Concord Ave.
Cambridge, MA 02138
Software tools

Jeffrey Perrone & Associates, Inc.
3685 17th St.
San Francisco, CA 94114
Consulting

Level 5 Research
503 Fifth Avenue
Indialantic, FL 32903
Expert systems tools

Logicware, Inc.
1000 Finch Ave. West
Toronto, Ontario Canada M3J2V5
Prolog

Palladian Software
14 Munroe St.
Cambridge, MA 02142
Financial expert systems

Radian Corp.
8501 Mo-Pac Blvd.
Austin, TX 78766
Consulting & expert systems

Silogic, Inc.
9841 Airport Blvd., Suite 600
Los Angeles, CA 90045
The Knowledge WorkBench (software)

Smart Systems Technology
6870 Elm St.
McLean, VA 22101
Consulting, training

Solution Systems
335 W. Washington St.
Norwell, MA 02001
Prolog & LISP

SRI International
333 Ravenswood
Menlo Park, CA 94025
Research, consulting & expert system tools

Syntelligence, Inc.
1000 Hamlin Court
Sunnyvale, CA 94088

System Designers Software, Inc.
5203 Leesburg Pike, Suite 1201
Falls Church, VA 22041
Prolog + LISP

Teknowledge, Inc.
525 University Ave.
Palo Alto, CA 94301
Expert systems tools, consulting, design

Teknowledgy Sources, Inc.
11915 Latigo Lane
Oakton, VA 22124
Consulting

Texas Instruments, Inc.
12501 Research Blvd.
Austin, TX 78769
Expert systems tools & LISP machines

Conferences, Seminars, Workshops, and Courses

The ATHENA Group
575 Madison Avenue
Suite 1006
New York, NY 10022

Continuing Education Institute
10889 Wilshire Blvd.
Los Angeles, CA 90024

Gartner Group
72 Cummings Point Road
Stamford, CT 06904

George Washington University
Continuing Engineering Education
Washington, D. C. 20052

Harmon Associates
151 Collingwood
San Francisco, CA 94114

The Institute of Artificial Intelligence
1888 Century Park East, Suite 1207
Los Angeles, CA 90067

Integrated Computer Systems
6305 Arizona Place
P. O. Box 45405
Los Angeles, CA 90045

International Joint Conference on Artificial Intelligence
A A A I
445 Burgess Drive
Menlo Park, CA 94025

Massachusetts Institute of Technology
Center for Advanced Engineering Study
MIT Video Course
77 Massachusetts Avenue, Room 9-234
Cambridge, MA 02139

McDonnell Douglas Knowledge Engineering
Mail Stop VG2-B01
20705 Valley Green Drive
Cupertino, CA 95014

Mystech Associates, Inc.
Mark Center Office Park #14
1900 N. Beauregard Street
Alexandria, VA 22311

Purdue University
Division of Conferences
Stewart Center
West Lafayette, IN 47907

Smart Systems Technology
6870 Elm Street
McLean, VA 22101

Software Architecture and Engineering, Inc.
1500 Wilson Blvd., #800
Arlington, VA 22209

Sperry Corp.
P. O. Box 2191
Princeton, NJ 08543

Technology Transfer Institute
741 10th Street
Santa Monica, CA 90402
Tower Conference Management Co.
331 West Wesley Street
Wheaton, IL 60187

U. S. Professional Development Institute
1620 Elton Road
Silver Spring, MD 20903

Yourdon, Inc.
1133 Avenue of the Americas
New York, NY 10036

AI Market Studies, Reports, and Directories

Artificial Intelligence: Reality or Fantasy?
Information Industry Association
316 Pennsylvania Avenue, S.E.
Washington, D. C. 20003

Cutter Information Corp.
1100 Massachusetts Avenue
Arlington, MA 02174

DM Data, Inc.
6900 East Camelback Rd, #1000
Scottsdale, AZ 85251

Electronic Trend Publications
10080 N. Wolfe Rd., Suite 372
Cupertino, CA 95014

Expert System Strategies
Cahners Publishing Co.
P. O. Box 716, Back Bay Annex
Boston, MA 02117

FIND/SVP
500 Fifth Avenue
New York, NY 10110

SEAI Technical Publications
P. O. Box 590
Madison, GA 30650

Sourcebook on Artificial Intelligence-Products and Vendors
Graeme Publishing Corp.
P. O. Box 549
Wilbraham, MA 01095

Who's Who in Artificial Intelligence
WWAI
P. O. Box 620098
Woodside, CA 94062

Expert System Tool Vendors

As this book was written, the following list was up-to-date. It is not an exhaustive list of vendors, but probably covers 90% of them. In this dynamic field, companies come and go and new products are introduced almost daily. To get the latest word, read the magazines and newsletters and go to the conferences.

Abacus Programming Corp.
14545 Victory Blvd.
Van Nuys, CA 91411
818-785-8000
ESI

Artelligence, Inc.
14902 Preston Rd., Suite 212-252
Dallas, TX 75240
214-437-0361
OPS5+, $3000
Prodigy, $450/950

California Intelligence
912 Powell St., #8
San Francisco, CA 94108
415-391-4846
XSYS, $995

Dynamic Master Systems, Inc.
P. O. Box 566456
Atlanta, GA 30356
404-565-0771
TOPS I, $175

ExperTelligence, Inc.
559 San Ysidro Rd.
Santa Barbara, CA 93108
805-969-7874
ExperOPS5, $325

Expert Systems, Inc.
868 West End Ave., Suite 3A
New York, NY 10025
212-662-7206
Expert Ease, $475

Expert Systems International
1150 First Avenue
King of Prussia, PA 19439
415-924-3644
ES/P Advisor

EXSYS, Inc.
P. O. Box 75158
Contra Station
Albuquerque, NM 98194
505-836-6676
EXSYS, $295

General Research Corp.
7655 Old Springhouse Rd.
McLean, VA 22102
703-893-5915
TIMM, $9500

Human Edge Software Corp.
2445 Faber Place
Palo Alto, CA 94303
800-624-5227
Expert Edge, $795
Expert Ease, $475

Inference Corp.
5300 W. Century Blvd.
Los Angeles, CA 90045
ART

KDS Corp.
934 Hunter Rd.
Wilmette, IL 60091
312-251-2621
KDS, $795
Playback, $495

Kemp-Carraway Heart Institute
Birmingham, AL 35234
205-226-6697
FLOPS, $195

Level Five Research, Inc.
503 Fifth Ave.
Indialantic, FL 32903
305-729-9046
Insight, $95
Insight−2+, $485

Lightwave Consultants
P. O. Box 290539
Tampa, FL 33617
813-988-5033
ESIE, $145

Micro Data Base Systems, Inc.
P. O. Box 248
Lafayette, IN 47902
317-463-2581
GURU, $2950

Mountain View Press, Inc.
P. O. Box 4656
Mountain View, CA 94040
415-961-4103
Expert-2, $100

Neuron Data, Inc.
444 High Street
Palo Alto, CA 94301
415-321-4488
Nexpert, $5000

Potomac Pacific Engineering, Inc.
P. O. Box 2027
Gaithersburg, MD 20879
307-977-4103
Expert System Tool, $20

Production Systems Technologies, Inc.
642 Gettysburg St.
Pittsburgh, PA 15206
412-362-3117
OPS/83, $1950-$25,000

Programs in Motion, Inc.
10 Sycamore Rd.
Wayland, MA 01778
1st Class, $495

Radian Corp.
8501 Mo-Pac Blvd.
P. O. Box 9948
Austin, TX
512-454-4797
Rule Master, $5000

RK Software
215-436-4570
Small-X, $225

Software A&E, Inc.
1500 Wilson Blvd., Suite 800
Arlington, VA 22209
703-276-7910
KES, $4000

Software Intelligence Laboratory, Inc.
1593 Locust Ave.
Bohemia, NY 11716
516-589-1676
WIZDOM, $250

SRI International
333 Ravenswood Ave.
Menlo Park, CA 94301
415-859-2464
SeRIES, $5000

Teknowledge, Inc.
525 University Ave., Suite 200
Palo Alto, CA 94301
415-327-6640
M.1, $5000

Texas Instruments, Inc.
P. O. Box 809063
Dallas, TX 75380
800-527-3500
Personal Consultant Plus, $2950

Ultimate Media, Inc.
275 Magnolia Avenue
Larkspur, CA 94939
415-924-3644
Advisor, $100

Xerox
250 North Halstead St.
P. O. Box 7018
Pasadena, CA 91109
818-351-2351
Humble (Smalltalk)

AI Language Vendors

LISP

Automata Design Associates
1570 Arran Way
Dresher, PA 19025
215-355-5400
UNXLISP, $86

CRIL
12 Bis, Rue Jean-Jaures
92807 Puteaux, France
1-776-34-37
Le LISP, $3000

Cybermetrics
P. O. Box 1194
Los Gatos, CA 95031
408-725-1344
UNXLISP, $69.95

Digital Equipment Corp.
146 Main St.
Manard, MA 61754
806-DIGITAL
GCLISP, $495
ISI-Interlisp, $10,000

ExperTelligence
559 San Ysidro Rd.
Santa Barbara, CA 93108
805-969-3345
ExperLISP, $325

Franz, Inc.
1141 Harbor Bay Parkway
Alameda, CA 94501
415-769-5656
FranzLISP

Gnosis, Inc.
4005 Chestnut St.
Philadelphia, PA 19104
215-387-1500
P-LISP, $79.95
Apple

Gold Hill Computers, Inc.
163 Harvard St.
Cambridge, MA 02139
617-492-2071
GCLISP, $495

Integral Quality, Inc.
P. O. Box 31970
Seattle, WA 31970
206-527-2918
IQLISP, $175

IOTC
P. O. Box 1365
Laramie, WY 87070
307-721-5818
PC-LISP, $125

Levien Instrument
Box 31
McDowell, VA 24458
703-396-3345
BYSO LISP, $150

The LISP Company
430 Monterey Avenue, #4
Los Gatos, CA 95030
408-354-3668
TLC-LISP 86, $169

Microsoft, Inc.
10700 Northup Way
P. O. Box 97200
Bellevue, WA 98009
800-426-9400
muLISP, $300

Norell Data Systems
P. O. Box 70127
3400 Wilshire Blvd.
Los Angeles, CA 90010
213-748-5978
LISP/88, $49.95

Northwest Computer Algorithms
P. O. Box 90995
Bellevue, WA 98009
800-426-9400
UO-LISP, $150

PC/BLUE Users Group
The New York Amateur Computer Club Inc.
Box 106
Church Street Station
New York, NY 10008
XLISP, $7

Pro Code International
15930 SW Colony Place
Portland, OR 97224
800-LIP-4000
Waltz LISP, $169

Software Toolworks
15223 Ventura Blvd., Suite 1118
Sherman Oaks, CA 91403
LISP/80, $39.95

Solution Systems
335 - SL Washington St.
Norwell, MA 02061
617-659-1571
TransLISP, $75

System Designers Software
5203 Leesburg Pike
Falls Church, VA 22041
703-820-2700
(LISP + Prolog)
POPLOG, $1950

University of Utah
3160 MEB
Salt Lake City, UT 84112
801-581-8224
Portable Standard LISP, $750

Prolog

Arity Corp.
358 Baker Avenue
Concord, MA 01742
617-371-2422
Arity/Prolog
Interpreter, $495
Compiler, $1950

Automata Design Associates
1570 Arran Way
Dresher, PA 19025
215-355-5400
Prolog, $29.95

Borland International
4585 Scotts Valley Dr.
Scotts Valley, CA 95066
408-438-8400
Turbo Prolog, $99.95

Chalcedony Software
5580 La Jolla Blvd.
Suite 126C
La Jolla, CA 92037
619-483-8513
PROLOG V, $69.96

CRIL
12 Bis, Rue Jean Jaures
92807 Puteaux, France
1-776-34-37
Prolog/P, $400

Expert Systems International
1150 First Avenue
King of Prussia, PA 19406
215-337-2300
PROLOG-1, $395
PROLOG-2, $1895

Interface Computer GmbH
Oberfoehringer Str. 24a
D-8000 Muenchen 81
West Germany
0049-89-984444
IF/Prolog

Logicware, Inc.
20 William St., Suite 200
Wellesley, MA 02181
617-547-2393
MPROLOG, $725

Programming Logic Systems
31 Crescent Dr.
Milford, CT 06460
203-877-7988
LPA Prolog, $395
(MicroProlog) APES, $395

Quintus Computer Systems, Inc.
2345 Yale Street
Palo Alto, CA 94306
415-494-3612
Quintus Prolog

Solution Systems
335-L Washington St.
Norwell, MA 02061
617-659-1571
Prolog-86, $125

Smalltalk and Others

Digitalk, Inc.
5200 W. Century Blvd.
Los Angeles, CA 90045
213-645-1082
Smalltalk, $250

Productivity Products International
27 Glen Rd.
Sandy Hook, CT 06482
203-426-1875
Objective-C

Verac, Inc.
9605 Scranton Rd. Suite 500
San Diego, CA 92121
619-457-5550
GeoFlavors

Decision Software Vendors

Decision Support Software, Inc.
1300 Vincent Place
McLean, VA 22102
703-442-7900
Expert Choice, $495

Kepner-Tregoe, Inc.
Research Road
P. O. Box 704
Princeton, NJ 08540
800-223-0482
Troubleshooter, $250
Decision Ade, $250

Index